# Jimmy Mac

## Prince of
## Inside Forwards

# Dedications

*To my father who took me on the road to Burnley many years ago.
He could never have imagined, and would have been quite astonished,
that here I am today, writing Jimmy McIlroy's biography.*

*To Tommy Cummings, with 479 appearances, a distinguished servant of
Burnley Football Club.
1928 - 2009.*

*To Ray Griffiths, 1931 - 2009, who as one of the Directors of
Burnley Football Club helped to ensure that the Wembley win of
May 2009 was not just a dream, but real.*

# Jimmy Mac

## Prince of
## Inside Forwards

*A Jimmy McIlroy Biography*

*by*

Dave Thomas

Hudson and Pearson

Published by Hudson & Pearson Ltd. 2009

10 9 8 7 6 5 4 3 2 1

First published in Great Britain in 2009 by
Hudson & Pearson Ltd.

Hudson & Pearson Ltd.
Bradwood Works, Manchester Road, Dunnockshaw,
Burnley, Lancashire BB11 5PW

A CIP catalogue record for this book
is available from the British Library

ISBN No. 978-0-9554017-4-9

Typeset by Hudson & Pearson Ltd.
in Berling

Printed and bound in Great Britain by
Hudson & Pearson Ltd., Dunnockshaw, Burnley, Lancashire BB11 5PW

The Early Fifties

# Acknowledgements

Chris Baldwin in Stoke.

Ken Bates for finding time to see me.

Stewart Beckett: for his help with the Oldham section and pictures.

Gerard Bradley: For photographs.

Billy Bingham MBE.

Dr Malcolm Brodie MBE: for access to his reports and articles.

Alastair Campbell.

Sir Bobby Charlton C.B.E.

Brenda Collins: Lisburn Museum.

Simon Doyle: for all his help and research in Belfast.

Pete Ellis: For his wonderful story.

Roy France: For the outstanding *Glentoran a Complete Record*.

Norman Giller: For his immediate permission to "lift/borrow/edit" any of his material.

Brian Glanville: For long chats and immediate permission to use his material.

Spurs fan Les Gold: For all the contacts and help he gave me.

Hudson & Pearson Ltd.

Simon Lowe: For immediate permission to use his material.

Simon Marland: Bolton Wanderers secretary and historian.

Jimmy McIlroy in particular: For his permission to include and adapt chapters from *Right Inside Soccer,* and for the many hours we talked.

Burdwaz Mungur: in Mauritius who saw Burnley play there in 1954.

Paul Plunkett: *Lancashire Telegraph*.

Ivan Ponting: For his introductions and early help.

Eddie Rawlinson: For photographs.

Tony Scholes.

Ray Simpson: for his knowledge of "all-things Burnley F.C."

Mike Smith: for his help with pictures.

Keith Wales: The Stoke Sentinel.

The *Burnley Express* and Edward Lee and Chris Boden.


All the Burnley fans who let me look through their scrapbooks and photograph collections.

Burnley Football Supporters' Club.

And Mrs. T. who is my computer technician.

# Contents

# Author's Note

WHERE POSSIBLE in this biography I have used parts of chapters from Jimmy Mac's own book *Right Inside Soccer*. I am grateful for his permission to do so. There seemed little point writing sections of this book when his own chapters fit into the narrative perfectly. But, what I have done with them sometimes, again with Jimmy's permission, is to adapt them by slightly altering the style, occasionally changing the verb tenses, and amending the words so that they read a little more like Jimmy would say them. I think this is what Brian Glanville, one of the great football writers, meant, when he once said that *Right Inside Soccer* was too much David Jack (his ghost writer) and not enough Jimmy McIlroy.

The chapter I wrote about Jimmy in the first *No Nay Never* provided a good prologue without much need for change, other than moving some paragraphs to other parts of the book. Similarly, the pages I wrote about his transfer in *Harry Potts Margaret's Story*, are used in their entirety, save for a small number of minor changes or additions. There seemed little point in re-writing them.

I grew up with Jimmy McIlroy, in that my boyhood and youth coincided with his years at Burnley. For over four years I was able to see him play. For that reason, even though I never met him personally until 2003, I feel like I have known him all my life. Maybe all we football fans feel this way when we have a particular favourite or hero who dates back to our formative years. They are just such an integral part of our lives. Say their name, years later, and we see them again in an instant, and our minds flood with memories of the games we saw them play, and what we were doing with our own lives at that time. It is a theme I have tried to incorporate into the book. The writing took a year and I have also tried to incorporate the events of that year into the chapters.

We separated in 1963. He went to Stoke City and I went to college. His name continued to crop up over the years and I was an avid reader of his sports columns in the local Press during his years as a journalist.

And then I met him face to face for the first time ever. I remember it was a Sunday evening when I picked up the phone to speak to him to arrange the visit. I hesitated for what seemed an age, nervous as a kitten. Years of being a Headteacher doesn't prepare you for moments like this. Our heroes do this to us. But such talk embarrasses him enormously. This book is my tribute to him and a heartfelt thankyou.

*Dave Thomas September 2009*

Versus Charlton Athletic

Versus Luton Town

# Jimmy Mac
## ACTION GALLERY

Competing against England international Don Howe of West Bromwich Albion.

Looks like a rare Jimmy Mac header but just wide.

The anguish of a chance missed.

Forcing a save against Blackpool.

Goalmouth scramble. Number 9 is Peter McKay.

Almost but not quite.

The very early 50s versus Liverpool.

# Foreword

## By Sir Bobby Charlton C.B.E.

WHAT A SURPRISE it was to receive an invitation to introduce Jimmy McIlroy's biography. When I heard his name again after all these years my mind went straight back to the memories of games when we played against each other at Old Trafford and Turf Moor.

In the late fifties and early sixties, before the abolition of the maximum wage, our paths crossed many times and in those days our two clubs, in terms of ability and competitiveness, were very much on a level footing.

There were no easy games against Burnley; in fact we rarely looked forward to playing against them during a period when they had such wonderful players and a marvellous winning team that eventually became champions in 1960. As often as not they beat us. Jimmy McIlroy played a huge part in that success and Sir Matt Busby was a great admirer of his. In fact he thought he was a genius with the ball at his feet.

I remember the wins Burnley had in the European Cup, and had Jimmy McIlroy not hit the post in the dying minutes against Hamburg they may have progressed even further. They had another opportunity to win the title in 1962 but faltered near the season's end. Sadly for Jimmy and Burnley, Manchester United were victors by three goals to one at Turf Moor during that final period that saw Ipswich pip them at the post.

Jimmy was a marvellous player, a terrific opponent, and an absolute gentleman. I cannot remember him ever retaliating in an age when heavy treatment was given to any star players who posed a threat. He always believed that skill would prevail and few players were more skilful than he. He was an absolute artist with the ball at his feet and like many others at the time I was mystified by his transfer.

Football was simpler in those far-off days but no less competitive than now. In today's game he would still be a world class player and clubs as big as Manchester United, Real Madrid and Barcelona would bid millions for him. He played at a time when pitches were often mudbaths and the ball felt like it was made of concrete. In today's conditions I fancy he might be unbeatable.

He has served both club and town with distinction and the award of Freeman of the Borough of Burnley is richly deserved. I know he still attends games at Turf Moor and I share his pleasure and pride in seeing the club doing so well during 2008/09.

Well done Jimmy. I wish you and the book great success

*Sir Bobby Charlton C.B.E., April 2009.*

Spot The Ball. The legendary Longside in the background ... caps and grey overcoats.

# Prologue

H<small>E CAN WALK</small> through Burnley and football supporters of a certain generation will stop and smile when they see him. He can be in one of the town's supermarkets, Tesco or Sainsbury's, or in Marks and Spencer's, and he will be stopped by tongue-tied admirers who engage him in conversation as he tries to do his shopping. He can be approached for autographs by grandfathers who will then tell their grandsons who this man was and what he meant, and still means to the town of Burnley.

He arrived in 1950 and has been in the town ever since. From the first game he ever played in the club's first-team he became an instant fixture in the side for the next 13 years. He played not far short of 500 games for Burnley Football Club, when footballers made no great fortunes, and 55 times for Northern Ireland. In a football age when there were so many great players and football heroes he was one of the greatest of them all. In 1999 he was recognised by the Football League as one of the 100 best-ever players. One of the great stands at the football ground is named after him. His name is on the plaque of legends on the outside wall of that stand. In 2008 he received a special achievement award from all the Burnley supporters' clubs. He is a Freeman of the Borough of Burnley. At club dinners when he speaks, you can hear a pin drop as people listen to his soft, gentle Irish brogue. His name is Jimmy McIlroy, but just say Jimmy Mac and everyone knows who he is.

Ask him about football and the modern game and he will say he doesn't understand it. When he played, two teams went out and both went out to win. Now he sees it mostly as a game where two teams don't go out to win, but simply to avoid losing. He valued skill as a player and as a coach and manager. Now he bemoans its absence other than in just a very small band of the top players. Where once he loved the players who could dribble with the ball and take chances, now all he sees are players who are told to pass the ball and not risk losing it. Football has changed since he played and little of it for the better. Other than Manchester United and Arsenal there are few teams he looks forward to watching. It is a sad indictment of the game today.

The first time I ever picked up the phone to contact him was several years ago; I hesitated for an age before I plucked up the courage to speak to him. Then, years later when I suggested we write this book, the first thing he said was, "But who on earth wants to read about an old has-been like me?" A little later he added, "Does anyone today have any idea who I am?" He was genuinely apprehensive.

With a wry sense of humour he will say that the only people who remember him now are the senior citizens of Burnley and he will tell the story of how one day he was walking down the street near his home and was approached by a little old dear who was 80 if she was a day. She stopped a few yards in front of him and was clearly awe-struck. "Jimmy Mac, my hero," she exclaimed wide-eyed. "Ah, you can't possibly be old enough to have seen me play," he replied smiling, making her day. He always was a charmer.

Jimmy's own book *Right Inside Soccer* was published in 1960. It was a typical football book of the age, slim, only 128 pages, and short on detail. But what it did include were many of Jimmy's own opinions about the game, some of them quite controversial, even radical. But it certainly never gave a rounded portrait of him. How could it? Stopping in 1960 it did not cover the Cup Final or his totally unexpected transfer; they would come later. Although there was a chapter called 'Limping along the road to the Championship', in fact the chapter was mostly about one particular Cup game against Blackburn Rovers. The ghost-writer was David Jack, a leading football writer of the time, but the eminent writer Brian Glanville's comment to Jimmy was that "it was too much David Jack and not enough Jimmy McIlroy." It was reportedly the Italian speaking Brian Glanville who once spoke at length to Jimmy about moving to Italy, acting almost as a go-between. Nothing happened.

As soon as his book was published a whole crowd of us who formed the football team at Todmorden Grammar School bought and devoured it from cover to cover. The man was our idol. We played for the school team in the morning and then rushed to Turf Moor for first team and reserve games on alternate Saturdays. If there was a tough game coming up we'd simply say "Jimmy Mac will win it for us."

Brian Glanville, always a McIlroy admirer, penned a piece about him that is as fresh now as it was then. He called it *The Magic of McIlroy* and wrote it at a time when Jimmy Mac was at his absolute peak.

'Burnley's Jimmy McIlroy, at 28, is almost unquestionably the finest inside forward in Britain; more versatile and fluent than Johnny Haynes, more consistent at international level than Ivor Allchurch, more mature than Bobby Charlton, Denis Law and Jimmy Greaves. McIlroy is above all a stylist and a perfectionist, with an utter mastery of technique. Every pass, every flick, every swerve is studied and controlled. His speed off the mark is amazing. Few who saw will have forgotten his magnificent burst, half the length of the field, in a League game at Tottenham a year ago. Burnley were a goal down, there was a minute to play and all seemed over. Suddenly he got the ball in the inside-right position and accelerated like a racing car, leaving man after man behind him, boring irresistibly into the Tottenham half. Then, he flicked the ball accurately across goal, where Cheesebrough had only to put out a foot and touch it over the line'. *(For full article see appendices)*

My abiding memories of him are his delicate way of taking penalties and sending goalkeepers the wrong way; the way he could work his way along the goal line into the penalty area, fooling them with a shake of the hips and a shimmy, and his ability to take a ball into the corner by the flag, shield it, keep it, and while away precious minutes towards the end of a game. The legendary Everton hardman Jimmy Gabriel called it "doing a Jimmy McIlroy" when he did it himself in a Wembley Cup Final. Perhaps only Leighton James since then at Burnley has had the ability to ghost his way past an opponent as if he wasn't there. He was never known for sustained pace but what Jimmy possessed was a burst of speed over the first few yards that got him round his man on countless occasions. Matt Busby wrote the foreword to his book, which is tribute indeed, mentioning his subtlety, the ability to find space, to take command of a game, and his sheer skill. His use of the word 'dazzling' is not inappropriate, nor is the word 'genius'.

In a family where there were five girls and just one boy, himself, it is perhaps surprising that he became a footballer. But, with a football every Christmas and his father and uncle being players themselves of some ability, the foundations were laid. It was by quirk of fate that he joined Burnley, not Bolton Wanderers as a teenager. The promise of a visit from someone from Burnden Park was never kept.

His first impressions of Burnley were less than favourable. All he could think of were the green hills of Antrim. It took him months to understand the accent, though it has to be said, it was a problem that worked both ways.

The chapters of his own book look at his early life and the early days at Turf Moor. For this book some of them have been expanded and more detail has been added. The ones chosen look at his early life, being a rookie at Turf Moor, his first season, FA Cup disappointments, the Championship season, the rumours of transfers, and his international career. Much of this introduction has been adapted from material in *No Nay Never Volume One*.

For me, 1959/60 was the first full season of watching the McIlroy magic. With a gang of pals I was there at a baking hot Elland Road for the first game of the season against Leeds United. I can still remember the steam train journey and a long walk from the station to the ground. Burnley won 3 – 2 and it was a first sighting of a long, tall, gangly, giraffe-like centre half called Jack Charlton. I have a recollection of a disallowed goal in the final seconds of the game just after the whistle had gone, except that we didn't know whether it counted or not, and we came home thinking it had been a 3 – 3 draw. None of us could have had any idea that by the end of that season we would be champions or that in the final nail-biting game, a half-fit McIlroy would spend several of the last minutes doing what he always did well – "doing a Jimmy McIlroy," screening and holding the ball by the corner flag to wind down the clock.

I had no chance of seeing that final game but sat by the radio all night waiting for the final result. Burnley scored within four minutes but then City equalised. For the first goal there is a memorable picture of Pointer, arms wide in jubilation, watching the ball cross the line. For the second Burnley goal there is a memorable picture of Meredith shooting it home with this time McIlroy watching. From that point on Jimmy Mac tried all he knew to slow the game down and retain possession. But by the end, nerves were raw and voices hoarse as Manchester City did their utmost to score again.

The Burnley chairman Bob Lord once said that Burnley was famous for two things – cotton and the Burnley Building Society. Supporters might add a couple of others – the Championship and Jimmy McIlroy.

My father always vividly remembered another season, season 1952/53 when another good side might have won the title. Jimmy Mac was in that side as well. Once he came into the side in 1950 it would be an amazing 13 years until 1963 when he lost his place.

At the Millennium Celebration game on 28th December, 1999, he was publicly honoured when he officially opened the 'Jimmy McIlroy Stand'. The emotion in his voice as he made his speech from the pitch was obvious to all. It was typical of the graciousness of the man that he suggested that it should have been named 'The Champions Stand' in honour of all the team. In an interview with Frank Keating a week later in *The Guardian* he spoke about the ceremony. He talked about how unbelievable it was that he and the team should be together again on the same field where they'd had all their triumphs. Only Angus and Adamson were missing. Each one came out for an individual reception from the crowd. On the field his imagination took him back to a pass here, a tackle, a goal or a shuffle. He spoke glowingly of his fellow players. He talked about one particular game against Leicester City where it seemed they could do no wrong, when the football they played was perfect and their display was so magnificent that neither crowd nor team wanted it to end. When it clicked into perfection it must have been breathtaking to watch, he said.

The game at Leicester he referred to was on September 9ᵗʰ, 1961 and was won 6 – 2 with goals from Connelly (2), Robson (2), Pointer and Harris. This was the season when Burnley were frequently magnificent with scores of four, five, six and seven throughout the season until near the end when they just ran out of stream and adrenalin. A second title slipped tamely away. In the final four games they took just two points. In the League alone they scored a phenomenal 101 goals most of which were scored in the first thirty games. There was the Wembley Cup Final and they were so close to a wonderful Double achievement.

Throughout that season how privileged I was to have seen him play so often and to be able to recall the things he did; his beautiful passing skills, the penalties he put away, the rough treatment he received without ever retaliating, the dummies with which he used to send a player one way whilst he went the other, the way he schemed and controlled a game and always had so much time and space, the mark of a truly great player. He was never a man mountain like Emile Heskey, or a player with pace over distance like the early Anelka. To look at he was quite middling, quite average (perhaps just a little on the stocky side) but his average appearance belied his inherent skill and magic.

One thing not often mentioned is his stamina. These were days of relentless rough treatment, mud bath pitches, playing on with injuries,  and three games in four days at Easter.

The nearest comparison you might make in recent times is Zinedine Zidane, except Jimmy never head-butted anyone in a World Cup Final. Players like this go past others as if they just aren't there. There is no flamboyance or elaborate ostentation. There were none of the Ronaldo circus tricks or triple step-overs with a somersault and twist for Jimmy Mac. There was just a touch, a flick, a feint: or show the ball to an opponent and then with a short burst of acceleration whip it past him. Sometimes there was a shake of the hips so subtle you might miss it. And on top of all this were the superb passing skills. The talents of people like this are instinctive and natural, but there they are in the thick of things, pulling the strings. They are the schemers, the generals, the magicians, and they make it all look so easy. They run the game and dictate the play. Where once every team had such a player, today it is so different.

He was forever in demand for games outside of Burnley. A letter discovered in a pile of folders in the ancient Albert Maddox office under the old Cricket Field stand politely requests that he be allowed to play in a testimonial at Sheffield United for Jimmy Hagan. There were many others when his gracious presence was sought. He played for the Football League as well as a Great Britain Xl. In another file was a whole heap of correspondence relating to the Burnley versus Reims European Cup game. One of them relates to the insurance cover needed for the trip to France. All the team except McIlroy were valued at £20,000. Significantly, Jimmy's insurance value was £30,000.

My first visit to see him was in 2003 at his immaculate home in Burnley. I asked him the questions that he must have been asked countless times and become tired of answering. But he answered with unfailing politeness and patience. The '59/60 title win at Manchester City "still brings goosebumps just to think about it," he told me. "In all honesty I don't know how we did it. I remember my thigh being strapped up, and the day before I said to Billy Dougal that no way would I be able to run or sprint. Dougal just looked at me and announced I'd be playing no matter what. What a night it was, although it didn't sink in at the time. Little Trevor Meredith one of our reserves scored the winning goal. In any other team he would have been a regular."

In '61/62 when the club were in sight of both League and Cup he explained, "We just ran out of steam. Most of us felt like physical wrecks. There were too many games crammed into one hectic period. We just couldn't sustain it and it all faded away." His simple explanation was that their legs and energy just gave out at the end. There was just one win in the last ten games and the final result was a humiliating 0 – 4 defeat away at Sheffield Wednesday. "The sparkle had gone," said Jimmy omitting to mention that he had missed five of them because of injury.

He lived and played in an era when the financial rewards were nothing like those of today, but he doesn't begrudge what modern players earn. Nor were there high definition televisions with huge screens in the corner of every living room spotlighting misdemeanours, fouls, flare-ups and confrontations with referees. The worst and most disgraceful of these was perhaps a few seasons ago when Manchester United's Van Nistelrooy was set upon by half the Arsenal team led by Keogh at Old Trafford. "But it happened all the time in my day," Jimmy commented. Today's hardmen have nothing on Eddie Clamp, the ex Wolves and Stoke City halfback. Jimmy played both against him, and with him.

"There's nothing new going on. Players were just as 'naughty' then as they are now in fact off the field probably worse. But there weren't tabloids and reporters intent on revealing and publishing all. There weren't cameras everywhere and it never made headline news. In fact, more often than not, the reporters who travelled with the players joined in. And the other difference was that in my day the Grosvenor Hotel was way beyond the footballer's pay packet. Girls hung round footballers then just as they do now. I can well remember a night out with the boys in my younger days of course. Maybe it was the dancehall or somewhere like that and there were always girls coming up to us. One of our players was approached by one girl after another and he asked each one 'do yer do owt?' If the answer was no she was told to 'bugger off'." Jimmy in his younger days could certainly have taught George Best a thing or two.

On the subject of wages Jimmy recalled that his dealings with Bob Lord were generally short and sweet. "When the maximum wage was abolished and it was announced that Fulham were going to pay Johnny Haynes £100 a week Bob Lord asked me what I thought I was worth. Hopefully I said £60. He looked at me and I waited… and waited… and then he spoke. 'And there'll be tax to pay as well I suppose,' he said. 'So you'd better have £80'. I left the room smiling."

In a career that was so long and glittering, Jimmy McIlroy finds it hard to single out particular occasions that are significant or extra special. One of his favourite stories that he often tells is about one of his first ever games as an 18 year old. "It was against Portsmouth at Fratton Park and Portsmouth had some great players then and they'd recently been champions. They had Jimmy Scoular who was one of the hardest ever players. Scoular was built like Desperate Dan with legs like tree trunks and he'd obviously decided to leave an impression on me." (The tackle by Darren Purse on Andrew Cole in the Burnley Cardiff game in April of 2008 pales into insignificance in comparison.) "I had the ball on the touchline and in he came at me. Well, he took me over the edge of the pitch, across the track round the edge, and even over a low fence that separated the spectators. You can tell the force at which I was hit because the spectator my boot struck had to be taken away for treatment. After treatment of my own by our trainer, a cold sponge on the back of the neck to bring me round, I came back on. Not long after Scoular comes up to me and says, 'Listen you little Irish Fenian bastard that's nothing to what I'll do to you next time'. But I'm a Protestant I told him wide-eyed. Well, Scoular looked at me open-mouthed, quite aghast, with a look of anguish on his face. Gently he put his arms around me and said, 'Ah God son, did I hurt you?' After that I never had any trouble from him, in fact I can't remember him ever tackling me again."

In that first meeting I ever had with Jimmy I can well remember sitting facing him as he retold these tales. As he spoke I looked at him like a small schoolboy might sit in awe of his headmaster (if that's what they still do these days). He must have been so weary of talking to yet another fan about yesteryear and this was at a time when football in general was pretty wearisome to him. But he never showed it. The word gentleman would not go amiss.

"Do you know," he said, "the one thing I regret is that I never had the chance to play on the perfect pitches that players have now. The progress that has been made with all-year grass is astonishing. If there's been one major change other than the money it's the quality of the grass and any old player will tell you that. I remember some of the conditions we played in just wouldn't be allowed now. There was the Cup-tie at Bradford. It was a game when with twelve minutes to go and us losing 2 – 0 I actually pinched myself to make sure it was really happening. I've never known mud like it. When we came out it had been rolled quite firmly and we passed the ball around quite easily for the first 20 minutes or so. But then it just became a soggy nightmare. I remember the last minute equaliser. Pilky floated a free kick across and I jumped like everybody else did. All I remember is landing flat on my face in the mud and seeing the ball trickle over the line. And then in total contrast a few days later the replay was played on a pitch so frozen it was like a skating rink.

"Then there are the lighter balls used today. They bend and swerve and go in from 30 yards. In my day they were so heavy a 20 yard goal was a rarity and any goalkeeper would be annoyed if he let one in. Today it can be in the net from way out before a goalkeeper can even move. They can bend shots so much that it starts out heading straight at the goalkeeper but it can finish up in the top corner of the net it's swerved so much."

Today Jimmy McIlroy lives in an elegant semi-detached house on the edge of Burnley not far from the spot where the Tottenham team coach years ago was coming down the hill in mist and fog and Jimmy Greaves uttered the immortal words: "Blimey, where are we going, Brigadoon?" It is something that has never bothered Jimmy who professes that from the day he arrived he has never wanted to leave. He still watches the Clarets, (enthusiasm and interest very much rekindled by the entertaining play of Owen Coyle's attacking team and Carling Cup exploits) plays golf and is a skilled painter. He smiles when he says he can't walk 20 yards without someone wanting to chat about the old days or wanting to know if he thinks they will win on the coming Saturday.

On Saturday February 7th, 2004 he was given a standing ovation as he walked round the pitch at the finale of the parade of Legends. At 2.00 pm the plaque had been unveiled outside the ground honouring 25 Burnley 'greats'. 45 minutes later he received a marvellous

# JIMMY SCOULAR (*Newcastle United and Scotland*)

"Built like Desperate Dan with legs like tree trunks", and left his mark on a very young Jimmy Mac.

reception from the thousands of people inside the ground. The town and people love this man for what he has given to them, for the loyalty he has shown and the affection and dignity with which he always speaks of the place. At the dinner later that evening in the James Hargreaves Suite over 300 people again gave him a rapturous welcome as he took his place at the high table. "If only Bob Lord could see me now," he began, as he made a short but moving speech, going on to ask "why me" and to suggest that there were so many other worthy legends who should be honoured – Halley, Boyle, Watson, Dawson, Kelly, and many more upon whom the club's history had been built. What he wanted to do, he said, was to thank the supporters for the honour. And of course he spoke of Burnley the town, of how he had never in his life contemplated leaving, and that even playing for Stoke City, he had travelled every day from Burnley rather than move. There were more than just a few moist eyes as he sat down to more rapturous applause.

Let the next paragraphs of this introduction be a tribute to the man's genius, for that is surely what he was, and it is what Ken Bates who saw him play many times, still calls him. If he played today, what price would he command if pursued by the likes of Chelsea, Manchester United or Real Madrid? In December 1958 this was written about him:

'McIlroy illuminated the murk of Manchester with one of his star performances. He was the mentor, the master magician whose sorcery conjured the ball round, through, between heavier bodies and left them sprawling. They tackled him in pairs, they crowded him in threes; he showed them the ball, flicked it away from them, worked it on with little skips and feints and shuffles, while the crowd gazed on in silent wonder. He was so baffling that one received the impression that had the laws of football allowed it, he would have waved one of his magic feet over the ball three times, and produced it, reduced in size from the referee's pocket.'

And then in November 1959 of the Championship season, Burnley demolished Wolves 4 – 1 at Turf Moor with goals from Pointer (2), Connelly and Robson. 27,793 people witnessed another masterclass described by Noel Wild a local journalist.

"He funnelled the ball to every tactical advantage in midfield. He plotted and charted the course of practically every Burnley attack. He juggled at the corner flag, wiggled wickedly, slowed the game down one minute and then streaked away like an electric eel with a sprint which rivalled the acceleration of even Stanley Matthews and Tom Finney. He sometimes jabbed short passes forward, and other times swung 40 yarders out to the left wing. That day Jimmy McIlroy cascaded all soccer's arts and graces before his baying audience. It was Rhapsody in Claret and Blue."

After the 4 – 1 thrashing of Wolves, Alec Johnson wrote:

'If ever there was a one-man show, this was it. After 15 minutes Jimmy McIlroy kindled a soccer flame and kindled it with wafts of soccer greatness. By the end of the game the fire had roared through the Wolves' house and burned it to the ground. McIlroy stands 5' 8". Put him in football boots and give him a ball and there is a giant. Players have never stumbled and staggered in front of one man like this. After 22 minutes he arrived dramatically on the scene dancing past Flowers. Then, again he went round Flowers, who, a few seconds later became so confused, he passed to Pointer – and the ball was slammed in the net. Ninety seconds later the extraordinary McIlroy did it again. Weaving through, he sent a pass to Connelly, who angled it to Robson… and it was in.

Yes, they should really have hung a sign outside the ground before the match reading – 'Presenting McIlroy and his magicians, turning Wolves into lambs'.

And then, in 1963, this charismatic player, this exquisite performer, this man who could inspire such prose and rapture, and who some said *was* Burnley Football Club and was the club's greatest ever player, was placed on the transfer list and within days, with almost indecent haste, was sold. Some supporters swore they would never attend another game. A Burnley side without the incomparable McIlroy; the town was stunned and disbelieving. Little else was talked about for days. It filled page after page in national and local newspapers. People gathered on street corners to talk and read the headlines. After nigh on thirteen years of wonderful service, he was going.

But what was the cause? It came quite out of the blue. What could have prompted it? Exactly what was it that happened?

Ronnie Clayton of Blackburn Rovers and England captain – a "one club" player.

# Chapter One

# Sold

THE BEST players in the game today hold all the high cards. They can name their price and choose their clubs – or at least their agents do it for them. They can dictate their terms and as good as decide when they want to leave. Contracts can be meaningless. Loyalty is an expression seldom used any more; long service even less so. Even at levels below the Premiership, players move around and chop and change and the days are very much gone when a top player would give most, if not all of his playing career, to the club where he started as a boy. There are exceptions; Scholes, Giggs, Gary Neville at Manchester United, Gerrard and Carragher at Liverpool. But they are a rarity.

Jimmy McIlroy belonged to a time when loyalty and long service were prized and were the norm. Tom Finney spent the whole of his career at Preston, Nat Lofthouse at Bolton and Ronnie Clayton at Blackburn. Eventually, however, as players began to reap the benefits of the abolition of the maximum wage, the shackles of subservience were loosened – but only a little. The manager and chairman of a club still reigned supreme and a player still did as he was told. To ask for a transfer was a bold decision on the part of any player. If the chairman or manager took exception to that, then that player could be as good as ostracised, banished to the reserves and made to train on his own. Taken to extremes, his career could be frozen, as good as over. Contracts were binding.

But conversely a player could be placed on a transfer list and sold by a club and there was little he could do about it. When his sell-by-date came, that was it. The player had little or no say in the matter.

At Burnley, players had long been sold as a matter of course, partly because there were so many to choose from, and so many coming through the youth system, and partly because money was always needed to meet the costs of running the club and an increasingly ambitious chairman, Bob Lord. But players sold so far had been either peripheral players or those who had reached the end of the best of their careers. One or two went because they might just have irked Bob Lord or the manager – Peter McKay for example, even though his scoring record was exceptional. Jimmy McIlroy rated him the best finisher and poacher he ever played with, able instinctively to score from whatever angle or direction the ball came to him. But, if a player annoyed the chairman of Burnley Football Club, Bobby Seith in the Championship season, he was sold.

But no one of the category and ability of McIlroy had ever been sold that spectators could recall. There had been the young Tommy Lawton just before the war, and way before that, Bob Kelly in the 1920s. But at post-war Burnley, the sale of an ever-present iconic player like McIlroy was unheard of.

The three main characters in the saga were the manager Harry Potts, the chairman Bob Lord, and of course McIlroy himself. Only the latter remains to tell the story and he professes to be baffled by it even now after all these years. In recent times perhaps only the Beckham sale at Manchester United, prompted by a manager who had lost all patience with his celebrity status can compare for surprise and shock value. But whereas the McIlroy sale is still talked about in Burnley over 40 years after the event, it is hard to imagine Mancunians talking about the Beckham transfer 40 years from now. The Beckham saga filled the newspaper pages but within a year he had been replaced by other 'galacticos' and the fuss subsided. Does anyone at Old Trafford bother about it today; since his departure more titles and trophies have been won and other great players have joined the club one after the other.

The world outside of Burnley still asks who shot Kennedy, or what happened to Princess Diana but it cares little about why one player was sold in 1963 at Turf Moor. But I'd hazard a guess if the answer was available to just one of those questions, Burnley fans of that particular era would choose to know the reason why McIlroy was sold.

The reasons for this sale remain, to fans, as big a mystery today as they did then and the stories and rumours have grown over the years. There's a varied selection:

1.  There was a major fall-out between Harry Potts and McIlroy about his playing role.

2.  "Just what have you done to upset Bob Lord and Harry Potts? What have you been up to, and who with?" asked his great friend Danny Blanchflower who telephoned him immediately.

3.  "Either he goes or you go," said Bob Lord to Harry Potts.

4.  "We want the same money as he gets," said a posse of the emerging Burnley younger star players knocking on a worried Bob Lord's door when the last thing Lord wanted was everyone on McIlroy's wages.

5.  He was good friends with an ex director, Reg Cook and his son, whom Bob Lord didn't like. "I'll choose my own friends," said McIlroy to Adamson who warned him that Lord did not approve.

6.  The club was desperate for money after two months of inactivity due to a bad winter.

7.  He wasn't performing any more and was past his best, said several Press reports.

8.  "He doesn't try and doesn't train, we're fed up," said a group of team mates in an early display of player power.

9.  "You're not playing to your own high standards any more," Harry Potts told him.

10.  He had a poor game, according to Press reports, against Liverpool in the Cup replay in February and then returned home, not on the team coach but with his friend Reg Cook's son and this was the last straw for Bob Lord.

11.  'Selling Mac will balance the budget', wrote Bob Lord in the Evening Telegraph in a lengthy piece, (full article in appendices). Yet this clearly contradicts Lord's continual insistence that it was always Harry Potts' decision, since Potts never had any input into the financial decisions at the club. Nor did Potts' eventual explanations for the transfer ever include the need to balance budgets.

You take your pick from any of the above stories from the rumour mill. But the further puzzle is that if Jimmy Mac's own explanation is correct, that is to say his friendship with the Cooks; then it was clearly and solely Lord's decision, even though Lord always maintained that it was Harry Potts who made the decision. To this day, Jimmy Mac and John Cook remain the closest of friends.

All that is known for certain is that Lord held a board meeting on the Sunday after the Tuesday evening Liverpool game. "We're selling him," Lord informed them all.

It was, incidentally, round about this time that Lord (forever in the back page news) and Potts might have been lampooned mercilessly on the TV satire show, *That Was the Week That Was*, in a script written by football writer Brian Glanville. The sketch making fun of Lord in the role of the 'tyrant' and Potts in the role of the subservient 'yes man' was never shown. Glanville has always believed that the title win was less to do with Harry Potts, than the presence of great players at their peak like McIlroy and Jimmy Adamson, and the foundations laid by Alan Brown.

The only certainties in the saga, however, are that the Cup-tie was lost, the club was desperate for money, an impromptu board meeting was held, and McIlroy was informed by manager Potts that he was being transfer listed.

It was in 1999 that he spoke to what was then the *Lancashire Evening Telegraph* about the decision that had been made years earlier. "It was the worst day of my football career. I can remember Harry Potts calling me into the office at quarter-to-ten to break the news and say he was putting me on the list. Immediately I knew it wasn't Harry's decision because he looked in pain. He looked more stunned than I did, so obviously he had been told by Bob Lord that I had to go. In fact some time afterwards I learned from a Burnley director that Lord had called a meeting at his factory on the Sunday morning and he said to Harry Potts, 'McIlroy must go'. And I gather then Harry said to him 'I still need him' and Lord is supposed to have said, 'Well either he goes or you go'. I was very friendly with the family of a Burnley director who everyone knew Bob Lord detested. He was called Reg Cook. At one time he was vice-chairman of the club and I was very friendly with his son and in fact in away games his son used to bring me back in his car. I can remember Jimmy Adamson saying to me one day that Bob Lord won't like this, being so friendly and seeing so much of the Cooks. But I thought, 'I'm not going to let Bob Lord choose my friends for me'. I'm convinced that's the sole reason why Bob Lord put me on the transfer list. I feel sure that my friendship with the Cooks ended my career here."

Possibly Jimmy's explanation is partly correct in that the Cook friendship was simply the last straw for Bob Lord. It is doubtful that it was the sole reason and was probably one of several.

Even without the transfer controversy it was a season not without its problems including; the bad weather, a brutal Cup-tie at Tottenham (which Burnley won 3 – 0), Press and FA criticisms of Harry Potts, and a training incident when Gordon Harris assaulted Jimmy Adamson.

It was after the Spurs game that Burnley were next drawn against Liverpool and the first game in Burnley was a 1 – 1 draw. The replay did not take place until midweek on February 20th. It was the catalyst for the bombshell that was to follow.

The story is well known. In extra time Adam Blacklaw as good as gifted the game to Liverpool. He was an outstanding goalkeeper and had very much kept them in this tie at Turf Moor. But even the best goalkeepers are not perfect. He elected to kick a back pass from Alex Elder straight back up the field from the edge of the area. It hit Ian St. John who was just yards away. St. John was onto it in a flash and would have scored but for Blacklaw bringing him down. The penalty was put away by Ronnie Moran. Burnley, fancied for Wembley again, were out and McIlroy according to Press reports had not played particularly well. He was described as spending most of his time dropping deep, ineffectively meandering in no-mans-land and never living up to his reputation. Newspapers pointed to

Bob Lord, along with Harry Potts, probably the only person who really knows why Jimmy Mac was sold.

Burnley's uncustomary defensive style and that they had abandoned their usual sweet-moving attacking style and Liverpool were never put under any pressure. McIlroy later defended himself saying that he had only been playing to manager Potts' instructions.

There hadn't been a League game since December 29th and there was no game on the Saturday following the Liverpool game. On the Monday McIlroy was called into Potts' office and given the news. Little elaboration at this stage came from Harry Potts to journalists and it was the player who gave the gist of the conversation to the Press.

"I went into Harry Potts' office and he told me straight out that the board of directors had decided on his recommendation to place me on the transfer list. I asked him why and he told me he was disappointed with my playing efforts and that there was nothing more to it."

McIlroy added that it had then been explained to him that it was purely to do with the playing side of things. It was nothing to do with finance (in contradiction to what Bob Lord later said) and that there was no friction between himself and Harry Potts, the directors or Bob Lord. If this was the explanation he was baffled. Surely if this was the reason the normal thing would have been to play him in the reserves for a while in order to recover his best form.

After the meeting Potts suggested to McIlroy that he should go home and miss the rest of training. This he did and gave the news to his shocked wife Barbara. Within 24 hours supporters were starting petitions, holding meetings, bombarding the Press, demanding answers, threatening never to set foot in Turf Moor again, and daubing graffiti around the town.

Granville Shackleton recalls being at the club and being told the news. He also recalled that an astonished Ray Pointer was in the vicinity and on hearing what was going on, rushed off to tell the other players. John Connelly was on his way to an England gathering, and remembers saying a shocked "bloody hell" to himself when he heard.

It seemed that everyone who possessed pen and paper wanted to have their say and put down their views, including Tom Finney and Danny Blanchflower. "Burnley must speak up," wrote Finney, noting that no official Press statement had yet been made. He added that McIlroy had commented to him that he was perhaps caught up in club politics, possibly in connection with helping his father-in-law buy and sell club shares, not something that Bob Lord would welcome. Or perhaps it involved his friendship with the Cooks and that it had not gone down too well that after the traumatic Liverpool game he had disappeared all too quickly in the Cooks' car.

Blanchflower's lengthy, thoughtful piece in a Sunday newspaper hinted at financial reasons and that other players were resentful of his star status and backslaps he received. They resented his higher salary, he suggested. He implied that because of this, the financial balance of the club was being undermined as other players sought parity and clearly the only way to nip this in the bud was to sell McIlroy. Blanchflower alleged that he had spoken at length to his colleague, and dwelt in the article on how McIlroy would now feel until the transfer was resolved. He would be in a vacuum, feel isolated, and there would be a definite uneasiness in the dressing room.

"It must be finance," he said.

'When they beat Tottenham, Bob Lord and his merry men probably thought they would win the Cup. But Liverpool had other ideas. Another Cup run to Wembley would have put thousands of pounds in the Burnley kitty. Maybe they were counting on that. And on the added support that a good Cup run would bring to their League matches. It's been a hard winter. Funds are low all round. McIlroy is getting more money than the others. Perhaps the others are starting to ask for the same. Simple solution: sell McIlroy; get some cash, cut the feet from under the others with regard to asking for more. That's better for the club in the long run or at least it would seem to be'.

*(For complete Blanchflower article see appendices)*

Blanchflower as ever spoke good sense. He certainly phoned Jimmy Mac; maybe he phoned other players. And McIlroy himself, not long afterwards, in a daily newspaper alluded to the possible discontent felt by other players that he was on a higher salary.

Were these the reasons then that he was transfer-listed; a combination of the club being in desperate need of money, and player unrest? Lord had plans to build a giant new stand. No club can build stands without money, nor can it pay wages. And, if player unrest was a factor, this was certainly not something the club would have wanted to make public. How badly it would have reflected on the legendary family spirit.

At last the club spoke. "POTTS ENDS HIS SILENCE" was the *Burnley Express* headline on March 6th after Burnley and Stoke had sealed the deal that took Jimmy Mac to the Potteries. It had taken this long for anything to come from Potts or Lord, the silence being another factor that aggravated supporters.

'When I first told Jimmy McIlroy last Monday that Burnley had decided to put him on the transfer list, it was agreed between us that there should be no public slanging match. I have seen that this has not occurred and because of it I have been unable to say to the Press until now any more than that this was a club matter. Now I can tell you our side of the story. Jimmy McIlroy has left Burnley and the only person responsible for this is Jimmy McIlroy himself'.

Potts could make it no clearer than that, and then went on to say that he had not been giving 100%, that Jimmy on his own admission had become complacent and that no club could afford the luxury of a player not giving every effort. McIlroy could have stayed at Turf Moor for the rest of his playing days with a third benefit and testimonial game to be arranged, Harry explained, but it was his lack of playing effort that was the reason behind the decision to sell him.

Potts' statement is therefore plausible, but if there are indeed other reasons as suggested by McIlroy himself in the *Daily Express*, they are left out. They are not what a manager like Harry Potts with his multitude of loyalties would want to make public.

Lord stayed silent and it was left to the manager to make the statements. As a result, it was Potts, as much if not more than Lord, who was subjected to abuse and criticism from Burnley people. His wife found slogans and insults on their car and was greatly upset by it. Their children were taunted at school. Not much more than two years earlier he had won a Championship for them, played in Europe and less than a year earlier had reached Wembley. Now he was being pilloried.

More than 40 years on, Jimmy McIlroy maintains that he is still baffled by the whole thing. "When I asked him why I was being transfer listed he replied that he didn't think I had been doing it on the field. So, I asked, well why not drop me and put me in the reserves? He answered that you don't drop players like me. Since then I have always thought, well then why sell me?"

But sold he was, to Stoke City, after several days of wrangling and haggling over the price; his friendship with the Cooks and return home to Burnley with John Cook after the Liverpool defeat probably the last straw for an irate Bob Lord. We in Burnley can still speculate and talk about all the theories and rumours that abound regarding the reasons for his sale. Perhaps Blanchflower's finance theory was correct, perhaps Potts' part of the story was correct, perhaps Jimmy is correct about the Cooks. Maybe there were a number of contributory reasons and it all came to a head after that devastating Cup-tie result.

Jimmy McIlroy can have the last word. "As far as I'm concerned, only two people know why I was placed on the transfer list and that secret will remain with them. By coincidence they lie close by each other in the graveyard at Read Church."

He has had a remarkable impact on the small town of Burnley and its people. It is for that reason that his story is worth the telling.

## Chapter Two

# Boy With A Tennis Ball

IT WAS our first face to face meeting to talk about the book. It had taken me a while to bring him round to the idea that people would value it and that it was worth doing. I had said to him that, in fact, I would be able to write about him without his help, not that I wanted that to sound arrogant or conceited or that he, Jimmy McIlroy, was unnecessary. Far from it; without him, how could I get to the heart of the man, delve into his opinions; tease out his stories and all the experiences of his magical years in football. To write this book without him, how could I possibly put flesh on the bones and bring it to life?

From his initial lack of enthusiasm when I first broached the idea little seeds of interest began to appear, but it took some time to bring him round. I drove over from Leeds not entirely confident or certain of his agreement. I knew from talking to his daughter Anne that he had genuine reservations. I'd met him several times since 2003 when I wrote about him in *No Nay Never*. Regarding this new book, we had spoken by 'phone several times, but not until the first meeting did he agree to go ahead. Three things concerned him, that firstly it would not sound like him; secondly that it would be a rush job, and thirdly that his memory would let him down. I knew by the end of the morning that the latter would be no problem as he related a dozen stories. He was relieved to hear that it would take probably a year from start to finish. And as for sounding like him, (he speaks softly and quietly, the gentle Irish brogue still firmly there after all these years in Lancashire), all I could say was that I would write it in plain simple English, or maybe I should have said plain simple Irish, and anyway it would be a biography, not an autobiography, so the bulk of it would be in my voice or those of other contributors.

When a book is about a man like Jimmy McIlroy, the writing of it is like a journey. Somehow I wanted to take him back in time to how and where it all began. Once there, at the beginning, I wanted Jimmy to bring me back on the return journey to the present. In this case both of us could relive our past, for whilst Jimmy was at Burnley playing and enthralling the crowd, I was one of that crowd. I have scrapbooks that narrate those times and the programmes of games he played in. There are landmarks in my own life that I can remember and they relate to the events in his story. He and I are not two distant people who have come together simply to write this book. Though the first time we met in person was in 2003, I have in fact known Jimmy McIlroy all my life from my schoolboy days, through watching him play, reading his book, and then seeing him leave. He is, quite simply, one of my great heroes. I grew up with him. My boyhood and teenage years coincided with his greatest times.

It was when I was leaving and we stood just outside the front door of his house that I realised that before this visit, he must have intended to go ahead. He had already given thought to wanting to write about his early years in Ireland and knew what he wanted to call the book. "I've thought of a title. I'd like to call it *Why Me?*" The reasons for that title I hope will emerge. As it turned out much later, we changed this name when it became clear the 'Prince of Inside Forwards' were the words that best summed him up.

The 1931 wider world he was born into was not an easy one. There was a deepening economic crisis particularly in Europe. Britain was verging on bankruptcy and civil unrest. 12,000 sailors mutinied over pay. A new coalition government raised taxes and reduced unemployment allowances. Against this background Oswald Mosley launched his fascist 'New Party'. In Germany the Nazi party was growing stronger by the day against a background of 5million unemployed. In the USA Al Capone was put behind bars, and the Empire State Building was finally completed and opened its doors. But all of that was miles away from the Ballyskeagh that Jimmy came to describe, especially as news from afar was something seldom heard in a place, where in 1931, not one person in the village possessed a radio.

Jimmy Mac with teenage team mate Billy Bingham at Coop Recreation. For years Northern Ireland right wing partnership.

All the history books say that Jimmy McIlroy was from Lambeg. "But that's probably because they didn't know how to spell Ballyskeagh," he says with a smile. He was born in Greenhill a mile or so from Ballyskeagh in his Grandmother Maguire's house. But he was brought up and raised in his Grandmother McIlroy's house in Ballyskeagh, a tiny place that in 1931 could hardly be described as even a village. Close to Lambeg and Lisburn, the latter today a city of over 70,000 people, it consisted of just four rows of terraced houses, with only earthen lanes in between. Only one of them, a row of houses that ran alongside the main road, affectionately known as the 'parlour houses' by the villagers, had running water. They were called the 'parlour houses' because they had a front and back room with a front and back garden.

He was the eldest and the only boy of six children, and was "the reason why my mother and father married." Harry McIlroy and Matilda (Tilly) didn't have a suitable property so Jimmy was born in Grandma Maguires house. Thus, after he was born, Grandma McIlroy suggested that Jimmy should live with her in Ballyskeagh until his mother and father found their feet. "When he was 19 my father could have become a professional footballer but my grandmother said to him that he couldn't afford now he had a wife and baby. There wasn't enough money and in the summer there was even less if you were a footballer".

As one by one the five sisters were born, Jimmy stayed with her until he was thirteen. It was only on her death that he moved to live with his parents when his grandfather moved to live with one of his other daughters. In villages such as this whole families lived side by side. In the house next to his grandmother lived her sister; in the next house was her daughter, and then next to that another sister. His mother and father lived in one of the other rows. He saw them once or twice a week when he called in on them, or they called at his grandmother's. To him it was all so very normal.

"The village was full of cousins and aunts and uncles, it was so small you knew everybody and we were always in and out of each others' rows of houses."

These were the rows without running water and electricity. Rainwater collected in a barrel from the roof of the house was used for washing. The village pump provided drinking water. It was under a corrugated tin hut with a tin roof that projected outwards to keep waiting people dry. People had their set time for fetching their water. It was a great place for gossip.

"I could lie awake in bed at night, the pump was only 30 yards away, and I would know who was there filling up their containers. As soon as I was big enough it was one of the jobs I did." Baths in the tin bath were rare and Jimmy well remembers "in the one hot week of the year we seemed to have in May, we'd all just dive in the river. For some of the lads it was their only bath of the year and they were black with dirt."

"Why me?" is a question Jimmy asks himself sometimes as he looks back on his life. "Why did I become a footballer, why did I become so successful, when there were other boys who might have been just as good, just as successful?" Maybe one reason is simply that his grandmother had the end house in one of the terraces and he was able to spend hours kicking a tennis ball against the gable end without anyone telling him to stop. Had someone else lived in that house it is more than likely they would soon have become tired of the constant sound of the ball being kicked against the wall. He and his pals played football constantly in the nearby fields but when they were called in for their tea Jimmy was more often than not straight back out to play on his own kicking the ball against the gable end. "Just how often do you see this today?" he asks, "A boy playing and practising with a tennis ball."

"This was 1930s rural Ireland, today you just can't imagine what it was like," says Jimmy. "It seems to me now it was just one step above the poverty line of a Third World country. It's hard to convey and describe just how primitive it was. I can remember the first electric lights and the first radio that someone had in their house. We all crowded into the hall or stood outside to listen to Big Bill Campbell's Rocky Mountain Rhythm. The first sports programme I heard was a flyweight world championship boxing match between Rinty Monaghan and Dado Marino from Mexico. Rinty was the world champion and after every fight sang 'When Irish eyes are smiling'. Years later in 1958 we sang it in Sweden. His nickname came from his fondness for dogs and frequently bringing injured dogs home, resulting in his grandmother calling him Rin Tin Tin, after the famous film dog."

Jimmy's beginnings were poor; his mother didn't work. "Too busy bringing up five girls," says Jimmy. His father Harry left school at 14 and was a labourer until he found work in a Belfast paint factory. He had a wonderful knack for the blending and mixing of colours, becoming highly skilled. Today Jimmy smiles wistfully remembering all this and wishes that he had the same skill in the mixing of his watercolours when he is working on his paintings. Many of the other villagers worked in Churchill in the weaving factory that was near enough to walk to.

It was when Jimmy moved to his parents' house following the death of his grandmother that his father began to make sure that Jimmy had the meat, when there was any, and the girls according to Jimmy "got the vegetables." It was clear by now that he was a talented and gifted footballer and his father wanted to make sure he grew stronger. But by now it was wartime, making food even scarcer still. Belfast suffered from bombing raids and an air raid shelter in Ballyskeagh provided four more walls against which a ball could be kicked and skills developed.

Belfast, just a few miles to the north, was a total contrast, with its university and government buildings, grand shops, elegant streets, and all its industry and busy shipyards. A village like Ballyskeagh might have been a million miles away. Life and amenities were basic and luxuries were few and far between. Hunger, poverty and hardship were widespread. Entertainment was home made. Close as it was to Belfast, this was rural Ireland, a place of small farms, green fields, meadows, streams and woodlands. Available work was based around agriculture or the linen industry of which Lisburn was a major centre. The mills, general labouring and the Belfast shipyards were the biggest employers for many years.

The climate was ideal for the growing of flax and Irish linen was world famous. The River Lagan flows through the vale and it was because of the river and the damp climate that flax was first grown there. Nearby Lambeg was known for its bleaching greens, these being large areas of grass where the linen was laid out to be bleached by the elements. Woven linen cloth is a pale beige colour and must be bleached to achieve the crisp whiteness for which it is famous. Before chemicals were introduced this was done by exposure to sunlight and weather. The cloth would be pegged out and turned over regularly to attain an even bleaching on both sides. Spreading it out and collecting it all in was an endless backbreaking task for those involved. Watchmen were employed to ensure that no cloth was stolen or grazing animals intruded. Small as it was, Lambeg became a place of some importance in 1921 when the Government of Northern Ireland set up a Linen Research Association but as the industry declined it closed in 1993. By the end of the 1950's the competition from other textiles produced in poorer countries was too great.

Today, Ballyskeagh is the home of Lisburn Distillery Football Club, Distillery having moved there from Belfast in the early 80s, and changing its name from Distillery to Lisburn Distillery in order to associate itself with new potential supporters. Next to it is McIlroy Park. The boy who grew up with all the difficulties and hardships of such a humble, although happy boyhood, brought up for most of that time by his grandmother, today has a park named after him. "Why me?" he asks again. "How did life manage to pick me out to be such a success?"

*In retrospect, I feel now that my life in football was the inevitable outcome of a Christmas gift from Uncle Willie McIlroy; to be correct, a succession of Christmas gifts. Most youngsters collect a ration of toys from their uncles, books and other welcome presents – but not me. I always received a football. With almost monotonous regularity, 25th December, the most exciting day in the calendar for every youngster, yielded a ball for Jimmy McIlroy. I cannot remember when I was given my first; it seemed there was no beginning to the ritual. The footballs had always come for Christmas.*

*Uncle Willie had a great influence on my early development as a footballer. He had the background, being a professional player, a centre half with the Irish League club Portadown. My father, Harry, also possessed considerable ability as a player, being with Distillery at one time, though most of his games were played in the reserves.* (Right Inside Soccer 1960)

When Jimmy still wonders today how it was that he went on to become a player, he

# Growing up in 1940s Ireland

Top left: This was supposed to be a family photograph but somehow Francis Spence sneaked on the picture. Jimmy is on the left and cousin Willie Brown is on the right.

Below left: Glentoran's nursery side, The Coop, which produced several professional players.

Top right: Jimmy centre with two school friends.

Bottom right: Studio portrait taken after first youth international game aged 16.

points to other happy accidents. In a family of six, the law of averages might suggest that five sisters is unusual and the fact that he was the only boy of the six children meant that it was he alone who received most attention. Not that his sisters were neglected but another boy in the family might just have diluted the focus he got when it became clear to his father and uncle that he possessed a rare talent. The only boy therefore, with a footballing father and uncle, gave him the belief that he was destined to become a footballer, and the opportunity to fulfil it. He would have loved a brother in fact, and when his final sister arrived, he was hugely disappointed.

*Many outstanding footballers claim they learned their trade with a tennis ball, or even a bundle of rags tied together with string. Constant practice with a tennis ball is the finest coaching ever devised. The 'real' ball was reserved for 90 minutes on a Saturday afternoon; the tennis ball was the tool for practice and we hoped might lead to perfection. As I gradually mastered ball skills, my dad became even more keen that I should not be hampered by my physique. There wasn't very much of me which is why he made the unselfish decision – especially in the days of wartime rationing – that the best had to be fed to young Jimmy. Meats, eggs, bacon were all terribly scarce, but it was taken for granted that I should go short of nothing. I owe a debt to the other members of my family.* (Right Inside Soccer 1960)

*I'm certain I owe a lot to countless hours spent kicking a tennis ball against the wall of my home, when my pals tired of soccer, and using my imagination as an opponent, conjuring up all sorts of incidents I was likely to encounter in a match; such as a defender rushing in to tackle and being forced to play the ball first time from all heights and angles. I'm convinced this 'self-coaching' developed my skills, timing and balance, because in my imaginative wonderland I captured the pace and excitement of a real game, and it's only in matches that skills are nurtured into peak performance. It's possible, too, Irish as it may sound, that I was fortunate my schooldays happened during the war years, when footballs were practically non-existent, and touch and ball-sense was fostered with the only balls occasionally available – tennis balls.* (See appendices for full article: Gillette Book of Cricket and Football 1963)

"I never doubted that I would become a footballer," wrote Jimmy in 1960.

The conditions and background for his development and the growth of his talent were in place. He and the village boys played from morning till night and he laughs now to think that one part of the fields where they played was where the earth toilets were emptied every so often. Other than in the 'parlour houses' a flush toilet was unheard of in Ballyskeagh and the 'night soil' as it was known, was periodically collected from every house and tipped down one of the sloping fields.

What else was there to do then in the village but play football, with most people not even possessing a radio? But what do young lads do today when they are surrounded by so many other available activities and distractions, glued to their TV's and computers in their bedrooms, whilst outdoors, the places where they can play dwindle, and  Saturday morning school football led by eager teachers is almost a thing of the past in so many areas. Jimmy and hundreds like him developed their wonderful individual skills without any coaching. Today the scouting net is cast far and wide and youngsters are attached to clubs from as young as ten and even eight years old. They are coached on a regular basis. Yet, one of the most prolific eras of football in the UK, the 40s, 50s, and 60s, was a time when there were legions of supremely gifted, individually great players. A list of their names would fill several pages, yet this was a time when such early systematic coaching did not exist. Skills were

A smartly dressed young Jimmy Mac.

honed in the backstreets, the fields, and the school playground and if you were lucky, against the gable end of your house, like Jimmy McIlroy's.

He ran back home every night from school. "My fitness in later life must have had something to do with that." It was in Drumbeg just a couple of miles away and they walked there in all weathers, winter and summer, but ran back. There were three teachers to teach the pupils who came at five years old and left at fourteen. "There was Mrs Allen and Miss Gordon. Then there was Mr Connor who taught us from age twelve to fourteen. He had white hair and was quite distinguished looking. He had travelled a lot to America and places in Europe and told us all about those places. He was interesting and I remember he cycled to school a distance of two to three miles.

"Mrs Bunting had the village shop and it was the kind of shop where she'd have oil for the lamps we needed in one hand, and a loaf in the other when you went in. The shop sold everything from candles to sweets and groceries to cigarettes.

"My grandmother's house had a hall which opened into just one biggish living room. This room had what we called a 'bunk', a sort of, not really a cupboard, but a floor to ceiling space that was boxed off with a bed inside it. Upstairs there were two bedrooms. We had oil lamps and in winter we lit the coal fire and sat round it to keep warm. It was used for cooking and my grandmother always seemed to be baking soda bread, and wheaten bread.

"The one holiday of the year and a highlight was the annual trip to the seaside. For those who went to Sunday School regularly there was the special day out, just the one day. A coach would take us and that was our one treat of the year. The Orangemens' March on July 12th was always special and spectacular. They would use the Lambeg Drum, famous because it's the biggest drum there is. On a Saturday I used to go the 'pictures' in Lisburn for the afternoon matinee. There was Gene Autry; I think he was 'the singing cowboy', and Roy Rogers and his horse Trigger. Then there was Tarzan. Once I was working, we went to Belfast on a Saturday night for the dancehalls or the cinema.

"My grandmother had never been anywhere further than Belfast in her life. There was a morning bus to Belfast and one in the evening. At weekends there would be a few more. In wartime, Belfast suffered a number of air raids. We could see them from Ballyskeagh ten miles away. Whenever we could see and hear a raid we all ran down to a relative's house to shelter together in the one room. I laugh now to think that's what we did instead of spreading out, all of us hiding together. If one bomb had hit that one house we'd have all been blown up.

"There was no organised football at this time. There was no school football at all and we organised games amongst ourselves. But at the school in Lambeg the headmaster was Tom Priestley and he had played for Northern Ireland. He had played for Chelsea as well. He was bald and wore a wig, but if he was playing he took the wig off. I met him when I signed for Burnley. He had his wig on that day."

Jimmy never saw his father or Uncle Willie play but his father always told him the story that on one occasion he was walking towards the Belfast Oval; who was coming towards him but Peter Doherty then playing for Glentoran. Jimmy says his father told him that story so many times and always counted it as one of his greatest thrills. At that time Harry McIlroy would never have guessed that his son Jimmy would play for Glentoran and Northern Ireland, the latter with the legendary Peter Doherty as manager.

One particular friend of Jimmy's was a lad called Artie Taylor who lived in Greenhill.

Artie too was a brilliant footballer; in fact Jimmy says he was the best of all the lads he knew. He was a wonderful dribbler and no-one could ever get the ball off him. His memories of Artie again prompt Jimmy to ask "why me" when he contemplates his career. "Artie was so good, why was it me and not him who found fame? Artie played for Luton and still lives there I think."

It was Artie who persuaded Jimmy to join him playing for Craigavad which was way past Belfast on the road towards Bangor. It was a walk into Lambeg for the bus, the bus to Belfast and then change to another bus to Craigavad. "I'd be at work in the morning, rush home, grab something to eat, rush to Lambeg – and then to Craigavad. It seemed to take hours to get there, but we thought nothing of it. It's what you did."

*At 14, I'd won a scholarship to Lisburn Technical School, where one of my fellow pupils was Norman Drew, who later became a distinguished member of the Great Britain Ryder Cup golf team. Norman swears to this day that it was playing behind me in the 'Tech' football team that made him switch from football to golf. He thought his own limitations as a footballer became far too obvious.*

*My stay at the Technical School was brief, only six months in fact and then I thought it was about time I did some work for a living, to repay all that my parents had done for me. My father, dedicated to helping me becoming a footballer, insisted that whatever I did should not be strenuous and that living on double rations I should avoid anything too laborious. We decided I would be an electrician.*

*But, a cousin of mine then suggested that what I really needed to build me up with man-sized muscles was an outdoor job. I should do something physical – like building, or tree-felling.*

*I became a bricklayer.*

*The sacrifices my family made continued. When sandwiches for lunch were made in the morning, mine were filled with meat and the first to be made. Food was still short even when the war ended and my parents continually tried to get extra eggs from the local farms. As a famous politician might have said, "I'd never had it so good."*

*It was a wonderful, glorious summer. I stripped to the waist and worked hard. Muscles developed everywhere and the sun gave me a deep brown tan. The family was delighted.*

*But that was the summer and then the winter came. For months I froze and tried to warm my hands over an open brazier. My fingers were numbed, the circulation seemed to stop. All I wanted to do was find some other job, anything, any job, instead of bricklaying. One of my workmates was Tommy Casey who one day would also play for Northern Ireland alongside me. He would become a star player with Newcastle United. On cold, frosty mornings as we shivered and grumbled each of us would try to get the newspaper first and look at the jobs section. Even today I shudder to think of those wintry days, the cold, the damp and our icy fingers. I decided you couldn't pay bricklayers enough in these conditions, and it was impossible to overpay a man who laid bricks for his living. "I'd rather be a rag and bone man," said Tommy one morning.*

*The only thing that made up for this was football. I had become a member of the Craigavad club near Bangor.* (Right Inside Soccer 1960.)

## Chapter Three

# No Suitcase

I'D TAKEN Jimmy Mac a few things to show him; souvenirs, memorabilia, magazines, photographs, some old annuals in which he was featured, and the programme of the Stoke City versus Real Madrid centenary game in which Jimmy scored in a 2 – 2 draw.

"Oh blazes," he said. "Blazes" is the nearest thing to swearing I have heard from him whereas the dreadful 'F' word seems to be the first word the modern footballer learns as a toddler. "Where did you get these things from?" He looked at one old action picture of himself in the green Irish shirt. It was one of those lovely old pictures you found in 1950s annuals where they took a black and white photograph and then hand coloured it. Some of them are works of art but accuracy and facial features can get lost in translation.

"Oh blazes," he said again with the tiniest smile on his face. I couldn't blame him, even in the Irish green he looked more like John Wayne than Jimmy McIlroy. I passed him an old September 1966 *Soccer Star*. On the front cover was the Oldham Athletic team. Jimmy is on the back row. He looks cold and fed up, mind you so do half of them. There's just the hint of a smile on the rest. Maybe it's to do with how I remember him in earlier years, but he looks ill at ease and out of place. Another of the magazines featured him on the front cover in the red stripes of Stoke City. He had seen it once before on the wall of the Border Bookshop in Todmorden.

Victor from the shop told me Jimmy had been there a couple of times and had seen the picture on the wall. He'd said how he never liked it and that it was a shirt in which no-one ever looked good. He looked at it again when I showed it to him. "I never looked good in it, never felt smart in it. I always thought it looked an untidy shirt. Not even Stanley Matthews looked good in it."

The Stoke v Real Madrid programme I bought on eBay for less than a fiver. I thought it would set me back far more and if I'd spent four times that, it would have been worth it. Jimmy looked through the pages and the team lists. The game was played not long after he moved from Burnley.

"Did I tell you about Puskas?" he asked. I settled back. Puskas had been in the Real Madrid team that night.

"One of the best moments of the night was when I beat Puskas and got past him. I feinted and he fell for the dummy. I remember there was a look of acknowledgement on his face and appreciation of what I had done. He was still one of the greatest players in the world and he showed me with the look on his face and in his eyes that he recognised that bit of skill."

What I wanted to talk about that morning was his time at Craigavad and then Glentoran. But first, another little story came out and again it was all to do with the recurring question, "Why me, how was I picked out to do well, how did the luck come my way?

"I had been picked to play for the Irish youth team against Scotland at Ayr. But I had no suitcase. We were to sail across from Larne to Stranraer in Scotland, play the game, and then come back the next night. But all I could think was I have no suitcase for my clothes and without a suitcase how could I go; in fact I didn't want to go. How could I go with my things packed in just a bag or a parcel? I would have looked like an evacuee. I would just be so embarrassed. Well, word must have got round the village and there was just one person with a suitcase. 'Can I borrow it?' I asked. I still remember it was nothing special because it wasn't leather; it was a sort of thick cardboard. But it was a suitcase and it saved me because I would have been too embarrassed to go without one. And I still think even today what I would have done? I was just lucky that one person had a suitcase."

Jimmy's first serious team was near Bangor. "It was Artie Taylor who persuaded me to join him playing for Craigavad which was way past Belfast on the way to Bangor. It was a walk into Lambeg for the bus, the bus to Belfast and then change to another bus for Craigavad. I'd be at work in the morning, rush home, grab something to eat, rush to Lambeg, then to Craigavad. It seemed to take hours to get there, but we thought nothing of it. It's what you did then." In fact, as well as Craigavad, Jimmy turned out for any team short of a player.

Scouts from the big clubs were always watching their games and Fred Steadman had followed his progress since Technical School. One night with Artie he was stopped by Steadman who asked the pair of them would they like to sign for Glentoran? He didn't need to ask them twice. They signed the forms there and then and received their first signing on fee – a fish and chip supper. He was put in the Co-operative Team and also in this team at the time was Danny Blanchflower's brother Jackie and Billy Bingham. The Co-operative team was in fact the Glentoran Third team by another name.

*My foot was at last on the ladder at Glentoran and without doubt I couldn't have joined a better club to begin my career. Glentoran at that time were making the first serious attempt to develop young players. They weren't allowed to enter teams in any amateur league but they got round that by taking over the Cooperative Club and used that club to give young Oval players competitive football. It was Glentoran Juniors in all but name. In that side I first met Billy Bingham who like me moved on to the first team and was then transferred across to England where we both won international honours.*

*John Geary, an old Irish international was in charge of the Cooperative team and deserves a huge tribute. He insisted at all times that we should play cultured football. His maxim was: 'Pure football counts above all else'. These words have stayed with me ever since and guided me. Enthusiasm, speed, hard work, all these have their place in football, but, I am certain that only skill provides the real test and is the essential basic need. It is all-important.*

*I remember one particularly rough match with the Glentoran Co-operative youngsters on the receiving end of some vicious first-half tackling. At half time John Geary warned us: 'There must be no retaliation from any of you kids. Any display of bad temper will be severely frowned on. Keep playing football'. We did, but it was difficult against grown men every week.*

*Many lessons are there to be learned between the ages of 15 and 20. I learned how to live with disappointment. After one game for the international youth eleven, I was dropped. Later, I won back my position and realised that faced with setbacks like this you have to take them in your stride.*

*It was during a youth international fixture in England at Hull that I was first approached about joining an English club. Ireland lost 2 – 4 but I must have had a good game. As I left the ground I was approached by a stranger who asked me would I like to sign for Bolton Wanderers. I was immediately over the moon and replied immediately that I would love to. The stranger promised me that someone would be over to Belfast to see me. But no-one ever did. They must have decided I wasn't good enough to justify the journey. By that time, anyway, I had signed professional forms for Glentoran.*

*Towards the end of the 1948/49 season I was promoted from the Co-op to the Glentoran first team, it was the very last match of the season. A week later Glentoran went to Dublin for a friendly game against Bohemians at Dalymount Park, and I kept my place. Allegedly, two directors from Burnley were at that game with most of their attention fixed on myself and Billy Bingham. I'm told they reported back that we were no better than the young players already at Turf Moor. I could have been signed for £10 that day and so could Billy Bingham. I later cost them £8,000 and Billy Bingham went on to become another great player.*

*At the start of the next season I reported to the Oval expecting to be in the reserves again. Instead, with Billy, I was straight into the first team for the first game against rivals Linfield. This was always a 'needle' match and there was a huge crowd for this opening game. They were probably attracted more by Linfield stars like Alf McMicheal and George Hannah, rather than the young Jimmy McIlroy.*

*I kept my place for the next half a dozen matches but felt something was missing, I felt something was wrong with my performances. I was still bricklaying and trying to be a footballer at the same time. There was no way this was possible and it bothered me that I wasn't physically or mentally strong enough to make the progress I wanted to make. We worked on a bonus system in the building trade so there was no chance to take things easy. If I'd done that and slowed down I would have cost my workmates hard cash. Working so hard laying bricks all day I seemed to have little energy left for the football and the training. It was just too much. I had a hard decision to make and chose to give up the job and become a full-time footballer on £5 a week, less than what I earned as a bricklayer with the bonuses.*

*Most of the other players were part-timers and there were days when there was no-one there to train with so I made another decision. I would spend two days every week hiking round the hills overlooking the Lagan Valley. With the family mongrel, 'Darkie', I covered at least ten miles a day, building up stamina and fitness. Going full-time was the best decision I made, the new fitness and readiness for Saturday showing in my game. (Right Inside Soccer 1960.)*

Jimmy played just the one league game for Glentoran in 1948/49. Danny Blanchflower was still there but left for Barnsley at the end of the season and another great player, Bertie Peacock, left to go to Glasgow Celtic. Billy Bingham was another new, rising star in the team. He would be sold to Sunderland. McIlroy played just the one game plus a friendly but in the following season 1949/50, he came into the team to play 25 games and score nine goals. He was quick, incredibly sharp and was clearly a major talent.

Glentoran were a club with a great history, part and parcel of the life and fabric of Belfast since 1882, one of the most successful clubs in the province; their roll call of players sent to England impressive, Bingham, McIlroy, both Blanchflowers, Casey, Peacock being just a few. Their most romantic achievement was perhaps winning the Vienna Cup in Europe in 1914. They won the league title, the Irish Cup, the Gold Cup, the Antrim Shield and other trophies on countless occasions.

They had in fact returned to the Belfast Oval in season 1949/50. In the wartime

"I'd taken Jimmy a few things to show him. One of the magazines showed him in the red stripes of Stoke City". Not Jimmy's favourite picture or shirt. "The least flattering jersey I ever pulled on".

bombing raids on the city, the ground had been reduced to rubble along with the shipyards. Somehow the club had raised £20,000 to restore the Oval, a huge amount for those days. Most of it was the result of the supporters' clubs and scores of events organised in conjunction with the 'Back to the Oval' appeal. Excitement mounted in Belfast as August 20th approached and it was seen as the dawn of a new era. 25,000 fans turned up. It didn't matter that they lost 2 – 3 to Linfield. They were back at home where they belonged.

By the end of 1949, Glentoran with Jimmy Mac stood second in the table having played eight Irish League games. There had been just one defeat. Billy Bingham was the man playing out of his skin. Record crowds followed their progress. For the first game of the fifties Linfield were again the opposition. Another 25,000 fans crowded in but Glentoran lost 2 – 3. At the end of February Glentoran and Linfield were level on 23 points.

Meanwhile scouts were turning up to watch the newest star – Jimmy McIlroy - in a 2 – 0 win over Derry. They came from Bolton, Tottenham, Sheffield Wednesday, and the club that would sign him a week later, Burnley. In 1949, Burnley had missed out on signing goalkeeper Bert Trautmann from St Helens Town by a matter of hours. This time they were not going to be beaten. McIlroy played 25 games during the season scoring 9 goals, scoring twice against Cliftonville in December '49 and then twice against Crusaders in the following February. His first ever goal came in October against Coleraine, just before his 18th birthday. He had arrived. His last goal for them was in March against Distillery in a 4 – 1 win.

Glentoran eventually finished runners-up in the League that season, losing to Linfield yet again, in a play-off. Later in May there was a friendly against Doncaster Rovers then managed by Jimmy's great hero Peter Doherty. Jimmy missed him of course, but they would meet again in international fixtures.

*My game came on in leaps and bounds; I scored goals, was quick and sharp, could make a telling pass and covered all the pitch. After one very successful game in February 1950, the manager Frank Grice introduced me to the Burnley chairman Mr Kay. I'd had a good game but Frank was a wily character and suggested to Mr Kay that it had not been one of my better games. He wanted a decent transfer fee.*

*I became a 'marked man', and after a game a week later as I came out of the Oval I could see a stranger pointing to me and telling a companion. "That's him, that's the one we want." I assumed the pair were from Burnley. Things started to move the next week because having played my best against Distillery at Grosvenor Park, I was told: 'Frank Hill the Burnley manager was here to watch you today'. That was wonderful news. I knew that I'd had a good game and if it needed something special to attract Burnley, I felt sure I had produced it that day.*

*Sauntering home at about 11 o clock at night having spent the evening in Belfast, I was met by my sister Doreen, breaking all speed limits on her bike. She jumped off and gasping told me there were two Englishmen waiting to see me at the house. She told me to hurry so I grabbed the bike, left her to walk home, and got there as fast as I could. The two men were Frank Hill and a Burnley director, Wilf Hopkinson. Frank Grice was with them who told me that terms had been agreed between the two clubs and all they needed was my agreement. Football-minded boys in Northern Ireland have only one real ambition in life. They live for the day they can join an English club. I needed no persuading.*

*I was however a novice in the transfer business. There were no agents in those days. You only had your own wits. I could have made, or attempted to make, a considerable amount of money out of the move. All I collected however was the £750 signing on fee. I thought I was a millionaire overnight. But then when I heard of other players who had made far more out of their moves; I heard that one player pocketed a third of his £12,000 fee, and others gained amounts from £1,500 to £2,000, I felt rather disillusioned. They had the sense to play 'hard to get' when they were asked to sign. I, on the other hand, was too flattered to think I was wanted and was too eager. I made no attempt to push my good luck further by seeking anything extra.*

*But, those thoughts came later. For now I was delighted and excited. I had got a move. I was going to England.* (Right Inside Soccer 1960.)

It was the Burnley chairman, Mr Kay who sanctioned the deal. He was playing snooker in the Mechanics Institute recreation room when he received an urgent phone call from the club representatives in Ireland. He interrupted his game, took the call and the deal was clinched. That decision must surely be the best he ever made for the club.

"You remember the strangest things," said Jimmy. "The night I was signed by Burnley it was the manager Frank Hill who came, and one of the directors, I think it was Mr Hopkinson. They were in the house waiting for me. I'd played at Glentoran against Distillery in the afternoon and not come home until about 11 o clock. My sister met me on my way home on her bike. I grabbed the bike off her and left her to walk back. But, what I realise now, years later, is that they must have been waiting for me there for some time. And I think now, what if one of them had wanted to go to the toilet. All we had then was an earth closet in the outside yard, dark, with no lights, how embarrassed I would have been. And now what I wonder is, if one of them had needed to use that closet, would they still have wanted to sign me?

"Funnily enough, Frank Grice the Glentoran manager was a cockney and I could never understand a word he said. But then I don't suppose he could understand us either. He had once been at Tottenham and Frank told me that Arthur Rowe at Tottenham had given him an absolute rollicking for selling me to Burnley and asked him why he had never told him about 'this promising young player'."

Of course Jimmy has happy memories of his short stay at Glentoran. His talent was obvious but it was clear his future lay elsewhere. He returned to the Oval in early August, 2008, when Burnley and Glentoran played a pre-season fixture and was presented to the crowd and the players. Between March, 1950 and August, 2008 he could never have imagined that so much would happen.

# Chapter Four

# To Burnley And Early Days

THE TRUTH is someone should have written this book years ago. He's in his late 70's now and his memories, though many remain, are sometimes not crystal clear. We fans who watched our heroes play make a big mistake. Today, we still see them as they were, not as they are, and for us they will never grow old. They were part of our youth and growing up and we don't want to let go of the images that remain.

He remains busy and often goes to Spain with his longstanding friend John Cook. He is in constant demand to attend local functions, dinners, presentations, charity events, and he rarely refuses. Just prior to our first meeting to talk about this book he had been to Belfast as a guest of the Sportswriters' Association who were honouring the remaining members of the team of '58, the one that did so marvellously well in the World Cup in Sweden, bringing honour and glory to Northern Ireland. Shortly before that he had been honoured at the Burnley Football Supporters' Clubs awards evening. He was about to embark for Northern Ireland again for another football function. He plays golf regularly. But it's hard on some days now to do something like work on a book.

I tell him he can do as much or as little as he wants. The last thing I want is that he feels pressured, stressed, 'bothered'. That was a word my grandmother used a lot. "Stop being a bother," she'd say when I was being troublesome on Friday nights when I was a nipper and stayed with her.

"If ever I am a bother, Jimmy, you must tell me," I said to him one day. He laughed. The trouble is he's just too nice a person to say so. And always his worry is, "Will what you write sound like me?"

He has the most quiet, gentle, lilting, almost quizzical, Irish voice. He pauses every now and then, while he thinks carefully of the next words. He still can't imagine why anyone would want to read about him. He thinks there are far too many football biographies.

The paradox is that when we sit down, or when I telephone, some of the memories do come back, some of the stories and tales are still there, and there is much he has to say.

But age can be cruel and confusing. Some of the distant past can still be sharp and clear. But, the yesterday and the 'now', make us panic when we can't remember something that happened just a day ago or week ago, or an arrangement that we have made. We struggle to make quick decisions and tire easily, "Sometimes Dave I just want to sleep. I haven't picked up a paintbrush now for eighteen months. I come back from a holiday more tired than when I went."

When I telephoned to check it was OK to come over for the second visit, it had slipped his mind. We talked on the 'phone instead; the call lasted an hour as I knew it would, and I scribbled rough notes furiously. The 2008 European Championships were taking place at the time. Much of it left him totally disinterested and bored. He watched very little of it

JIMMY McILROY
Burnley and Ireland

A European tour was an adventure in 1951. Transport was slow and hardly luxurious. Such tours were often a test of endurance and patience, with uncomfortable coach journeys and long days.

although occasionally, Spain, Portugal and Holland lit up the gloom. As for the rest, it was all about not losing (I can hear his voice again saying "in my day we went out to win"), the Greeks just appalling, the score 0 – 0 as they pass the ball over and over again across the back four, deep in their own half, for fear of making a creative pass which may go wrong, and fear of losing. Even their own fans boo them. It didn't work anyway. They lost 0 – 2; poetic justice, there is a football god.

The modern game: hold the ball, pass it around in your own half, sideways, backwards, players bunching, bore spectators to death, hope for a set piece goal and then hang on. It won Greece the tournament four years ago. Danny Blanchflower would turn in his grave. And in Danny and Jimmy's day they wouldn't have called it a set piece, they'd have said free kick or corner. Today they call the wings, 'channels'. What on earth for? Who thinks up these things? Jimmy Greaves once listened to a manager giving a team talk sprinkled with jargon. There was a blackboard and it was covered in arrows. "Which of us are the bloody Indians?" Jimmy quipped.

And what did Danny Blanchflower once say? "The game's about glory. It's about doing things in style, with a flourish. It's about going out and beating the other lot, not waiting for them to die of boredom."

In 1950 when Jimmy Mac arrived, Burnley was a grey, smoke-filled industrial place; and Britain, in general, a drab and gloomy place wherever you went. It was a nation still suffering from the lingering, debilitating effects of World War Two. National Service in the army was compulsory. Petrol rationing had only just ended. The country was still a place of austerity and hardship. Central heating, washing machines, fridges, telephones, televisions, what were they? Half of all homes had no indoor bathroom; one in five had no electricity and made do with glimmering gaslight. In winter you awoke unable to see out of the window because of the ice on the inside. Colour was in short supply although the Eagle comic and Dan Dare made their first appearance. The Festival of Britain that year was dreamed up to bring light and cheer into this pervading gloom, to remind people of what they were good at, to restore optimism. The joke was, however, that the slender symbolic Skylon tower had no visible means of support – like the still near-bankrupt Britain, people commented. Winston Churchill was re-elected Prime Minister. In sport Randolph Turpin beat Sugar Ray Robinson in the world middleweight championship. In the greatest football upset of all time the USA beat the mighty England 1 – 0 in the World Cup. England were shocked and humiliated and it was seen as a national disgrace. The West Indies beat England at cricket for the first time in England. And far away from these shores, the Korean War began.

The official 1950 Burnley Corporation handbook, however, made fine reading, making little mention of the conditions of poverty and deprivation that existed in many Burnley areas. It began by suggesting that if coal had not been discovered in the region, then Burnley might well have become a fashionable spa town instead of one of Lancashire's cotton towns. Before the mills and line upon line of terraced rows filled the vale, springs with excellent medicinal qualities had been found in the town. Had these been developed, as opposed to industry, there was the potential to develop a most beneficial inland watering place, not unlike Harrogate on the other side of the Pennines. In the places surrounding the town the area had, and still has, some of the most beautiful countryside imaginable, miles of wonderful stretches of scenery, and picturesque villages and hamlets.

But, had that happened, then there would certainly have been no football club. Burnley Football Club grew from working men, not the affluent gentry dipping their toes into healing waters. The football teams born in the 1880's grew from industry and the prosperity it brought, and from working men who needed leisure activities. As industry then thrived in the early 1900's, so the football club in Burnley grew and developed, albeit with mixed fortunes along the way. Harrogate never became a strong base for football. Neither would Burnley have done so without coal, canals and cotton.

Burnley in 1950, industrially, was still a thriving place with an official population of 84,590. 'John Grey Limited', for example, employed 500 people. In addition to the cotton weaving mills, there were attendant engineering firms and loom makers, bleachers, dyers and sizers. An aerial photograph of the town shows acres and acres of factories, mills, chimneys and workers housing. But, it was not all cotton. There were numerous coal pits. There were leather tanners, rope manufacturers, hosiery and underclothing firms, glass bottle makers, paperworks, sheet metal works, tin and copper works. There were manufacturers of shuttles, steel springs, washing machines, scales and weighing machines, raincoats, 'Prestige' kettles and kitchen tools, uniforms, metal toys, surgical appliances and furniture. There was electrical engineering, a brewery and brickworks.

Entertainment was provided by two theatres, the Palace and the Victoria. There were cinemas in most parts of the town, The Savoy, Grand, Odeon. Roxy, Empire, Pentridge, Alhambra, Tivoli and the Imperial. The Empress Hall catered for roller skating and dancing. Thompson Park and boating lake covered 480 acres.

What the handbook does not mention is that the Burnley in which Jimmy McIlroy arrived from the green hills and spaces of rural Ireland was more often than not clouded in a thick pall of smoke and soot belching out of the tall mill chimneys and the coal fires of hundreds of back to back houses. Nor does it mention that wages were low for those in work and for those who were unemployed there was a hopeless despair.

Once a year the whole town seemed to decamp and vanish. It was 'Wakes Week,' and they went to Blackpool for a brief respite from factory drudgery. On a Saturday they wanted their football team to do well and to entertain them. They streamed in from the town and the surrounding areas, clambering aboard the 'football special' buses, then to alight and surge like a human tide underneath the canal bridge and up Yorkshire Street to Turf Moor. No man could have had a bigger culture shock to his system. The first time Jimmy McIlroy saw the town his eyes were wide with disbelief, his comprehension system struggling to cope. But he came to love the place and is still here today. Jimmy Greaves couldn't shame him into moving, Danny Blanchflower could not persuade him, and nor could Sampdoria, who tried to tempt him away to the glamour and money of Italy.

*First impressions are very important, and to be perfectly honest, I must say that my first impressions of Burnley were distinctly unfavourable. Frank Hill drove me from the ferry terminal at Heysham near Morecambe. The miles we drove through the countryside were pleasant enough, but then we approached Burnley. When I saw what I was coming to all I wanted was to get the next boat back. I thought it was like nothing I had ever seen before. For the first time in my life I was surrounded by grey, stone buildings, cobbled streets and the shawls and clogs of Lancashire. It looked awful. From open green fields and the hills of the Lagan Valley to a place where there seemed nothing but rows and rows of featureless houses, factories and huge chimneys. In my innocence I had always imagined that such places only existed in the writings of Priestley or*

DRINK

# MASSEY'S BITTER ALES

GOLDEN in COLOUR

GOLDEN in QUALITY

Massey's Burnley Brewery Limited

BREWERS in BURNLEY

SINCE 1750

SATURDAY, 20th OCTOBER - - 1951

BURNLEY Football Club

Official Programme Price 2d

**BURNLEY FOOTBALL CLUB.**

*Fixtures for Season 1951-1952.*      *First Team*      *Fixtures ... ral League*

| Date | Opponents | Ground | Date | Opponents | nd |
|---|---|---|---|---|---|
| Aug. 18 | Charlton Athletic | away | Aug. 18 | Chesterfield | home |
| ,, 21 | Liverpool | home ... | ,, 20 | Blackpool | away |
| ,, 25 | Fulham | home ..... ... | ,, 25 | Sheffield Wednesday | away |
| ,, 29 | Liverpool | .. away . | ,, 28 | Blackpool | home |
| Sept. 1 | Middlesbrough | away | Sept. 1 | Leeds United | home |
| ,, 3 | Tottenham Hotspur | home ... | ,, 4 | Everton | home |
| ,, 8 | West Bromwich Albion | home | ,, 8 | Bolton Wanderers | away |
| ,, 10 | Tottenham Hotspur | away | ,, 15 | Newcastle United | home |
| ,, 15 | Newcastle United | away | ,, 22 | West Bromwich Albion | away |
| ,, 22 | Bolton Wanderers | home | ,, 29 | Stoke City | home |
| ,, 29 | Stoke City | away ... | Oct. 6 | Barnsley | away |
| Oct. 6 | Blackpool | home | ,, 13 | Sheffield United | home |
| ,, 13 | Arsenal | away | ,, 20 | Huddersfield Town | away |
| ,, 20 | Manchester City | home | ,, 27 | Wolverhampton W. | home |
| ,, 27 | Derby County | away | Nov. 3 | Bury | away |
| Nov. 3 | Aston Villa | home | ,, 10 | Aston Villa | home |
| ,, 10 | Sunderland | away | ,, 17 | Derby County | away |
| ,, 17 | Wolverhampton W | home.. | ,, 24 | Manchester City | away |
| ,, 24 | (1) Huddersfield Town | away | Dec. 1 | Liverpool | away |
| Dec. 1 | Chelsea | home | ,, 8 | Blackburn Rovers | home |
| ,, 8 | Portsmouth | away | ,, 15 | Chesterfield | away |
| ,, 15 | (2) Charlton Athletic | home | ,, 22 | Sheffield Wednesday | home |
| ,, 22 | Fulham | away | ,, 25 | Preston North End | away |
| ,, 25 | Preston North End | home | ,, 26 | Preston North End | home |
| ,, 26 | Preston North End | away | ,, 29 | Leeds United | away |
| ,, 29 | Middlesbrough | home | | | |
| **1952** | | | **1952** | | |
| Jan. 5 | West Bromwich Albion | away | Jan. 5 | Bolton Wanderers | home |
| ,, 12 | (3) | | ,, 12 | | |
| ,, 19 | Newcastle United | home .. | ,, 19 | Newcastle United | away |
| ,, 26 | Bolton Wanderers | away | ,, 26 | West Bromwich Albion | home |
| Feb. 2 | (4) | | Feb. 2 | | |
| ,, 9 | Stoke City | home | ,, 9 | Stoke City | away |
| ,, 16 | Blackpool | away | ,, 16 | Barnsley | home |
| ,, 23 | (5) | | ,, 23 | | |
| Mar. 1 | Arsenal | home | Mar. 1 | Sheffield United | away |
| ,, 8 | (6) Manchester City | away .. | ,, 8 | Huddersfield Town | home |
| ,, 15 | Derby County | home | ,, 15 | Wolverhampton W. | away |
| ,, 22 | Aston Villa | away | ,, 22 | Bury | home |
| ,, 29 | Sunderland | home | ,, 29 | Aston Villa | away |
| April 5 | Wolverhampton W | away | April 5 | Derby County | home |
| ,, 11 | Manchester United | home | ,, 11 | Manchester United | away |
| ,, 12 | Huddersfield Town | home | ,, 12 | Manchester City | away |
| ,, 14 | Manchester United | away ... | ,, 14 | Manchester United | home |
| ,, 19 | Chelsea | away | ,, 19 | Liverpool | home |
| ,, 26 | Portsmouth | home | ,, 26 | Blackburn Rovers | away |
| May 3 | Open | | May 3 | Everton | away |

*Cronin. At the old Empress Hotel in the market place, I stood and looked at the street carpeted by filth, waste, rubbish, rotten fruit and the general garbage left by stallholders. It was depressing and for this I had left the beauty of Antrim. It was paradise lost with a vengeance.*

*With the clogs and shawls went the accent. It took me months to get used to it and translate the things that people said. But, in fairness, my own Irish brogue was no more understandable to the locals. In an early game Reg Attwell and I wondered if we really did speak a common language. I asked him if I should take a throw-in. He said he didn't understand a word I'd said. Again I asked him. Again he didn't understand. In exasperation he shouted: "I can't tell a word you're saying, just take the throw".*

*But since those early days and the awful first impressions I have become truly attached to Burnley. My worries were unnecessary because, in truth, beneath the grey, drab, exterior of this colourless, industrial town, there is a heart of gold.*

*As early as October, in my first full season, I would wear the claret colours in the first team. In football, every player needs luck and the breaks going his way. Such an early promotion to the team was my biggest stroke of luck perhaps. Harry Potts was transferred to Everton for a fee of £20,000. There was no obvious replacement and the manager threw me in at the deep end. Perhaps Frank Hill felt that I just had to be good enough having paid that fee. I was only 18 and unknown. It was a gamble on his part.*

*As so often in their history, Burnley were then a mediocre, middle-of-the-table team. Mediocre results, plus mediocre gates added up to a mediocre club. Of course I had not known that when I signed but it would probably have made no difference. I was 18 and had burning ambition. The mediocre state of the club was of no consequence to me. I was in the first team.*

(Right Inside Soccer 1960.)

He was in the first team and 'on his way'. But there were ambivalent attitudes to football in 1950. It was the game of the masses and the crowds attending football were still benefiting from the slow release from austerity that the war had imposed. But, as Maurice Edelston so eloquently wrote it was not everyone's cup of tea. Snobbery and the class system, although eroded by the war years, were still rampant and football heroes were not everyone's favourite.

'What might be called the Henley-blazer, or bound-copies-of-Punch attitude to football, still lingers in the English air like the faint expensive flavour of an old pair of riding-boots in a box-room. Cricket is a sacred institution. Rugger is a man's game. Golf is full of legend and pawky wisdom. Eton Fives and Real Tennis are solemn mysteries. The techniques of all of them can be discussed, gravely or wittily, in the most proper company. But football is low. Professional football is lower than amateur football. Professional players shake hands after goals. They have even been known to embrace and leap about ecstatically, instead of trotting back to their own half without looking at each other. Their shorts have no side pockets. Their supporters wear, not scarves but mufflers. They come from the North to gape at London, 'Oop for t'Coop'. Sometimes instead of cloth caps, they wear painted toppers bearing such mottoes as 'Up the Trotters' and 'Wor Jackie'. It is all rather undesirable.'

As Jimmy himself would later write, there was more kudos in being a member of the golf or the tennis club in Burnley, than being a footballer. Nobody then from the middle classes or above wanted their daughter to marry one. Today, with the money in the game and the astronomical wages it is almost the opposite and quite de rigueur to bag a wealthy footballer for a husband, the ultimate accolade being ten pages in *Hello* magazine and more money for the bank account.

### A ROOKIE AT TURF MOOR, MY FIRST BURNLEY SEASON

*Burnley had the reputation, despite efforts to shed it, of being an 'ordinary' football club. Seldom collecting any of the game's honours, and rarely in relegation trouble, we were often what was commonly called a 'middle of the table' outfit. This was quickly brought home to me when I was transferred from Glentoran in the spring of 1950. Burnley ended that season with the figures of an average team; played 42, won 14, drawn 14, lost 14. I played no part in first team games, concerned only with adjusting to a completely new way of life and at the same time finding my feet in the Central League team.*

*The first team forwards were Jackie Chew, Billy Morris, Bill Holden, Harry Potts and Jackie Hayes. There seemed little likelihood of me challenging them for their positions. In the reserves I found the pace of the football quicker than it had been in the Irish League. But roughly the same as far as skill went.*

*At the start of the 1950/51 season I was considerably alarmed when the club decided to convert me from an inside-forward to a wing-half. Manager Frank Hill thought I could be successful in this position but it had always been my impression that moving from a forward role to a half-back role or from half-back to full-back, needed less skill and was a backward step. I treated these experiments as personal relegation. Fortunately, another inside-forward, Jimmy Adamson, was undergoing similar switches as this time, to such good effect that, as we know, he developed into one of the finest wing-halves in the Football League. He became captain of the club and I remained a forward.*

*When I ask the question 'why me' I know that luck is so important. I was lucky when Burnley felt they could not refuse an offer of £20,000 for Harry Potts from Everton. Harry signed for the Goodison Park team leaving a gap at Turf Moor that could be filled in one of two ways. They could either buy a replacement, or they could promote me – at least as a stop-gap. I was promoted and from then on until I was transferred to Stoke City, was never really pushed to retain my first-team place. Luck is the most valuable thing in football. I was so lucky to make the move from the obscurity of an Irish League team and so quickly win a place in the First Division in England. I had the good fortune to be given a few months in the Central League, an ideal training ground to raise the tempo of my game, at the same time as allowing me to develop skills at a level I was used to. I was lucky again when the conversion of Jimmy Adamson to wing-half ended any thoughts at the club of making a wing-half out of me. I was lucky when the transfer of Harry Potts gave me my place in the first-team. And on top of all this I had the breathing space to consolidate my place because there was no-one better there to displace me.*

*The first twelve months in the first team is of tremendous importance to every footballer. These are the impressionable, learning months. A good game can lift a youngster to the heavens and a poor one can make him despair. Supporters seldom take into account the feelings of a young, raw, inexperienced player, trying to establish himself in the game.*

*An Irish friend and I decided to try our skill at a game of bowls soon after I made my first team debut at Turf Moor. I have, by the way, tried every ball game possible, but still can't play any of them to my satisfaction. This was my first game of bowls. On the bowling green I recognised a neighbour of mine, but he obviously didn't realise who we were. He heard our accents, developed many miles from East Lancashire, and the following conversation took place.*

*"You youngsters are Irish aren't you?"*

*"We are."*

*"Perhaps you're footballers on trial at Turf Moor?"*

*"That's right."*

*"I've got an Irish footballer in lodgings near me. Fellow called McIlroy."*

*"What sort of player is he?"*

*"Well when he first arrived he looked pretty useful. But I'm afraid he'll never make the grade. He's just not good enough."*

*After all these years, I suppose I should apologise to the chap for keeping up the deception during the conversation. But his summing up of my ability, which seemed to me to be complete condemnation, didn't really bother me. A footballer usually knows himself whether he has what it takes to reach the top of his profession. Without being conceited, I felt I was gradually conquering the problems of English football. I had confidence in my own ability and that confidence meant more to me than the opinions of someone in Burnley. I was convinced of my ability to make good. At the same time I knew that much hard work lay ahead before I could impress people like my neighbour. No doubt there were others who thought 'McIlroy will not make the grade'.*

*Maybe I was thick-skinned. Maybe I possessed the sort of confidence that provided insulation and protection against critics. But If I'd been more sensitive when I had that chat on the bowling green, its effect on my subsequent career might have been disastrous. Youngsters are impressionable and very easily distressed. They need encouragement not criticism and should be given every chance to settle down before the critics jump on them.*

*My immediate reaction was to prove, in the only possible way, that I was right and my critics wrong. Another youngster might have taken it differently; even to the extent of packing his bag and taking the next boat home. This is something that has happened many times to first-season professionals. Supporters would do well to remember this.*

(Right Inside Soccer 1960.)

Mrs Hesketh was his first landlady at 6 Stoney Street, up Todmorden Road. There was the traditional outside loo in those days, a perilous place on a freezing cold winter's day, or a night when the rain was lashing down. But he enjoyed his time at Stoney Street; Mrs Hesketh being a homely woman in her fifties who had lost her husband just a couple of years before Jimmy arrived. "She was a lovely lady and her daughter worked at the Town Hall. Paddy Corr came afterwards and we shared a room. He was from Ballymena but only played in the reserves. I was well looked after there and it was just right for me. At Mrs Hesketh's it was the first time I had eaten rabbit. There were still food shortages and rationing but we had a lot of rabbit which tasted like chicken."

Very occasionally his mother and father came over and on their visits stayed there too. When uncles and cousins came they came on the morning boat to Heysham and went back on the evening boat – no simple journey. Mrs Hesketh and he often played cards and on the morning of his home debut game against Aston Villa, Jimmy says he simply lost track of time and realised he was late for the bus he needed. All the buses that came by were filled with supporters so that there was no room for him. Panicking slightly, he set off to half walk, half jog to the ground and arrived in the dressing room, late, sweating, after the 2.15 deadline that players were expected to be there. The players were half stripped and into their playing kit. Nothing was said until the Tuesday after when Billy Dougal called him in for a chat.

"I remember he called me Muckilroy. Why were you late on Saturday, did you want everyone to see you come in?" he asked. Jimmy explained that he had missed the bus. "He

thought I was being big-headed but didn't make a song and dance," said Jimmy, "Billy just knew that a quiet word was enough, but he didn't know how I had rushed to get down to the ground."

"I can't praise Billy Dougal enough," he continued. "He was the shrewdest man I ever knew and never got the recognition he deserved for what he did for this club."

Jimmy talks fondly of his father and the support he gave him during this early period. "A story my father, who stayed quite trim and youthful looking, never tired of telling was how he was mistaken for me at Everton when he had gone there with friends. Someone passing by heard his name mentioned, "McIlroy," and asked him wasn't it time he was getting changed. On the first occasion I came over he and an uncle came across with me and we were met at Heysham by Frank Hill. My father and uncle were quite concerned at how I would cope with the rough stuff in English football. Frank who had played for Arsenal and for some years after that just rolled up his trouser legs and showed them his legs. 'Look at these,' he said 'not a mark on them after all these years'. I told Billy Dougal this story in later years. 'That's because he never made a tackle in his life,' said Billy.

"One of my best pals back in the early days was a lad called Joe McNulty. He was another Irish lad and was reserve keeper for a while. He was a year older than me and had been here that bit longer so he took me under his wing; he'd been around a little bit. We filled our time either at the cinema, the dancehalls or the coffee bar in the centre of town called the Lubeck. It was a regular meeting place for young or unattached players. Let's just say the girls descended on us. There were never any problems finding girls. But then, no girl ever wanted to get pregnant, it was a stigma then to be an unmarried mother. On a Saturday after a home game we'd get back to our lodgings, have a meal, change, meet at the Lubeck and then go on to a dancehall, maybe the Imperial at Nelson. That place was always packed and you danced to top bands like Joe Loss.

"Eventually Mrs Hesketh decided it was time for me to settle and meet a nice girl. She was concerned I was meeting the wrong ones. 'There's a nice girl in the choir at the Methodist Chapel at the top of our road', she told me one day. So, I went to up there one Sunday, spoke to Barbara, arranged to meet – and that was it. She became my wife. She died just a few years ago and I still feel lost without her.

"I didn't visit home very often in those days, maybe once or twice a season. But then you went home for the summer break which could be as long as eight to ten weeks. We caught the ferry from Heysham and this was over the Irish Sea and this is a sea that can be very, very rough. There was one trip I did with Billy Bingham and I was in the top bunk and Binghy was in the bottom. This was a journey in a rough, rough sea. 'Oh please God let this ship go down,' Binghy moaned over and again. Billy still remembers the occasion. 'We were playing in Scotland and the journey was from Larne to Ardrossan. I actually had a blinder of a game'.

"My first pay packet was £10 in the reserves and £12 in the first team and it was less in the summer. I sent my mother £1 a week. Whenever I went back home I felt like a millionaire. I had to ask Mrs Hesketh how much rent I had to pay. She told me the last player had given her £2 a week. So I told her I'd pay her £2 and ten shillings. When I went back home to Ireland my mother wanted to know what I was paying for rent. When I told her it was £2 and ten shillings she replied, 'And you're only giving me £1.' I knew what she was hinting at and from then on I gave her £2 and ten shillings."

Legend tells that Jimmy helped build Gawthorpe but he actually escaped the rigours of digging ditches, laying drains, building brick walls, and levelling the grounds at Gawthorpe when Alan Brown oversaw, as foreman, the conversion of the green fields to a much envied training centre.

"By then I was in the first team and we escaped those jobs. The younger players did all that. Training was far more enlightened in the fifties at Burnley than at other clubs where running and endless lapping of the football pitch without a ball at your feet was the usual training routine," said Jimmy. "We always had a ball at our feet.

"I was quite happy with my two first games, away to Sunderland and then home to Aston Villa. In both I was up against international players, Willie Watson at Sunderland who also played cricket for England, and against Aston Villa against a Welsh international. In the home game I laid on one of the goals, it was Attwell or Holden who scored. I felt comfortable; I had no nerves, and held my own."

From that point on Jimmy Mac developed and shone until the cataclysmic events of 1963 ended his time at Burnley. When Frank Hill brought him from Ireland he knew he had brought a rare talent to the club. He could never have imagined just how much that talent would grow.

# Chapter 5

# The Team Of 1952/53
# Nearly The Title

"THE FIRST game I ever went to see at Burnley was in 1955," I told Jimmy during a visit when we talked about his time with Frank Hill and Alan Brown. "My father took me along hoping that it would make me into an instant Burnley supporter, keen to go again. It was a rite of passage in that he'd decided I was ready for the initiation. September '55, and it was against Manchester United. That's probably one reason why I went along. I was eleven, quite excited but only because it was the Busby Babes, but disappointed when United played in blue not red. All I can recollect is that it was a 0 – 0 draw and I wasn't bothered about going again. I still remember I was bored and not too impressed."

It would be another four years before I became a committed regular and if I said earlier that I've felt like I've known Jimmy since my schooldays then it was the game in '55 and the day that our paths first crossed. In truth it was Peter McKay and Tommy Cummings that I recall my father talked about a lot, especially the great goal Cummings scored against Newcastle. Les Shannon was another of his favourites.

What I know now, but didn't then, was that it was one of the rare games when Jimmy Mac wore the number nine shirt. Peter McKay was missing. I looked up the records and Jimmy Mac didn't manage to score as a centre forward. There have been some great games between Burnley and Manchester United over the years but the 0 – 0 draw wasn't one of them. Perhaps I was bored because I couldn't see much either. These were the days of big crowds and you paid something extra to get into the enclosure at the front of the Longside. There were over 26,000 for this game and when adults stand in front of an eleven year old you don't get to see much.

"I don't remember much about it either," said Jimmy, "though I do remember wearing the number nine shirt occasionally. Alan Brown had this idea that I might do some damage there."

And so, after the game, my father drove us home passing The Kettledrum and The Fighting Cocks, the latter now an Indian restaurant, through Cliviger and then down through the Cornholme Valley behind the convoy of green buses filled with supporters to Todmorden. I felt let down by the blue shirts. He felt let down no doubt by my lack of interest.

Jimmy and I talked for a while about how different things were then. There was hardly a foreign player to be seen. The ball was heavy, laced and made of stitched leather panels. Players lived next door to the supporters, walked to the ground on matchdays, came on the bus or got lifts with a friend or even a supporter able to afford a car. They were still seen as working class; still on a maximum wage no matter how big their name, and a reduced wage in the summer, still at the beck and call of a manager, or chairman and directors. Footballers were still very much the bloke next door; many had other jobs, a favourite was painting and decorating. But it was an exciting age and exhilarating when wingers flew down the touchlines dribbling and beating the full-back and entertaining the fans. Physical contact was the norm yet on the terraces opposing sets of fans mixed happily. Hooliganism hadn't been invented. The game was tough and uncompromising on pitches that were more often than not a quagmire. Referees rarely took names. And in the fifties Burnley, the town, was filled with smoke and smog, the cotton mills still clanking away, the rows of terraced houses still filled with mill workers. Demolition and decay and ultimate regeneration were still years away.

Eminent author Norman Giller writes that the fifties were "when the beautiful game was in black and white… they were the best of times and the worst of times." The pressure to win games was but a fraction of that which exists today. Raich Carter, Wilf Mannion, Len Shackleton, Tom Finney, Stanley Matthews, Tommy Lawton were among the prominent names. Tottenham, Manchester United, Arsenal, Wolves, Chelsea, all won the title during the 50s. This then was the background against which Jimmy Mac played and blossomed as the fifties progressed.

It could be argued that the only reason manager Frank Hill is ever remembered at Burnley is because he signed Jimmy McIlroy – and even then there is always the caveat that it was another player who was the target and McIlroy was 'discovered' by accident. In fact Hill is more important than that, having given the club a firm footing and making a number of astute signings whilst he was manager from 1948 to 1954. Sandwiched in between the success of Cliff Britton in 1947 and the huge influence of Alan Brown for the three years following 1954, Frank Hill merits more than just a passing mention. As a player he had won three title medals at Arsenal and whichever club he joined later, he was a natural captain. He had also won three Scotland caps. He was a shrewd and wily character but likeable. There is the story that one particularly new and shiny pair of shoes he wore one day was paid for with the proceeds of Cup tickets he sold. As soon as he himself went to Ireland and saw McIlroy play, he snapped him up and gave him his chance recognising that when Harry Potts left he was good enough to replace him without the need to look elsewhere.

By the beginning of season '52/53, McIlroy was still not 21 years old but had played 28 games the previous season and was already an Irish international. He was lightning sharp and clearly a very special talent. In today's football industry he would most certainly have been bought within a season from Burnley by a bigger, wealthier club, a Liverpool or a Manchester United. It is also probable that he might never have arrived at Turf Moor in the first place.

However, at Burnley he was part of a team that came, under Frank Hill, so very close to winning the First Division Championship by the end of '52/53. Hill had inherited several good players and had also gathered a group of very fine players whom he could call his own. Tommy Cummings from the Northeast was a young and outstandingly quick centre half and in the season before had scored possibly Burnley's best ever goal when he took the ball from the edge of his own penalty area, beat man after man and scored with a thunderbolt shot. This was unheard of from a centre half. Author David Wiseman's father turned to his son and told him it was the greatest goal he would ever see. My own father

Willie Cunningham, the Preston North End and Scotland full back, given a gruelling time by Billy Elliott.

used to describe it to me. In an age when he was up against players like Len Shackleton, Jackie Milburn, Trevor Ford, Nat Lofthouse and Stan Mortenson, Cummings with his pace and interceptions rarely put a foot wrong.

Harold Mather was still putting in crunching tackles at fullback. He was not only well known for that but also for the greyhound he used to keep under the Cricket Field Stand at the club on account of his landlady not allowing it in the house when he was in digs. It was a great favourite with all the players who constantly spoiled and fed it. As a result it never won a race. After one race meeting when along with Reg Attwell he had lost all his money, Mather was so fed up with the dog as he walked back home along the canal to Burnley, he contemplated throwing it in and running away. He and Attwell decided against it thinking that, slow as it was; it would only climb out and catch them up.

Also in the team was the young and stylish Jimmy Adamson, making his mark at half back. He would eventually develop into one of Burnley's greatest players. Alongside him was the superb Reg Attwell still at the peak of his cultured powers. Jackie Chew, 'Cowboy', was at outside right and Les Shannon was another very fine player at inside forward who could score goals; twice he scored a hat-trick during the season. Bustling, but not an unskilful centre forward, Bill Holden scored 22 goals during the season. Holden had been overlooked by Bolton and discarded by Everton after a trial. Hill snapped him up and took him to the fringes of the England team over the next couple of seasons. He was big enough to be physical when necessary but was two-footed and mobile using the full width of the pitch instead of being the proverbial battering ram.

And then, at outside left, was the incomparable Billy Elliot. It is the much later Mike Summerbee at Manchester City who is often seen as the first winger who decided that roles should be reversed and wingers should stop being delicate little orchids belted and kicked black and blue by hard-faced full backs. It was Elliot who decided that it would be he who ferociously tackled the full-backs and give them a taste of their own treatment. It was Billy Elliot, one of the hardest men in football, who turned the role upside down long before Summerbee, and at Burnley the crowd loved him for it. He was signed by Hill from Bradford Park Avenue for a then record fee for Burnley of £25,000, and whilst at Burnley won five England caps. Hill could most certainly spot a good player. One of Elliot's caps was against Austria in Vienna when Nat Lofthouse was dubbed 'The Lion of Vienna' for his two goals in the legendary 3 – 2 win. Even by the standards of 1950s football he was a hard man, and his confrontation with Preston's Willie Cunningham during one game resulted in the Preston captain moving Cunningham to the other side of the field, something quite unheard of in those physical times. He became the first player to be sent off for Burnley after the war when he simply 'looked' threateningly at an opponent. He could do that to his own team as well and Jimmy McIlroy remembers one game when his terrifically hard, low crosses were coming across regularly but no one was getting a head to them. Elliot was fuming and after one of them, he came across to the penalty area glowering. "Which of you fuckers ducked?" he demanded to know, and would certainly have thumped anyone who owned up.

Before one game, Jimmy McIlroy remembers him sitting in the changing room holding his face clearly in pain. "Elliot asked Billy Dougal if he had a file. 'What for?' asked Billy. He told Billy his teeth were killing him. Some of them were missing and he had dentures. He took out the dentures; blood was trickling down the sides of his mouth, and using the file

BILLY ELLIOTT
Burnley and England

There was a time when it was the full back's duty to kick the winger into the stands. Billy Elliott reversed the process

**LES SHANNON, Burnley**

A cultured and stylish player and one of Jimmy's favourites.

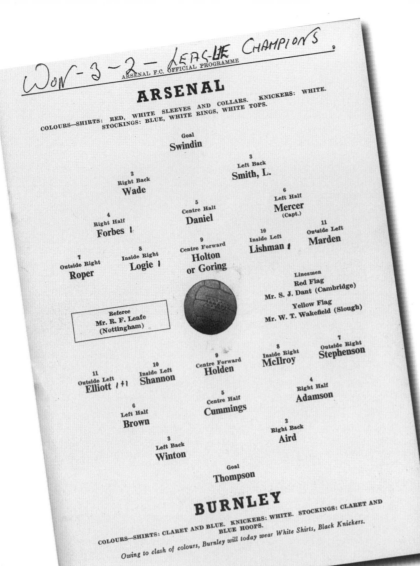

WON—3—2— LEAGUE CHAMPIONS

# ARSENAL

COLOURS—SHIRTS: RED, WHITE SLEEVES AND COLLARS. KNICKERS: WHITE.
STOCKINGS: BLUE, WHITE RINGS, WHITE TOPS.

Goal
**Swindin**

2
Right Back
**Wade**

3
Left Back
**Smith, L.**

5
Centre Half
**Daniel**

6
Left Half
**Mercer**
(Capt.)

4
Right Half
**Forbes** I

9
Centre Forward
**Holton
or Goring**

10
Inside Left
**Lishman** I

11
Outside Left
**Marden**

7
Outside Right
**Roper**

8
Inside Right
**Logie** I

Referee
Mr. R. F. Leafe
(Nottingham)

Linesmen
Red Flag
Mr. S. J. Dant (Cambridge)

Yellow Flag
Mr. W. T. Wakefield (Slough)

9
Centre Forward
**Holden**

8
Inside Right
**McIlroy**

7
Outside Right
**Stephenson**

11
Outside Left
**Elliott** I + I

10
Inside Left
**Shannon**

5
Centre Half
**Cummings**

4
Right Half
**Adamson**

6
Left Half
**Brown**

2
Right Back
**Aird**

3
Left Back
**Winton**

Goal
**Thompson**

# BURNLEY

COLOURS—SHIRTS: CLARET AND BLUE. KNICKERS: WHITE. STOCKINGS: CLARET AND
BLUE HOOPS.

*Owing to clash of colours, Burnley will today wear White Shirts, Black Knickers.*

Arsenal clinched the title in this final game of the season. Burnley were top in March but faded.

The team came so close to success but is seldom mentioned in the Burnley history books. It had some great players and manager Frank Hill was extremely shrewd. To him goes the credit for signing Jimmy McIlroy.

SATURDAY, 23rd AUGUST, 1952.        No. 1.

# BURNLEY
## Football Club

SEASON        1952-53

WINNERS, F.A. CUP ... 1913-1914        FINALISTS ............. 1946-1947

CHAMPIONS: Div. I ... 1920-1921;        RUNNERS-UP: Div. I ... 1919-1920;
Div. II ............ 1897-1898;        Div. II ... 1912-1913, 1946-1947
Central League 1948-1949

WINNERS, LANCASHIRE CUP ...1889-1890, 1914-1915, 1949-1950, 1951-1952

## OFFICIAL PROGRAMME
3ᴰ

# HUDDERSFIELD TOWN
*Association Football Club*
Ltd.

OFFICIAL
PROGRAMME
3ᴰ

LEEDS ROAD, HUDDERSFIELD

smoothed down one of the teeth that was rubbing into his gums. He looked at them, decided they were ok and put them back in his mouth. 'That's better', he announced and went out to play as normal."

Elliot played at Burnley for just two seasons before moving to Sunderland. He eventually became a coach and manager and worked in football until 1983. It might only have been two seasons at Turf Moor but he did enough in that time to justify the label 'legend', and the mere mention of his name makes Jimmy McIlroy smile with affection and nostalgia.

Twenty players were used in all during the season but just twelve of them played the bulk of the games, resulting in a very settled team, so that the players knew each others' game instinctively. Just a small number of reserves played a handful of games between them. In goal, Jimmy Strong was replaced by Des Thompson midway through the season. McIlroy played 38 of the League games scoring 11 goals. If the previous season had been one of consolidation for him, this one was where people sat up and took notice. All in all, this was a very fine team, a mixture of youth and experience, and of power and skill. The balance was exactly right and for almost a month, in March 1953, it was top of the Division and on course for the title.

With McIlroy and Les Shannon leading scorers with three goals each, five of the first six games were won and made everyone well aware what this team was capable of. With Billy Elliot then away playing for the Football League, a future star was drafted in, the very young Brian Pilkington. The game against Tottenham was lost but Pilkington played supremely well against Alf Ramsey. Another player who came in for just a handful of games was Joe Brown who later progressed through the ranks of the backroom staff to become manager, albeit briefly.

It was significant that this game was lost to an 89th minute goal. Two games during the season were lost in the 89th minute, one was lost in the 88th minute and another two games lost to goals in the final ten minutes. Add these points lost to those taken from Burnley by eventual champions Arsenal, and it would have been Burnley crowned as league champions. Ironically it was in the very last game of the season at Arsenal against Burnley, that the 3 – 2 Arsenal win clinched the title for them.

In December, Burnley played a friendly game against Distillery for whom Jimmy's Uncle Willie had played. They had been formed in 1880 by employees of Dunville's 'Royal Irish Distillery' and at that time were still based in Belfast. It would be 30 years before they moved to their new ground in Ballyskeagh. Burnley won 3 – 2 but Jimmy did not make the score sheet. Needless to say members of his family were in the crowd to watch him play.

The success that came Burnley's way up until March 14th seemed to come in short runs of games where there were consecutive victories; a run of five at the beginning of the season, a run of four in October/November, and then a run of three in February. There was a run of eleven unbeaten games spanning late November to the end of February but six of these eleven games were only draws. Sadly however, there were only two more wins to come following the victory over Manchester United on March 14th, only six points from a possible twenty.

March began with a visit from Blackpool who proceeded to win and do the double over Burnley, the only side to do so that season. Wins against Chelsea and Manchester United saw a return to form, top place and Press predictions that here were the champions, but then anti-climax set in. A last-minute goal at Fratton Park gave Portsmouth revenge for their FA Cup defeat at Turf Moor and a run of five games garnering only one point saw the Clarets disappearing from contention. Manager Hill shuffled his pack and brought in fresh players from the reserves, Stephenson, Brown and Winton. Hope came with a 5 – 1 demolition of Sunderland with Bill Holden scoring four times. Inconsistency reared its ugly head again and Burnley were hammered 5 – 1 at Wolves. The season was fading rapidly.

The title slipped away and it was Arsenal who claimed it. They had also ended Burnley's Cup run in February. (In their three home Cup games Burnley were watched by a staggering 143,000 people). In the league, a golden opportunity was missed by the side that had only conceded 52 goals all season, the second best defensive record. But whilst Arsenal scored 97, Burnley only scored 67. It was consistency that they lacked resulting in the six point gap between them and Arsenal.

Disappointment was the key feeling but Hill had achieved success, limited though it might be. Sixth place was no mean achievement. Entertainment had replaced the defensive 'iron curtain' of previous seasons. Crowds had come back to watch with an average attendance of over 28,000. Bill Holden was the first player since the war to score over 20 goals. And in McIlroy, who was only 21 by the end of the season, Adamson and Cummings who were only 24, and Pilkington a mere 20, a third of the team that would win the title in 1959/60 had emerged.

At the end of the season the players dispersed. This was a time when there was a proper 'close season'. Football was properly over until August. There was even time for some of them, though no-one from Burnley FC, to be professional cricketers.

Though he was never seen as an out and out goalscorer, nevertheless he scored 17 goals in the following season as Burnley developed into a side that was fancied by more than one expert to win honours. Though that never happened under Hill, they became an attractive side to watch and received many compliments, one of them being written by Frank Osborne in *Soccer Star.*

'One secret of manager Frank Hill's success at Turf Moor is the unity and comradeship both on and off the field. The lads who don the claret and blue may not be the boys with the glamour of big-money football, but they can be credited with switching the spotlight to the drab and colourless streets of the Lancashire mill town of Burnley. Providing the vital link-up in attack at inside right or left is Jimmy McIlroy, with Brian Pilkington at outside left – a combination which at times has produced flashes of brilliant craftsmanship that has left the opposing defence bewitched, bothered and bewildered. Outstanding as one of Burnley's youngsters is McIlroy, who was signed from Glentoran for a fee of around £7,000 in 1950.'

Two years later Hill had been replaced by Alan Brown who had once captained Burnley in the late 40s when there had been a Wembley appearance and promotion to Division One. Brown was an innovator, strict and stern. McIlroy looked up to him and admired him enormously, even playing a handful of games at centre forward for him when Holden lost his place. But 1955/56 was a season when he was absent for three months with a bad ankle injury, the first real injury of his career. He played four games at centre forward early in the season but then Peter McKay was brought back into the side and McIlroy reverted to his more normal role. Today, any conversation with him usually comes round at some stage to a mention for McKay. In the previous season he had only played four games – yet scored four goals and McIlroy rated him then, and rates him still, as the best natural goal scorer and poacher he has ever played with. He was only at Burnley for a little over two seasons and was already 29 when he arrived. He gets few mentions in the Burnley history books and few supporters today have probably heard of him. Yet he was a quite phenomenal goalscorer and had he arrived at Burnley when he was younger, who is to say that the title that came so close in 1952/53, would not have been won. He would have been worth millions in today's game.

Alan Brown – a huge influence on Jimmy McIlroy and Burnley FC, laying the foundation for the 1959/60 Championship season.

"Once in training at Gawthorpe," says Jimmy remembering one funny moment, "the idea was that Brian Pilkington, our left-winger, was to sprint down the line and whip over a cross for little Peter to thump into the net. Now Brian won't mind me saying that terrific player that he was, he wasn't the most accurate crosser of a ball, and Peter wasn't too fond of running after anything. On this particular occasion after sprinting from the halfway line only to see the cross drop behind the goals, the wee Scot looked up, gasping, 'Pilky if your brains were made of dynamite and I put a match to them, they wouldn't blow your cap off'."

McKay was small and razor sharp, with the ability to 'ride' the roughest of tackles and lunges, the complete opposite of someone like the bulldozer Nat Lofthouse. When he was a boy he used to listen to stories about Scotland's Hughie Gallacher, one of Scotland's greatest centre forwards. When McKay saw pictures of him though, what struck him was his size. McKay described him as looking like a small schoolboy and he wondered how it was that such a small man could be such a great centre forward. Gallacher was McKay's inspiration and from him he realised that nobody needed to be big to be effective. When, like McKay, you were only 5' 6" you need brains not brawn. McKay was a natural at finding gaps and spaces. He had an instant snap shot "and seemed to be able to score from any angle. No matter how the ball came to him he could strike the ball," says McIlroy. His best season was in 1955/56 in a team where all the forwards were small so that this was never a team that was going to sling high balls and crosses over; it was on the ground as often as possible. In such a team, McKay thrived. This was a rare season when McIlroy was the biggest player in the forward line at 5' 8". To cope with this, McIlroy remembers how Brown and trainer Billy Dougal developed all kinds of new free kick and corner routines which had never been seen before. "A portion of every day was spent practising routines and timing," says Jimmy. "And Dougal took to me because I listened to every word he said."

McKay started his soccer days in Newburgh, a Fifeshire village. Scouts flocked to see him play as a juvenile. Both he and his mother were thoroughly fed up of the constant knocks at the door and the question, "Will Peter sign for us?" He turned down the chance to join several clubs before at last joining Dundee United as a part-time professional training just two nights a week. Joining United meant he could still live at home. He had seven years

# BACKSTAGE AT BURNLEY

"Delicious!" says Burnley's Jim Adamson as he tastes the soup made by his wife, Mary.

Winton and Pilkington watch an acrobatic turn by Jimmy McIlroy, popular Irish international forward.

Trainer Bill Dougall passes on a few hints. Listening to him are Adamson, Cummings, Holden, Pilkington, Thompson, Aird and Gray.

there, happy with the club and the people. He was popular which was not surprising considering that he scored over 200 goals in just under a goal a game. In two of his seasons there he was the league's top scorer and one game in particular always stuck in his memory. "We were drawn against the mighty Celtic in the Scottish Cup and most people wrote us out of the competition before the kick-off. But we won 4 – 3, and had another three goals disallowed. I managed to bag a pair in a victory which set the town alight."

In the mid 50s he became restless and asked for either a benefit or the chance to leave. During the close season he learned that Burnley wanted him and just days later he was in Burnley and straightaway liked the look of the place.

In his first season he played only four senior games. In the words of the locals he says, "I did nowt." But in 1955/56 he came in for the fourth game and scored a hat-trick. "Our nippy team was playing quite well and I seemed to fit straight in this time. Goals came fairly regularly and I soon established myself as first-choice."

He had in fact found the change from part time football to full time quite difficult initially but once he adjusted he scored 25 goals in just 34 games. That he didn't stay longer than just the following season is down to Alan Brown who demanded a greater work ethic from his players that McKay was unable to give. McKay was an out and out poacher and basically lived in the penalty area, like a Jimmy Greaves or an Andy Payton. Exerting himself all over the pitch was just not his style. Priceless though his talent was he was discarded and in January '57 returned to Scotland. The memories of him, however, still stay strong and clear in Jimmy McIlroy's mind. 25 goals from him, along with Holden's 22 a few seasons earlier in 1952/53, might well have won the Division One title for Burnley.

By this time, early 1957, Jimmy McIlroy was a 'name' player and more than one other club would have been glad to take him from Burnley. One of his first ever written pieces appeared in the December 1955 edition of *Charles Buchan's Football Monthly*. Parts of it show that he was already a deep thinker about the game with some very firm opinions.

*Can you imagine anything more likely to take the gloss off winning a first international cap than to return to your club to find you are dropped for the next league game? That happened to me in October, 1951. I was within a few weeks of my twentieth birthday when I was selected for Ireland against Scotland at Windsor Park, Belfast. I must admit I did not have a very good game, but to return to Turf Moor and find I was out of the team was a shock. As a result I did not have much hope of being chosen for the next big game against England. I was not surprised when Sammy Smyth got my inside-right position. Yet I played in that game after all. Bertie Peacock, the other inside-forward, cried off and I was brought in. To top off a memorable season – I think I had only two more outings in the league team – I also played against Wales at Swansea.*

*So there I was – good enough for three successive internationals but not good enough for my club team. It was a strange position. All those internationals brought defeats to Ireland and a number of forward changes. I had three wing partners – Billy Bingham, Johnny McKenna and Norman Lockhart. Soon afterwards, Ireland began a policy of making as few changes as possible and I have been a regular choice since then.*

*Although I prefer the right flank, especially for shooting, my recent caps have all come on the left, as partner to Villa's Peter McParland. He is the type of winger I like to play with. He is clever, persistent, fast and always looking for a half chance. Not only good with his centres, Peter also likes a smack at goal. We first teamed up in the surprise win against Wales at Wrexham*

Windsor Park, Belfast, was the venue on 13th August 1955 to celebrate the 75th Anniversary of the Irish Football Association. For this reason, the IFA United Kingdom team appeared in the traditional Irish green shirts, and were selected from the the home countries of England, Wales, Scotland and Northern Ireland. Sadly for the United Kingdom team the Europeans ran out 4-1 winners. The photograph above shows the assembled United Kingdom team with trainer Gerry Morgan, back row left, and Walter Winterbottom, team manager, back row right. Jimmy is seated front row third from the right.

75th Anniversary Match

UNITED KINGDOM
VERSUS
EUROPE

WINDSOR PARK Belfast
13TH AUGUST 1955 at 3pm.

OFFICIAL SOUVENIR PROGRAMME

6D.

1880
1955

## HOW THEY WILL TAKE THE FIELD

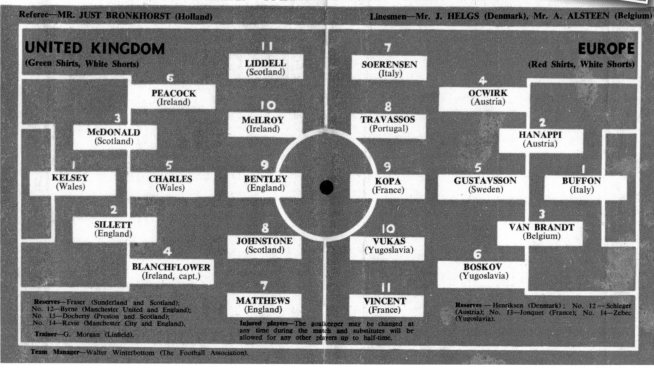

Referee—MR. JUST BRONKHORST (Holland)    Linesmen—Mr. J. HELGS (Denmark), Mr. A. ALSTEEN (Belgium)

**UNITED KINGDOM**
(Green Shirts, White Shorts)

**EUROPE**
(Red Shirts, White Shorts)

11 LIDDELL (Scotland)
7 SOERENSEN (Italy)

6 PEACOCK (Ireland)
4 OCWIRK (Austria)

10 McILROY (Ireland)
8 TRAVASSOS (Portugal)

3 McDONALD (Scotland)
2 HANAPPI (Austria)

1 KELSEY (Wales)
5 CHARLES (Wales)
9 BENTLEY (England)
9 KOPA (France)
5 GUSTAVSSON (Sweden)
1 BUFFON (Italy)

2 SILLETT (England)
3 VAN BRANDT (Belgium)

8 JOHNSTONE (Scotland)
10 VUKAS (Yugoslavia)

4 BLANCHFLOWER (Ireland, capt.)
6 BOSKOV (Yugoslavia)

7 MATTHEWS (England)
11 VINCENT (France)

Reserves—Fraser (Sunderland and Scotland); No. 12—Byrne (Manchester United and England); No. 13—Docherty (Preston and Scotland); No. 14—Revie (Manchester City and England).
Trainer—G. Morgan (Linfield).

Injured players—The goalkeeper may be changed at any time during the match and substitutes will be allowed for any other players up to half-time.

Reserves—Henriksen (Denmark); No. 12—Schleget (Austria); No. 13—Jonquet (France); No. 14—Zebec (Yugoslavia).

Team Manager—Walter Winterbottom (The Football Association).

*in March, 1954, when Peter had a remarkable debut and scored both our goals. On this occasion Ireland had chosen a youthful attack for the first time. I can still recall some of the younger players listening to team manager Peter Doherty. He impressed them so much that their eyes nearly popped out. I think had he told them to kill our Welsh rivals one by one they would have done so.*

*Talking of internationals reminds me of Danny Blanchflower. When he left Aston Villa for a reported £30,000 it was considered too big a sum for a wing-half. I'm completely against these mammoth fees, but if anyone is worth such cash it is Danny. He is the most constructive player I have played with or against, a wonderful team man and grafter. You can always rely on him to be around ready to get you out of trouble. On international trips we bunk together and it is a remarkable experience to hear him talk soccer theory and tactics for hours on end. Danny certainly rates top wing-half in my opinion, just as Wilf Mannion gets my vote as the best inside forward.*

*I've heard of the legendary play of Peter Doherty and Raich Carter, but was too young to see them in action. Mannion, however, I have watched and played against. If I ever become half as good as Wilf I will consider myself very good.*

*I'm told that when Burnley signed me in March, 1950, they had to pay Glentoran £8,000, a record for an Irish junior. Yet they could have had me for nothing. When I was an amateur, a Burnley official decided I was not good enough. I had been a professional for eight months when they had another look at me. Like every other Irish player I was keen to go to England and was immediately ready to accept their offer.*

*The glamour of joining an English club got a jolt when I looked out of my bedroom window on my first morning in town. A market had been held and the square was in a terrible mess. I got over that but I soon became bewildered again. The trouble this time was coaching. I tried to take everything in but it was a job to absorb it all. Perhaps I was too impatient and expected results immediately. It was months before the coaching showed effect.*

*One final point: I often wonder whether we can hope to match the brilliant Continentals while our clubs are so competitive. Often in five-a-side practice games I see players bring out the most brilliant ball play because they know nothing is at stake. But on a Saturday afternoon the same players make a hash of similar chances. They fear to make a mistake because it may mean the loss of a vital point.*

(Jimmy McIlroy December 1955)

Over 50 years later Jimmy still asks the same questions and has the same opinions. Players fear to lose the ball, players are drilled to do the simple risk-free things, players are coached to avoid taking chances, players are instructed to make the safe pass rather than try to beat a man. Managers berate their players for errors and failure. Points are everything. The game today is based on going for the safe option. Not losing is the priority; going for the win is secondary. Where is entertainment? Where are the entertainers? Messi, Zola, Ronaldinho, Ronaldo, Henry and maybe one or two others can (or could) light up a game and get us on the edge of our seat. But it is a small list and none of them are English or Irish.

At the mention of the money in the game today he simply shakes his head in disbelief. £30,000 for Danny Blanchflower in the mid fifties provoked his condemnation. Real Madrid paid £80 million to Manchester United for Ronaldo. The idea of John Terry receiving a reported £150,000 a week is beyond his comprehension.

There is a very fine line in Ian Ridley's book *Floodlit Dreams:* Clubs, "making fortunes out of players treated as slaves, players now making fortunes out of clubs treated as cash cows."

Jimmy McIlroy never had the opportunity to be a member of the second group. He benefited from the eventual abolition of the maximum wage but certainly made no great fortune. It is remarkable to hear from him that when he finally did leave football, he returned to his old trade – bricklaying, and spent two years bricking up the windows of condemned, abandoned, terraced houses in Burnley, and salvaging lead.

## Chapter Six

# With Northern Ireland

JIMMY HAD been to Belfast again, this time as guest of honour at a pre-season friendly between Glentoran and Burnley. It was easy to see why he had been invited. It was Glentoran's 125th anniversary season and this was where he had started his career. This was where he had been spotted, and Frank Hill had decided he was good enough for Burnley. Both he and Billy Bingham were introduced to the teams before the kick-off to rapturous applause. Not only had they started their careers at Glentoran, with Bingham then signing for his first English club Sunderland, but they had both been heroes of the 1958 World Cup team in Sweden.

Links between the two clubs go back many, many years, in fact long before Jimmy Mac. Tom Morrison came over to Burnley in 1894 and went on to play 195 games. Then, following Jimmy Mac came Alex Elder and Sammy Todd who both went on to play for Northern Ireland. Englishman Glen Little came to Burnley via Glentoran where he had been playing, and went on to become one of the great Turf Moor crowd favourites of recent times.

On a warm Monday night in July the players lined up on the pitch to welcome Jimmy Mac. Earlier he had been on local TV. He in turn applauded and waved to the crowd in which there were more than just a few moist eyes. Ade Akinbiyi, dwarfing him, gave him a huge and affectionate hug. Jimmy's Glentoran debut had been way back in the late forties and now here he was 60 years later being acknowledged again as 'the prince of inside forwards', the title awarded him by the great *Belfast Telegraph* football writer, Doctor Malcolm Brodie. Brodie is well qualified to award this accolade, having reported on every World Cup since 1954.

Simon Doyle of the *Irish News* was there and met Jimmy after the game when he was signing Burnley Chairman Barry Kilby's programme. Doyle was greatly moved by the experience of seeing elderly supporters whose eyes welled with tears of admiration. "The teams formed almost a guard of honour for him on the pitch lining up side by side as if they were preparing to be greeted by royalty. The PA announcer then welcomed him as he walked out to a standing ovation. The prolonged applause lasted for as long as it took Jimmy to greet each of the Glens' players. Both sets of fans rose as one to applaud and there were chants of 'oh Jimmy, Jimmy'."

After the game Jimmy spoke of how moved he had been by the reception; that he had felt like a little boy on Christmas morning just like he did when he first came to the ground all those years ago. "I feel it's wonderful. It's a lovely feeling. Sometimes I do feel like an old has-been when I walk into a room but when I hear the applause I lap it up." He went on to say that as he gets older the applause seems to get louder each time he hears it. He had hoped nobody would ask who he wanted to win. 1 – 1 would have been the ideal score but he was pleased he had seen Burnley win well, (5 – 0 in fact) and that he had the feeling that a really good season lay ahead.

Jimmy is proud of his roots and especially of his time playing with Northern Ireland. For many years they had been a 'joke' international team. "To say that Ireland ran their international affairs a little haphazardly at that time would be putting it mildly," wrote Billy Bingham in *Soccer with the Stars*. "We had no team manager, no set tactics, in fact no team plan at all. Jack Vernon our captain was the only regular choice and in our matches against the other three home countries some of us knew our opponents better than we knew our team-mates. If we had any plan at all it was only what Jack had told the Press on the eve of the match. And we had to read the papers to find out what that was."

But the great Peter Doherty changed that. Doherty, one of the very best inside-forwards with quick feet and a razor-sharp football brain, once described as 'the Van Gogh of football,

It was Malcolm Brodie who dubbed McIlroy "Prince of Inside Forwards".

his red hair burning bright in the mist', created a football plan that was based on the strengths of Danny Blanchflower, along with Jimmy McIlroy filling one of the two inside-forward places. His team talks were inspirational; he devised a double-spearhead plan that overcame the endless problem Ireland had finding a good centre-forward. And he drilled the team in tactics and free kick, corner and throw-in routines until they could perform them instinctively. 'Doherty made us feel nine feet tall', wrote Jimmy.

*When I was a boy my father used to take me to internationals in Ireland. "Watch that red-haired fellow," he would say. "That's Peter Doherty. If you want to be a footballer, study him – you won't go far wrong." I couldn't have known then that this was the man who was going to take Ireland to the 1958 World Cup Finals and me with him.*

*When Peter first started wearing the green shirt our national team was a shambles. Discipline was non-existent because there was no-one to administer it. And if there is one thing an Irish side needs it is discipline. Without it, our independent spirit has us flying in all directions. To put it bluntly, an Irishman can go crazy quicker then most, and without a team manager to keep the boys in check the temptations must have been enormous.*

*That then was the background to Peter's brilliant career. When he was appointed team manager for the game against Scotland in Belfast in 1951/52, he was determined that a new era was about to start.*

*Gone were the days of no policy, no planning, with the team meeting each other the night before a big match. Ireland were organised and it was Doherty who had done it. He injected us with a new spirit. Earnestly, persuasively, he made us realise the size of the job in front. "Ireland is looking to you," he told us, and we all felt about nine feet tall at the thought. What is more, he inspired such a bond of respect between us that we went out on the field aiming to satisfy not only Ireland but Peter Doherty too. He demanded that we train hard and play hard, and we obeyed*

Peter Doherty, manager of Northern Ireland and Jimmy Mac's hero.

One of the big successes of the Northern Ireland team which reached the quarter-final of the World Cup was Burnley's Jimmy McIlroy, here shown playing inside-left in the Wales-Ireland match in April which resulted in a 1—1 draw.

*him willingly, for nobody gave more to football in his playing days than Doherty.*

*I don't recall much from the times when I watched him as a boy. I was too young to recognise his body-swerve, his split-second sense of timing, his play when he was not in possession of the ball. But I realised when I saw him play during our five-a-side practices during training, how great he must have been. I envied him his grace with the ball at his feet and his brain that still worked at lightning speed.* (Right Inside Soccer 1960.)

Ireland's resources were limited with, at the most, eight regulars. In other positions it was always a struggle to find players of real international class. For the '58 World Cup they were unable to nominate an initial 40 players. Eventually 14 players were identified who formed the basis of the team for a successful two-year period. During that time one of their great triumphs was in beating England 3 – 2 at Wembley on November 6th, 1957. Gregg, then with Doncaster Rovers, was in inspired form, some of his miracle saves still living in the memory of people today. McIlroy was one of the scorers.

Jimmy's debut game came in 1951 with a 0 – 3 defeat by Scotland. His first goal came in 1956 when there was a 1 – 1 draw with England. He scored again in 1957 against Portugal in a 3 – 0 win. But it was with the 3 – 2 win over England, and another goal in the same year, that the brief spell of Northern Ireland glory began. His final cap came in 1965 when he was at Stoke City.

1958 was a glorious year for Northern Ireland and it was almost unimaginable that they had become "one of the mighty powers in world soccer." In the summer they reached the last eight of the World Cup Finals in Sweden. It was the last time that all four of the home nations would reach the World Cup final stages. Jimmy Mac tells the story in his own book.

*In the qualifying tournament Northern Ireland were grouped with Italy and Portugal, a grouping that was regarded by the Italians as something akin to a free passport into the tournament proper in Sweden. On the Continent, Ireland, like Wales, were known only because results of matches against England and Scotland in the British Championship were reported each season. Portugal, though capable of shocking a strong country perhaps once in every five years, were of no more importance then Ireland. Only one nation could qualify from our group. It had to be Italy, unless all known form took a somersault. The Italians, their own native soccer strength – which is considerable – augmented by costly imports from all over the world, were being backed to win, not only from the group, but also the World Cup itself.*

*Thus the scene was set. The stage was prepared for the greatest show ever performed in the history of Irish international football. I admit now, though it would never have done at the time, that I was among the unbelievers. I didn't think we had a hope. Believing that Ireland's sole motive for entering this magnificent tournament was the financial gain to be wrung from the four qualifying games, I philosophically decided to treat the matches (home and away) against Italy and Portugal as another step in my soccer education. It would be valuable experience.*

*As I walked along the promenade at Estoril on a January day, I also realised the trips themselves would be recompense for our anticipated speedy exit from the World Cup. On the day of our first game, the players were killing time in the company of exiled royalty and a few dozen millionaires in the playground of Portugal. More serious business awaited that night, at the match in Lisbon.*

*We kicked off at the odd time of 10 p.m. The line-up was Gregg, Cunningham, McMichael, Danny Blanchflower, Jackie Blanchflower, Casey, Bingham, McIlroy, Coyle, Cush and McParland.*

*Within 12 minutes, my old Glentoran pal, Billy Bingham, had scored Ireland's first ever World Cup goal, and I had visions of a win for the old country. But, it was not to be. The Portuguese, seldom penalised for constant obstruction and tripping, managed to scrape a draw, with a goal that looked likely to cause civil war in the Irish camp.*

*Goalkeeper Harry Gregg could hardly have anticipated criticism when he dropped a high ball that led to the equalising goal. As so often happens, in the heat of the game, Tommy Casey shouted to Harry, "What's the matter with you?" "The lights dazzled me," said Gregg. That excuse didn't satisfy Tommy, who cracked, "There are 21 other players here who manage to see the ball." Harry Gregg exploded: "YOU come in if you think you can do any better." Tommy did not take the goalkeeper's jersey but we all pulled their legs about the cross-talk act when the game ended.*

*There was no censure, even in fun, for Harry Gregg after Ireland's next match in the qualifying tournament, against the glamorous Italian maestros in Rome. Harry was brilliant, giving a performance which only those who have seen him at his greatest could possibly describe. We lost 0 – 1, although I blame myself for not salvaging a point with a clear chance of scoring 10 minutes from time. From 12 yards range, I beat the goalkeeper, and hit the crossbar. The only goal of the game was a silly one, although I must give the scorer credit for thinking just a little quicker than we did. Facing a free-kick just outside the penalty area, Billy Bingham lined up four Irish forwards to form a solid wall as cover for half of the goal. The other half could be safely left in the very capable control of Harry Gregg. Just before the kick was taken, an Italian moved the ball a yard and a half to the right – and that was enough to allow the scorer a clear view of the empty half of the goal, between Gregg and the wall.*

*Coming off the field, I realised for the first time that Northern Ireland were good enough to qualify for the World Cup. We had invaded enemy territory twice to discover we were every bit as good as Portugal and Italy. We had seen the best they had to offer, and I couldn't wait to get them back to Windsor Park, Belfast, for the home matches. It was heartening, too, to hear those Roman spectators giving their own blue-shirted gladiators a verbal thumbs-down as they left the arena, disgraced because they had not massacred the unknowns from Ireland.*

*Looking back on the difficulties faced by Ireland in Rome, I still feel there should have been a massacre. The game had been arranged for the Thursday after Easter, which meant the Irish players were in action for their clubs on the Friday, Saturday and Monday before meeting their most severe assignment only two days later. In addition, Aston Villa's Peter McParland, always a potential match-winner, could not travel because his club would not give him permission.*

*At the banquet following the match, Eddie Firmani, the South African transferred from Charlton Athletic to Italian club Sampdoria, spoke about these things. He told me, "The Italian players would all go on strike if they had to put up with your preparation for such a big game. They'd think you were mad if you told them to play four games in seven days." Well, it is said that all Irishmen are a little 'touched', so perhaps Eddie Firmani was not far off the mark. This was Ireland's team for the game in Rome: Gregg, Cunningham, McMichael, Blanchflower D, Cush, Casey, Bingham, Simpson, McMorran, McIlroy and Peacock.*

*In the following May, we beat Portugal comfortably in Belfast 3 – 0, the only feature of the meeting worth recalling, being my first penalty kick for my country. I scored, but a penalty against England at Wembley I missed. Penalty kicks, in my view, are converted, or missed, depending on the mental reactions of the taker: in other words the important factor is how you tick, not how you kick. It is well known that, even in Continental countries, the distance between the goalposts*

Billy Bingham, one of Northern Ireland's greatest ever players and a boyhood team mate of McIlroy.

is always the same: but never try to convince a taker of penalty kicks that this is so. When you are having a confident day, the goal looks so wide and high, you cannot possibly avoid scoring; indeed placing the ball on the spot, the penalty-taker can almost summon up a certain sympathy for the goalkeeper about to be beaten. On a not-so-good-day, however, the scoring area has shrunk to such an extent that the man taking the kick is left wondering how the goalkeeper does not constantly complain of claustrophobia, being confined to such a tiny space.

Portugal then did Northern Ireland a very good turn by surprising everyone and beating Italy in Portugal. As the Italians had won their home game against the Portuguese the position in our qualifying group in the summer of 1957, was Italy played three and four points. Ireland had played three and had three points. Portugal had played four and had three points. Ireland **had** to beat Italy to gain those coveted passports for our trip to Sweden. Defeat or even a draw, in the last match, in Belfast against the Italians, would see us eliminated from the competition.

The big match was arranged for 4th December, and without any question, it was regarded as the most important 90 minutes ever undertaken by the footballers of the Emerald Isles. Feverish excitement, almost unbearable tension, desperation on the field, celebration or heartbreak off it; these things were expected; but more much more, awaited the players and the onlookers as the drama unfolded.

The British climate is blamed, unjustly, for many things; but on the weather man's shoulders must rest most of the infamy at Windsor Park, Belfast, on the day Italy met Ireland. Fog at London Airport delayed a very important traveller to Belfast, Mr Istvan Zsolt, a Budapest theatre manager, who, in his spare time won fame as one of Europe's most respected football referees. Mr Zsolt was the official deputed to be in charge of the Ireland Italy match. In the dressing room at Windsor Park, the Irish players were told, a bare 40 minutes before the scheduled kick-off that as the referee still had not left London the match would have to be controlled by an Irish referee, Mr Tommy Mitchell, and in the circumstances, it would be a friendly international, robbed of the World Cup label.

The information was conveyed, even later, through the loudspeaker systems to the capacity crowd, and it is to put it mildly to say they took the news badly. At times, Belfast spectators can be very ugly spectators, as boxing enthusiasts who have visited King's Hall would testify. They were at their ugliest as the teams took the field. Ireland represented by: Gregg, Keith, McMichael, Blanchflower D, Blanchflower J, Peacock, Bingham, McIlroy, McAdams, Cush and McParland.

The Italian players had my sympathy as a wave of booing accompanied the playing of their National Anthem. The 50,000 Irish spectators knew, full well, that the real culprit was the fog. But the fog could not be booed. The Italians could, and they were – most brutally. With such feeling prevailing, the game started, inevitably in a keener atmosphere than is normally associated with a friendly international. One incident, I felt, could supply the spark to ignite a fiesta of football fireworks. That incident occurred when the costliest footballer in the world, Juan Schiaffino, a Uruguayan international in the national shirt of Italy, made a nasty tackle on Billy Cush. I thought Cush was fortunate not to break a leg, or at least suffer a severe injury, yet it was not the offence itself which really did the damage. Rather, it was Schiaffino's shrug of the shoulders and broad smile which so angered the crowd. I could have willingly taken the Uruguayan by the throat, despite the fact that I like to think I never lost my temper on the field.

The game deteriorated from that moment into the most 'unfriendly' game ever seen in Britain. An Italian player, not Schiaffino this time but Chiapella, ran a good 20 yards before jumping with both feet into Billy McAdams's back. He was sent off. I could see that while the Irish players

Strolling in Athens in 1961, Jimmy with Peter Doherty. The "Prince and the King of Inside Forwards".

# OF A WEMBLEY TRIUMPH TO REMEMBER
# and no blarney

FOUL!

**Billy Wright fouls Billy McIlroy and concedes his first international penalty**

Ireland failed in their bid to win the Home International Tournament because they were held to a draw by Wales at Ninian Park. Here are two of the reasons why they did not win – Welsh defenders Kelsey and Hopkins, who are foiling McIlroy as he tries to shoot.

*had only a 50 – 50 chance of finishing the game without serious casualties, it was heavy odds against the Italians reaching their dressing room safely, so incensed were the spectators at the rough play. The score was 2 – 2 when mercifully, the referee blew his whistle to signify the end of the roughhouse. Warily watching for flying bottles, I edged towards the tunnel where I heard the crowd hurling filthy abuse at an Italian player. He, in turn, shouted at them, until Dick Keith motioned to him in sign language, to get off the field while still in one piece. Misinterpreting the advice, the Italian tried to throw a punch at Dick, but fortunately missed.*

*Eddie Firmani, a reserve for the Italians, did understand the shocking insults from the spectators as he sat on the trainers' bench, but even if he hadn't, Eddie was left in no doubts about their intentions when he collected a black eye after being hit through the wire netting. Later, I must admit, it was impossible to suppress a laugh when he showed me his 'shiner' and complained, "And I wasn't even playing."*

*Not until I was safely in the dressing room did I learn of the most serious incident: the personal assault on Italy's centre-half Ferrario by fans who invaded the playing pitch. Although I hold no brief for the fanatics who shamed all Irish sport at the friendly, in fairness it must be pointed out that they were provoked by a combination of circumstances. It should be borne in mind that a Windsor Park international match is not staged solely for the benefit of Belfast folk. People travel from all over the six counties, perhaps the 32 counties on such occasions. The majority of them, this time, had lost a day's wages for the doubtful privilege of watching a match that counted subsequently for nothing. They felt, justifiably, that they had been taken in and robbed of their hard-earned money. Anger had to be worked off on someone. Italy's footballers were selected as the obvious target.*

*Yet, had it been a clean game, there would surely have been no invasion of the pitch. If only Juan Schiaffino had not smiled as Billy Cush lay injured on the turf at Windsor Park. As would be expected, the happenings at Windsor Park carrying the tag, 'Battle of Belfast', created something akin to an international incident. Italy appealed for the match to be replayed in a neutral country, even going so far as to nominate Paris as the venue that would best suit them. While such talk infuriated all Irishmen, it cannot be denied that the Italians had several good reasons, 50,000 of them in terms of spectators, for not wishing to return to the scene of their misfortunes. The Italians went to the length of asking FIFA, soccer's world governing body, to ban Northern Ireland from all international soccer, as it was not safe for any visiting nation to play in Belfast.*

(Right Inside Soccer 1960.)

Malcolm Brodie wrote about the game as recently as 2007 in the Belfast Times.

'Fifty years ago this week – Wednesday December 4th, 1957 to be exact – the Battle of Belfast between Northern Ireland and Italy, a 2 – 2 draw, raged at Windsor Park in one of the most bizarre and shameful afternoons in Irish football history…

Two months earlier on a cold, bleak night in Lisbon, Northern Ireland had drawn 1 – 1 with Portugal…

A flash in the pan? Not at all, with the emergence of a new Irish international football concept inspired by Peter Doherty the manager and former prince of inside forwards, and skipper Danny Blanchflower. Moves of fascinating beauty both in creation and execution came from players who benefited from being kept together for prolonged periods. They possessed flair, inventiveness and repeated tactical experiments were carried out…

On the eve of the game a behind-the-scenes drama unfolded. Hungarian referee Istvan

Zolt, manager of the Budapest Opera House was fog-bound in London and alarm bells rang. Irish FA general secretary Billy Drennan arranged for English referee Arthur Ellis to travel by ship from Stranraer as a stand-by, should the circumstances be unchanged. Italian President Ottorino Barassi would not agree and preferred to leave it until the morning but the fog never lifted. Behind closed doors at the Old Midland Hotel a compromise was reached when the match was reduced to a friendly and re-arranged for January...

What a furore arose when fans, most of them taking a half day from work were informed... there was an atmosphere of distrust, anger and antagonism which affected the players...

Italian right-half Guiseppe Chiapella caught Blanchflower with a lightning hook which would have been applauded at Madison Square Gardens; Schiaffino, contrary to his normal cultured play, brutally hit Wilbur Cush and Blanchflower, realising the danger, told him to forget it and get on with the game. Cush nodded, but shortly afterwards, tackled the Uruguayan with a ferocity which made even those who knew the toughness of the little man from Lurgan wince.

In the midst of the mayhem was the giant centre-half Rino Ferrario who pleaded with Danny Blanchflower to keep the peace, but then became engaged in acts of fury and during a corner kicked all around him with the ball nowhere in the vicinity.

Italian goalkeeper Ottavio Bugatti lay prostrate after diving at Peter McParland's feet, Chiapella went berserk jumping with his feet into the small of Billy McAdam's back and at the end of the 2 – 2 draw (Cush got both Northern Ireland goals) the crowd invaded the pitch attacking the Italians including Ferrario the villain of the peace. Police had to baton charge the crowd on the pitch to restore order. Questions were asked in the Italian Parliament...

*Fortunately FIFA ruled that there was only one place for the match, and that place was Belfast. It was arranged for 15th January, 1958. All Ireland waited impatiently. Once again, fog prevented one of the star attractions from putting in an appearance. Harry Gregg, needed by his club Manchester United for a European Cup-tie against Red Star Belgrade on 14th January, was stranded at Manchester Airport on the morning of the Belfast match. Harry could never have dreamed at that time of the disaster destined to overtake his club when they played the second leg of their tie against Red Star, the Munich air crash.*

*Ireland, deprived of Gregg's brilliance, had, nevertheless, a most capable deputy, Norman Uprichard, standing by in Belfast. The team was: Uprichard, Cunningham, McMichael, Blanchflower D, Blanchflower J, Peacock, Bingham, Cush, Simpson, McIlroy and McParland. With everyone on their toes, not least the Royal Ulster Constabulary, hoping for the best, yet fearing the worst, Ireland's manager, Peter Doherty, played a trump card. In a newspaper article, Peter made a moving appeal to everyone going to the match, asking them to behave like sportsmen. Win, lose, or draw, the Italian footballers must be given a square deal, insisted Peter. "Spectators, do not let Ireland down," he wrote.*

*The progress of the match also contributed, to some extent, to the important business of keeping spectators in good spirits. Within 14 minutes I had scored the first goal, a real piledriver, the sort of screaming shot that goes in perhaps once a season. No better occasion could have been reserved for this one. Soon after came another tonic when Danny Blanchflower put Billy Cush through to make it 2 – 0. Ireland were decidedly on top, a state of affairs due in no small measure to a muddy pitch, on which Italy grovelled and Ireland revelled. Those Latin ball artists were quite unsuited to the conditions.*

"Now I am approaching football in a more philosophical manner", says Jimmy McIlroy. And here, suiting his actions to his words, Ireland's great inside-forward just smiles ruefully as England goalkeeper Ron Springett safely gathers the ball in last season's international match at Wembley.

*Individually the Italian players were brilliant, particularly the forwards, and despite our heartening lead, many an Irish heart stopped when Italy's forward line had possession of the ball. A quarter of an hour from the end, Norman Uprichard took his eye off the ball for a second, long enough for it to hit him and rebound to Da Costa who smartly reduced Ireland's lead to 2 – 1. Those last 15 minutes were the longest I have ever known, yet somehow, we held on until the final whistle put us out of our misery. Feeling I was living the greatest moment of my life, I straightaway turned a cartwheel on muddy Windsor Park.*

*Suddenly I looked at Ferrario's face. It was contorted in agony. The famous Italian centre-half, victim of a savage assault on his only previous visit to Belfast, was leaving the pitch, this time in tears. My heart went out to Ferrario. If this was my greatest footballing moment, it was surely his most disastrous. It does no harm, in such moments of elation, to consider the less fortunate.*

*Having said that, I must stress; that most of my thoughts dwelt on Northern Ireland's achievement of a footballing miracle. We had won on merit in a cleanly fought game, despite the ordering off of an Italian player, Ghiggia, who had apparently taken a very mild kick at Alf McMichael. Poor Alf tried to stop Ghiggia leaving the field, and for his compassion, was nearly sent packing too. That incident apart, nothing untoward happened at Windsor Park on the day we qualified for Sweden.*

*Now soccer politics took a hand. As the players bathed after the game, their good spirits were tempered, somewhat, by the knowledge that certain people connected with the Irish Football Association were determined to prevent us travelling to the World Cup Finals because of a longstanding ban on Sunday soccer. These bigots, and I see no reason to apologise for the use of the word, were, unfortunately, in the majority. The enlightened legislators would be up against it at voting time.*

*The Irish League clubs and the important IFA officials were pretty well unanimous in their opinion that the Sunday veto should be scrapped, at least for the purposes of World Cup competition. On the other hand, the representatives of clubs in sundry amateur, junior, and church leagues were equally agreed that Northern Ireland should never play on a Sunday. As I was being congratulated in the dressing room by an IFA official, I asked him, "Is all this effort going to be wasted? Have we qualified for the World Cup simply to withdraw?" He made a pledge, "You boys have done your bit out there on the field. Now we'll carry on the fight in the legislation chamber."*

*What a sad commentary on Irish football that such a fight should ever have been necessary. Yet the first round went to the small men, the narrow-minded fraternity who thought it would be a good idea to request the World Cup organisers to arrange Northern Ireland's Sunday fixtures for Saturdays. That was out of the question, indeed it was an insult to ask FIFA to consider such an arrangement for the benefit of one member nation.*

*The wrangling, the lobbying and the voting are now, all history. It was eventually decided, don't ask me how, that we should travel to Sweden, having worked so hard for the privilege of qualifying.*

*Before the 1958 World Cup, Northern Ireland were soccer nonentities, known only in the British Isles. Through playing in Sweden we became a world soccer power. Those three weeks in Scandinavia did more for Irish football than all the seventy-odd years that went before. Northern Ireland, having fought to earn a place among the world powers, would have retired immediately to the backwoods if the suicidal decision, wanted by so many, had been taken.*

(Right Inside Soccer 1960.)

Jimmy Mac was scathing in his criticism of the attempts to deny the team entry to Sweden. He was aghast that even though the majority of senior clubs were in favour, the majority of players were in favour, the majority of spectators were in favour, and the people running the international side were in favour, it was touch and go whether their participation would continue, thanks to the views of small amateur leagues. He wondered, too, if the small leagues accepted part of the proceeds paid to Northern Ireland for their participation, when the IFA made bumper payments to their members.

Northern Ireland entered the 1962 competition, but the entry was again delayed due to the obstructive tactics of the same people who had nearly succeeded in sabotaging the 1958 venture.

And how were they allowed to enter the final stages in Sweden? To cut a long story short, so it goes; if they were allowed this one time to travel to the Swedish World Cup Finals, they promised not to do it again.

# Chapter Seven

# An Irishman In Sweden

THERE IS no doubt that Peter Doherty was the man who took Northern Ireland to the moment of fame in 1958. He had galvanised not just players, but officials and supporters as well. His right hand was Danny Blanchflower, assistant manager in all but name and on the field entrusted to make decisions and change tactics as and when necessary. Before that, the appointment of a young man called Billy Drennan as secretary in 1952, had also been a catalyst for change and as the players said at the time, it became a real honour to represent the country. Players like Jimmy McIlroy and Billy Bingham were spellbound by Doherty and hung on his every word not just because he was an inspirational manager but also because he had been an outstanding player they had looked up to as boys. Maybe it was a lucky coincidence that Doherty and Blanchflower emerged at the same time. They were both outstanding personalities.

Blanchflower was a master of wit and riposte. In Sweden he said, "If *we* don't know what we're going to do, how can the other side." On the problems of the Sunday football ban he said, "A majority 75% of the Irish FA decided we could not go to Sweden, but being Irish, we did." His newspaper columns were wonderful pieces of writing.

Between them, Doherty and Blanchflower tried to devise tactics and systems that no-one else had thought of. Blanchflower claimed that it was Northern Ireland who first thought of defensive walls at free kicks. They were one of very few teams to use short-corner routines. Another such team was Burnley where the winger playing the ball to a close-by McIlroy was a regular feature of play.

The band of players that gathered together was small in number but huge in team spirit and togetherness. They knew each other's strengths inside out. The camaraderie and bond between them was second to none. They were heartbroken by the injury to Jackie Blanchflower in the Munich air crash and a vital part of the team was now missing. But the small squad shuffled round to cover the loss and he was always in their minds as they played on.

The Swedes took them to their hearts for their openness and joy. If there had been a poll to measure the popularity of all the countries visiting Sweden, wrote John Camkin, there is little doubt that Northern Ireland would have topped the list.

They were especially popular with the authorities because their players and officials, unlike those of every other country, were always accessible to discuss match arrangements and the abundance of problems which occur in a competition of this nature. They met the Swedish authorities halfway in one of their major difficulties and accepted without argument a tufted, bumpy practice pitch secluded in a pine forest about a mile inland from Tyosland. Ireland took everything in their stride. There was no, more happy, more friendly, training camp anywhere in Sweden, with players and selectors on Christian-name terms, dining together, talking together, joking together. They were one big family.

Because they were the underdogs, the unexpected, the unfancied, they were relaxed and at ease, out to enjoy themselves, free of the pressures to win the tournament outright. They fraternised with the locals, had their sing-songs, served in local shops, adopted a young Swedish boy as a mascot, and mixed with their supporters. They recognised that it was a fairytale that they were there and were put further at ease by more of Blanchflower's maxims where he always told them to equalise before the other team scored and always retaliate first.

Jimmy McIlroy was certainly recognised as one of the players in the team who would have graced any other, the others being Gregg, Bingham, Blanchflower and McParland. McIlroy alternated between styles, wrote Albert Sewell, at times having to play deep and at others joining Cush in a double spearhead style of attack. If there were occasions when he seemed caught between the two, the attack nevertheless functioned mainly around him.

Derek Dougan later commented: "There was only one footballer in my lifetime who became a legend while he lived, and that was Peter Doherty. He, more than anyone, realized Danny's strong points, and he played to them. They made a great combination, Blanchflower, McIlroy and Bingham were a little trio who worked things out for themselves and the rest of us reacted to them and the way they played."

Peter McParland: "We were free and easy in our ways, we sang our way to the grounds, 'When Irish eyes are smiling', or whatever. The people took to us in Sweden, especially Tyosland, a village just outside Hamstad, where we were staying, where we'd go and have a cup of coffee, or whatever. They were all behind us and when we played, the Swedish public were on our side. We admired their way of life and we were grateful for what they did for us and their support."

Today, Jimmy Mac says he can remember little of what happened in Sweden other than the blondes on the beach (laughing while he said it) and the endless travelling. He devoted a whole chapter of his book to the events that took place in Sweden.

*Often when I am asked to explain the creditable performances of Northern Ireland in the 1958 World Cup in Sweden, I reply: 'It was the inspiration of the beautiful girls on the beach at Tyosland, because the Irish players knew that as soon as they were knocked out of the competition it would be the end of 'Les Girls'.*

*Tyosland… now there was a quiet place. The Irish team could not have chosen a better spot for their headquarters; just a collection of chalets and beach huts and a luxury hotel overlooking a sandy beach. All this was within about half a dozen miles of Halmstad where Northern Ireland were to meet Czechoslovakia and Argentina, and also within fairly reasonable reach of Malmo where we had to play West Germany.*

*Much criticism was hurled at England's team manager for taking his side to Sweden a bare 48 hours before their opening World Cup engagement, and for billeting players in the ever-so-grand Park Avenue Hotel in the centre of busy Gothenburg. In the case of Northern Ireland, we reached our HQ on the Monday, six days before the first match, an ideal time for acclimatisation.*

Preceding this, Billy Bingham remembers three weeks of hard training led by Doherty and Blanchflower, at Windsor Park. There were long runs, sharp sprints, exercises, "physical jerks" and the 5-a-side games that McIlroy set so much store by. They all felt as fit as fiddles and in great spirits. But Bingham also remembers a confrontation about 'spending money' when they got to Sweden. "The only jarring note was a slight tiff about whether or not we were allowed spending-money during our stay in Sweden. Earlier it had been agreed that

no spending money would be allowed. But, a visiting Press man told us that the English players over at Gothenburg were getting two pounds a day, so we asked for the same. Our officials were sympathetic but asked us to wait until the matter had been raised at a meeting of the International Board the following week. What happened at that meeting I do not know, but we got our spending-money." The international associations were particularly niggardly with their players in those far-off days.

Jimmy Greaves sitting in a station with a cup of tea and a cake whilst on the way to an England international game remembers being admonished by Sir Stanley Rous for daring to purchase a cake. "You will be fed on the train," he was informed in no uncertain terms.

'International soccer is a grim, competitive business. There were 16 international sides in Sweden in June 1958, and there is no denying that fifteen of them were living on their nerves, dedicated to the serious soccer assignments that faced them. But Northern Ireland were different. Wherever we went, the locals, and our opponents were amazed by our light-hearted approach to the business in hand, they could not understand how a national team could appear to be so completely unconcerned about a great tournament. The Irish had been criticised for this happy-go-lucky philosophy, but ever since I won my first international cap, the team had had such an approach to the game'. *(Billy Bingham 1962)*

But Bingham also added that the relaxed and easy-going fun they had, masked a determination to do well. With a man like Blanchflower as captain they could not do otherwise.

*We were a happy family. Though nobody took his soccer more seriously than our manager Peter Doherty, he was able to make, and take, a joke as well as anybody. Our normal routine at Tyosland involved training in the mornings, lounging on the beach after lunch; and in the evenings letter-writing, a hand of cards, and an occasional round of golf. When football writer Jack Milligan and Peter Doherty challenged Danny Blanchflower and me to 18 holes for a few*

Doherty and Blanchflower two of the greatest ever football thinkers.

*kroner sidestake, we accepted – even though we knew we would be up against it. Manager Doherty experienced difficulty keeping his drives on the tree-lined fairway, frequently disappearing into the forest for 10 minutes or longer, in search of a missing ball. After one such excursion, Danny shouted to him: "Hey Robin Hood how's Maid Marion?"*

*Peter had the rub of the green on several occasions when his slices hit the trees and bounced back leaving him excellent lies on the fairway. After this had happened for the third or fourth time, Danny Blanchflower, always the joker, told Peter: "No wonder your Bristol City team isn't doing well. They need some trees down the touchline to keep the ball in play."*

*At the 10th hole, dusk was drawing in. At the 13th it was just a case of hitting, and hoping the ball could be found. Danny and I were two down coming up to the 14th and were being ribbed constantly by Peter and Jack. Conditions were impossible, it was dark as pitch. So, as our opponents with the scent of victory in their nostrils, played the next hole, Danny and I quietly headed back to the clubhouse for a nice shower, and refreshment.*

*At least an hour later, two Irish golfers emerged from the darkness. Peter and Jack were livid as they saw us enjoying the clubhouse hospitality and Peter was quite serious when he told me: "Ireland haven't got a chance in the World Cup when we've got types like you two in the team. What an attitude, just because we were licking you."*

*To the day he died, Peter Doherty claimed I owed him 10 Swedish Kroner and refused to play golf with either Danny or me.*

*I could not write about Northern Ireland's Swedish expedition without bringing in our 'mascot', a 13 year old Halmstad youngster called Bengt Jonasson. He was constantly in our hotel helping trainer Gerry Morgan and the players, while as an interpreter Bengt was invaluable on shopping expeditions. Bengt also joined in our training sessions, and sang the old Irish songs as lustily as any 'Paddy' when we travelled by team coach. This boy fell in love with Ireland's World Cup team. We liked his company so much that he was guest of honour at every one of our matches, sitting on the trainer's bench just like any other twelfth man. He even travelled to Norrkoping for our final game against France, though it meant his being away from home for two days. When Northern Ireland were finally eliminated, it was pathetic to see our mascot crying bitter tears at our departure. We cheered him up by offering to have him over to Belfast in the following season as our guest at the Ireland v England international match. What is more, we kept that promise and Bengt duly made his appearance at Windsor Park.*

*Although I believe the Irish FA deserve great praise for getting us to Sweden in good time and also for their choice of headquarters, I must rap them over the knuckles for their handling of the internal travelling arrangements during our last week. It was chaotic. We played, and drew with West Germany in Malmo on the Sunday, arriving back in Tyosland at 3a.m. after a four-hour coach journey. On the Tuesday, this tiring business was repeated for the play-off match against Czechoslovakia. Then, there was a very short sleep in the early hours of Wednesday morning followed by a ten-hour coach journey across Sweden to Norrkoping on the same day. Not surprisingly the footballers of Northern Ireland turned up for their vital quarter-final meeting on the Thursday against France, regarded by some people as the best in the tournament, in a completely exhausted condition.*

*If we had stayed in Malmo after our match against Germany, and flown to Norrkoping following the Czechoslovakian play-off, I am sure we would have done Ireland far more credit in our final match. With four very hard games behind us, plagued by a series of injuries to Billy Simpson, Harry Gregg, Tommy Casey, Norman Uprichard and Bertie Peacock, we were in no condition to challenge the Frenchmen.*

*Our first game was against Czechoslovakia in Halmstad. Peter Doherty and Danny Blanchflower had watched the Czechs playing a club team in Copenhagen, and had reported back on their excellent football. It was ruled entirely by a smooth, flowing rhythm. We decided we must upset this rhythm, making our opponents play faster than they really liked. Ireland sacrificed much creative football to become chasers, hounding the Czechs persistently. Billy Cush scored the only goal of the game with a header from my pass and we held on to collect two valuable points although the game must have been pretty dull to the spectators.*

*There was nothing dreary, though, about our second game, also at Hamstadt, with Argentina providing the opposition. Even though they failed to qualify, I am sure the Argentinians were the finest footballing team in our particular group. I was apprehensive about playing them because, when meeting South American club sides in the past, the games had deteriorated into brawls. The Argentinian players, however, really love their football, and on that evening in Hamstadt they made a tremendous impression on me and on Northern Ireland.*

*We scored first with a typical Peter McParland goal, and they equalised from the penalty spot. After that, those scintillating South Americans soccer scientists toyed with us, teased us, and despite having only three goals to show for their superiority, did a fine job in 'taking the micky' out of Ireland. I would hate to have met them every week and suffer the humility of watching them put the ball through their opponents legs, laughing while they did so. Once on top, the game was great fun for Argentina. They even dispossessed their own team-mates as they turned on the exhibition stuff.* (Right Inside Soccer 1960)

Today, Jimmy remembers just a couple of things; that as the two teams came out together for the game the Argentina captain admired the Irish shorts which had a glossy, silky look. He touched Blanchflower's shorts and asked, "Silk?" Then his own shorts and said, "Cotton."

Secondly he remembers that after the defeat the Irish were still in high spirits and returned to the hotel singing. When they went in, all with their hands on the shoulders of the person in front, in a sort of crocodile, the people there thought they were mad.

*The Germans, a hard-fighting, tough bunch of footballers would have, I reasoned, a fair chance of beating Argentina, but I was completely flabbergasted when the Czechoslovakians gave the South Americans a 6 – 1 hiding. The only explanation for that result must lie in the Latin temperament. The Argentine players are either truly brilliant, as against Northern Ireland, or if the game is going badly, are liable to be reduced to a despondent state which makes them appear almost non-triers.*

*As Ireland lined up for the third match of the tournament, at Malmo against West Germany, we wanted a victory if we were to qualify for the World Cup quarter-finals. The Germans with three points seemed as good as through. Argentina and Northern Ireland had two and Czechoslovakia were in bottom position with one. With the brilliant Argentina team meeting Czechoslovakia, the bookmakers laying odds against Germany and Argentina being the two qualifiers from the group, were asking for trouble.*

*The West Germany v Northern Ireland match had much in common with a typical English Cup-tie. The tackling was hard, too hard at times, as when Tommy Casey collected a severe gash on his shin following a vicious tackle from a German.*

(The first goal from McParland came from a McIlroy pass, recalls Billy Bingham. The second goal came from a short corner, Bingham swung the ball into the middle and again McIlroy set up the goal for McParland).

*We led 2 – 1 until a few minutes from full-time, when Seeler of Germany tried a speculative hit-or-miss long shot. It turned out to be a hit, and we surrendered one of the most vital points in the history of Irish football. As we trudged off the field we were convinced the only job now left for Northern Ireland in Sweden was the packing of the bags for the return journey home. Germany had qualified and we felt certain that Argentina would accompany the Germans into the final stages. Suddenly, a few hundred of the supporters rushed onto the Malmo pitch shouting; "We're still in. Czechoslovakia have beaten Argentina 6 – 1." Elation succeeded despondency as the truth dawned. The wonderful South American team had been completely eliminated and Ireland were faced with a play-off against the Czechs to decide which country would join West Germany in the last eight.*

*I was certain the Germans could not hope to retain their World Cup trophy with the team they had in Sweden. We had gained a moral victory over them, even though the fantastic Harry Gregg had, at times, seemed to be playing Germany on his own.*

*Malmo was again the venue for our play-off fixture. But the injury list was mounting. Harry Gregg paid the penalty for his fearless exhibition against Germany, being ruled unfit to face the Czechs. Norman Uprichard, always a most capable deputy, was also nursing a hand injury, but it was decided he should play. He had to; there was no alternative, despite his injury.*

(Right Inside Soccer 1960)

The Irish were a goal down after nineteen minutes, wrote John Camkin, Zikan heading through a free kick from the centre circle which dropped in no-man's-land behind Cunningham and in front of Uprichard. McParland equalised precious seconds before half-time, meeting a loose ball after three shots by Cush had rebounded quickly from the goalkeeper. (It was McIlroy who had put Cush through in the first place.) When extra-time came, the Irish were reduced to nine fit men. Uprichard in the first place, twisted an ankle early in the game in the manner of Gregg two nights before. Around the hour, he broke a bone in his left hand, and then Peacock hobbling painfully but pluckily, had to be pulled out of defence and sent upfield with little more than nuisance value after eighty minutes. At the end of normal time, the full extent of Uprichard's hand injury unknown, Doherty and Blanchflower held a hurried conference to discuss the possibility of replacing Uprichard between the posts. But, despite rapid swelling, the Portsmouth goalkeeper courageously insisted on continuing. He suffered a thousand agonies every time he touched the ball. In fast-fading light, incident filled almost every minute of extra-time. The winning goal came in the 99th minute when, from a curving free-kick over the defence, McParland hurtling in from the left volleyed the ball into the net and almost through it before poor Dolesji sensed what was happening.

So, Northern Ireland, battered as they were, hauled themselves off the field and jubilantly into the arms of selectors who rushed to the touchline to acclaim their heroes. Irish eyes smiled that night seldom as before, and every heart was happy. They were the only British team to have won two matches in Sweden. Yet 48 hours later, the dream was ended. The motor bus that took the Irish party on their 300-mile journey from Malmo to Norrkoping for the quarter-final resembled an ambulance as five players who were either out of combat, or nearly so, struggled to be ready for the next day's game against France. "Gregg will play if we have to carry him on," Peter Doherty declared when Uprichard became the second goalkeeper casualty, and though such dire action proved unnecessary, Irish officials admitted that before he went on the field against France that Gregg was no more than 85% fit. Neither was Casey but circumstances enforced his inclusion and, even when his leg wound reopened, he gamely carried on.

For 43 minutes the Irish held out, mostly defending, rarely attacking. But, after France scored once, they scored four times, as their mobile darting forwards, with Fontaine, Kopa and Piantoni an electrifying inside trio, overran an exhausted defence. At last, the final blow had come to Northern Ireland but there was no disgrace for this little county.

Billy Bingham remembered one moment when Ireland might have scored before the French ran riot. "For nearly half the game we held France and might even have taken the lead. Our big chance came when the opportunity arose to try a move we had rehearsed in practice. The idea was that when we got a throw-in level with our opponent's penalty area, Danny Blanchflower would throw the ball to my head and I would flick it inside for McIlroy to run on to. It worked perfectly up to a point. But then Jimmy Mac, although inside the box and with an obvious shooting chance, decided to play the ball square across the goal. There, a defender gave it the boot, and that was that.

*Opinions about the French team in the World Cup vary enormously. There is no doubt that with brilliant forwards like Kopa, Fontaine and Piantoni on song, the Frenchmen could have beaten any team in the world. Yet I still believe their defence was poor, so poor in fact, that this defensive weakness coupled with forward strength, gave France a lopsided look in the team sense. I felt France were no better than other teams we had met in the early stages of the competition. That is what made our defeat so hard to bear. It is history now that we were heavily beaten 4 – 0, but had we not been handicapped by travel tiredness and injuries, I am sure Ireland would have beaten France. We had practically no chance, even before the teams kicked off.*

(By the time they took the field they were dead on their feet, and Peter McParland was also rueful about the state the Irish team were in when they played the final game. "I would have liked us to have had a go at them on level terms. While we were playing the play-off matches and travelling here, there and everywhere, the French had got their feet up for four days just waiting for us. They were a very good team, but if we'd been as fresh as they were we could have given them a game.")

*After the game though, the Irish party still managed to enjoy a celebration meal, much to the amazement of the Norrkoping locals. We had embarked upon the World Cup trip as a happy bunch. We were leaving in similar spirits, singing, 'When Irish eyes are smiling'. This song is the finest insulator against despair I have ever known, as was emphasised a couple of days later when the players flew from Stockholm Airport on the return journey to Britain. We had been airborne only a few minutes when Billy Cush, sitting by my side, looked at me with a worried expression and whispered: "There's something wrong with this plane. We're not climbing."*

*He was right. As we flew only a few hundred feet above the Swedish countryside, the pilot's voice warned us. "I am afraid I cannot retract the undercarriage. We must return to Stockholm but as we cannot land with full fuel tanks, we shall have to circle for some time."*

*Let me say right away there were no brave men on that plane. The memory of Munich and the Manchester United disaster was still fresh in our minds as we circled for at least half an hour burning some 200 gallons of petrol. Eventually we made a safe landing thankfully and I shall always consider it an act of providence that Harry Gregg, a Munich survivor, had left Sweden on the previous day on a sudden impulse. He had actually travelled to the World Cup by boat, swearing that he would never be tempted into a plane again. But when he heard that there was one vacancy on a plane to London, 24 hours before the Irish players were due to leave, he decided to take the plunge.*

*Though gratified that Gregg had been spared a second flying mishap so soon after Munich, the passengers on our plane were, forgivably, more concerned with their own problems as we landed. There was an immediate rush for the bar to sample the medicinal properties of the airport brandy. After two and half hours of 'medicine', we again boarded our plane.*

*As we took off, the strains of, 'When Irish eyes are smiling' filled that plane. Some of the passengers must have thought we were terribly brave, but credit for our high spirits should really be accorded to Messrs Martell and Hennessy.*

(Right Inside Soccer 1960)

On their return home the Irish party were feted and congratulated. The England team were not. They had had a poor tournament and Jimmy McIlroy was clear as to why this was. He felt, quite firmly, that they simply had not picked their best players, or the players best suited to playing World Cup football against 'footballing' nations whose emphasis was on skill. The forwards had made a hash of things and ball-playing forwards had been neglected. At fault was the selection system. A committee of 'selectors' were responsible for naming the players in the squads, Ireland as well. But whereas the Irish team as good as picked itself, England had a large number of players from which to choose. Selectors argued as to which players to select. Each had their favourites, and on some occasions a player might be selected purely because of his "physical strength and manly physique." It was for this reason that, for so long, selectors had adhered to the notion that the traditional 'battering-ram' type centre forward was always the best.

Jimmy McIlroy's views were powerful and outspoken in 1960 and he echoed those of Tom Finney who said, "There is an amateur approach to the vitally important business of team selection. The present selection committee of nine individuals is far too big. It should be drastically streamlined."

"I have an inherent dislike of selection committees," said McIlroy. "They should be done away with leaving the business of team selection to one qualified man."

Astonishingly, it was not until Alf Ramsey became England team manager, that the job of selecting the players was left entirely to the manager.

McIlroy was equally critical of the Scottish selection process. Scottish players who 'defected' to England were largely ignored by Scottish selectors as a matter of principle and this policy was endorsed by the Scottish Press.

Next, he criticised the 'age' factor where players (with just one or two notable exceptions) were deemed to be over the hill once they reached the age of 30. Then there was the 'honest endeavour' factor whereby 'power' teams like Wolves, Bolton and Sheffield Wednesday were filled with players who could run all day and would give their last drop of blood for the cause. "But when searching for international success," said Jimmy, "the ball artists should be admired far more. I have yet to see a great football team made up of 90-minute triers."

*Inside forward is one position about which I should be qualified to write. The inside man is the architect of victory, or defeat, because upon his creative prowess rests the main hope of goalscoring chances for his colleagues. His first requirement should be subtle skill with the ball, the sort of skill that can leave an opponent, or defence, flat-footed.*

Jimmy cited Tommy Harmer the Spurs inside forward as the example of what he meant.

*England desperately needed an inside-forward able to hold the ball, a match-winning schemer who did not mind attracting the wrath of those misguided spectators who congregate under the banner of the 'get rid of it' school. Tommy Harmer the cockney lad who had twinkling feet was doing it for years at Tottenham… his reward, not one international cap. Too many experts faulted him for not being a worker, not being at his best in three inches of mud and his inability to retain possession after bone-shaking tackles. Tommy Harmer's frame was built, not to withstand 90 minutes of non-stop energy; it is suited for the body-swerve, the delicate touch, the impeccable balance and the sleight of foot, of the soccer artist.*

Over the years, since Harmer, a procession of gifted and highly skilful forwards were overlooked, given at best just a handful of caps, and then seen as luxury players – Albert Quixall, George Eastham, Peter Osgood, Alan Hudson, Mat le Tissier. Even back in 1960, McIlroy decried the emphasis on full-backs who were just stoppers and able to clout the ball 50 yards upfield. He noticed that more and more of the continental full-backs had pace, were often the fastest man in the team, could distribute the ball cleverly with short passes, and were constructive and agile. The Burnley full-back Alex Elder was one of the first English league players to demonstrate an ability to make storming runs up the touchline, either to cross the ball or get in a fierce 20-yard shot.

In midfield he questioned the use of players like Ron Flowers, Eddie Clamp, Wilf McGuinness, Maurice Setters and Tony Kay; all fierce in the tackle and fierce in their belief that frills were unnecessary in a half-back. Was the powerful Duncan Edwards really 18 caps better than his midfield partner at Manchester United, Eddie Colman, he asked?

*Let's have football for a change* was the title of an article he wrote for the 1961 *Empire News Football Annual*. "I wish we could interest every club in the country in FOOTBALL. I mean football which doesn't include 'getting stuck in', 'fighting for the ball', or 'belting the ball'. Before Burnley leave the dressing rooms, the final instructions from Harry Potts are nearly always the same: "Play football, but above all enjoy your game." What a pity other managers don't think the same way. Critics bewail the lack of ball-players. So do I. Yet the blame rests entirely on the people who control the teams. What chance has a boy to concentrate on skill as he avoids crunching tackles, and hard robust play? I believe skill and 'fight' are the opposites. The complete footballer possesses a blend of both, but the emphasis should be very much on skill. If we are to equal the best in Continental football the tough stuff must be erased from our game to make way for subtlety, delicacy and softness of touch."

His criticisms were correct and just as valid in 1962 as they were in '58. "England, though, will continue to muddle merrily along until the next inevitable set-back in Chile in 1962," he wrote. How prophetic he was. England were indeed a failure in Chile in 1962.

Jimmy McIlroy's concerns that toughness, power, strength, and stamina take precedence over skill remain as strong as ever with too many clubs and managers. Ask him today what he considers the vital ingredient in any footballer's make up, then his answer will be the same now, as it was then - skill.

# The Turf Moor Stage ...

... upon which Jimmy Mac performed in the 1950s and early 60s.

... when the Longside was filled to capacity and noise cascaded down from the terraces.

... when Bob Lord worried that the Brunshaw Road Stand would collapse with age.

... when the fans stood shoulder to shoulder at the uncovered Beehole End in all weathers.

... when the mud was sometimes inches deep and yet still the foobtall flowed.

... it was the Turf Moor that staged epic games in League and Cup and magical performances on European nights against Reims and Hamburg.

... the people who were there when the ground was packed to the rafters are part of the club's history. Those who never felt or witnessed the power and noise of such crowds when it filled all four sides of the ground, but especially the Longside, have missed something that can never be recreated.

Jimmy recalls running round the cricket field every day before Gawthorpe, sprint training down the touchlines and 5-a-sides across the pitch when groundsman Tommy Danns allowed it.

# Chapter Eight

# Limping Along To The Championship

IF MY OWN story as a Burnley supporter is inextricably linked with the story of Jimmy McIlroy, then I know exactly the season my Burnley support began, and it couldn't have been a better one. It was 1959/60; Burnley won the League Division One title and I was 15. We had an ancient Ford Prefect, DHG 232, with just three crunching, grinding gears as cars had in those days, and it was a thirty minute journey to Turf Moor, 40 maybe if we got stuck in the lines of special buses that started from near the market on Burnley Road. We always parked on Mizpah or Lebanon Street in the days before restrictions, yellow lines, surly traffic wardens, and residents who look out of their parlour windows to watch and laugh when wardens slap a ticket on the windscreen. This little car only ever touched 50 going downhill, and as we chugged to the ground in this magic season there was always the sense of anticipation and excitement because we sat there thinking Jimmy Mac will surely win us the game. And so he did, or so it seems now through my rose-coloured spectacles. In fact he was injured for much of that season and he always says he limped through the final months. He takes us through that season in his own book *Right Inside Soccer*, although, strangely, his ghostwriter, David Jack, spends most of the time writing about the Cup game against Blackburn Rovers.

His longstanding injury that season makes Burnley's achievement all the more remarkable, for they used in addition to the regular eleven, just a handful of other players who barely played a dozen games between them. And with Jimmy Mac playing with the injury in many games, it means they didn't have a first eleven, they had a first ten-and-a-half. Today's top clubs insist on a squad from which, in effect, they can field two first teams. That was unheard of in 1959. A player carrying an injury today would not play.

If Jimmy Mac was my hero, then my father always reserved his admiration for Chairman Bob Lord. They were just about the same generation, give or take a few years, with the same values I guess. "There's Bob Lord in his pork pie hat," he'd say and point across to the great man in his seat in the opposite stand. In his voice was a sort of admiration-from-afar that signified his deep appreciation of this man. If he was in the national papers again, which he frequently was, grumbling outspokenly about something, pater would ruffle the broadsheet and announce: "Ee, he's in the paper again, but it's all good publicity for Burnley." But I doubt my father knew that the Cobbold brothers, who presided over Ipswich, usually with a few drinks in their hands, always called old Bob, *Bollock Chops*.

At a dinner to celebrate Ipswich winning the title in 1962 neither the Cobbolds nor Alf Ramsey smiled or applauded when Lord sat down, after he'd said that Ipswich only won because Burnley threw it away - which they did, as Jimmy McIlroy will testify. But the difference is that Jimmy would never have stood up at an Ipswich dinner and said that.

Of course this was a time when I bought *Charles Buchan's Football Monthly* and if they had pictures of Jimmy Mac, Pilky, Connelly, McDonald, Pointer and all the rest, they were treasured items. Sometimes there'd be a double page spread or a written feature. I think I learned to read with *Football Monthly*. It was also the tradition to race down to buy the *Sports Pink* on a Saturday night. The routine was to get back home from the game, gulp some tea down, usually potato pie, (I was 18 before my mother realised that cigarette ash wasn't supposed to be part of the ingredients), then run down to the lad who sold *The Pink* from the steps of the ice cream parlour near the huge railway viaduct by Tod Market.

One particular issue of *Football Monthly* included a wonderfully evocative piece by Geoffrey Green about Jimmy McIlroy's town, Burnley, the place he has never wished to leave.

'Burnley the town is no beauty spot. It forms part of a backcloth of tall chimney stacks and slagheaps that scar the Lancashire countryside. On the surface it looks dingy and dirty, a cotton town that has known better days. Yet beneath the surface, a warm, friendly, dignified heart beats. And outside, just out of sight, there are some fine, cold moors where even the sheep look drab. And when the mist drifts in from the hills there is soot in it, hanging at times like a thick garland in the sharp floodlights of Turf Moor, the home of Burnley Football Club, where once in 1924 a crowd of 54, 775 thronged to see the tykes of Huddersfield Town.

It is here that the real heart of the community quickens these days. Those tall pylons throw out their beams like candles in the night and towards them these sturdy Lancastrian moths flutter.

Come out of Burnley railway station and you find a little pub just across the road. A Southerner hardly dares open his mouth there at first, feeling like an intruding foreigner. The ale flows. Stained hands grip the jug handles, moving the amber nectar towards grimy faces. These are the men who now find themselves part of a new industrial revolution that has come to town.

Half fearful, you dare to ask the quickest way to Turf Moor. The response is magical. Through the dirt, friendliness gleams. Half a dozen men are your brothers at a stroke, each giving different directions. Little maps are drawn on envelope scraps. Some will even walk you to the corner and point. And on those occasions of a night match you can't, of course, go wrong. Those beaming searchlights direct you over the dark sea, with the rest of the seeping tide.

Burnley with its population of 82,000 is the smallest town to support a club in the First Division. And perhaps nowhere in the country is there quite the same relationship between the community and the team that bears the banner of their hopes and achievement. It is a true community because Burnley FC have seldom delved into the transfer market. They catch them young, on the moors, or in the hills. And if these mills at times seem to grind long and exceeding small, they grind them true, home grown products in the main. Here evolves the deep affinity between actor and the audience. They are friends. They grow up together'.

Half of Todmorden used to trek to the match on a Saturday in those unique, green, double-decker buses that loaded up outside the Abraham Ormerod Medical Centre opposite the railway viaduct. It was inside the Medical Centre that the infamous Doctor Shipman first decided that disposing of the ill, was more fun than curing them. The buses were low with a peculiar squashed look, and that was to enable them to get under the low

SATURDAY, OCT. 3rd, 1959

COPYRIGHT

VOL. LII. No. 10

ALL RIGHTS RESERVED

Secretary:
R. S. JARVIS

Team Manager:
W. E. NICHOLSON

Medical Officer:
Dr. A. E. TUGHAN

Chairman:
FRED. J. BEARMAN

Vice-Chairman:
FREDK. WALE

Directors:
F. JOHN BEARMAN, D. H. DEACOCK
S. A. WALE

# TOTTENHAM HOTSPUR

## FOOTBALL AND ATHLETIC COMPANY LIMITED

## Official Programme

### AND RECORD OF THE CLUB

# WELCOME TO BURNLEY

TO-DAY we give a hearty welcome to our visitors, Burnley, the third Lancastrian club we have met this season in the space of a month. Our visitors have made an excellent start to the season, and when the table was made up after last Saturday's games they were in fourth place in the League bracketed with Wolves and Arsenal with 14 points from their 10 matches. An exciting match is in prospect this afternoon, although neither side will be at full strength owing to International calls on Blanchflower, Brown and Mackay from our club and McIlroy from the visitors who will be on duty at the Ireland v. Scotland match in Belfast.

The following is the record of Burnley's performances in the League to date. It will be seen that they have scored 22 goals from their 10 matches as against 17 conceded, which indicates that they are no longer a side relying upon their tight defence, as they were a few seasons ago, but are putting more emphasis on the attack.

Home
| | | | | |
|---|---|---|---|---|
| Everton | .. | .. | .. | won 5—2 |
| West Ham United | .. | .. | .. | lost 1—3 |
| Preston North End | .. | .. | .. | won 2—1 |
| West Bromwich Albion | .. | .. | .. | won 2—1 |
| Birmingham City | .. | .. | .. | won 3—1 |

Away
| | | | | |
|---|---|---|---|---|
| Leeds United | .. | .. | .. | won 3—2 |
| Everton | .. | .. | .. | won 2—1 |
| Chelsea | .. | .. | .. | lost 1—4 |
| Preston North End | .. | .. | .. | lost 0—1 |
| Newcastle United | .. | .. | .. | won 3—1 |

It is evident that our visitors are a side to be treated with considerable respect, and that their Manager, Mr. Harry Potts, himself a former Burnley player, has assembled a team which is capable of extending the strongest opposition. In addition to building up the senior side there is also an adequate reserve strength, and several of the younger members of the Turf Moor staff who have stepped into the League side at one time or another have shown considerable potential. So much so indeed that such severe blows as the loss of their

English International goalkeeper, Colin McDonald, and experienced full back David Smith, owing to injuries, have not been felt so keenly as might have been anticipated. Alan Blacklaw has proved a most capable deputy for McDonald, while veteran Tommy Cummings, and more recently Alex Elder, have taken over at full back for Smith.

Burnley's policy in recent years has been to develop their own talent, and of their regular line-up only Elder and Jimmy McIlroy, both signed from Glentoran, cost more than their signing-on fee. They have always found the North-East a prolific source of talent, and two of their best acquisitions from that area have been Tom Cummings, a native of Sunderland, and Jimmy Adamson who hails from Ashington. Others are right-back John Angus, Jimmy Robson, inside-forward, and fair haired centre-forward Ray Pointer who scored 27 goals for them in the League last season.

During the summer months there have been some departures from Turf Moor, and these have included Albert Cheesebrough now with Leicester City, and winger Doug Newlands who joined Stoke City. Now that these two experienced players have gone Jim Robson and John Connelly have established themselves at inside-left and outside-right respectively. Both have made rapid strides in the last 12 months or so, and Connelly's progress was rewarded recently by a Football League representative honour against the Irish League. He is their leading scorer this season with eight goals to his credit, followed by Pointer with six. Their other scorers have been Robson, and his partner Brian Pilkington with three each, while McIlroy, who nowadays concentrates chiefly on providing the ammunition for his colleagues to fire has two goals to his name.

### LONDON CHALLENGE CUP

The draw has been made for the First Round of the London Challenge Cup, and we shall be playing Brentford here next Monday, October 5th, kick-off at 7.30 p.m. our opponents and the London F.A. having agreed to our suggestion that the match be played under the floodlights.

**In the Interests of Ground Conditions, Players on either side will not sign Autographs on the Field**

**PRICE TWOPENCE**

Printed by Thomas Knight & Co. Ltd.,
The Clock House Press, Hoddesdon, Herts.

bridges that dotted the Calder Valley. Sometimes I went on the bus if there was a gang of pals going. We had names like Ed Cock, Winny, Podge, Fat Stan, Jammy, Dicken, Spon and Sugar. Mine was Tommy. Most of us dreamed of being John Connelly, Ray Pointer, or the great man himself, Jimmy Mac. Today, not one green double-decker special makes the journey to Burnley from Todmorden and therein is a visible, or should it be invisible, symbol of the decline of a once famed club in the years before 2008/09 and promotion. Sometimes when I drive through on the way to a game there might be just one or two young lads in their claret shirts by the bus stop.

When my father died I was less than impressed when all he left me was a fob-watch that didn't work. But, he took me to the Turf all through that wonderful championship season when the abiding memory of the final game at Maine Road, for the many who were there chewing their nails, is still Jimmy Mac sticking his bottom out to shield and screen the ball by the corner flag, using up the final dwindling minutes to hang on to victory.

I thank them both.

'A 1990s footballer *(wrote Jimmy Greaves)* finding himself dropped into 1960 would feel as if he had landed on another planet. We even spoke a different language in the soccerland of 1960. There were wing-halves, inside-forwards, and wingers, two points for a win, and shoulder-charges were allowed against goalkeepers who had never heard of the four-step rule. Words and phrases like striker, overlap, workrate, tackling back, centre-back, man to man marking, substitutes and the professional foul had yet to enter our vocabulary.

We played with five forwards, including two wingers who used the full width of the pitch. The most common playing formation was 2 – 3 – 5, two full-backs, three half-backs and five forwards. The more progressive teams were experimenting with the 4 – 2 – 4 line-up that served world champions Brazil so well in the World Cup in Sweden. On the packed terraces they waved rattles and cheered, and about the most imaginative chant they stretched to was 'two four six eight, who do we appreciate'. There was not a hooligan in sight and Liverpool's fans had yet to introduce the 'ee-ay-addio' singing sounds that were to transform terraces throughout the land. These were the good old days when we still had threepenny bits and tanner coins, and it cost you just a couple of bob (10p) to stand on the terraces to watch your favourite team, and for an Oxford scholar (a dollar, five shillings. 25p) you could sit in comfort in the stand. A programme cost you between twopence and sixpence, and you could expect long queues at the turnstiles because the average attendances for the First Division clubs stood at 31,000, with Tottenham and Manchester United both topping 47,000. Floodlit football was just seeing the light of day, and Saturday was the big football day when millions of listeners would tune in to 'Sports Report' on the BBC wireless Light Programme on which Eamonn Andrews would introduce the 5 o clock results and reports. Television hardly got a look in.

It was being suggested that football was going crazy because, in March, 1960, a British transfer record fee of £55,000 changed hands between Manchester City and Huddersfield Town. In return City got a skinny, 19 year old goal hunter called Denis Law. If this had been the nineties, £5million would not have bought him. Yes, he was that good. The 1990s player would have mostly felt the difference in the two worlds in his pocket. The maximum wage that a player could earn in 1960 was £20 a week, regardless of how talented he might be. Thousands still flocked to watch Stanley Matthews perform his dribbling wizardry with Blackpool, but his weekly wage packet was still the same as that paid to young Johnny

Byrne, who was on the first rungs of his career with Crystal Palace down in the Fourth Division. But there were rumblings of discontent over what was to be known as the 'soccer slave' system. A smell of revolution mixed with the aroma of embrocation in dressing-rooms up and down the country as the sixties dawned. And the face of football was about to be changed beyond recognition. As we entered the football world of the sixties the old guard were coming to the end of their reign. Billy Wright, the heart of the Wolves, had recently retired after a record 105 matches for England. Wolves would win the FA Cup at Wembley that May, but it would be the last gasp of a giant that had trampled on the opposition throughout the fifties. Manchester United, rivals to Wolves, as the kings of the last decade, were rebuilding after the horrific Munich air crash of 1958 that claimed the lives of eight of their 'Busby Babes'.

Exceptional players of the previous 20 years like Tommy Lawton, Tom Finney, Raich Carter, Stan Mortenson, Len Shackleton, Billy Liddell, Jackie Milburn, Wilf Mannion and Nat Lofthouse had recently retired or were about to fire their final shots. There was a new wave of players coming through, and I was lucky to be one of them. We were the wartime babies who had grown up on ration book food and with bomb sites as our playgrounds. Many of us were born to the accompaniment of falling bombs and into a world that was off its head. We learned our football in the traffic-free streets, with tennis balls and old tin cans at our feet and with our coats on the ground as goalposts. Little did I realise that, as 1960 arrived, I was standing on the doorstep of the most exciting era in the history of British football. The age of austerity was over. The land of plenty was about to arrive'. *(Jimmy Greaves with Norman Giller: The Sixties Revisited, Queen Anne Press 1992)*

Jimmy Greaves both as a player and then as a writer and TV presenter was always full of admiration for Burnley and the football they and McIlroy played, during their years as rivals. There is the story that in one game when there was a sprawling melee and a mass set-to between the players that the two Jimmy's sat in the centre circle having a convivial chat while the brawl carried on around them. In another game, with Burnley casually stroking and passing the ball around, and Tottenham totally unable to get it back, Jimmy plaintively asked McIlroy and Adamson to let him have a touch and promised he would then give it back to them. Jimmy McIlroy was quite simply one of Greaves' all-time favourite footballers. He saw McIlroy and Adamson as the main motivators for the title win and that their positive football would have brought them more honours if Tottenham had not been emerging as such a good side at the same time. He saw that it was in the midfield where Burnley "purred with power and precision like a Rolls Royce engine." Greaves had the utmost respect for all the clever free-kick routines and short corners, the "mesmerising variety of free-kick scams" he called them. And all the time there was "McIlroy, stocky and almost arrogant, inspiring everybody around him with his wonderful, imaginative and intelligent positioning and passing."

Ray Pointer also gives some insight into McIlroy's skill. "When Jimmy got the ball, he'd keep it for quite a while. He would only release the ball if you had a chance of running on to it. We were the runners. He was the brains. If you couldn't pick up a pass he would turn back. If Jimmy Mac was heavily marked then Jimmy Adamson would move up and help find the wingers. Jimmy Mac hardly gave the ball away even though opposing sides would try to put a man on him. He was difficult to tie down, though. He was so quick from a standing start. He would create so much space for the rest of us. But our success was based

**BOLD, BRAVE BURNLEY**

JIMMY ADAMSON
... great captain

BRIAN PILKINGTON
... great winger

JIMMY McILROY
... great inside-forward

# Dogged resistance

A black and white dog gives light entertainment to the Turf Moor crowd when Burnley play their vital end-of-season game with Fulham (0-0)

on a lot of practice. We sometimes didn't wait for him to find us. There were a lot of times during a game when we would already be moving into position just as Jimmy was releasing the ball."

Of that winning season McIlroy said: "In our championship season manager Harry Potts nearly always gave us the same final instructions before we left the dressing room. 'Play football but above all enjoy your game'. It was a refreshing attitude and one that would certainly bring an improvement if it were adopted in the modern game. Skill was always our priority. Phrases such as 'get stuck in' and 'belt the ball' were not in our vocabulary. We had a great sense of achievement because we won the championship by playing football pure and simple."

*In fact, the strangest thing of all in 1959/60 was winning the Football League Championship. Strange; because the great honours in the game then, were reserved in the main for the so-called glamour clubs. Consistency is the paramount virtue when a team goes in search of the League title or the FA Cup. In post-war soccer, one thought of Manchester United and Wolverhampton Wanderers as being the type of teams able to produce consistent results throughout a full season. Burnley on their day were often superior to such teams, but good results were seldom sustained from August to May.*

*As season followed season, we seemed well placed to win either the Cup or the League, the latter particularly in the 1952/53 season. But we missed both targets due to vital lapses in a few matches, or in the Cup, due to just one bad game. I had the feeling in the 1959/60 season that Burnley would be proved to be one of the finest teams in the game – but win nothing. I was wrong.*

*At the start of January Burnley were perfectly placed among the first three clubs in the League. I believed that the bookmakers were being unnecessarily cautious when they made our team a short-price bet for Cup success. I had no thoughts of Wembley, despite our Third Round draw which was to take Burnley to Lincoln City, a very ordinary Second Division side.*

*But my own personal injury problems contributed to this outlook. I was suffering from a deep-rooted groin strain, the type of injury which can handicap a footballer for months, or even a complete season. On December 12th, playing against Arsenal at Highbury, the groin first went. Previous to the Arsenal match I had been on the table daily with a pulled muscle for nearly five weeks, and from Highbury I returned to the Turf Moor treatment room for concentrated treatment.*

*As Christmas approached, I was out of action, but Burnley did well enough without me on Boxing Day with a win against Manchester United at Old Trafford. My deputy Ian Lawson was a success, but it was agreed that I should play in the return game at Turf Moor on December 28th. That match was only five minutes old when I realised I had made a bad decision in electing to play. In those days there were no substitutes and I stayed on the pitch. United beat us 4 – 1 and the Burnley club came in for considerable criticism for playing me half fit. But even though I played in many matches during the second half of the season when I should really have been resting, at no time did I play against my wishes. The decision was invariably left to me.*

*These were depressing days. I had reached my peak as a professional footballer at the age of 27, feeling at last that I had sufficient experience to use whatever skill I possessed to the very best advantage. I had matured in time for what should have been my best season. Instead, suffering the anxiety of constant injury, it developed into my most unhappy one. A permanent resident in the Turf Moor physiotherapy room, I sometimes wondered how much electricity went into that* troublesome left thigh of mine, particularly when Billy Dougall who mends the players' injuries so expertly, told me: "Residents in the town are complaining that you cause interference in their TV sets whenever you take a walk."

I met Tom Finney at our training headquarters in Blackpool one day. Tom has been a great friend and adviser over the years. I talked to him about my injury troubles, hoping he could suggest the best way to make a full recovery. His advice merely depressed me even more. "I had exactly the same trouble last season," said Tom. "And like you I played when I was 50% fit. That nearly put me out of football permanently, so eventually I did the only thing possible. I didn't kick a ball for 14 weeks."

Our Cup run of 1959/60 ended at Ewood Park, Blackburn. Disappointed at the time I also felt an illogical relief that there would be no further Cup battles until the next season. It was as if a great weight had been lifted off my mind, because in truth, my injury had not allowed me to enjoy any game in the Cup. The league matches, those in which I had played, had been no better, either. Had Burnley been halfway down the league table, I might have been able to take the long rests needed, or even ignore all league games to give the leg maximum relief for vital Cup-ties. All this time, however, we were on the heels of Spurs for the Championship: consequently league matches were just as important as Cup games. There was no letting up and no period of respite. As each Cup-tie and replay approached, I kept feeling that an extra week of rest would restore me to fitness. Unfortunately the Football Association did not change their Cup fixture dates to suite Jimmy McIlroy. I played and each time, the recovery period was slowed down.

Between December 12th and the end of March I felt fit in only one match – the important league game between Burnley and Spurs at Turf Moor. For the opening six or seven minutes I moved about the field completely mobile; far faster than I had for weeks. At last, I thought, I am going to enjoy a game of football. I was wrong. Stretching for a ball with the left leg, the old pain returned and I had to limp off to get the thigh strapped up. As I settled in the trainer's box I felt like getting dressed and giving up football for the season. This was the fourth time I had broken down during the actual course of a game. I was sick to death.

In the closing weeks of the 1959/60 season, our Cup blues were relieved considerably as we joined battle with the mighty Spurs and Wolves for the League Championship title. Though Burnley were destined to win that battle, it is an amazing fact that we were never actually in the top position at any time during the season until after the 42$^{nd}$ and final game. In addition to Spurs and Wolves, other clubs like Preston North End and West Ham had enjoyed brief periods at the top – but never Burnley.

At Easter I thought Spurs would take the title. Having beaten Chelsea, away from home, on Good Friday, they should, in theory, have collected another four home points against struggling Manchester City and in the Chelsea return game in the two remaining holiday fixtures. They lost both, and with those points lost the League Championship. This established Wolves as favourites. Yet in a surprise result at Molineux, Spurs' last desperate efforts produced an away win which was to prove the death knell for Wolverhampton. Meanwhile, Burnley were quietly collecting vital points. Every game was a Cup-tie virtually. We drew at Blackpool, won the most important game of all at Birmingham and on what should have been the last Saturday of the league season, frustratingly could only manage a draw against Fulham at Turf Moor.

One re-arranged game remained, at Maine Road, against Manchester City. Spurs with all fixtures fulfilled, were out of the race. Wolves were one point ahead of Burnley, with a superior goal average. We HAD to win at Maine Road. Even a draw would have been useless to us. In

JOHN
CONNELLY

JIMMY
McILROY

Men
of
Burnley

TOMMY
CUMMINGS

ALEX
ELDER

One of the iconic Burnley F.C. pics. Pointer watches the first goal roll home at Maine Road, May 1960.

*the first few minutes Burnley were a goal up when Brian Pilkington caught Bert Trautmann going the wrong way. City soon equalised. Then, a few moments before half-time, Trevor Meredith, who had taken over from the injured John Connelly in our last few games, scored the goal that was destined to take the Championship to Turf Moor. The half-time score was 2 – 1. And that was the final result at the end of 90 minutes which must have been absolute torture to the followers of Burnley.*

(Right Inside Soccer 1960)

Supporter Peter Burch well remembered the night. The coach he travelled on was abandoned some way from the ground, the queues were immense. He was 17 at the time but managed to talk his way through a 'junior' turnstile. For a shilling he was in and managed to get right to the front. He missed the first goal but watched in agitated agony the remainder of the game as the final minutes ticked by with Burnley 2 – 1 up. The second half felt like two days. With just minutes to go it looked like Denis Law would score a certain equaliser but Adam Blacklaw pulled off a magnificent save to keep out the header.

Former Burnley MP Peter Pike drove up from London for the final home game but was unable to get to Maine Road as he was chairing a young socialist meeting. He had what was quite a rarity in those days, a pocket radio which he listened to as soon as he could get away from the meeting. He remembers shouting at the radio in those final moments for the referee to blow the whistle.

*I could pay tributes to each Burnley footballer individually, but that is hardly necessary. They played as a team, and won the Championship as a team. Nevertheless I must give a special pat on the back to Trevor Meredith and Tommy Cummings for coming late into the side from the reserves and playing with all the ability and confidence of regular first team performers. The most important thing that happened during that season was the establishment of Burnley as one of the really big name clubs in British soccer.*

*There had been big changes since I had arrived from Glentoran. In the fifties Burnley were described as an 'unglamorous' club, a lonely soccer outpost dropped in a hole in the Lancashire hills. But times changed so that in 1960 Burnley were a headline club, worthy representatives of the game and chosen to be England's ambassadors in the New York international club tournament.*

*Bob Lord, the chairman, because of his outspoken manner was not everyone's friend. But he did much to effect the transformation. Publicity-minded, his name, and consequently that of Burnley Football Club, appeared almost daily in the national newspapers. He admitted that he was setting out to put the club on the football map, and he did just that. I used to chat with other players at other clubs and was often amazed to hear them complain about the way they were treated. There were many unhappy footballers in the game, because they played for clubs that couldn't treat them as intelligent people. The more complaints I used to hear, the more I realised I played for a great club. Off the field we were not subjected to petty restrictions. The manager Harry Potts was 'one of the boys'. He trusted us. He knew that at all times we would give everything for Burnley and for him. He seemed to have the complete confidence and backing of the board of directors.*

*Not many years before the title win, Burnley were a dull, defensive side. We conceded few goals but we didn't score many. The style changed. In place of the stodgy, stopping soccer so often associated with Burnley in the fifties, Burnley became an attacking side. It was obviously appreciated by the most important people – the club supporters. Bob Lord made great improvements at Turf Moor. Cover was built down the full length of one touchline to protect the fans and floodlights, the equal of any in the game then, were put in. Bob Lord ended the Cinderella days. At Gawthorpe we had our training headquarters, set in delightful, rural surroundings, the sort of spot to make even the most reluctant-to-train footballers feel good to be alive. There were three training pitches and possibly then the only all-weather football pitch owned by a league club. When direction from the top is inspired, tremendous changes can be made, even at a club which was one of the 'lesser-lights'. Harry Potts and the players, too, helped rid the club of any negative and defensive complexes. Burnley supporters were at one time the hardest to please. I sometimes used to wonder if we were playing away, not at Turf Moor such was their condemnation. But in 1959/60 the supporters roared us on with treble the volume of earlier years.*

(Right Inside Soccer 1960)

At the end of this momentous season Chairman Bob Lord was elated and announced that he would not part with McIlroy for £100,000. But he was far from pleased that it was Bill Slater of Wolves and not Jimmy Mac who was voted Footballer of the Year by the Football Writers' Association. McIlroy came second in the poll much to the surprise of my father and everyone in Burnley.

"The award should have gone to Jimmy," announced Lord. "Slater is a nice fellow, a gentleman, but fair do's, he hasn't shown the brilliance or consistency of Jimmy, who in my book, is the unchallenged footballer of the year. He's been consistent all season whereas Slater came into the Wolves first team much later. The writers' votes are influenced too much by the Cup Final."

Sitting at Jimmy's kitchen table reminiscing and talking about the Championship win led us to Harry Potts, whom, like McIlroy, will always be associated with the winning of the League title and the manic scenes at Maine Road. Looking back all those years, McIlroy always instantly smiles at his memories of him. "Harry… he was just one of the lads, a lovely human being, it was impossible for him to bear malice," was his instant response in a previous interview, but these are only a few of the things that he says about his genial old boss. Nor is he the first to say that Harry was the son that Lord would have liked for his own. McIlroy is keen also to talk about the immense influence and importance of Alan Brown, Ray Bennion and Billy Dougall in his career.

It was McIlroy who replaced Harry Potts when the latter moved to Everton. He has few memories of him as a colleague, though he recalls they must have played against each other in practice games. "But we didn't meet at all, the first team used one dressing room and the reserves used the other one." But he remembers manager Alan Brown well, especially his strong mind and iron will, personality features that did not go down at all well with Bob Lord. "The future is looking good at this club, and you must feel that I'm deserting you," said Brown to McIlroy. "But one day you'll realise why I left." Fifty years later he is sure this is a reference to the fact that Brown and Lord clashed several times, but in such a situation it is inevitable that it will be the chairman who will win. Lord could never have lived with any man with a mind and will stronger than his own. The club's training facility at Gawthorpe will be forever linked with Bob Lord's determination to purchase the area, but it was Brown's vision and with apprentice players to do the labouring, it was Brown who developed it.

Then there was Billy Dougall who had immense influence on McIlroy. He was a player

McIlroy, inside right of Northern Ireland and football perfectionist, with Bob Lord, Burnley chairman and uncompromising soccer administrator.

for Burnley before injury cut short his career. From Charlton Athletic he came back to Burnley as reserve team trainer in 1932. In '34 he became first team trainer a position he held until Alan Brown left for Sunderland. He was briefly manager until Potts arrived and then became club physiotherapist. This role is unique at any club. The physio often becomes a sort of father/confessor figure as the relationship between him and player becomes so close during the healing of any injury process. Jimmy McIlroy spent long hours with him on the treatment table especially during the latter half of the Championship season talking about all kinds of things. His injuries were never career threatening but sometimes were of a nature that could easily cause dejection and immense frustration.

Ray Bennion was another huge influence, joining Burnley in 1932 as a player and then becoming one of the trainers on his retirement. He and Dougall were such longstanding fixtures at the club. They had everyone's respect and with Potts had their 'boot room' where they talked for hours long before such a thing was invented by Bill Shankly.

"It's true to say I worshipped Billy. Jimmy Strong used to say 'he knows what we're thinking before even we do'. The bootroom was where Dougall would often summon a player, and quietly talk things through with us. Later in his role as physio he could just feel and squeeze a muscle and say 'right that's a ten day job, or that's a two-week job'. Burnley and me owe Billy Dougall such a lot. He had such wisdom and knowledge and is one of the great unsung heroes of Burnley Football Club. All his words made sense. 'You do what the opposition don't want you to', was one of his great pieces of advice. He was always looking for us to play the perfect ball. Even if a pass created a goal, if the pass wasn't quite inch perfect he'd say 'that was almost a good ball'. He always sought perfection. Billy Dougall was a great influence on Harry Potts as well and Harry relied on him a lot when he was manager."

A grin appeared on Jimmy's face as he recalled Ray Bennion's response to the way the single lads would discuss their latest sexual exploits on the team coach. "Just heat and friction boys," he would say, "just heat and friction."

Whilst talking about Harry Potts, it was a smile of affection. "You never saw him despondent, he was always cheerful. I can't remember him ever shouting at a player or swearing. You knew yourself if you'd had a bad game, he knew he didn't need to tell you. He was always the optimist; he loved the game so much and never lost the joy the game can bring. At Gawthorpe he joined in everything. What he loved were the 5-a-side games. Jimmy Adamson and I used to say he was the best paid 5-a-side player in the country.

"If Harry had one thing it was passion and involvement. During a game he would gesticulate, point, wave and shout out messages – which you could never hear. I saw him doing this in one game and said to Jimmy Adamson 'what the hell is he on about?' For some games I sat in the dugout with him when I wasn't playing. He'd start off quietly and in control, then as the game went on you'd hear these little grunts and groans and gradually they got louder and by the end of the game he could be quite out of control. Then there was the incident at Reims when he ran on the pitch and moved the ball. That was the most hostile crowd I've ever experienced but I remember trying to calm Alex Elder down by saying it was nothing compared to Lisburn on a Saturday night back home.

"Being a great diver himself in his day, he appreciated others winning penalties. There was one occasion when I won one. I managed to fall over the other player's leg and it was against Sheffield Wednesday. As I lay on the ground I could see Harry was so pleased, dancing up and down on the touchline. But next to him was the Wednesday manager screaming 'he dived, he dived'."

Jimmy laughed as he related the next story. "Billy Dougall was manager for a short while before Harry came, and I remember he used to smoke cheap, little Woodbines. But when he became manager Bob Lord told him to smoke something better. He told him, as manager, he shouldn't be smoking something as cheap as those."

The smile of nostalgia stayed on Jimmy's face for quite some time. Dougall clearly meant a lot to him, and still does.

Maybe the innocence of football began to disappear after season '59/60. Nearly every game played was in an attacking and open manner, but all that would change as tactics and teamwork and organisation

became more evident. Many teams didn't even have a coach. Players lived in club houses, largely because they couldn't afford mortgages. Tottenham Hotspur with their big-money buys were maybe the first 'glamour' team. It was becoming a fashionable sport. Short back and sides were being replaced by something more stylish. John Moynihan wrote:

'The mood of football began to change in England. There was more money in the country now and rationing had finally gone. The footballers themselves began to change. They seemed to be younger, more handsome with a show-business look about them."

Old baggy kits were being replaced by something more continental, sleek and sophisticated. Television was beginning to bring more games into peoples' homes. In our armchairs we watched the one night when football changed forever; the night of May, 18th, 1960 when Real Madrid, with di Stefano and Puskas, put on one of the most devastating, mesmerising displays of club football ever seen, beating Eintracht Frankfurt 7 – 3 in the European Cup Final. "It was as if their football came from another planet," said Jimmy Greaves, "sending shock waves through the British game." Jet aeroplane travel made European games easier. Where once, the players walked to the ground or came on the bus rubbing shoulders with the fans, they now came in their newly-purchased cars funded by the end of the maximum wage.

Words like 'homely' and 'homespun', perfect in any description of Burnley or Jimmy Mac, were used less and less, and after the Ipswich title win in 1962, disappeared forever. In a way, McIlroy himself was emblematic of that change; a wonderfully talented and gifted but modest player, one of the very best in all of Europe, one that every top club in the league coveted; yet content to stay in a little place like Burnley. But his era was done.

# Chapter Nine

# Better Money and Dreams Of The Cup

IN 1959 THE average national weekly wage was not much more than £11 a week. The maximum weekly wage of a professional footballer at £20 was significantly higher. Yet, it was considerably lower than the figures earned by the top entertainers. Comedian Tommy Trinder was paid around £100 a week as compere of 'Sunday Night at the London Palladium'. In fact, £20 a week would only be paid to the top football performers, or if they were a first-team regular. The minute a player was dropped from the team, his wages might well go down with immediate effect. In the summer there was an automatic reduction to the 'summer-wage'. With all this came minimal security, the clubs dictating the terms, and the club determining whether to retain or transfer any player, irrespective of that player's wishes. If a player refused to comply, (George Eastham became the test-case at Newcastle in 1960), the club could simply refuse to select him to play or refuse to relinquish his registration. Within this context, Sepp Blatter's claim that Manchester United were treating Christiano Ronaldo as a soccer slave because they would not sell him to Real Madrid, becomes simply laughable. Today the wheel has turned full circle. "If this is soccer slavery," retorted Sir Bobby Charlton, "then give me a life sentence."

Jimmy McIlroy recalls that any player during his early days was at the complete mercy of the club as to what he could earn. Players might do some summer coaching or some temporary summer work but it didn't amount to much. Harry Potts for example took football groups at Butlin's Summer Holiday Camps. Jack Charlton earned 30 shillings an hour in schools as a qualified FA Coach in the afternoons. But freedom to earn extra money outside of football was extremely limited and it was mostly players at London clubs who had that opportunity. Dennis Compton of Arsenal and also an England cricketer was able to make use of his fame with adverts for 'Brylcream' a hair product for men.

McIlroy was unable however to make his way to London and the opportunities it offered, but Bob Lord did arrange for him to write a newspaper column in order to increase his income. Nevertheless he might have been forgiven for looking enviously at his near neighbour Tom Finney at Preston. He had a football boot deal that brought him over £1000 a year; he endorsed a brand of football, and shinpads, with payments linked to sales. For one day's work making a Shredded Wheat commercial he earned £500. These were considerable sums of money in the 1950s and Finney was an exception to the rule that extra earnings were hard to find outside the big clubs and London.

Jimmy McIlroy was able to put things in perspective, acknowledging that whilst he earned £20 a week, local tradesmen were earning less than half of that. He did not buy his first car until 1957, and that was a second-hand Austin 7. At that stage few footballers had cars, and relied on public transport or friends to get to the ground for a game in which they might well perform in front of 40,000 and more. He remembers his first holiday on the

120

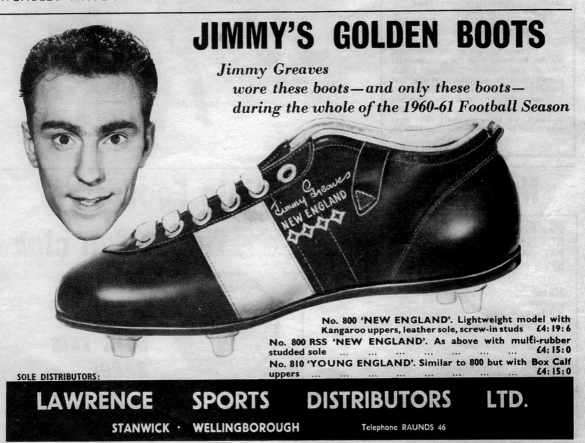
Jimmy Mac was unable to cash in on lucrative advertising. Few players outside London were used.

# SPOTLIGHT ON BURNLEY

JIM SCOTT     BILL JOYCE.     TREVOR MEREDITH     BILL MARSHALL

RAY POINTER     DOUG NEWLANDS     BRIAN PILKINGTON

RONNIE FENTON     JOHN CONNELLY     JOHN TALBUT     IAN LAWSON

Continent, a week in Ibiza for £52. That was a huge amount at the time, he recalls. The club helped with housing. Married couples at Burnley were offered a club house at a rent of £1 a week. Marriage was encouraged. Settled footballers make better footballers was the adage. There are unconfirmed reports that potential wives were quietly vetted by the club. When McIlroy took his first club house in 1954 he thinks he was then earning around £15 a week. There was an allowance for decorating and a director of the club complained that the McIlroy expenditure had been too extravagant.

"When the maximum wage was abolished our wages were doubled immediately. I knew that Johnny Haynes had been awarded £100 a week so I thought I should look for more. I eventually received £80 a week."

The 'why me' modest and unassuming part of the Jimmy McIlroy personality kicked in immediately when he wondered if he really was worth all that money. Looking back, he thinks he could have held out for £100 a week if he had had more confidence.

"But Bob Lord must have thought I was worth it. He liked to show that everyone at the club was well paid. He was proud of that. It gave him and the club some status and reflected well on him."

McIlroy at that time was not aware of any resentment that some players were paid more than others (although this would emerge in a much later newspaper article he wrote after his transfer). "We were close as a team. We all got on well together. Success helps make that bond closer along with good results and reading good things about yourselves in the newspapers."

But higher salaries for Burnley footballers certainly had no effect on the social strata of the town. Footballers then did not have the celebrity status they have now. Supporters might have held them in high esteem, but among wealthy Burnley folk, the 'middle classes' and 'upper middle' classes as we knew them by, in those still class-conscious days, footballers were still definitely 'working class'.

"For example, at this time you were considered to be more important locally if you were a member of the Burnley Belvedere Tennis Club, than if you were a professional footballer. It was quite a catch if you happened to be friendly with a girl from that club," said Jimmy.

The Mecca Dance Hall in Burnley was more in line with the social status of Burnley footballers and an impressive number of Burnley footballers met their future wives there. Marrying Burnley girls is what strongly linked and identified the players with the area. As a result, many of them still live in the town decades later, even though they came from the Northeast or even further. Few of them after football returned to their roots.

By 1962, however, the new brand of footballer had emerged and Brian Glanville wrote about one of them in the first edition of the *Sunday Times Supplement* on the 4th of February 1962.

'The wage limit has gone but the new footballer was emerging before it went. He's a product of his age, of the blue-blazered middle-class revolution, and the honing away of differences and eccentricity. Snobbish hotels no longer reject him. He blends with the background; speech and mannerism grow more unexceptional year by year.

Jimmy McIlroy of Burnley may not be typical, but in background and behaviour he is still a product of the New Wave. Thirty years old, inside-right for Burnley and Ireland, he became this season one of the two or three best paid players in the country. Burnley are said

The mid 50s. Ray Bennion and Billy Dougal, back row left, and Alan Brown, end right.

Burnley F.C. 1956-57. Back row, left to right: R. Seith, T. Cummings, C. McDonald, J. Adamson, J. Winton, L. Shannon. Front row, left to right: W. Gray, J. McIlroy, P. McKay, A. Cheesbrough, B. Pilkington.

Burnley F.C. 1958 team group.

Burnley F.C. 1958-59. Back row, left to right: B. Miller, T. Cummings, D. Winton, C. McDonald, R. Seith, J. Robson, D. Smith, L. Shannon. Front row, left to right: D. Newlands, A. Shackleton (now with Leeds United), J. Adamson, R. Pointer, J. McIlroy, B. Pilkington.

to pay him £80 a week; with other earnings, he must be making close on £5,000 a year. On and off the field, one is struck by his absolute self-containment. Haste, to him, seems the ultimate vulgarity; lack of purpose, anathema. He's a dark-haired, pink-cheeked, good-looking man, shrewd, self-deprecating, a humourist. If one can criticise his play, with its absolute technical mastery, it can only be on the grounds that perfectionism has its own Nemesis; virtuosity without bite.

His situation is one now of double paradox; in the first place because, like every athlete, his career is circumscribed, he will be on his way down when other men are just on their way up; secondly, because the New Deal has arrived when he is thirty, not twenty. "Only now," he says, "is a little fear creeping in. This money at first was the answer to all my prayers. I could see myself saving £2,000 a year, but now I'm finding my standard of living is creeping up. And the fact that I'm thirty and my earnings are at their peak and must start to come down makes it all the more frightening."

Married, with a son and daughter aged seven and five respectively, he had moved into a large, new, semi-detached house a year before he got his new contract. His first reaction to his wealth, other than "stepping up from a Morris to a Hillman," was to set himself a savings target which meant that he would have less money to spend than he had previously had on a quarter of the salary.

This Spartan resolution gradually lost strength. He bought an infra-red lamp to keep his muscles supple, in the hope of prolonging his career. He is planning to buy a hundred guinea pick-up to listen to classical music. "Often in my travels I've heard stuff and I've been spellbound, thinking this is the type of music I want to listen to." Such aspirations are again a characteristic of the most intelligent of the new professionals. Some of them went to Grammar School; more of them, like McIlroy, bitterly lament the fact that poverty caused them to miss it. He had won a scholarship to a technical school in Ulster, but had to leave so that he could help his family.

The New Deal has odd psychological by-products. McIlroy, for instance, is much more ready now to wear the club uniform – grey flannels, grey, crested blazer. "In the past," he says, "travelling first class by rail or air, I felt inferior to the other passengers. Now I've lost a lot of the complex. Sometimes I have a quiet chuckle to myself when I see a chap with a bowler hat or briefcase, and I say to myself, he looks to be earning the money that I know I'm earning. I wonder, is he?"

He's found no jealousy among his colleagues, but one feels that so far, the New Deal has brought him more anxiety than satisfaction. He worries, not only about his rising standard of living, but about the fact that, though he has "enough money to start a business," he doesn't really know where to begin, nor does he feel that he has "the business drive, the enthusiasm, and the know-how."

A younger, unmarried player, of course, a player like Johnny Haynes, the captain of Fulham and England, who is earning £100 a week from his club, has fewer preoccupations. But even Haynes has become a more sober figure this season. "He's grown," as the Fulham Chairman, Mr Tommy Trinder, says. Thirty is the turning point, the watershed, and every footballer must reach it. The brevity of his career suggests that there'll be no profound change in the direction of the British player. Like McIlroy, he won't send his sons to public school; nor will the public schools now send players into football. Like McIlroy, he may not employ an au pair girl, because "that would be a luxury beyond my means", clearly a

Son Paul visits Jimmy in the treatment room along with Jimmy Adamson and Les Shannon.

With Doug Newlands, Jock Winton and Jimmy Adamson.

subjective feeling, when one is earning £5,000 a year. Meanwhile McIlroy is trying to convince his wife that his new hundred guinea pick-up is essential to have in the house as furniture.

The irony of the situation isn't lost on him. 'At quiet moments, I think I've been robbed, the new salary coming at thirty instead of twenty. But then I think of Matthews and Finney and the colossal sums they have lost.' *(Brian Glanville Sunday Times Magazine, 4ᵗʰ February, 1962)*

Jimmy Mac's first ever Cup game for Burnley was not a happy one. Burnley lost 0 – 2 at Aston Villa. Before the game they'd remembered that the last time they had played Villa in the Cup's 3ʳᵈ round they had won 5 - 1, and then gone on to Wembley. Footballers look for things like that. But the omens this time were wrong; it would not be another visit to London, nor would the streets of Burnley be deserted with everybody away in the capital. That would come in 1962 and for Jimmy it would be a long wait. Aston Villa came out of the hat again in '57 and '59 but before those games there was the memorable Cup game in January, 1954, when Burnley beat Manchester United 5 – 3 at Turf Moor. There are old film clips of this game that show the goal that Jimmy Mac scored. It's a half chance in the box, the ball is loose, and he is in like a flash to score. It's possibly the earliest bit of film of him and shows just how sharp he was as he slides in like lightening. It's a poacher's goal, the sort that is there for just one second, if you see it and grab the chance.

Jimmy wrote of two more Cup games against Aston Villa and one of his favourite players Peter McParland in *Right Inside Soccer*. In both 1957 and 1959 Jimmy Mac, as the Cup games went by, harboured hopes of a Wembley appearance. This was an age when the FA Cup meant something; players and fans saw it as a truly dazzling trophy. The tournament was undiluted by other factors and competitions. No club would have dreamed then of playing a reserve side. Wembley was Mecca and it was a player's dream to appear there. A Cup Final was the only opportunity for dozens of players to play there and the kudos and prestige it brought was immense. The third-round draw on the radio would have millions listening in, including players who huddled round a crackling radio at the training ground or at the club. It was a magical competition where players dreamed of a medal. Today it is a competition where at least a dozen of the Premiership teams play their reserves or blood their younger players.

It was Aston Villa who ended Burnley hopes in the fifties. 1957 was the season that Ian Lawson emerged and scored four goals in one Cup-tie at home to New Brighton, and before that scored three goals in the home tie against Chesterfield. He was hailed as the new Tommy Lawton but the rest of his career never lived up to that billing.

*When the sixth round draw came through, with Burnley at home to Aston Villa, I started thinking for the first time of a Cup Final appearance at Wembley. Burnley invariably beat Villa at home and I was convinced that we were heading to Wembley. Against Villa we took an early lead and without playing really well held it until a few minutes from the end of the game. Then, the most dangerous man in soccer at converting the pass to the far post, Peter McParland, popped up to head in the equaliser from his favourite position.*

*But there should never have been a replay. In the first ten minutes or so, I squared two passes across the face of the goal, both taken by Ian Lawson in his stride. From very close range, Ian sidefooted the ball wide each time. Without wishing to upset him, I could not help thinking that had Lawson been out and Peter McKay in, at least one of those chances would have had goalkeeper*

Is this the perfect swing?

*Nigel Sims retrieving the ball from the back of the net. Against a great centre-half like Jimmy Dugdale, Lawson was given very little chance to shine, but McKay would surely have escaped Dugdale's attentions for long enough to have won the match.*

*I hope that this doesn't read as some sort of dig at one of my Turf Moor colleagues, because I had the greatest respect for Ian Lawson and he eventually matured to challenge for all three of the inside-forward positions. But Lawson was not quite ready in March 1957 and Burnley had to travel to Villa Park for the sixth round replay.*

*The pitch at Villa Park was in a shocking state. There were pools of water on the surface and where there was no water there was mud – gallons of the stuff. In one corner, in fact, there was a patch of filth giving off the most nauseating odour, causing us to wonder if this famous football ground had been used for sewage disposal. Thus the stage was set for one of the most vital Cup-ties in the history of either club.*

*Aston Villa at that time were being assailed on all sides for their vigorous style of football. They tackled hard, used their weight to maximum advantage, and generally bothered little with the frills of soccer, although their manager Eric Houghton repeatedly refuted charges that Villa were over-robust. There was no denying they were formidable opposition. In marked contrast, Burnley were a team of flyweights, with one of the smallest forward lines in the entire league. The Midlanders, who later went on to win the FA Cup, beat us 2 – 0, with goals coming from Johnny Dixon and inevitably my old Irish pal Peter McParland.*

*Burnley were out of the Cup, well beaten on a terrible pitch by an efficient workmanlike team. The match was not a classic, my main recollection of it being the rather odd-looking playing strip worn by Burnley. We wore navy blue shirts and navy blue shorts, and with the referee in his customary black outfit it was not surprising that he was given more passes than anyone in our team and we wondered at the time why return passes never came. He changed into a white shirt at halftime.*

*Two years later, Burnley again set out for Wembley only to be halted again in the sixth round by the same foe, Aston Villa.*

*Our third round task was one I did not fancy, an away game against Stockport County. The game was played on a very bad ground, hard as concrete under a layer of snow, with a covering of sand running the full length of one side of the pitch. We conquered both the conditions and Stockport County, winning decisively 3 – 1.*

*I felt sure that having beaten Stockport County we would survive the fourth round hurdle, the meeting with Blackburn Rovers at Ewood Park. Once again, the pitch was in a terrible state, far worse in fact, than at Stockport. This time we were faced with hard ice, which was a mass of wicked-looking jagged edges and also patches of packed snow. Ewood Park on that Saturday afternoon was a death trap; both teams courting disaster when the game started in such conditions. It was yet another game that would never have been played today. After ten minutes of slipping and sliding, I felt certain the match would have to be abandoned. So did our captain Jimmy Adamson, who recommended such a course of action to the referee, without success. Jimmy then asked the rival captain, Ronnie Clayton, to make a similar approach to the official, but still the travesty of a game continued. All the time I feared a goal for either side. Once that had been scored, I knew that human nature being what it is, at least one team, plus manager, plus directors, plus supporters, would insist that the conditions were perfect for the match to be played to the finish.*

*Mercifully, halftime was reached with no evidence of fractured limbs, and no goals for Burnley or Blackburn Rovers. During the ten-minute interval, the managers, Harry Potts and Dally Duncan, went out to inspect the pitch with the referee. The sensible decision was taken, the match being abandoned. After 45 minutes of play the ground was no better or worse than it had been at the start. If it was obviously unfit at the interval, it was equally unfit at the kick-off. This Cup-tie should never have started in my opinion.*

*We tried to settle it again on the following Wednesday when Ewood Park was in slightly better shape. Rovers led 1 – 0 but I managed to equalise. Jimmy Robson headed the winning goal in the dying minutes.*

*Burnley's fifth round tie was at Turf Moor with struggling Portsmouth. Jimmy Adamson scored the only goal with a wonderful run followed by a scoring shot. We were in the last eight again and it appeared as if only Bolton or perhaps Nottingham, Forest would stand in our way. They were drawn against each other and the outlook was exceptionally encouraging. We were due to meet Villa again, this time away from home, but with the Midlanders suffering one of their poorest seasons in their long, illustrious history, there was no despondency in the Turf Moor camp about the trip to Villa Park. It was a difficult match but it produced a goalless draw and a replay at home.*

*There may be people who remember the anguish of that replay in March 1959. In the first half we played extremely well giving the Villa defence a terrible drubbing. Just one thing was missing – goals. Despite the Burnley pressure, we could not get the ball past the capable Nigel Sims. Peter McParland, meanwhile, was having a very poor outing. Yet so unpredictable is this goalscoring winger, he can never be left alone at any stage of a game. This lesson was brought home to us in the most amazing fashion. With the score sheet still blank in the second half, McParland took possession of the ball near the halfway line and set out on a diagonal run towards the opposite wing. He wanted I am sure, to pass to his right-winger. But, he kept running with the ball getting nearer and nearer to our goal. David Smith, the Burnley left-back, moved out to cover the Villa outside-right, so that he could be positioned to intercept McParland's pass. That pass never came, and all the time, big Peter kept running with the ball at his feet. Before anyone could appreciate the danger, he shot from the inside-right position from about 20 yards. It was a goal from the moment the ball left his foot. My hopes of Wembley died again.*

*A young team, very short of experience against the unorthodox; Burnley lost a match which they should have won because our forwards could find no solution to a retreating defence. Neither could we counter a character called Peter McParland.*

(Right Inside Soccer 1960)

# Chapter Ten

# Ever Closer To The Cup

STILL VIVID in Jimmy's mind all these years later are the memories of the 3 – 3 draw against Blackburn Rovers in 1960 when Burnley had been leading 3 – 0 with just 15 minutes to go. He had played in it, I had watched it. The image of the moment when the ball hit Alex Elder's arm, and there was nothing he could do about it, is still crystal clear in my mind, though it was so long ago. Some things you just don't forget and who is to say that this one incident, this one moment in time, didn't prevent Burnley doing the double that season.

*Having struggled through every round with injury, we reached the last eight of the FA Cup in 1960. It was then that I started visualising a trip to the Final. The draw could not have been better for Burnley. Drawn at home at last, we had avoided a clash with Aston Villa, our constant nemesis, and with Wolves, the team nobody wanted to face. Blackburn Rovers, not particularly well-placed in the First Division, had done nothing to suggest undue strength – apart from a Pools-shattering victory over Tottenham Hotspur in London.*

*I had no worries about the Blackburn Rovers team. My only problem was with the same thigh muscle injury which had caused me to play at half-speed in all my games since December 12th. By this time, however, I felt that even on one leg I was getting away with things so often, there was no reason why I should not continue to do so, at least for the Blackburn Rovers game. Subsequent events were to prove me wrong.*

*Little of consequence happened in the first half. Cup-tie tension, plus the added nervous strain of a 'local derby' produced 45 minutes of indifferent football, with Rovers slightly the better team. Who could have visualised the second-half scoring spree? It started when I spotted Brian Pilkington standing unmarked near the corner of the penalty area. I swung the ball over to him. Brian half drove, half lobbed his shot over the clutching fingers of goalkeeper Harry Leyland, and Burnley were in the lead 1 – 0. A few minutes later we led 2 – 0 after I found myself in possession of the ball a few yards from the corner flag surrounded by about three opposition players. This position, in theory, is not a dangerous one, yet it is surprising the number of times it has given me the chance to create Burnley goals. I know, providing I can beat my immediate opponents and still retain possession, I can then approach the goal along the by-line, a situation which can strike terror into any defence; as Stanley Matthews of Blackpool demonstrated in the 1953 Cup Final against Bolton Wanderers.*

*On this occasion I managed to beat the Blackburn defenders, two, three, more, according to which paper you read. Please don't ask me because I wasn't counting those blue and white shirts. Instead of then bringing the ball in, I parted with it quickly, knowing instinctively that Ray Pointer would be dangerously placed to snap up the chance. I didn't actually see him, but having teamed up on this move hundreds of times in practice, I took it for granted Ray would be there. He was – and he glided the ball neatly into the net.*

*From an indecisive 0 – 0, we now had two goals in hand, but the scoring still had not come to an end. Another pre-arranged scoring move brought success with a goal to John Connelly. During training sessions we felt that a long pass beating the full-back could give Connelly just the sort of chance he thrived on, because Rovers were particularly vulnerable to the move. It worked like a charm with Jimmy Adamson making the pass, and Connelly getting the goal that made the score Burnley 3 Blackburn 0. Every player knew then that the Cup-tie was virtually over. We were in the semi-final. Blackburn felt that way too at the kick-off following the third goal. They were thoroughly dejected and restarted the game as if all subsequent play was just a waste of time and effort. I knew we had won – provided nothing crazy happened. Unfortunately it did.*

*Mr J Hunt, the referee, gave Blackburn Rovers the most fantastic penalty I have seen in my entire football career. This is not sour grapes on my part, or the biased verdict of an embittered*

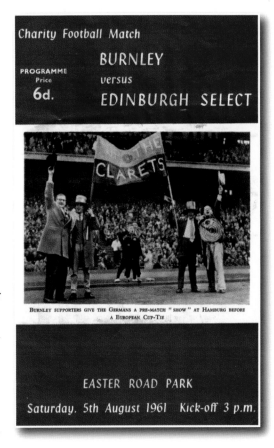

Charity Football Match

**BURNLEY**

PROGRAMME Price **6d.**

*versus*

**EDINBURGH SELECT**

BURNLEY SUPPORTERS GIVE THE GERMANS A PRE-MATCH "SHOW" AT HAMBURG BEFORE A EUROPEAN CUP-TIE

**EASTER ROAD PARK**

Saturday, 5th August 1961  Kick-off 3 p.m.

*man. I have never been a bad loser. I have never been a referee baiter. But I would have been less than honest if I hadn't added my condemnation of that strange decision to similar criticism from the mouths of so many neutral observers. The incident was simplicity itself. A harmless looking shot from McLeod struck our left-back Alex Elder on the boot. The ball was deflected up on to his arm. There was nothing in the world that young Alex could have done to get out of the way of the ball. Hands? Yes. Deliberate hands? Certainly not.*

*As was expected, the Blackburn officials endorsed Mr Hunt's decision after the match. Yet even they unanimously stated that the ball **hit** Elder on the arm or hand. According to the laws of the game, this is the only relevant point. Whether or not Burnley gained an advantage through the incident or whether or not it gave Elder possession of the ball, did not enter into the case. Unless a player **intentionally** plays the ball with his hand, no offence has been committed. Mr Hunt, however, had his own strange interpretation of the incident, and to my amazement, he awarded a penalty kick. I thought then, as I have thought since, that he might have been less inclined to blow his whistle had the score still been 0 – 0 or even 1 – 1. It seemed almost akin to an act of kindness to a team already three goals down, a decision which could not apparently affect the ultimate result of the match. It was to prove decisive though. Bryan Douglas scored from the penalty spot. New life entered the dispirited Rovers' ranks, but spirit being drained from the Burnley players. Blackburn realised, suddenly, that they had a slim chance of survival. Forgotten, from that moment, was the hopelessness that had faced them while they trailed 0 – 3, only 18 minutes from the final whistle.*

*Peter Dobing tried a speculative shot from about 20 yards. Too late, Adam Blacklaw, who must have been unsighted, realised the danger but the ball beat him and entered the net. Now the score was 3 – 2. Rovers were fighting like demons for the equaliser and a fearful panic had*

Bob Lord loved his grand social occasions at the club. Above: Brian Glanville talks to Jimmy Adamson at one of Lord's celebration banquets. Below: 1959 – a grand time to be at Burnley Football Club.

*spread through the complete Burnley team. Now Burnley, not Blackburn, were the beaten team, even though still leading by a single goal. The equalising goal arrived via a free kick from Matt Woods. With the penalty area packed, the ball floated into a crowd of players. I am not being uncharitable when I say that the ball had to bounce well for Rovers, for anything to come of the scrimmage. And bounce well it did. Mick McGrath stabbed hopefully at it; the ball went through the bunch, hit a post and crept into the net. This was not unlike the desperation goal which had saved Burnley at Valley Parade in the mud at Bradford in the earlier round, and apparently one which had rescued Blackburn Rovers in an earlier round against Blackpool at Ewood Park. I am sure Rovers were as concerned about the artistic merit of McGrath's goal as Burnley had been in the last minute of our Bradford City Cup-tie.*

*It was an amazing result for Blackburn Rovers, yet it might have merited even bigger headlines. During the closing few minutes it would have come as no surprise to me if Rovers had actually scored a fourth and match-winning goal. They nearly did and it is a fact that the Turf Moor team, virtually in the semi-final of the Cup 18 minutes previously, were struggling like madmen to remain in the sixth round as the whistle blew to end this extraordinary Cup-tie.*

*Afterwards, the inquests raged throughout East Lancashire, if not farther afield. Alex Elder enjoying a fabulously successful initial season in the First Division was in tears in the Burnley dressing-room. I am certain all his many outstanding matches meant nothing to him in those moments of all-consuming misery as he sat and said to himself, over and over again, "It was an accident, it was an accident." He was due to go out that night. He stayed at home. He could not face his friends and all their well-meaning sympathy. He blamed himself. I prefer to blame a gentleman with a whistle called Mr Hunt.*

(Right Inside Soccer 1960)

Even after this catastrophic final 18 minutes there was confidence in the Burnley camp that they could go and win at Ewood Park but when the day came defeat awaited. For McIlroy it was a nightmare game as the injury reared its ugly head yet again and he was unable to cheat the inevitable by performing on one leg. On the morning of the game the club doctor gave him an examination and asked how he felt. "I wouldn't play if this was a League game," he replied. "I've got away with it in seven Cup-ties; maybe I can in an eighth." But no, by his own admission he had a poor game. Another player, Jimmy Robson had spent the day in bed with stomach trouble. Blackburn were worthy winners and McIlroy still wonders how they managed to take them into extra-time without conceding a goal. But in extra-time Dobing, in another scramble, put Rovers a goal up. McLeod scored the second when Burnley had thrown caution to the winds and gone all-out for the equaliser. McIlroy's contribution was minimal. He couldn't move quickly, couldn't shoot and his passing was ineffective. Burnley hardly ruffled Blackburn. Add to that the booing of McIlroy by the home crowd and his night was complete. He accidentally kicked Derek Dougan the Blackburn centre-forward. Dougan went down theatrically, hopping, and then rolling along the ground. It looked dreadful. The crowd booed McIlroy mercilessly. But Dougan was fine and arrived for the second half alone, after the other players, in a blaze of dramatic glory, to the cheers of the fans.

So the Cup-run of 1959/60 ended at Blackburn Rovers and there was great disappointment. Yet, on the other hand, McIlroy admitted to a sense of relief that there would be no further sapping Cup battles. "It was as if a great weight had been lifted from my shoulders, because in truth, my injury had not allowed me to enjoy any game in the Cup."

The Cup Final of 1962 was the second Cup game in a row of three that Burnley and Spurs played in consecutive seasons between 1961 and 1963. In 1961 they lost the semi-final tie at Villa Park 0 – 3 against Tottenham.

This was a game not without controversy and two goals for Spurs that came from Burnley mistakes. A perfectly good Jimmy Robson goal was disallowed and the Spurs players afterwards admitted to being baffled as to why it didn't stand. Cliff Jones was actually on the way back to the centre circle as the ball went into the net, and thought to himself, that's it, Burnley will go on and beat us. But it wasn't to be Burnley's day. One Spurs goal came from an Adamson misjudgement and another from an Elder mistake.

In 1963, the year after Wembley, Burnley beat Spurs 3 – 0 at White Hart Lane in a real rough-house game. The physical game was totally out of character such was the respect these clubs had for each other. Jimmy puts it down to the conditions, slippery ice made it into a skating rink and that meant that players simply careered into each other unintentionally. But a collision between Gordon Harris and Dave Mackay was the start of all the trouble, and after that things got out of hand. When yet another fracas started, Jimmy Greaves went over to McIlroy and said, "Lets get out of the way of this Jimmy, we're just two cowards."

Jimmy's biggest memory, he said in the local Press, of the games leading up to the 1962 Cup Final, came seconds after the start of the second half at Everton. "We worked our way down the right and I squared the ball to Brian Miller. There's never been a more thrilling sight than Albert Dunlop, Everton's goalkeeper, being at full stretch and being unable to stop Brian's shot. That goal was a real thriller."

According to Bob Lord the team was relaxed and sure of themselves; League disappointments were over and done with. They were ready for the big occasion which the football public hailed as the one that everyone wanted.

'We were at least playing opponents respected for their type of football... Already in the ground were thousands of Burnley supporters. All had spent many hours travelling to London; some had had no sleep on Friday night. 'Oop for the Cup', as they call it. But it raised a lump in the throat to see all these good lads from home – cheery, excited and bedecked.

I spoke to the players individually, dithering with emotion and pride... 'We all want to win, of course, but so long as we reach peak form, even in defeat, I'll be satisfied'.

But, there was Tottenham's sensational opening goal in the third minute. This was a real jolt. Half an hour of dejection and somersaults in the stomach so recently patched up... the trying pause during the interval when you have to put on a big, bold smile for all and sundry... and then, before you have settled in your seat and know where you are, our equalizing goal. Up in the heavens, down with a dramatic pulverising drop sixty seconds later when the Spurs go straight down the field and snatch the lead again. You are just numb. But in the remaining play the claret and blue gained a million friends. How we lost by debated incidents concerning a linesman's signal for a free kick before the referee awarded the knock-out penalty decision does not now matter.

Our players, of course, were down in the mouth. Two honours lost on the post. But their sportsmanship in defeat crowned a glorious season. When the referee pointed to the penalty spot not one of Burnley's players made a protest.'

*(Bob Lord: My Fight for Football, 1963)*

The Golf Fan. Still as keen today as he was in the 50s and 60s, in fact even more so.

Sadly for Bob Lord they did not reach 'peak form' and it was Greaves' goal that was the catalyst for the Spurs win. Sam Leitch wrote:

'It was the opportunism of Jimmy Greaves after just 180 seconds that put Spurs in complete command of the FA Cup Final against Burnley. How he got that goal still mystifies me. A hefty clearance from goalkeeper Bill Brown was nodded down perfectly by Bobby Smith to the galloping feet of Greaves. He charged on to goal but lost control through the momentum of his own pace. Then, wheeling to the left, he blasted the ball all along the ground past five thunder-struck defenders'.

*(Sam Leitch Sunday Pictorial May 5th 1962)*

Greaves, who certainly had a mutual admiration society with Jimmy McIlroy always denied it was a blast. "I couldn't burst a paper bag from more than fifteen yards," he once said. The goal gave him great satisfaction. Before the game he had pledged to score a goal within five

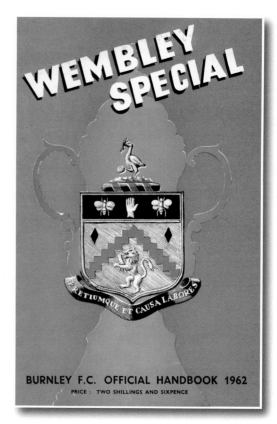

BURNLEY F.C. OFFICIAL HANDBOOK 1962
PRICE : TWO SHILLINGS AND SIXPENCE

minutes, he wrote later. Greaves and McIlroy had common views about the game; that constant tough physical training and endless running, then the norm at many clubs, was unnecessary, that the game was all about skill, and above all that it was about fun and enjoyment. Geoffrey Green in *The Times* bemoaned its disappearance. "Play with a chuckle in your boots," said Harry Potts to McIlroy and the rest. In today's game, chuckles are few and far between.

Down in the mouth they might have been in the dressing room, but by the time McIlroy and all the rest had reached the Café Royal, they were ready to have a wonderful evening, and that they certainly did. Margaret Potts can still remember what a magnificent evening it was and how someone who came across from the Tottenham celebrations commented that with all the noise they were making and the smiles on peoples' faces, it sounded like they had won, not lost.

Jimmy McIlroy now thinks back to the game and the day and says how it all felt so flat. "Wembley to me was disappointing," he recalls. "When I got on the field all I felt was that it was just another match. I should have felt excited and raring to go. But, there was no electric

Cup Final here we come, 1962. Back row: Potts, Cummings, Miller, Blacklaw, Elder, Adamson, Angus. Front row: Connelly, McIlroy, Pointer, Robson, Harris.

TOTTENHAM HOTSPUR F.C.

 **UMBROCHURE 1962/63**

BURNLEY F.C.

Our cover shows Tottenham Hotspur and Burnley
Football Clubs in the Umbro Jerseys, Shorts and
Hose they wore in the F.A. Cup Final, 1962

*sportswear by* **UMBRO**

The Choice of Champions

**supplied by**

Arthur Denn Ltd.,

4, Bridge Street,

BURNLEY, Lancs.

atmosphere that you got in the early rounds with a packed ground and the fans close to the pitch. There was no Cup fever like there was in the mud at Bradford City. To me it was disappointing. I waited my whole life to play in an FA Cup Final and when it happened it was a let-down. There was a long gap between the semi-final and then Wembley and in those few weeks everybody wants you. Danny Blanchflower on the way out onto the pitch said, 'I bet you wonder what all the fuss is about'. I've few memories of the game itself except for me pointing to our goalkeeper where I thought Danny would place the penalty. Danny saw me doing that and said, 'Do you want to take the bloody thing?'

"On the morning of the Cup Final I met with the manager of Italian team Sampdoria. He promised me all kinds of things; a villa overlooking the Mediterranean, an international school for the children, wages beyond my dreams. But when I went told my wife she said, 'What would we want to leave Burnley for?'"

It seems astonishing now all these years later that a star player could be blatantly 'tapped up' and approached by another club on the actual day of the Cup Final. But that is what happened he says, even leaving the team hotel in the morning to meet up with the people from Sampdoria. Fast forward to today and imagine the same scenario. Manchester United are in the Cup Final. Rooney leaves the team hotel on the morning of the game, only hours before kick-off, to meet up with Real Madrid officials in another hotel where they invite him to join Real Madrid. It is an unthinkable situation. If Jimmy Mac was not at his best in the '62 Cup Final he can be forgiven for having been distracted in the most blatant manner, with his mind perhaps on other things.

Perhaps some of the team just weren't 'up for it'. Ray Pointer agrees inasmuch as he thinks that some of the players just didn't perform. Much might have been said in the Press about how Burnley had regained their spirit and resolve; the club might have put on a brave face, but Jimmy would disagree. It was not one of Burnley's best days. The truth is they had peaked earlier in the season and by the end Jimmy thinks that the adrenalin and their legs had gone. In short, they were mentally and physically weary. The celebrations at the Café Royal banquet, in fact, celebrated relief, the end of a long season, and the lifting of a great weight.

Jimmy Adamson had been voted Footballer of the Year. McIlroy was second. Adamson would go to Chile as assistant manager to Walter Winterbottom. The rest of the group would go back to Burnley to a tumultuous reception. Before the end of the next season, however, McIlroy would be gone, something that no-one would have thought possible. Bob Lord always claimed it was Harry Potts' decision to sell McIlroy. Potts said later it was because Jimmy "wasn't doing it on the field." He didn't play well on Cup Final day, and you wonder, just wonder, if the first seeds of concern were sown in Potts' and Lord's minds when they thought about the game in the following days.

"But Burnley will be back," wrote Jimmy in the 1962/63 *Empire News Annual*, following the failure to land the 'double'. "Why then did Burnley, whom I consider to be every bit as good as Tottenham, fail so narrowly? My conclusion was that there was little between the teams." He went on to say that they were prepared for another assault on the 'double' and that maybe in the following year he would be in a position to tell people how they accomplished it. He would not get the opportunity. By that time, he would be gone. *(Empire News 1962/63 for full article, see appendices)*

Jimmy Mac and I were both at Wembley in '62. But, the difference is that whilst he had a good night out afterwards at the *Café Royal*, me and my pal Ed Cockroft were pretty downhearted, and funnily enough not that far away. Prior to the game it was always a family joke in our house that my mother, who didn't have much of an idea about football, and even less interest, thought we were playing Wembley.

In Jimmy Mac's kitchen I told him how Ed and I, over 45 years ago, went down on the Friday, two lads from the sixth form bunking off from school. My father too would have come but his absence at Castlehill Junior School where he taught wouldn't have gone down too well with the sombre-faced headmaster. So Ed Cockroft and I got the train from Todmorden to Manchester and then changed for London with accommodation fixed at Ed's brother Gerald's flat. He was a doctor at one of the big hospitals and Ed's father was a millowner, not that the mill would

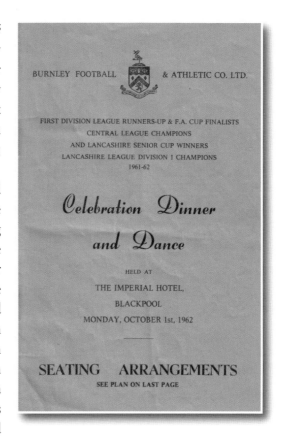

last much longer as one by one they all closed down, and Gerald was under instructions to take us out for a celebration meal at the renowned Simpson's Restaurant in the evening. It was famed for its roast beef and Yorkshire Puddings, which still surprises me because I never knew they could make Yorkshire Puddings south of Doncaster.

On October 1st, 1962, the club held its prestigious Celebration Dinner and Dance at the Imperial Hotel, Blackpool, to honour the achievements of the previous season. They had been runners-up in Cup and League. The reserves had won the Central League Championship and the Lancashire Senior Cup. The 'A' Team were champions of the Lancashire League Division One. Established players were still in their prime and several fabulous young players, the next generation, were coming through to make their mark. Bob Lord revelled in these splendid banquets. He could show off his club and his players and their achievements. A huge hall filled with players and guests dined on Ightenhill Clear Vegetable Soup or Padiham Thick Mock Turtle Soup. There was Brun and Calder Rainbow Trout in Butter or Turf Moor Veal and Peronace Spaghetti along with Gawthorpe Chicken and Irish Bacon Waldorf Salad. The wine flowed, speeches were made; toasts were proposed. Tommy Trinder one of Bob Lord's few friends provided the entertainment and then people danced the night away, before a bacon and eggs breakfast in the early hours. These were grand days and a wonderful time to be at the club.

But this grand Celebration Dinner in October of 1962 was almost the beginning of the end of the truly great years, although the team of 1965/66 would provide brief hopes of a revival. The dinner at the Imperial Hotel, in truth, was almost the last hurrah.

# Chapter Eleven

# Foreign Travels And European Nights

FOR FOOTBALLERS, a summer tour at the end of a long hard season was one of the perks of the trade. During the 1950s Burnley visited several European countries including; Germany, France, Switzerland, Spain, Czechoslovakia and Austria. But this was an era when foreign travel was decidedly slow and not at all easy or straightforward. Travel was certainly not available as it is today in the form of instant mass-market package holidays. Journeys abroad could in fact be a test of determination, stamina and fortitude. A trip overseas at this time was not just a simple journey where passengers could sit back in comfort; it was a genuine adventure. This was a time when a trip to France, meant a coach or train to Manchester; then the train from Manchester to London, possibly an overnight stay; then change stations again for the train to Dover or Tilbury, and the ferry across to Calais. If it was known as 'the golden age of travel' it did not apply to a party of 20 footballers and officials making their way painstakingly across Europe. That soubriquet was applicable only to those who travelled in first-class luxury, more often than not still with a manservant or two.

Perhaps the most fascinating tour Jimmy Mac enjoyed was to Mauritius and Madagascar in 1954 with the first game against Tananarive. There was a 14 – 1 win. For the only time in his professional career McIlroy scored four goals. Bill Holden scored six of the others in that game. A total of 28 goals were scored. Even goalkeeper Colin McDonald got in on the scoring act when he played as a forward after being injured in one of the games. The Cup presented to Jimmy Adamson on behalf of the Mauritius Football Association during that tour is still on display in the Turf Moor trophy cabinet. Clarets fan Andrew Firmin, in connection with his work, actually met someone who was from Mauritius who remembered the games. Not only that, he could remember the immense interest that Burnley's visit inspired, how people spent hours walking to the matches, and how at one game people outside the ground climbed trees in order to see. One tree branch was unable to take the strain and a number of people fell to the ground. Enterprising entrepreneurs sold posters in the streets of the Burnley players.

Jimmy remembers the Mauritius trip as being his favourite of all the tours he did. The team flew to Paris on a Tuesday afternoon. It was Thursday evening by the time they finally arrived having flown the length of Africa, stopping several times for refuelling. Each time they stopped the plane was fumigated with fly sprays. "Here come the bug sprays," announced Harold Mather on each occasion. "The plane was very cramped and I remember a child crying all the way down," Jimmy added.

Bhurdwaz Mungur is a resident of Mauritius and was a young boy when Burnley made the tour. He writes:

'Before 1954 nobody living in the Indian Ocean islands knew anything about English

European travels. Sometime in the 1950s.

football clubs. It was announced in our newspaper that an English club was to play six matches, three with Mauritius B and the other three with Mauritius A. There was a high demand for tickets. Before the arrival of Burnley bamboo hedges were cleared and very hastily seating accommodation was made to contain a total of about 15,000 spectators. In those days there was no electricity. There was no TV. Only the rich could have radios run by batteries. There were three newspapers which spoke lengthily about the club. The Mauritians were ignorant of English football and were sure to beat Burnley. The day arrived and Mauritius B were beaten by 4 – 0. On the following Sunday a large crowd turned up to attend the match. Needless to say King George V Stadium was packed to capacity and many returned home to follow the match by radio. The fans expected our A team would do better and amend the defeat of the B team. Their expectations were quashed as Burnley gave a better performance and beat the A team by six goals to one. They made a very great impression which has lasted to date among people of the older generation. During the 50s Burnley were the most popular club on the island. Many names are still remembered. The most popular is undoubtedly Jimmy McIlroy. There are still many Burnley fans among the older generation'.

Since then Burnley FC has been close to his heart and he has visited Burnley. In his possession is a letter which he treasures, written to him by Jimmy Mac some years ago.

*Of all my football tours that took me to many parts of the world, without question the three weeks I spent in Mauritius with Burnley was far and away the most enjoyable of all. Even today half a century later I still get a warm glow just thinking about it – which is not surprising considering the warm welcome we received from the people of this beautiful little island in the Indian Ocean.*

*Even the date we arrived, 6th of May 1954, is unforgettable because it was the day Roger Bannister made world news by becoming the first man to run the mile in under four minutes.*

*The many delightful memories are still vivid, though strangely, not many of them involve the games we played, which may not be too surprising as the opposition consisted of young keen amateurs against one of the top English sides. In fact from the football point of view just about my only recollection was listening to the radio recordings of the game commentated by an Irish Sergeant in the Kings Own African Rifles and his repetitive description of each goal: "and the ball – is in the back of the net."*

*Our trainer, a lovely Scotsman called Billy Dougal undoubtedly also enjoyed his time in Mauritius because before each game he would be at the ground studding boots. Every time there was a pause in the hammering a voice would call out, "Whisky Billy?" No wonder Dougal so often spoke lovingly of Mauritius.*

*It was the most relaxing of all my soccer tours, allowing the players lots of time to socialise and see so much of this intriguing island. There were invitations galore, and one that stands out for me is fishing beyond the reef at Grand Bay on a yacht along with my room mate Jock Winton. To this day Jock and I still argue about who actually caught the 90lb hammerhead shark on just a line with a baited hook. Certainly it took both of us to haul the fish in, resulting in burnt fingers and a near heart attack as it surfaced.*

*On the first morning in Mauritius in my chalet in the hotel grounds, I heard this booming Irish voice asking, "Where's Jimmy McIlroy?" On opening the door I was confronted by this huge priest.*

*Now, hailing from Northern Ireland where centuries-old conflict between Protestants and Catholics is known world-wide, I managed to stammer, "Father I have to tell you I'm a Protestant." Only for him to roar, "Never mind, we'll soon change that."*

*For my sins the priest's name escapes me, but what a time he and his colleagues at the Presbytery gave me and a few of my pals in those three weeks. To this day I often wonder how Mauritius may have changed since 1954. But one thing has not changed – my conviction that this was my finest soccer tour.*

A 5 – 1 win over Bilbao in Spain in 1957 was perhaps the most memorable victory. It was a game tagged on to the end of a tour of France and was arranged by Alan Brown who simply informed the directors that there was an extra game. They were furious; all they wanted to do was get back home.

"The journey from France was through the Pyrenees by coach. That was a hair-raising journey with a lot of anxious moments going round all the hairpin bends and looking down the steep drops," remembers Jimmy. "Bob Lord was back in London and he was furious. But the day after the game, the Press said it was the best display by any English team seen in Spain."

It was also Alan Brown who made the players do exercises in the snow to impress the Germans one year. "It was May but there was a sudden snow flurry and the ground was covered. There was a group of Germans watching us train so Alan Brown ordered us to take off our tops and lie down. Then, flat on the floor in the snow, we did our exercises and the only reason he did this, I'm sure, was to let the Germans think how tough we were."

In the summer following the 1960 title win there was a long trip to North America, taking in a tournament in New York and then games in Canada. The club had been invited to participate in the New York tournament before they had clinched the champion's crown. That they went as champions added more glamour to this great venture. At home we followed its progress thinking how wonderful it was that Burnley were taking part in such a prestigious event. Bob Lord thought it was an honour. Today nobody thinks twice about tours of the USA or the Far East but back in 1960 this was something very new. They were all excited and the journey across was on the *SS United States*, one of the world's finest ocean liners. If the outward journey was made in high spirits and with great anticipation, by the time they came back they were weary, dispirited and Jimmy Mac was scathing about the actual games.

The party found themselves in a poor hotel in Brooklyn, the food and conditions far below the standards that Bob Lord always provided for his players. They moved hotel and were seen as ungrateful grumblers; the Press being critical of them both in New York and in the UK.

Summer in New York is hot, sticky and humid, certainly not the best time of year to be playing football. Those who can afford to get out of New York in the summer. Burnley went in. Well known in the UK, they were anonymous in New York. Their form was inconsistent, results mixed, and the razzmatazz irritating. As they journeyed over the Atlantic on a luxury liner, it was seen as one of the rewards of the job, like the tours to other countries in previous summers. But for this one they were away from home for longer than usual, travelling to Canada after some of the New York games. This involved a long coach drive, and then back to New York again. Weary and tired, by the end they couldn't wait to get home.

Not long afterwards Jimmy wrote, "It was a very excited team that gazed at the famous Statue of Liberty and sailed up the Hudson River into New York's magnificent harbour. We thought we should soon be seeing the bright lights of Manhattan, but instead we found ourselves in a dingy hotel in Brooklyn. We kicked up a fuss about it and luckily we were moved to a better hotel."

The local Press dubbed Burnley "the Cinderella team from Lancashire." Bob Lord was scathing, maintaining that Kilmarnock, who beat them in the second game, had kicked them from start to finish, the tournament was poorly organised, sponsors had not kept to the agreements, payments to players and expenses were inadequate, and the referees were incompetent. Jimmy Mac thinks that Kilmarnock wanted to bring Burnley back down to size after the fuss they had made over the hotel.

McIlroy commented, "As soon as the competition began we realised that it was impossible to take the games seriously. The crowd had come to enjoy themselves and what the players were doing was often of little interest to them. Before the games started an announcer would tell them, 'Ladies and gentlemen the ball game has started'. And he would proceed to give a running commentary on the whole match. If the whistle sounded he would yell, 'It's hands folks!' or, 'That means a corner shot for New York'. Often he would interpret the referee's decision quite wrongly but most of the crowd didn't know any better so they were quite happy about it. When a goal was scored he would announce, 'Scorer number nine with an assist by number ten', and in the final minutes of a game would

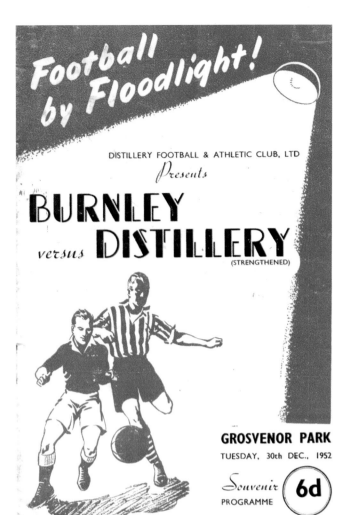

**Football by Floodlight!**

DISTILLERY FOOTBALL & ATHLETIC CLUB, LTD

*Presents*

# BURNLEY
*versus* **DISTILLERY**
(STRENGTHENED)

**GROSVENOR PARK**

TUESDAY, 30th DEC., 1952

*Souvenir*
PROGRAMME **6d**

**B.T.** **FODBOLD SERVICE**

# KØBENHAVNS IDRÆTSPARK

**STÆVNET**

**BURNLEY** FC

Torsdag d. 24. maj 62
kl. 19.00

*Burnleys stærkeste kort,
den irske innerwing Jimmy McIlroy
her fotograferet under
den afsluttende træning i går*

**DANMARKS BEDSTE SPORTSSIDER**

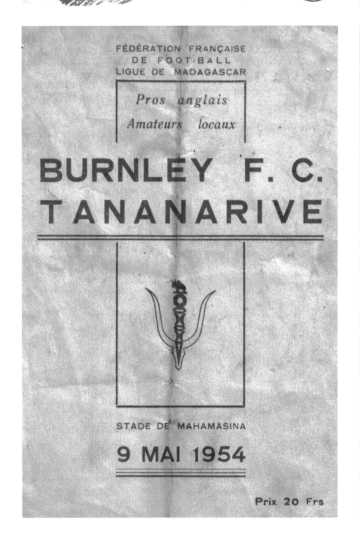

FÉDÉRATION FRANÇAISE
DE FOOT-BALL
LIGUE DE MADAGASCAR

*Pros anglais
Amateurs locaux*

# BURNLEY F. C.
TANANARIVE

STADE DE MAHAMASINA

## 9 MAI 1954

Prix 20 Frs

---

Official Programme — Price One Penny

## Burnley Football and Athletic Co., Ltd.

Season 1959-60
OFFICIALS
President: J. N. GRIMSHAW, Esq.
Directors:
R. W. LORD, Esq. *(Chairman)*     R. COOK, Esq., J.P. *(Vice-Chairman)*
W. HOPKINSON, Esq.; W. PICKARD, Esq.; F. R. KAY, Esq.; F. HARTLEY, Esq.
Medical Officers:
Dr. D. A. KER, J.P.
Dr. R. D. IVEN.
Manager: HARRY POTTS.          Secretary: HENRY SMITH.
Ground & Registered Office: Turf Moor, Burnley.

No. 14          **MONDAY, 19th OCTOBER, 1959**

**BURNLEY**
Colours—Claret and Blue
**BLACKLAW**

2                                 3
CUMMINGS          MILLER          ELDER    ADAMSON
4                  8                        MILLER
SEITH          ADAMSON

McILROY                        ROBSON
WHITE                        McILROY
7                  9                        10    11
CONNELLY          POINTER          PILKINGTON

Referee :                              Linesmen :
Mr. F. Carter                  Mr. H. Hodson (Red Flag)
(Burnley)                     Mr. R. Bracewell (Yellow Flag)

J. H. DEVINE          R. BROWN          A. McINTOSH
(Queen's Park & Scotland)   (Barnet & England)   (Birmingham University & Wales)
11                  9                        7

P. KANE                        J. R. WARD
(Queen's Park & Scotland)        (Northampton & England)
10                        8

H. FORDE          A. D'ARCY          R. SLEAP
(Glenavon & Ireland)   (Barnet & England)   (Barnet & England)
6                  5                        4

W. NEIL                        D. GARDENER
(Airdrieonians & Scotland)        (Crook Town & England)
3                        2

M. J. PINNER
(Queen's Park Rangers & England)

**GT. BRITAIN OLYMPIC TEAM**
Colours—Black and White.

HAMILTON PUBLICATIONS (BURNLEY) LTD

produce a countdown worthy of a space rocket launching; all very amusing but hardly helpful for playing soccer."

It was all ballyhoo, said Jimmy. He found it embarrassing that each player had to run on the field one by one to be introduced to the cheering crowd. The referee, an Irishman, joked to Jimmy. "Bet you wouldn't do this at Windsor Park for a fiver." Whilst only 11,000 watched them play the German team, 42,000 were at the nearby New York Giants baseball game.

But if there was one moment that touched Jimmy during the long trip it was the meeting between Billy Dougal and his brother who had emigrated to the USA 30 years earlier from Falkirk.

"This season will be the toughest for Burnley since 1921, when the Championship last arrived at Turf Moor," wrote Jimmy in the 1960/61 *Empire News Annual*. "Right now we are the bosses of English football, and as such, can expect every game to be a Cup-tie. All clubs will pull out that little bit extra to prove at least, our equal."

If Jimmy referred to every game being like a Cup-tie, there were two European Cup-ties in particular that had all of us enthralled. But before they were played McIlroy caused a controversy when he said he didn't want to play in the European Cup. On the eve of the new season reporter Frank McGhee had his 'bombshell' revelations splashed all over the back page of the *Daily Mirror*.

"Although he knows he will HAVE to play, he is frankly disgusted, and maybe even a bit scared, by the savage tactics and win-at-all costs methods of too many of the teams who take part. 'Some of the European Cup games I saw and read about last season made me shudder. If they are anything like that this season, I wouldn't want any part of them. It is too often the competition where only victory matters, with real danger to the footballers. I'm not looking forward to that sort of stuff. The original idea was great. It was to glorify the finest footballing club sides in Europe. But it hasn't always worked. Take just one instance last season, Glasgow Rangers, who reached the semi-final. It just isn't true to say they are one of the best four teams in Europe. And it hasn't always been the better side that has won some of the games'."

Jimmy went on to attack the Wolves style of play and their manager Stan Cullis; he said that they lacked skill, and he was scathing about Cullis' comment that Wolves could never win the European trophy by outplaying the opposition, which he saw as a terrible admission.

The backlash from Glasgow and Wolverhampton was considerable and McIlroy had to review his comments although without actually apologising.

I'm lucky. I saw the two European games that we played at home. There's just a dwindling band of us oldies left who were there and shared the glory. It's probable that those of us who were there, packed into the ground filled with the noise of wooden rattles, and the haze of drifting cigarette smoke, are now all in our sixties. The players, bless them, are in their seventies. They were night games and that made them better still. The Longside was at its vibrant, heaving best, a mass of people crammed down the full length of the ground, standing shoulder to shoulder, and the power and rolling sound it generated was inspirational to the home players, but terrifying to the visitors whose will it could break.

We all have our ideas as to the years and even the games when Burnley reached their peak. From 1959 to 1962 were the glory years, but within those three almost miraculous years, when everything came together, there were games that represented and symbolised the best of Burnley and McIlroy. The home games against Reims and then Hamburg were two of them and we won them both.

After the Reims game, and before the Hamburg quarter-finals, Jimmy says his thoughts were miles away with his parents and grandfather by then living in Dunmury, a few miles from Belfast. "I knew the excitement wouldn't allow much sleep for my parents and in the other house I could well imagine my greatest fan sitting, probably in tears of joy and unable to speak."

Jimmy McIlroy will be embarrassed when I say that each 40 mile visit to see and talk to him is like a pilgrimage. If he was special, he still wonders how it came about; in his own mind he is an ordinary, modest man who asks "why me," when he looks back on his football life.

My father too would have been astonished (and delighted) to know that this book is being written. Our father and son relationship was never close but the one thing that was the common thread between us was football. He had been a Burnley supporter all his life. But on nights like those against Reims and Hamburg we were a proper father and son, close, talkative, good pals. And on the journey home having seen the wonderful wins we'd talk volubly and excitedly. The next day we'd go through the papers, devouring the reports and reliving the game. Jimmy McIlroy was the common bond when we talked about him, how he'd pulled the strings, beaten his man, contributed to the goals, and calmed things down when it was needed. He was always the fulcrum, the focal point, the catalyst. It seemed to be so simple then, if he played well, we won. Of course there was John Connelly, and Ray Pointer and Brian Pilkington and Jimmy Robson and all the rest, but to us it was Jimmy Mac who orchestrated the moves, scheming his way tirelessly, in mud, mist, fog or rain, through the game.

Jimmy hasn't got a copy of the old *Radio Times* that featured the second leg of the Hamburg game. He has few if any mementoes and souvenirs at home. His daughter and a close friend keep what is left but she says he has given so many things away over the years. I showed him the *Radio Times* copy I have (bought from eBay, where else?) and he smiled. Such things can turn a clock back almost 50 years, in seconds. The game was to be featured on Peter Dimmock's *Sportsview* at 7.55 pm on Wednesday March 15th. Which of us today remember Peter Dimmock, then a household name? There would be the latest news of the game from Hamburg it said. Kenneth Wolstenhome wrote the scene-setting introduction.

'Every seat sold weeks ago; demands that Hamburg S.V. be excused all League matches before the big game; demands that their players be excused all international commitments until after March 15th. That is how seriously the West Germans are taking the European Cup match against Burnley. Burnley won the first leg 3 – 1 – Hamburg's first defeat of the season – so the Germans have given top priority to their preparations for the seemingly impossible task of handing Burnley a two-goal start – and a beating. This second leg to be played today in Hamburg is likely to be even more thrilling and dramatic than the first at Burnley where the Germans claim they were bogged down in the mud. This time, they say, they will play a lot better. But Burnley have set their hearts on winning the European Cup. They are pinning their hopes on their solid, unshakeable defence and on their attack, which strikes with a suddenness and a ferocity which are almost frightening. Hamburg who are running away with the North German title believe the Seeler brothers will be the ace and

After the Reims game in Paris. A feeling of job well done and quiet satisfaction.

king of trumps. Last season Germany's representatives Eintracht Frankfurt reached the Final. This season Hamburg intend to do even better. But if they are to beat Burnley they will have to play brilliantly. That is why today's game is attracting world-wide attention and promises to be the soccer match of the season'.

Sadly, though they played well, they did not play brilliantly and Burnley lost. Near the very end McIlroy hit the posts twice. But the win was not to be; the goal given away at Turf Moor cost them dear, and Jimmy would not have the chance to face Barcelona in the semi-finals or play in Europe again. There is a photograph that shows one of the occasions that the ball hit the post and McIlroy is watching with an anguished face. The goalkeeper is diving but is nowhere near. Such is football, so near but so far away.

On my shelf I have an old video, *'When We Were Kings'*. Its sub title is 'Burnley in Europe' and shows in grainy black and white film the triumphs we had when Turf Moor was at its peak. It's hard not to grow misty-eyed when you watch it, which I still do. They may be in their seventies now, but nights like these are how I remember them.

Kenneth Wolstenholme commentates and remarks about McIlroy, "A man on whom

Seit 15 Jahren das aktuelle Fußball-Programm

Herausgeber: Fußballfreund Hans Kranefeld
Mitarbeiter: Altinternationale u. Nationalspieler

Verlagsort: Gelsenk.-Buer
Gladbecker Str. 60, Ruf: 3 20 88

# Westdeutsche Sonder Vorschau

## FUSSBALL-STADION-BLATT

Jahrgang XVI          Mittwoch, den 15. März 1961          Preis 20 Pfg.

### Volksparkstadion gerüstet für Rückspiel um Europa-Pokal.

# HAMBURGER SV - FC BURNLEY

## Uwe Seeler

hat sich zu einem der gefürchtetsten Mittelstürmer in Europa mit phantastischem Kopfballspiel dank unwahrscheinlicher Sprungkraft im richtigen Moment, blitzsauberer Schußtechnik und einem instinktsicheren Erahnen von Tormöglichkeiten entwickelt. Er brennt mit seiner Mannschaft, im Rückspiel um den Europa-Pokal Genugtuung für die 1:3 Niederlage in Burnley zu finden.

## Deutscher und Englischer Meister

ins „Bild gerückt"

### Hamburger SV:

Neisner, Dörfel, Uwe Seeler, Krug, Stürmer, Pichowiak, Dieter Seeler, Dehn, Werner, Schnoor, Meinke.

### FC Burnley:

Angus, Blacklaw, Robson, McIlroy, Pointer, Connelly, Joyce, Elder, Miller, Pilkington, Adamson.

Numéro Spécial — Lundi 1er Avril 1957

PRIX : 5 FRANCS

# OLYMPIC

### ORGANE BI-MENSUEL OFFICIEL DU ROYAL OLYMPIC CLUB CHARLEROI

Affilié à l'UNBOC

# R. O. C. Charleroi - Burnley F. C.

## Mes chers Amis, amateurs de football

**BURNLEY Football Club (1956-1957)**

De gauche à droite. Debout : Angus - Seith - Blacklaw - Winton - Miller. — Assis : Newlands - Mac Ilroy - Lawson - Adamson (capitaine) - Cheesebrough - Pilkington.

C'est avec un grand plaisir que j'entreprends aujourd'hui de vous parler de l'équipe des Iles Britanniques BURNLEY F.C. que nous verrons tout à l'heure évoluer devant notre bon vieux OLYMPIC.

Pour la première fois à Charleroi, une g r a n d e équipe anglaise jouera devant les vrais amateurs du Pays Noir, et je crois être votre interprète à tous, en la remerciant d'avoir accepté notre invitation.

Trève de bavardage, je vous présente ci-dessous le club de BURNLEY et ses joueurs.

Tout d'abord, le club.

BURNLEY F.C., fondé aux Iles en 1881, possède un passé célèbre et est glorieusement cité dans les annales du football.

En 1914, Burnley a gagné la Coupe d'Angleterre et plus près de nous, en 1947, il en fut finaliste, n'étant défait que de 1-0 par Charlton A.C., après extra-times.

En 1921, Burnley fut champion d'Angleterre, établissant un record extraordinaire chez les professionnels, a p r è s avoir joué 30 matches sans défaite. En 1948 et 1950, ce club termina en 2e position.

Plus près de nous, la saison dernière, Burnley a battu Chelsea 5-0, Sunderland 4-0, Bolton Wanderers 1-0 et Arsenal (à Londres) 1-0.

En 1956, pendant une tournée à l'étranger, les victoires s'accumulent : contre le R.C. de Lens 3-1, Fortuna Dusseldorf 1-0, F. C. Nuremberg 3-1. Il évolue en Espagne en 1954 ; il joue 5 matches, dont 3 gagnés et 2 nuls, rentrant ainsi en Angleterre invaincu.

Je crois que ce palmarès est assez éloquent par lui-même.

Se déplaçant très souvent à l'étranger, est précédé d'une réputation d'équipe très disciplinée, jouant avec cran et faisant honneur au football britannique. Sa ligne d'avants, composée en majorité de joueurs de petite taille, est mobile et spectaculaire, de ce fait, Burnley est un adversaire très recherché pour les nocturnes.

Burnley, avec Manchester United, sont les équipes les plus jeunes d'Angleterre. L'âge moyen des joueurs est de 23 ans, et le plus âgé (si l'on peut dire) a 24 ans, est l'international Jimmy Mac Ilroy. Nos visiteurs de ce soir pratiquent la politique des jeunes, insufflant un sang nouveau et des bonnes volontés toutes neuves pour le bon renom du football anglais dont le nouveau slogan est maintenant : DONNONS LA CHANCE AUX JEUNES.

(Voir suite en 3e page)

Burnley depends so much." But the video is a reminder, and Jimmy is the first to agree, of just how good this Burnley side was, both as a team and individually. What comes across when you watch are the flowing moves, the instinctive passing, the glimpses of McIlroy, and in defence the tenacious marking. In the away game at Reims what you see is a truly dramatic, pulsating 90 minutes, one of the best games you could wish to see. But for Connelly's wonder goal, and Blacklaw's outstanding saves, one of them with ten minutes to go the equal of Banks from Pele in the 1970 World cup game against Brazil, Burnley would certainly have been eliminated. For the final 15 minutes Burnley hung on desperately. Before the game began McIlroy calmed Alex Elder down, telling him that the atmosphere was nothing like Lisburn on a Saturday night.

The home game against Hamburg had taken place on the 18th January, 1961. Jimmy had already scored one goal in the home game against Reims, but in this next game against Hamburg it was Pilkington twice and Robson with one. Though it was a mild night, the pitch was a mudbath and 46,237 turned up to see one of the biggest games in the club's history. It surely ranks as one of the all-time top ten Burnley games. Pilkington's second goal is one of those moments that stay in the mind as clear as yesterday. It was a perfectly struck 25-yard shot and the camera angle was right behind him as he struck the ball. So was my and my father's viewpoint, we were directly behind it and it went home like an arrow with us willing it home. I can still see it now, the perfect strike, the perfect trajectory, the perfect goal, and the crowd erupted. John McPartlin tells the story of an epic game when Jimmy McIlroy made light of the conditions.

'Among the 46,237 crowd was a party of exuberant, klaxon-sounding German supporters. Hamburg were initially concerned that they might have had to play on a hard pitch, but these fears were unfounded. What did face them, though, was a Burnley team at full strength and an impassioned crowd. After just seven minutes, Burnley seized the initiative. McIlroy's finesse freed Pointer who set up Pilkington to score. Confidence immediately spread through the team. At the back, Blacklaw was handling confidently and commanding his area. Adamson was also keeping a tight lead on the dangerous Uwe Seeler, the Germans' main threat, so Burnley were able to press forward with Pointer drifting wide to allow Robson and Connelly to run at the heart of the German defence. As the pressure increased, Pointer, too, became more prominent in the Germans' area. He only just failed to convert two sharp crosses and Robson was inches away from connecting with a third after Schnoor was caught off-limits. Pointer's quick lob left Schnoor scrambling to recover but he just managed to palm the ball over. Despite this pressure Burnley were still only one up at the interval.

After half time, Burnley made their superiority tell. In the 61st minute Pilkington ran onto Miller's pass and struck a splendid goal from 25 yards. Robson then had three chances to put the game beyond Hamburg but he failed with two close range shots and was unable to capitalise on Connelly's excellent centre. Hamburg then demonstrated that they still had some sting left. The effervescent Seeler began to put himself about with greater effect. It needed the agility and bravery of Blacklaw to deny him on three occasions. For all that, Burnley's passage to the semis should have been secured in the 75th minute.

McIlroy who had sustained much rough treatment centred. Pointer powered in a header, which Schnoor couldn't hold and there was Robson to knock in the third. A fourth should have followed, when Pointer, running onto Connelly's pass, was brought down from behind in the box. Incredibly the referee waved play on. As so often happens in these situations, Hamburg broke away for Doerfel to score. Even then, Burnley had a late opportunity to restore their advantage when Pointer was clean through but shot wide when he had only the 'keeper to beat. On March 15th, Burnley would find out how expensive these misses would be.

At the end of the game Burnley lined up to clap their sporting opponents off the field. In turn, the huge crowd applauded the Clarets ecstatically. The crowd had roared so loudly that no-one had noticed the German klaxons. It was the finest night of football ever played at Turf Moor'. *(John McPartlin)*

Life works in funny ways and a young man who saw that game was nineteen years old Jack Moore from Burnley. He later became Richard Moore of the Royal Shakespeare Company, and several television series. Wherever he performed he never missed a chance to watch Burnley and of course in those days the team of Adamson and McIlroy. Today he has a lovely tale to tell of his McIlroy watching days.

Charity Football Match

PROGRAMME
Price
**6d.**

**BURNLEY**
*versus*
**EDINBURGH SELECT**

Burnley's well-drilled defence, with Scottish goalkeeper Adam Blacklaw to the fore, deals with a Tottenham raid in this year's F.A. Cup Final at Wembley.

**TYNECASTLE PARK**

Saturday, 4th August 1962     Kick-off 3 p.m.

'At 19 years of age, I was a drama student-in-waiting, but still a photographer having served a somewhat curtailed apprenticeship on the *Burnley Express*. By the time of the Hamburg match I was working for the newly formed Burnley Press Agency which had the distinction of premises above John Collier – "the window to watch," and a hairdresser in St James' Street. The grubby studio we occupied was used by "amateur photographers" who learned how to photograph the scantily clad female form. Those films handed in for developing often showed a remarkable degree of camera shake. Anyroadup – such was the importance of the Burnley/Hamburg clash we received a contract from a London news agency to cover the event for them for syndication with German newspapers. They wanted pre-match stuff and of course the match itself.

Pre-match was simple. The Hamburg team would stroll up the road from the Keirby to take eine kleine peep at the hallowed Turf. Not that they'd been allowed to train on it. Chairman Bob Lord had seen to that and sent them off to be impressed by the training facilities at Gawthorpe. Our Bob – no slouch at gamesmanship where his beloved Burnley were concerned – had said he wanted the pitch to be "in the best possible condition." In the event 46, 237 fans turned up that night and saw a rolled swamp that, by the time Burnley had won a corner in the opening seconds, had turned into a quagmire. Not that this stopped McIlroy et al turning on a super-show.

Unplayable by modern standards but quite acceptable at the time, Hamburg were playing us in their mid-winter break designed to avoid such pitches.

Now then; in those pre-digital days before the advent of memory chips that enable

# EUROPEAN AND INTERNATIONAL TRAVELS

Two of the many games played in New York and Canada in the summer of 1960.

Not Jimmy Mac's favourite tour. In fact he was highly critical of the the New York tournament.

photographers to take hundreds of shots, I was sent to the pre-match armed with two rolls of film each of 24 shots. It was enough to fire off 23 of them but in the best tradition of the trade, I left one unexposed frame in the camera in case something happened on the way back to the office. And goodness gracious, it did.

I mean, when you're 19 and a football fan and you get to stroll along the street back to the Keirby with the great Uwe Seeler and the entire Hamburg team, you do it. Uwe Seeler! In my book along with Jimmy McIlroy, was one of football's pantheons.

Now, as we walked along, as fate would have it, he was possessed of a football and I, in my callow youth, was possessed of one frame of film in my camera and there, on a cobbled Burnley back-street, festooned with sheets hanging out to dry, were two grubby kids, one pretending to be McIlroy, kicking a bald, torn tennis ball about. And this no doubt, the same kind of nearly-dead tennis ball that Jimmy Mac himself might have kicked about at the same age.

Uwe stopped bouncing the football and turned to look at the boys. Then he dropped the ball at his feet and dribbled towards them over the cobbles and two astonished kids found themselves trying to defend their Burnley back-street against one of Europe's most dangerous strikers.

I raised my camera, focused, muttered 'please let it be sharp' and clicked the shutter. Mercifully it was a beauty and found its way into several newspapers.

Later, the Clarets famously won 3 – 1 but Hamburg's away goal was to cost us dearly in the away leg when McIlroy hit the post. At Hamburg, the second leg went against us and McIlroy's European dream was over'.

"They were two wonderful games," says Uwe Seeler. He also remembers how in the first game at Turf Moor the pitch was such a morass. "The night before the game the pitch was frozen but on match night it was ankle deep in mud. Was it prepared?" he asked, with a hint of a smile, perhaps tongue in cheek. "English teams play well in mud," he continued grinning a little more. But on matchday, during the commentary, Kenneth Wolstenhome pointed out that during the day there had been a very rapid thaw.

In Hamburg, after a two month interval between the two legs, Hamburg were outstanding and wiped out the deficit. But Jimmy Mac, incredibly, hit the posts twice in the final minutes with Burnley 4 – 1 down. To hit the post once was bad luck; to hit them twice within minutes was simply heartbreaking. Today referring to one of them he says, "I made a hash of it. I sidefooted it, hit the post and should have scored. We were naïve and played our normal game instead of putting the shutters up."

The great European adventure was over. Watching those near-misses and what should have been a penalty at Turf Moor, on video, all these years later, makes Burnley's exit from Europe all the more poignant. After the game, with a semi-final Cup game against Spurs just three days away, he was asked if there were any injuries. "No injuries," he replied, "just eleven broken hearts."

# Chapter Twelve

# The Great Players

JIMMY AND HIS daughter Anne had gathered together all his scrapbooks and albums for us to go through. While I looked at them he took up the local paper; turned the pages quickly and found the one he wanted. He looked up. "This is the page I always look at," he said with a wry smile. "I always look at the obituaries page to see if I'm in it."

It was a morning, too, when our talk followed no logical order. We looked at some quite beautiful poems he had written many years ago, the first one beginning:

'*Every man on earth has a book to write,*
*A tale to tell, however slight,*
*Of rights and wrongs, and unfair play,*
*Of conquests made. Of yesterday…*'

Every man has a book to write, prophetic indeed. Then we moved on to tours to Mauritius and New York, and then to the 1958 World Cup. Somehow a game that Stoke City played against Barcelona in Spain came up. Stoke had played somewhere in Africa first, and then in Barcelona they went out for some practice at the training ground the night before the game was due to be played. Of course there were quite a few spectators there and even some of the Barcelona directors. Burnley had played there many years earlier. "Ah," said one of the Barcelona directors, who must have seen this game, to a Stoke director. "McIlroy: his father opened our stadium I think."

Somehow the conversation got round to players he enjoyed playing with, or against, but the problem discussing with Jimmy McIlroy any list of the 'best' players is that there were so many of them in his day. Not only that, but Jimmy is sensitive and aware of others' feelings so that he is reluctant to make any list, for fear of upsetting anyone he has left out. Then there are the players who are not just good, but were also 'characters'. In today's game there is a dearth of these players who can light up a game with their individuality, cheek, flair, and humour. When was the last time you saw a player beat his man by playing a one-two off the corner flag like Len Shackleton used to do, or put the ball on an upturned coffee cup to take a corner like Mike Summerbee? When, in fact, was the last time you saw any player beat a man and turn him inside out for fun, and then go back and beat him again, in preference to playing the 'safe' pass? On the rare occasion a player does that today he is accused of being 'disrespectful' to his fellow professionals. How absurd that is. When was the last time a single player could put 5,000 or even 10,000 on the gate, like George Best, Finney or Matthews?

The game is now so serious; all humour has vanished. It is based on such a degree of super-fit athleticism and the demand for success that the laughter has gone.

Physical contact is penalised at every opportunity. Eddie Clamp or Andy Lochhead would receive a red card today every time they played. Jimmy Mac well remembers the

# Dynamic footballer Jimmy Greaves trains and scores on Bovril

RIGHT FROM THE START, Jimmy Greaves' football career has been an amazing success story.

He was one of the youngest players ever chosen for the England Under-23 International team, and he scored a goal within the first 10 minutes of his first appearance with the team in 1957.

As Chelsea's inside forward Jimmy has maintained his early promise, is now a full international player and one of the leading goal scorers in the Football League.

Jimmy, clearly marked for a great future in football, makes Bovril part of his training schedule. He says, "Like many other professional footballers, I take Bovril regularly all through the season. I thoroughly enjoy it – wouldn't be without it in fact. Bovril is a big help when it comes to keeping you at the top of your form."

## BOVRIL does you a power of good

physical side of the game and players like Tommy Banks and Roy Hartle. John Connelly testifies that it was no good swapping wings to escape Hartle, because on the other side was Banks. In one of his first Burnley games Connelly was told by Banks, "Look, lad, I don't mind thee coming past me, And I don't mind t'ball coming past me. But not both together."

Jimmy Greaves tells the story about Banks in a game against Chelsea when he tackled a Chelsea player with such power that the victim lay writhing on the ground. Roy Hartle came over to speak to Banks. "You're losing your touch, he's still wriggling," says Hartle to him.

In an England game against Brazil the manager Walter Winterbottom tells Banks to keep Zagalo quiet. "First tackle, hit him hard. Hurt him, is that clear?"

"Not really," says Banks, "when you say 'hurt' do you mean temporary or permanent?"

Willie Cunningham of Preston North End was another of that group of formidable, rock-hard fullbacks who put fear into any opposing winger. "Tommy Docherty," relates McIlroy, "always made sure to visit the Burnley dressing room at Preston to tell Brian Pilkington that Cunningham would be after him, and that he was either eating raw meat or shaking the bars of his cage to be let out. He varied the information one day, saying that Willie was shaving with a blow-lamp, because if he used a razor, the stubble on the first side of his face had grown again by the time he finished the second."

During his career Jimmy played with or against a whole procession of great names - Bobby Charlton, Jimmy Armfield, Denis Law, Stan Mortensen, Billy Bingham, Jimmy Scoular, Cliff Jones, John White, Brian Clough, Tommy Docherty, Bill Shankly, Ian St John, Tommy Taylor, Duncan Edwards, Bryan Douglas, Ronnie Clayton, Bert Trautmann, Nat Lofthouse, Dave Mackay and Billy Wright.

In his book Jimmy talks about Jimmy Mullen (Wolves), Tommy Thompson (PNE), Eddie Coleman (Man Utd), Tommy Harmer (Spurs) and Ernie Taylor (Blackpool). None of these are the best known names in football but he admired them greatly. But several names came up more than once as we talked about the fifties and early sixties.

"Wilf Mannion was a player I would liked to have played more against, how I would loved to have seen more of this little, golden-haired man," said Jimmy. He learned all his skills as a boy with a rubber ball back home in his native South Bank on Teesside.

But Mannion had no great love for Burnley. He was bitter for years about the defeat at Turf Moor in a 1947 Cup-tie on the snow and ice covered pitch. Burnley won by one disputed goal after the drawn game at Middlesbrough, and Mannion never forgot an alleged foul on the goalkeeper and then a Burnley player sweeping the ball into the net with his hand.

"Wilf played football the way Fred Astaire danced," said Brian Clough. He was a wonderful dribbler, displayed mesmerising ball control and skills; he was an artist with a football, but also very strong-willed. In 1948 he staged a one-man strike at Middlesbrough, unheard of in those days of soccer serfdom, because he wanted to get away. But in the end he had to back down. "There's more freedom in the army," he said bitterly. Towards the end of his League career, at Hull City, he was suspended by the Football League for articles he had written. He then turned out for non-league sides. A player who was capped by England 26 times played at tiny grounds like Earlestown, near Warrington, where he was player-manager. An uncle who lived there took me to see him and my uncle remarked how sad it was to see a great player like Mannion reduced to this. That must have been sometime in the mid-fifties when I had minimal interest in football anyway. He was called the 'Golden Boy' of English football in his prime and not without reason. His golden hair and golden touch made him an absolute star.

Tommy Lawton began his career at Burnley (see *No Nay Never Volume One*) and never ceased to sing the praises of Ray Bennion, whom he says, taught him all he knew.

"I only played against him once," said Jimmy, "and I can still see the way he just flicked the ball from the centre-circle and found his outside-right way out on the touchline. He just seemed to hang in the air as if he was held up by a rope."

He was six feet tall, strong and beautifully balanced; the power and spring in his legs was astonishing. He moved from Burnley to Everton while he was still a teenager, and was bought to eventually replace the legendary Dixie Dean, the greatest header of a ball of all time. He learned by watching Dean who taught him all he knew. Lawton's trick was to fool opponents that he was going for a long-range header at goal, but then in mid-air he would twist and head a short pass to a nearby colleague. He seemed able to climb ever so slowly, hover over the ball, and then head it in any direction he chose. He even claimed to be able to put spin on it.

He played for Burnley, Everton, Chelsea, and then surprisingly Notts County who were in the Third Division. From County it was to Brentford and at the age of 34 from there to Arsenal. His career was not without its controversies. He was a hard-headed businessman as well as a footballer and if he moved to surprising destinations, it was always reasonable to assume there were financial benefits.

But it is his marvellous heading ability for which he is remembered and this in an age of heavy leather balls with laces; the spin he allegedly put on a ball came from heading the lace. There is simply no-one today to compare with him; perhaps Alan Shearer at his peak is the nearest, but even he pales in comparison.

'Tom was the great professional, the goal getter, the towering athlete with the elastic head... unmistakeable on the field, shoulders slightly hunched, his hair greased back into a solid flattened, blob of black... cheeks puffed out when he unleashed a shot', wrote John Moynihan.

Len Shackleton was known as 'the clown prince of soccer' and "I'd have hit the roof with his antics," said Jimmy Mac. "He was the first player I ever saw bend a ball, which was no mean feat with the ball we used in those days. In an exhibition game in Belfast I saw him nutmeg three players in the space of 20 yards. In a game at Turf Moor, he trapped dead a long goal kick and then for fun just lobbed it back to the goalkeeper. He wasn't a big man but he had such huge feet."

"Unpredictable, brilliantly inconsistent, flamboyant, radical and mischievous, a footballing genius," said Stanley Matthews.

Billy Bingham played with him at Sunderland and saw at first hand his skill and how he could entertain. "He was so unusual and such a good dribbler. He had great control and with a long ball could change play so easily. He was only about 5' 8" tall but his feet must have been size fourteens. I never saw him head a ball he always brought it down with his feet. But we were so frustrated by his unpredictability. He would look to play a pass, dummy, and then take it on himself and leave us looking at him... then he'd go and score".

Maurice Edelman wrote: "For the greater part of his seventeen years as a professional footballer... he was incalculable, and occasionally outrageous. Shackleton was eccentric, an

Peter McKay, considered by Jimmy Mac to be the finest goal poacher he ever played with in his time at Burnley.

PRINCE OF INSIDE FORWARDS | 163

erratic genius, a gifted individualist; a showman who drew the crowds, entertained and astonished them… He was not discreet…He criticised the Football league, The FA, players' contracts, the transfer system, referees, managers and directors… He had an impish streak, when he caught himself being orderly; a perverse impulse took hold of him… to be well-behaved for the whole 90 minutes was beyond him."

If, for example, his side were 3 – 0 up, for the last 20 minutes he would just switch off and amuse himself… bewilderingly clever one minute, utterly selfish the next. He would trap a ball dead, pretend to comb his hair and then look at an imaginary watch on his hand and yawn. He would beat countless opponents in a mazy dribble, go round the goalkeeper, then stop the ball just before the line and taunt the goalkeeper.

Such a man could never fit into a pattern, and as a direct result, only played six times for England. Perhaps Stan Bowles was the last of his kind and certainly no-one will ever see his like again in the dull modern game. His is the famous autobiography which has a chapter entitled something along the lines of 'The Average Director's Knowledge of Football'. Then, there is a blank page, page 78, Chapter Nine.

In September, 1957, an ankle injury ended his career. Oh that there had been a SKY TV company to make endless films of his genius and tricks.

John Charles played both with and against Jimmy McIlroy. No one has yet decided whether he was better at centre-half or at centre-forward. He was superb in either. In the representative game where they were colleagues Jimmy remembers Danny Blanchflower taking it upon himself to switch Charles from centre-half to centre-forward during the game. When that happened they conceded two goals. Walter Winterbottom the manager was furious with Blanchflower. Without the appearance of Pele and Maradona it is possible that Charles would today have the label the world's greatest ever footballer. The Italians certainly thought so when he played there. He was hugely powerful both in the air and on the ground, and had a magnificent physique. He moved deceptively, far quicker than opponents anticipated; sometimes it looked a lethargic movement, but before you knew it he had won the ball or burst clear. In the air he was almost unbeatable. The demands of being a defender or a forward are so contrasting, yet Charles slipped from one to the other effortlessly. Whilst at Leeds there are stories that Burnley tried to buy him before other clubs cottoned on to just how good he was. But it was Juventus, where he is still revered today, who bought him for an incredible £65,000 in 1957. For a big man he was surprisingly nimble, had beautiful balance, was neat and skilled with either foot and could change pace effortlessly. And all this without really stretching himself, said football observers like Maurice Edelman and Terence Delaney; as if it was all so easy for him.

"Tom Finney was the greatest all-round player I have ever seen," Jimmy McIlroy said. "He had more skill and skills than anyone I've known. He had tremendous speed and could score goals. This is where he had the edge over Stanley Matthews."

He had speed off the mark, an exceptional ability to cross the ball at speed, wonderful ball control and a calm, unruffled demeanour. He scored goals, slipping the ball past the goalkeeper, as if he was just posting a letter, wrote John Moynihan.

No other player has played at outside right, outside left and centre forward for England with the ability to switch from one to the other. He was two-footed, nimble, had superb balance, was razor-sharp, and on the right wing could cut in and shoot with his left foot, or vice versa. His acceleration and timing of when to make a sprint, and then shoot with either foot, were superb. At Preston, in fact, he played in every forward line position. He was only 5' 7" tall with a slight figure, never lost his temper, and was totally unflappable even against the most brutal treatment. And, on top of all this he was the perfect team man, always unselfish, and seeing when to make the perfect pass or cross for someone in a better position. He was continually compared with the older Matthews in spite of being a far more rounded player and so versatile. Kicking, trapping, dribbling, beating a man, seeing an opportunity to score or a space to dart into, he was quite peerless. At his peak he was offered £130 a week to go to Palermo, a £10,000 immediate lump sum, a car and villa. He asked Preston to release him but they turned him down. Twice he was Footballer of the Year. Today, he and Jimmy Mac meet quite often at dinners or football functions. The respect and admiration they have for each other is immense.

Jimmy McIlroy played with Stanley Matthews, a once in a lifetime winger, 'the Wizard of Dribble', for two seasons at Stoke City. His essential secret, if indeed it was a secret, was his sudden sprint, once described as a shuffle and a spurt, so that no matter how often an opposing full back thought he could read when that sprint was about to take place, Matthews would leave him stranded. No matter how often the full back could read the way he thought he was going to go, he would drop a shoulder, wrong-foot his opponent, leave him unbalanced, sometimes even facing the wrong way – and then he was round him and away. And all of this, he was doing well into his forties. Over 60 yards or so many could outrun him, over ten or fifteen yards there were few, if any, who could stay with him. But, in spite of all that skill and his ability to beat a man, he could also simply stand and look and see a man in a good position and give the most perfect pass. His crossing of the ball was pin point accurate. Tommy Lawton claimed that Matthews would always land the ball on his centre parting. Neither was it any secret that Matthews loved to destroy an opponent. Gentleman he might have been but in taking opponents on, he was ruthless. If half the battle was to destroy confidence in the opposition, that is exactly what he set out to do. People travelled miles to see him. He put thousands on any gate. And when he played for Blackpool against Burnley, Alex Elder was instructed to follow him wherever he went all over the field. Elder did just that with Matthews walking him round like a dog on a lead. It was embarrassing to watch. We felt sorry for Elder who was clearly playing to instructions. If he is remembered for one special game, then it is the 1953 Cup Final, the 'Matthews Final'. With 20 minutes to go, Blackpool were losing 3 – 1. In those next magical 20 minutes Matthews transformed the game with sorcery, trickery and a display of wing-play the like of which we shall never see again.

Danny Blanchflower and Jimmy Mac were international team-mates, had huge respect for each other and spoke frequently. "He was the most intelligent man I ever met," said McIlroy. When Jimmy was put on the transfer list, Blanchflower was one of the first to telephone him. If he was a consummate player, he was an even better captain, making decisions on the field and changing things round as and when needed with the approval of Bill Nicholson the Tottenham manager, and Peter Doherty when playing for Northern Ireland. His physique, slender and wiry, was hardly that of a footballer especially in an age of mud and physical contact but he could tackle, distribute a ball, make fine passes, and drive his team on. When he played well, Tottenham played well. From him there was never a crude tackle, or a wild clearance or a loose pass. He was delicate, cool and measured. Somehow he always seemed to be in space to receive a pass. He prompted, supported, and rolled the ball through the gaps for forwards to run onto. For a man who carried no muscle, he was incredibly hard to shake off the ball. He would bring the ball out of danger skilfully and then make a neat forward pass. If there was such a thing as an intellectual footballer, then he was it and in 1957 he was Footballer of the Year. "We wouldn't have reached the World Cup Finals without him," said Peter Doherty. After football he was manager of Chelsea for a short period but his real forte was writing and his column for the *Sunday Express* was outstanding, and his analysis of the Jimmy Mac transfer essential reading (see appendices). He was eloquent and articulate and could discuss any subject be it football or anything else, appearing on BBC *Sportsview* and children's TV programmes. Nobody ever had to tell him what to say; quite the opposite in fact, the difficulty was making him stop. Jimmy Greaves called him the "Oscar Wilde of football."

He was once asked to describe George Best after a game. He replied, "George makes a greater appeal to the senses than Finney or Matthews did, his movements are quicker, lighter, more balletic. George offers grander surprises to the mind and the eye. He has ice in his veins, warmth in his heart and timing, and balance on his feet."

"Yeah but how did he play?" said the bewildered reporter.

Jimmy Greaves and Jimmy McIlroy undoubtedly formed a well-established mutual admiration society. There has never been any other goalscorer quite like him. "He was a real poacher," said Jimmy Mac," you never saw him thump or belt a ball. I can't think of any goal he scored from outside the penalty area. He prodded, poked, glanced, sidefooted, placed the ball, but never from 30 yards. He was just a genius at goalscoring."

In his prime he was just a small, slight figure, quite pale, but he was incredibly quick, cheeky and clever, time and time again the leading goalscorer at Chelsea and Tottenham. He could look so casual and disinterested but had this uncanny sense of when the ball would come through to him. His speed increased, it became a sprint, and he was there in the right place at the right time yet again to put the ball in the net. He had balance and incredibly sharp reflexes, could shoot with either foot, could take the ball in his stride with a lovely first, delicate touch. He had that priceless gift of anticipation. His touch was deft and subtle, he didn't kick a ball; he stroked it. In a game at Turf Moor when Burnley played their reserve team against Chelsea in the early sixties, the final score was 4 – 4. Without the magic of Greaves it would have been a 4 – 2 win for the Clarets. Of course it had to be Greaves who put Spurs on their way to a 3 – 1 win over Burnley at Wembley in 1962. In between Chelsea and Tottenham he went to Italy for a brief unhappy spell. His scoring statistics can be looked up elsewhere; the story of his decline because of drinking is a sad one. He faded away at West Ham and then Barnet. But redemption and recovery saw him take up a television and prolific writing career.

"How good Johnny Haynes was in his day, is brought home to me today," says McIlroy, "when I watch today's players passing the ball sideways, backwards, any way but forward, and making so many negative passes. Haynes nearly always played a forward ball, rarely backwards. His passing was so positive; they were always attacking passes, eight out of ten of them."

When you watched Fulham and Johnny Haynes you always knew you would see a masterclass in the art of direct, accurate passing, and of the long forward diagonal pass to the wings, Haynes had no equal. He had no special tricks; he wasn't especially quick, he rarely attempted to beat a man in a dribble, though he had the knack of sidestepping an

Jimmy Adamson, Footballer Of The Year, and assistant England manager in Chile, 1962.

Burnley's left-back Smith touches the ball back to international goalkeeper Colin McDonald during a league game with Spurs at White Hart Lane. McDonald was a great success in the England goal in World Cup games.

Key man in the England forward line is Johnny Haynes of Fulham. In these days of deep-lying schemers, whose job is to lay on the passes for four sharpshooting forwards, men like Haynes are worth their weight in gold.

opponent before releasing the ball. His game was all about passing, and no one was more accurate than he. His strength was his quick thinking and mastery of the long pass, twenty yards, thirty yards, into the path of a racing forward. Then there were the reverse passes he was able to make, him going one way, and then quickly sending the ball, sometimes forty yards in the opposite direction to a winger on the touchline. He continually looked around the field as if memorising where every other player was positioned. When he began to add goalscoring to his repertoire at Fulham he was almost the complete player.

"Bob Lord was always telling me I was far better than Haynes," laughed Mac during one of our interviews. "I still wonder then why Haynes earned more than me. He was the first £100 a week player, but I only got £80 from Bob."

Ferenc Puskas was known as 'the galloping major' and his team-mate Francisco Gento described how his shooting was unbelievable and that he could even juggle with the soap in the showers. "His left foot was like a hand, he could do anything with it." He is best remembered here for two games, the first being at Wembley when the Hungarians beat England 6 – 3 in 1953. From this there is a film clip of him doing a drag back with the ball and then rifling it home. And then in 1960 he was part of the Real Madrid team with Alfredo di Stefano and Gento that gave one of the most mesmerising displays of club football ever seen when they beat Eintracht Frankfurt 7 – 3. Several minutes of it can be seen on the Youtube website. In that game he scored four times and even though it took place nearly fifty years ago, it has not been bettered as a 90 minute display of club football. His left foot did the damage; his right foot was merely for standing on. No-one or any coach ever tried to make him improve his right foot. The left did the work of both. He could put spin on the ball long before the development of the modern lightweight ball that can dip and swerve a metre or more. Bill Shankly in his memoirs remembers offering the Liverpool training ground to Panathinaikos, managed by Puskas, on one occasion. He then witnessed Puskas practising shooting. "He put the ball on the 18 yard line and then shot it with his left foot just a foot inside the post. He repeated this 12 times in succession." He was then 45 years old.

The combination of him and Alfred di Stefano was almost unbeatable and the win over Frankfurt was the fifth year in a row that Real won the European Cup. Jimmy faced them both in the game that celebrated the centenary of Stoke City.

Jimmy Mac and I talked about these great players against the background of the modern footballer where he regrets the dearth of truly great individuals, particularly in the UK. Stewart Downing would have been an average left winger in the 70s, decidedly ordinary in the 60s. The same can be said for Defoe, Crouch, Wright-Philips and Jenas who have all featured in an England shirt. Today they are all in the £10million class. David Nugent, a journeyman centre forward was sold to Portsmouth by Preston North End for £6million. His name is rarely heard now. Kyle Lafferty a raw, undeveloped, 20 year old centre forward, moved from Burnley to Rangers for £4million.

It is hard to be critical; it is the football world we live in. But the modern player is often unapproachable, cocooned, protected by the gates to his executive home, and guarded by his agent and club. On the occasion I once telephoned Gareth Taylor, then the Burnley centre forward, I received a phone call from a club employee asking me not to telephone the players. I was incensed. "But I am the bloke paying these players' wages," I told her angrily.

Jimmy McIlroy in his 1960 book warned of the problems of young players starting out in the game being subjected to terrace criticism and how it can destroy confidence and belief at a critical stage in a player's development. Kyle Lafferty, so often described as "still learning his trade," in 2008, expressed a desire to leave Burnley because of that same terrace criticism. But in today's game and demands for instant success, he will be on the receiving end wherever he goes when a club has paid that amount of money for him.

In Jimmy Mac's day loud, merciless criticism and banter from the terraces was part and parcel of the game. In Shakespeare's day the groundlings were quick to vent their ire at a poor performance or a poor actor at the Globe. Rotten fruit was often the order of the day. Many a comedian has been booed off the stage by a hard faced audience. The Glasgow Empire was unforgiving. It is the same in football.

McIlroy was and still is a great admirer of the wonderfully attacking Manchester United team of '58, the one so tragically decimated at Munich; the Spurs Double team, and Tommy Docherty's electric, jet-heeled Manchester United 70s team. Today he admits that there are only two teams that inspire him to switch on *Match of the Day*, Arsenal and Manchester United.

He featured the United team of '58 in his book *Right Inside Soccer*. Brazil and Argentina in 1958 impressed him hugely at first hand, even though Argentina inexplicably lost 6 – 1 to Czechoslovakia. There is a common strand to all of these teams. They played with flair and skill; contained individually great players… and neither of them were cursed by the greed and money that taints the game today. These were still very much the days before business and corporate groups had invaded the game and enormous stands contained executive boxes, lounges and fine dining suites.

If 'innocence' is the right word then it was still there, certainly in 1958, and nothing probably signifies it more than the '58 World Cup. But it certainly began to disappear after 1960 and Burnley's title win.

I mentioned to Jimmy how well Colin McDonald had looked at the Harry Potts dinner and somehow that became a chat about whether he would have picked McDonald or Adam Blacklaw as the best he played with. His choice was McDonald (just) and that choice was accompanied by the opinion that had McDonald not had his career terminated by injury, Gordon Banks would not have become England's goalkeeper quite so soon. "He was so brave from any distance and in training even if we were blasting the ball at him from just six yards, he would never complain. He would have been England's goalkeeper in 1966 and you'd never have heard of Gordon Banks. He put absolutely everything into training, worked so hard, harder than anyone else and he never pulled out of any 50/50 situation. There was never a thought of being injured."

"But," Jimmy added, "the trouble with picking the best at Burnley is that you have so many to choose from. You're spoilt for choice and that shows what quality Burnley had. But, yes, I'd choose Colin as number one, but Adam would be in the squad."

Well, in for a penny, in for a pound, I thought; let's ask about full-backs and then go on to a full team. Trouble is though, he's probably been asked this so many times already. Plus I've always thought until now what a 'sad' exercise it is picking 'best elevens'.

Anyway, at full-back Jimmy settled on John Angus and Alex Elder, but into the squad came Harold Mather; the classic fifties full-back, solid, reliable, dependable, not much got by him and a few wingers finished up in Row Z. "He was not very quick but that was OK

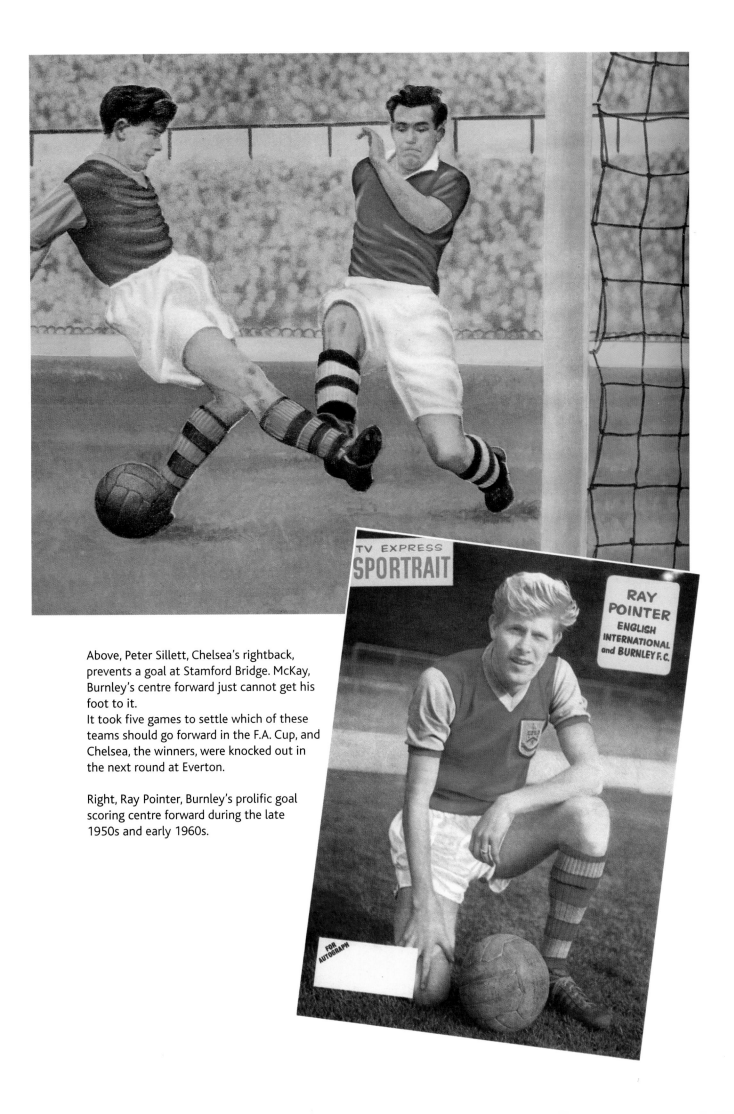

TV EXPRESS
SPORTRAIT

RAY POINTER
ENGLISH INTERNATIONAL and BURNLEY F.C.

FOR AUTOGRAPH

Above, Peter Sillett, Chelsea's rightback, prevents a goal at Stamford Bridge. McKay, Burnley's centre forward just cannot get his foot to it.
It took five games to settle which of these teams should go forward in the F.A. Cup, and Chelsea, the winners, were knocked out in the next round at Everton.

Right, Ray Pointer, Burnley's prolific goal scoring centre forward during the late 1950s and early 1960s.

Tom Finney, of Preston North End and England, was voted *Footballer of the Year* for the second time, during the 1956-7 season. A versatile player, Finney has been picked as outside-right, outside-left and centre-forward for England.

Tom Finney, considered by Jimmy to be the finest ever all-round player.

because fifties football was never about pace anyway. There was usually one winger on one side who was quicker than the other, and the other one would be the ball-player, the tricky sorcerer, who, like Burnley's Brian Pilkington could jink and shimmy and tie a full-back in knots."

Alex Elder however was a different kind of full back. If Mather belonged to an age when defenders rarely crossed the halfway line, then Elder was quite different. He made rampaging runs down the wing, got crosses over and had a thunderbolt shot. He was one of the first of the new breed of attacking full-backs.

"And John Angus, what can you say? He formed a wonderful partnership with any winger he played with. As a youth when he came down he was homesick and went straight back home but Alan Brown went up to Amble and brought him back down." All of us lucky enough to see him play will remember him. He was elegant yet hard as nails and had legs like tree trunks. He was a magnificent full-back although Bobby Charlton tells the story that there was one game when George Best gave him such a torrid time that the game should have been stopped.

Jimmy's full-backs would therefore be Elder and Angus (despite the blip against Best) and Mather would be in the squad.

When he played, there was just one centre-half as opposed to the current two centre-backs. The first to come to Jimmy's mind, although he never played alongside him, was the iron-man Alan Brown. Jimmy trained with him when he was manager in the fifties, nurturing the players who would become the side that won the title. "But I'm told he was ruthless, hard and fearless. When I trained with him, he could shake you in a tackle even then." At this point I mentioned the occasion of *that* legendary tackle by Brown on Stan Mortenson, when Mortenson was well and truly 'sorted'. Jimmy laughed. "Do you know I've heard the story of that tackle so many times I think there must have been 30,000 in the ground that day. I do believe Mortenson was airborne for some considerable time," he added with his characteristic understated, wry humour.

But it was Tommy Cummings he selected for his First Eleven. "Tommy was so quick and skilful and this was in an age of tall, lumbering centre-halves who were all very strong in the air. I remember the day I was playing in a reserve game and the news came through that Tommy had scored, early in the fifties, and we were amazed. Centre-halves never came across the halfway line in those days, let alone score.

"At right-half (midfield to us twentieth century folk) it would be Jimmy Adamson". But here, Jimmy had to think for a while, in fact the first name mentioned being that of Reg Attwell. By coincidence I'd been speaking to former club director Derek Gill the week before who mentioned what an elegant, cultured, player Attwell was, a lovely passer of the ball and Jimmy agreed with that. "But it would be Jimmy Adamson who would just shade it."

It was only at the end of this discussion that Jimmy suddenly remembered another midfielder Brian O'Neil, although having remembered him; it was O'Neil's trilby hat that intrigued him most, the one he wears now every time he returns to Turf Moor. "Brian had everything and he would be in my squad.

"And on the left side of midfield, it would be Brian Miller, the gentle giant. Do you know," Jimmy laughed," so many opponents always referred to him as 'that big dirty bugger Miller' but it was so unfounded. He was never a dirty player. I never saw him ever make one vicious tackle. If he'd have tried to hurt someone he'd more likely hurt himself. And he so loved getting forward."

For the forward line - first up was Ray Pointer. "He was so slight but so strong, tireless and fast. He was ahead of his time, the first of a new breed of small, mobile centre forwards. I saw Alan Shearer at his peak at Blackburn and I wouldn't know which one of them to choose as my all time best. Alongside him I'd have Jimmy Robson, so underrated. People don't realise what ability he had. Danny Blanchflower rated him highly as well and maintained that without Jimmy Greaves on the scene he would have played for England. But in my squad there would be Peter McKay, the most natural scorer I have ever seen, a genius in the box, so good at anticipating things and just being there. You can't teach that sort of thing Billy Dougal said. And also in the squad would be Andy Lochhead and Willie Irvine. Jack Charlton always said he came off the field black and blue after a game with Andy." (Charlie George in his book also lists Lochhead as one of the hard men of his time). Lochhead and Irvine would be in the squad but I'd have to go for Pointer and Robson.

"Alongside Pointer and Robson it would be Martin Dobson." (Of course in anyone else's team it would be Jimmy Mac himself but with characteristic modesty he elected not to choose himself).

"On the left wing there would be Leighton James who at his best was up there with George Best. And then there's Brian Pilkington and Gordon Harris. The first time Danny Blanchflower saw Gordon play he said 'you've got some player there'. He had this wonderful ability to accelerate by an opponent.

"On the right wing it would be John Connelly, good with both feet, twenty goals a season. There's also Dave Thomas, wonderful crosser of a ball and Glen Little who of all the modern players is the only one I enjoyed watching. He was the nearest to the old style wingers who could get to the by-line and get a cross over." (Who will ever forget the Carling Cup-tie when he came on with Burnley 0 – 1 down, tore Spurs apart, was virtually unplayable, and Burnley won 2 – 1). "And we haven't even mentioned Ralph Coates and Willie Morgan. Wonderful players and Burnley had so many of them all those years ago."

# Chapter Thirteen

# Transfer Rumours And Sold To Stoke

JIMMY AND I went our separate ways in '63. He went to Stoke City and I went to college. Jimmy knew exactly where he was going but when I went to Ormskirk I thought it was next to Southport on the coast someway midway between there and Blackpool. I was a lively lad and envisaged three years of fun and games. When I arrived there I discovered it was a small, sleepy inland market town surrounded by cabbage fields. (Doing 'A' level geography at school hadn't taught me much). The smell from those cabbages was sometimes so bad there were days when you could never open a window.

It would be 40 years before Jimmy and I met again when I wrote about him in the first *No Nay Never*. But even at college, after I had been there quite a while, maybe a year or so, his name cropped up unexpectedly. It was in a sports session on the playing field and we were doing football skills with a PE tutor called Ernie Wright. The assumption one day was that at some stage in our teaching life we'd maybe have a school team, or at the very least do some coaching during games sessions.

"Anybody here come from Burnley?" Ernie shouted to the assembled group. No-one responded. I came from nearby Todmorden but kept quiet like the rest. And anyway, you know what they say – never volunteer. "OK anyone ever watched Burnley?" he asked. This time I put my hand up, couldn't resist. I had claret blood.

"Ah Mr Thomas, good," he said. (Everybody was addressed formally. This was still the early 60s. Familiarity and first name terms hadn't yet been born in the seats of learning) "Great team, great football," he said. "Jimmy McIlroy, John Connelly, Ray Pointer, Jimmy Adamson, great players, always passing, always passing. Come over and help me demonstrate."

For a few minutes we demonstrated one simple move straight out of the Burnley coaching manual. It was the 'wall pass' where the man with the ball approaches the opponent, passes the ball to a colleague who is standing level with, but away from the opponent, runs by the opponent and receives the return pass from his colleague, who returns it to him so that he collects it without even altering his stride. How many times had I seen that simple move at Burnley?

So there I was, at Training College, miles from home, miles from Burnley, and yet there was the name McIlroy right out of the blue. It's a funny world, I thought.

From college when I returned home for holidays there was the occasional game to watch at Turf Moor, but these were the years of transition (according to Potts and Lord in the Press), or if we are more honest, the beginning of the end. When I left in '66 there was the World Cup and Burnley had just had a magnificent season where the likes of O' Neil, Harris, Morgan, Lochhead and Irvine et al came so close to another title, but the chance faded away, and later, one by one they were all sold. But they did finish third and qualified for Europe in the Inter Cities Fairs Cup.

Sometimes there was mention of Jimmy Mac who became manager of Oldham and had registered once more as a player. My father always thought it rather sad and said he couldn't imagine Jimmy having to play in this lower league with jobbing players who couldn't possibly be on the same level or wavelength. Of course he wasn't the same player that he had been at Burnley. How could he be as the years took their toll on his stamina, put an extra inch round his middle, and took the edge off his skills and sharpness?

But long before all this, of course there were frequent transfer rumours surrounding a player of his talent and magnitude. He wrote candidly about them in his book. Even as early as 1951 he asked for a transfer. He returned from his first game for Northern Ireland to find that he had been dropped from the first team. Not best pleased, he put in an immediate transfer request, (the impetuosity of youth perhaps); it was turned down immediately.

In October 1953 Manchester United made an approach to sign him. But as the fifties progressed, and certainly from '57 onwards, there were constant stories of impending moves or his wish to better himself. One of them in particular, again following an international game, was not without substance, and was only settled after long talks with Bob Lord and Harry Potts.

In the New Year of 1958 'Sportsman' in the 'Football Notebook' reported weekend stories of McIlroy's dissatisfaction, and of the Irishman wanting a move to another club. McIlroy was heading off to Ireland for the International game against Italy and rumours were rife that some big Italian club would make a huge offer for him. The potential loss to Burnley was a page one story and the player was reported as having commented that the current contract system caused him some uneasiness. He was a much coveted player and at a stage of his career where thoughts of his future security and a bigger pay packet to ensure that security, were emerging.

'McIlroy's name has been linked with Arsenal, Tottenham Hotspur and Manchester United, but the only comment has come from Arsenal, whose manager, Mr Jack Crayston, said that McIlroy was a fine player and they would be interested if any move was forthcoming, but they were 'sitting on the fence'.' (Burnley Express, January '58).

He was certainly 'tapped up' by Jimmy Murphy of Manchester United and it is only very recently that Jimmy Mac spoke of this when he told Radio Lancashire that he had turned down an approach from United's assistant Jimmy Murphy, when they met under unusual circumstances shortly before the Munich air disaster.

"I was injured and sitting on the touchline, we were playing Manchester City. He looked around to make sure nobody was listening and whispered in my ear, 'Our boss would like to sign you. All he wants is the OK, he will only make a move if he thought you would want to come to us'. For whatever reason I didn't give him any encouragement."

After the crash his thoughts turned immediately to the people he knew that were in the travelling party, Jackie Blanchflower and Harry Gregg, his international colleagues. "I could have been on that plane," he mulled.

A chapter in *Right Inside Soccer* was devoted to transfer issues. In it he admitted that he was the source of transfer rumours and in no way blameless on occasions. As a youngster coming into the game he had no worries about the future but as the years went by there was certainly the thought in the back of his mind that one day he would be finished with the game. He admits to brooding that once the adventure was over the open spaces that lay ahead would be dull and flat, and he had no desire to return to his first trade of bricklaying. In this there was a rich irony; it would indeed be bricklaying that he returned to for a couple of years when he left the manager's post at Bolton Wanderers. As a footballer he'd had money in his pocket, had seen the world, stayed in the best hotels and accepted adulation as if it were normal.

For these reasons there did come a time when he felt it appropriate to try and cash in on his reputation and seek a move. The maximum wage was restrictive and there were only two possible ways then in which he might gain more financial reward. He could play for a fashionable club in one of the major cities, London, Birmingham or Manchester. From this would come lucrative media opportunities, particularly newspaper columns. Or, secondly, the only other way would be to continue to play for Burnley, but only if they were successful and more fashionable. In this, however, he was convinced that Burnley would never become one of the country's most famous clubs. Then, when a reporter contacted him to suggest that only by moving to London would he benefit financially, he was even more convinced that a move was in order.

As a result of all this, at the back end of 1957, and then into '58 he had more or less decided that a transfer was the answer. It became a succession of front page news.

BURNLEY WILL SELL McILROY: It has been rumoured for ages.

WOLVES WANT McILROY

ARSENAL WOULD LIKE McILROY

REAL BID FOR McILROY: Spanish have eyes on Burnley's idol.

ITALIANS FEEL THE BURNLEY BOOT: Jimmy McIlroy will not be moving to Sampdoria.

NOT FOR SALE: "No-one has enough money to buy him."

"McILROY HAS BEEN GOT AT," was one huge headline when the rumours were at their height. "I am not mincing words. I say bluntly, McIlroy has been 'tapped'," said Bob Lord angrily.

"If I don't get any sort of satisfaction after a talk I intend having with Mr Lord tomorrow, I shall ask for a transfer and put it in writing," said McIlroy. "I am unsettled in Burnley and would like a change. I have no special club in mind – Manchester United, Wolves, Spurs, Arsenal, the sort of glamour club that might afford me some extra 'perk' outside soccer."

"The biggest soccer manhunt of the season will be sparked if the situation results in the player being placed on the transfer list… favourites could be Spurs, one of the richest clubs in the country," wrote top sports writer Henry Rose in the *Daily Express*.

Yet, it all came to nothing. Lord, announcing on each occasion, "Jimmy McIlroy will never leave Burnley."

By 1960, McIlroy was able to give a calm explanation for all the transfer talk and turmoil that had taken place two and three years earlier.

*In Belfast, for the Northern Ireland versus Italy World Cup qualifying match, a newspaper reporter spoke to me in an informal, 'fatherly' fashion. Whether he really had my welfare at heart, or whether he was really hard up for a story, I shall never know; but the trend of his conversation was that the streets of the big cities were paved with gold, the sort of gold I should never see while I remained in Burnley. I never believed that a move would bring riches galore, but I felt that there would be greater opportunities for me to pick up a few 'perks' with a glamour team.*

The reporter asked me if I would consider a transfer, and I produced my stock answer to that question: "I'd be happy to join any club which could put more money in my pocket than I was getting."

On the next morning, the headlines screamed at me... 'McILROY UNSETTLED AT BURNLEY – FANCIES A TRANSFER.'

This taught me one important lesson. It can often be dangerous to be candid with the Press. I always seemed to come off second best because I was seldom rude enough to say, 'No comment'.

When this particular storm broke I was a long way from home and that was my biggest regret. It seemed cowardly of me not to have discussed my problems with the club before they were aired in the papers.

The transfer story caused several people to add two and two together, producing five as the answer. On the Saturday before leaving for Belfast, Burnley played Tottenham Hotspur at Turf Moor. Naturally, my good friend and international colleague, Danny Blanchflower, called at my house for a meal before flying to Ireland. Although Danny and I were at home together for an hour at the most, it was reported that he had stopped the night, and it was also hinted, not very subtly, that he had been talking to me about joining Spurs.

Some good did come out of the transfer stories. I was given an opportunity to discuss my problems with Mr Potts and Mr Lord. With their sincerity, they convinced me that they would transform Burnley from just another club into one of the clubs. Between them, these two dedicated men reassured me about Burnley's future; and in consequence my future. When the interview ended I almost felt as they did that success was bound to come.

The 'knowing-ones' believed that Bob Lord gave me one of his shops as an inducement to stay at Burnley. There was a stock joke in the Irish team. "McIlroy is going to ask for a transfer again – to get another butcher's shop."

My name was linked with transfer stories several times but only once did I knock on the manager's door to demand a move. I was a fledgling of 21 at the time and was dropped after playing for Ireland. It came as a shock to play for my country one week and find, on the following Saturday that I was apparently not good enough for my club. I requested a transfer – the request being immediately rejected.

One or two football writer friends said I let them down by discussing a possible transfer on Saturday evening, and then denying it all on Monday mornings. But every footballer likes to have a moan now and then and in the company of Pressmen, such conversations are usually off the record. But football writers are under constant pressure. They either produce headlines or get a rocket from above.

In my case, having been caught out too often, I should have been guided by the maxim, 'Once bitten, twice shy'. Instead it was more like, 'Many times bitten and still no more shy'.

The last time I was alleged to have asked for a transfer was in April 1959 when a Sunday newspaper again used my habitual quote: "If I can earn more money with another club, I'd be glad to move." This brought the immediate response from Bob Lord. "If McIlroy leaves Burnley, we want £100,000 for his transfer. But he's not going."

Hordes of newspaper men besieged my semi-detached, and as some had travelled from Manchester, and even London, they had no intention of leaving without a story. I spoke to them in a friendly way. They didn't miss a single word, but, naturally, only used the comments that best suited them.

I weighed up all the advantages and disadvantages of being a Burnley footballer, and the *good points counted for more than the bad. My original problem of security remained, but I was grateful to the club for doing so much to help me earn a few pounds outside of the game in addition to the weekly wage.* (Right Inside Soccer 1960)

How could anyone, either then or now, blame McIlroy for wanting to seek the extra money that would allow him to save and secure his future? In contrast to the manoeuvrings of today's superstars, his actions, if indeed they were deliberate 'actions' were minimal. If he saw a small, select band of other top footballers being used for advertising in sports magazines, or writing newspaper columns, who can blame him for wanting to share in their good fortune? In the fifties and sixties, the age of 30 was seen, far more than today, as a definite watershed in the life of an expendable footballer. That watershed, when footballers began to realise that they had only a limited 'earnings' lifespan was slowly approaching for him. He could see the other side of the hill. In his book he referred to it as the other side of "an enchanted forest."

By the time Jimmy Mac's book appeared in 1960 he was settled and more secure. Bob Lord had arranged for lucrative outside work, namely a column in a national newspaper. What then emerged was that he was a skilled writer, perfectly capable of writing his own columns. Burnley had become nationally known; they were successful; both club and McIlroy profiles were sky high. The abolition of the maximum wage eventually gave a huge boost to his pay packet so that, as he penned his columns and book, he could never have imagined for one minute that, one day, he actually would be placed on a transfer list.

On 9th March, 1963, astonishingly, Burnley played their first home league game of the year, as a result of the dreadful winter. Manager Potts, several times accused of being a 'yes man' in his relationship with Bob Lord, but of whom no one could ever suggest insincerity or dishonesty, wrote extensively in his programme notes that day about the transfer. With pen in hand he could be extremely fluent and articulate. This same penmanship, however, could sometimes become wordy, over-elaborate and verbose. In these notes the attempt to calm the stormy waters failed; the nub of Potts' argument, buried within the rhetoric, clearly being that Jimmy Mac was not showing 'unrestricted dedication to the job', and that he was not displaying 'all-out endeavour'. Even supposing Potts' account of events were the correct ones, or even partially correct, nobody was convinced that there wasn't more to this than met the eye.

'It is my desire, and no less my duty, to set before you – our supporters – a review of the unfortunate development in our affairs in the last fortnight – the termination of Jimmy McIlroy's services at Turf Moor. After the happy association between him and our club during the thirteen years of his engagement it was never expected it would end this way. Naturally, the news of this, when it came to be disclosed, caused a more than ordinary sensation and immediately evoked an outburst of condemnation from a large section of the public. This was understandable for McIlroy enjoyed the favour of many people to a marked degree. To many he had become one of their football idols.

Most of those who rushed to his defence, I fear, were so obsessed with their own immediate reaction to the surprise decision that they completely overlooked the fact that for so long Jimmy had enjoyed the same appreciation within the club. They did not pause to reason that, in the light of that record, it could not have been other than unavoidable to break up the partnership. Obviously, and more and more of those who were shocked into bitter disappointment must surely be reflecting on this now, a club does not decide to part with a top capacity player without strong reasons for doing so. Most of the protest correspondence extolled the player and denounced the club, electing themselves judge and jury purely on evidence that had not come to their notice. Believe me, the decision to part with Jimmy McIlroy was not an appetising one for us within the club. We would have preferred to have him at Turf Moor to the end of his playing career and, who knows, perhaps beyond that.

But football is, after all, an important business in which clubs have to strive for success and if they find, in their judgement, that something that should be yielding a bigger contribution towards that end is falling below the level of effectiveness they consider possible and have the right to expect, then action has to be taken to remedy the position. Between management and players in the case of football, this is attempted through mutual concentration, in the hope that whatever defect has been cited, will be put right through intelligence, diligence and enterprise. Such matters do receive attention in all circumstances. If the purpose is not fulfilled then what are the alternatives?

Line up this idea as regards yourselves whether you hold executive or subordinate positions of responsibility to the organisation you serve. Would you expect your efforts to be accepted if those efforts in the view of those engaging you fell below the standard set and expected and for which you were held to be in receipt of complementary reward?

Now: the decision to place McIlroy on the transfer list and his ultimate transfer to Stoke City. His going has left no hard feelings; merely the sense of regret that our association had to end this way.

It came about because in my opinion Jimmy, in his latter days here, was not maintaining the consistency of ability we all know he is well capable to command. I hoped that the fault could be remedied by calm domestic approach, but unfortunately I eventually felt despair and that the necessary reciprocation was no longer a hope. I was demanding a standard of consistency in keeping with his ability and for some time I had seen it maturing only in spasms. Jimmy himself has stated that perhaps he had become complacent. But the situation did not rectify itself. The varying degrees of effectiveness in his performances left me disappointed.

Football success is not determined by brilliance here and there. Every game brings its challenge and in these days of not inconsiderable financial reward for those in the profession, there is a duty to club and patrons which calls for unrestricted dedication to the job. Degrees of skill vary in individuals, but the sense of ALL-OUT endeavour is possible for all and clubs cannot afford to lose sight of this need, match to match.

McIlroy may hold the view that he continued to measure up to these compelling factors. I have not held that view for some time and so we reached the parting of the ways – not in anger but regret, yet convinced that the problem had to be dealt with as it has been. The Burnley club, like all other clubs, is bigger than those who serve it. And the Burnley club is my responsibility.

In his new surroundings I wish Jimmy all happiness'. *(Harry Potts' Programme Notes)*

Jimmy responded to the transfer in his final article for the *Last Sports* saying that he was hurt by suggestions that he was "not trying on occasions" and that all he wished to do was to retain his dignity. He regarded the accusation as a blow to his pride and a deliberate stain on his character. Whilst his friends urged him to defend himself, he wrote that his wife Barbara urged him to rise above it "with dignity." He asked how it was that if Mr Potts had

# ANGRY FANS SAY 'POTTS MUST GO'

"SACK Potts! Sack Potts! We want McKilroy!"

The bitterness of Burnley—24 hours after the Jimmy McIlroy mystery explosion—was expressed by this demand for manager Harry Potts' head splashed in white paint on the wall of a mill near the works of butcher-chairman Bob Lord (writes STEVE RICHARDS).

I copied them down as I went along for an interview with Mr. Lord. But after a few minutes' wait, an employee returned to say: "He isn't in. He must have gone."

Lord, normally football's most verbose chairman, still held silence as fans attacked his manager, others hunted signatures for "keep Mac at Turf Moor" petitions.

Some fans even went so far as to threaten not to attend future games at Turf Moor until club directors explained the reason for their shock move.

Two 19-year-old shopgirls intend to personally deliver their petition to Turf Moor. The girls, Catriona Macadam, of Oaklands, Barrowford, and Cynthia Gall, of Church Street, Accrington, toured Burnley centre collecting names.

Both said: "This is not for us. It is for Jimmy McIlroy. We would do anything to keep him."

## IN HIDING

Last night everyone puzzled over the latest questions: Why did McIlroy go into hiding and miss training yesterday?

Has he left himself open to being disciplined, or was he given a second day off, since the first team, of which he is no longer a part, travelled to Peterborough for a friendly match?

Only mystery and suspicion have arisen from the sealed lips of Turf Moor since the announcement that McIlroy, Soccer king of Burnley, was up for sale.

## MUST SELL

Stars have been sold before by clubs without all this fuss, and it is generally known that Burnley have to sell players to exist comfortably.

A SIMPLE STATEMENT THAT IT WAS NOW CONSIDERED ECONOMICAL TO PART WITH McILROY, HAVING HAD THE BEST FROM HIM, WOULD, I AM SURE, WIN OVER SOME OF THE REBELS.

After all, 12 months from now it might be hailed as a slick business deal, even though the situation had been handled clumsily.

## After hearing Lord's argument..

# McIlroy, you made wise move

JIMMY McILROY has done the wisest thing in the world in getting away from Burnley FC as quickly as possible.

That must be the reaction of the millions watching an astounding interview on television last night when Burnley chairman, Bob Lord, gave the "low-down" on why his club had startled McIlroy and the Soccer world by placing the 31-year-old star on the transfer list.

Said blunt Bob: "McIlroy knows perfectly well he hasn't been playing as well as he can for the last 18 months. We can't afford to pay a man high wages if he's not giving 100 per cent."

The Burnley chairman hedged on the question why McIlroy hadn't been told about his deficiencies or even dropped into the reserves.

"McIlroy knows that wouldn't have worked at all," said Lord.

Then the Burnley chairman emphatically denied they had sacked the Irish international.

He said: "We placed him on the transfer list and Stoke bought him. That's not sacking a man."

Earlier, McIlroy had repeated that the decision was a complete mystery to him.

"It's big business, that can be the only reason I can think of," he said.

But here in the revealing eye of the television camera, Burnley's argument, if any existed, was exposed for what it was worth.

# 'BOYCOTT BURNLEY' CALL TO FANS

ANGRY football fans who claim Burnley FC are trying to sell Jimmy McIlroy "like a cow at market" are to hold a public protest meeting.

They will meet at Barnoldswick, Yorks, on Saturday, and call on the club to take him off the transfer list.

Mr. Bill Grace, a businessman, who will address the meeting, said supporters would be asked to boycott the club unless this was done.

"There are about 1,500 Burnley supporters in Barnoldswick,' said Mr. Grace.

"We can do without Burnley but they cannot do without us. The whole area is seething and we feel we should protest."

Burnley's chairman, Mr. Bob Lord, said yesterday: "These petitions can't do any good for McIlroy or the club.

"It has been revealed by McIlroy that our manager told him he wasn't satisfied with his play.

"We are 100 per cent. behind the manager, whatever may happen. The board felt that our manager, Mr Harry Potts, gave McIlroy the necessary explanations for his action.

"Even McIlroy can never complain about the treatment he has received from Mr. Potts.

"We have every thought for our fans, and are doing the job properly. Sometimes we have to make moves which are not popular."

## Officially, Not a Kind Word

PERHAPS the most incredible aspect about the whole incredible McIlroy business this past ten days has been the fact that not one spokesman for Turf Moor has taken the trouble even to thank the Irishman for his past service to the club.

McIlroy, himself, in all his writings and statements, has been generous in his references to the club.

But the generosity has not been reciprocated.

Last week the official reason for the transfer was that McIlroy's performances had not been good enough.

The gossips looked beyond that for the real reason.

Now, the transfer complete, Burnley release a longer statement. It boils down to this: that McIlroy, in the eyes of the club, has not been giving 100 per cent effort on the field and that anybody who does not give 100 per cent effort is a luxury which the club cannot afford. Therefore, the only person responsible for McIlroy leaving Turf Moor is McIlroy himself.

One's immediate reaction to this statement is that it has taken the Burnley club an awful long time to find out!

noticed this lack of effort, why had it not been seen by 28,000 supporters. He had refrained from mentioning to anyone the whispers and rumours that had preceded the transfer. He had been asked to continue writing for the *Last Sports* until the end of the season but felt that he couldn't. "With dignity I've tried to play for Burnley; with dignity I've written for you, and, with dignity, I shall leave."

So it was to Stoke City he went, with the shrewd Tony Waddington in the process of transforming Stoke from a struggling Second Division side, to an outfit that would win promotion and flourish in the top division well into the seventies. He did this initially by buying ageing but outstanding players, thought to be superfluous by their clubs. He blended them together, and then worked home-grown players into the team as well. His masterstroke was signing Stanley Matthews who was already 46 when he arrived from Blackpool. Matthews had started his career at Stoke and when he returned, Stoke went wild. Attendances rocketed in the very first game. It was a masterstroke. He could still dazzle, and was still superbly fit and agile. Even at the age of 46, and in fact because he was 46, he put thousands on any attendance at every ground.

Manager Alan Brown's programme notes for the Burnley game as long ago as August 27th, 1955, referred to Matthews as someone who drew in the crowds. Published statistics showed that wherever Blackpool played the attendance was higher than average. There had been a game on the previous Monday at Turf Moor with Blackpool the opposition for whom Matthews then played. Blackpool won 2 – 0.

'Thank goodness Stanley Matthews turned out (a lot of false rumours had been about during the day that he would not play) and we did not have his absence to explain away… what an example the wizard of soccer is to every young player coming into the game. Here is a man at 40 years of age who can still draw the crowds more than any other single footballer. Why? The answer is clear. He is always trying to put everything he has into the game, subordinating his own ability to the good of the side. What glamour it brings to both, and what an example for old or young players of his day'. *(Alan Brown August 1955)*

Gates soared at Stoke and Waddington's team was transformed not just by Matthews, but by players like Jackie Mudie, Eddie Clamp, Dennis Viollett and then in March 1963, Jimmy McIlroy.

'Where now for the nimble, quick-witted inside forward, who has been the architect of Burnley since 1950', the *Sunday Express* asked? 'He is 32 next October. His years as a top player may be numbered, but he would still be invaluable to half a dozen First Division clubs and any number of lower league clubs who need an 'old head' to get their young and virile players playing the right way. Leyton Orient, Stoke, Luton Town, Preston, Bury are all certain to be keen'.

His wife Barbara, a Burnley girl, was equally stunned on learning that he had been transfer listed. She revealed her thoughts in the *Daily Express*. "Even when he said 'Barbara I'm on the list' it didn't dawn on me what he meant. But from 2.30 when phone calls started and people began coming to the house I realised how serious it was. He told me about the interview at the club when Mr Potts, the manager, had given him the impression that a player of his ability should not fall below a certain standard. That to me meant the club thought he was not good enough. That was the moment I realised what a serious matter it was to the family. It's a problem for Jimmy because obviously he can't just play football one day and then suddenly not want anything to do with it. Perhaps if he could have been put in the reserve team it would have prepared us for the day when he would have to give up the game. You believe it just can't happen to you. I don't know what the future will bring. He is only 31. He used to be a bricklayer. We shall not starve. No. No."

In the *Daily Mirror* she added: "If they had dropped him or given him a good telling off then we might have been prepared for something like this. It makes you think that somehow there must be something more to it. But I can't think what. Obviously there is no sentiment in football."

In the game that came in the immediate aftermath of the shock, Burnley beat Peterborough 3 – 1 in a 'friendly' match but Mike Langley described them as like a chicken without its head, a team with no brain, a team with no Jimmy McIlroy to coax the old, sweet rhythm out of Burnley. Like the old Wolves up front, and Hartlepools behind, he described them. Jimmy Adamson, he said, passed the ball absent-mindedly to where Jimmy McIlroy might have been. "You have to adapt to the players available," said manager Potts, when he was asked if McIlroy would play on Saturday against Sheffield United. "I don't think so," said Potts. It was clear that in the space of just days, McIlroy had become almost an outcast, *persona non grata*, though he did put on a brave face and return for training a couple of days later. In his tracksuit he ran onto the pitch that was covered in ice.

Sheffield Wednesday were the next club in the rumour mill, but the name that kept cropping up was Stoke City. With several clubs, McIlroy's salary was a stumbling block, but Stoke were already paying big money to some players. Jimmy meanwhile spoke about giving up football to concentrate on a business venture in town run by himself, his sister and her husband. The one thing he didn't want to do was leave Burnley. A player-manager role, such as had been suggested at Mansfield, did not appeal to him. As the days went by it began to emerge on the grapevine that he would not object to a move to Stoke City. He would maintain a high salary and there was a good chance of promotion to Division One.

The wrangling over a transfer fee began. Burnley allegedly wanted £35,000 according to the *Daily Mirror*. Stoke said "no." Their offer was reported as £20,000. The Burnley board met for three hours. The Press reported that Oldham Athletic joined in the queue to sign him. Stoke upped their offer from £20,000 to £25,000. Just 13 days remained to the transfer deadline of March 31st.

Burnley lost 0 – 1 at Sheffield United. "All the talk was about the man who wasn't there." McIlroy kicked his heels without a game anywhere. Bob Lord issued a challenge to Stoke City. "If Stoke come along again they have only to be a little reasonable to take Jimmy McIlroy back with them within the hour." No other club was anywhere near approaching the sum Burnley wanted. Jimmy's father Harry came across to visit him. By this time Jimmy, he said, was resigned to not playing for Burnley again but that he was determined to stay in Burnley and run his business. Peter Doherty telephoned him and lifted his spirits, telling him he would come out of it a better player. Everyone was hoping that the Stoke transfer would go through. Danny Blanchflower telephoned him. Matt Busby wrote in the *Daily Express* about it all. He firmly stated that it was time Burnley made their price clear to all clubs concerned, and criticised the lack of any clear figure. His last sentence about the sale was telling. "It is so controversial an action it will leave the football public puzzled for a long time." His lengthy piece was written with tact, courtesy and moderation, but it did not mask his damning indictment of the saga.

And then at last the negotiations were over. Stoke made their final offer. The fee was

# £25,000-PLUS

## End of marathon negotiations

### Writes KEITH McNEE

PAGE OF WEDDING PICTURES
See Page 3

**J**IMMY McILROY is no longer a Burnley player. He parted company with Turf Moor shortly before 10 o'clock last night when he signed for Stoke City, the club who have been favourites to sign him since the inside forward was placed on the open transfer list nine days ago.

The fee is believed to be more than £25,000 — the biggest received by Burnley since they transferred Brian Pilkington to Bolton exactly two years ago.

McIlroy, happy last night to be settled again after a week of speculation over his future, is expected to make his debut at Norwich on Saturday in a league match. He is not eligible to play for Stoke tonight in their F.A. Cup third round tie against Leeds United at Elland-road because he has already played for Burnley in the competition.

McIlroy, however, will be going to Leeds to watch his new colleagues in action.

### Third time lucky

Stoke City officials paid two visits to Turf Moor at the end of last week to discuss McIlroy's future. Neither visit brought them any real success, but it was a case of third time lucky.

After more talks by phone yesterday afternoon, Stoke chairman, Mr. Gordon Taylor, and manager, Mr. Tony Waddington, set off immediately for Turf Moor. They arrived at 7-45 p.m. —a few minutes before McIlroy himself. Also present at the signing were Burnley chairman, Mr. Bob Lord, and manager Mr. Harry Potts.

McIlroy who, of course, had the final say in the matter, spent just over an hour talking to Stoke officials before agreeing to sign. The Irishman will receive £300 players' transfer fee—payable because he did not ask for a move—plus his accrued share of benefit.

### "I'm very glad"

After their talks in the Turf Moor boardroom, managers Potts and Waddington, and McIlroy, emerged all smiles. McIlroy said, "I'm very glad it's all over and all settled. I'm very happy with the terms that have been offered me in every respect. I shall be living in Burnley, but I don't know yet whether I will be doing any more training at Turf Moor."

Yesterday's developments ended what had seemed to be a stalemate situation between Burnley and Stoke.

On Sunday, Mr. Lord said: " It is up to Stoke now. They know the figure we want for McIlroy. If they want him, they should come and get him. Stoke only have to be a little reasonable about this."

At almost the same time Mr. Henshall was saying: "The ball is in Burnley's half of the field. There will definitely be no further increase to our last offer."

In between the two was McIlroy. He spent a quiet weekend at his home in Rosehill-avenue, altering his decision to watch a match when he heard that his father, Mr. Harry McIlroy, was coming to Burnley from Belfast to talk things over.

Before training on Monday, McIlroy made it clear that of the clubs that had shown interest in him Stoke was the only one he would like to join.

He told me on Monday: " I wish things would get moving because I am beginning to feel restless. I am itching to get back into action, and it was all the worse when I read the Sunday papers and realised how much I was out of things."

McIlroy did not have long to wait. Burnley and Stoke got together again yesterday, and the deal was settled soon after the arrival at Turf Moor of Stoke chairman Mr. Gordon Taylor and manager Mr. Waddington.

I estimate that with the cheque for McIlroy Burnley will have received about £140,000 in transfer fees in less than four years.

Since inside-forward Albert Cheesebrough joined Leicester City in June, 1959, for a £20,000 fee, the club has received big fees for Brian Pilkington (to Bolton for about £25,000 in March, 1961); Jimmy Furnell (to Liverpool for about £15,000 in February, 1962); Ian Lawson (to Leeds United for about £20,000 in February, 1962); and Ronnie Fenton (to West Bromwich Albion for £17,000 in November, 1962).

Additionally, Burnley has received fees for Bobby Seith, Duggie Newlands, Bill Marshall, David Smith, Billy White and Jimmy Scott. These have brought in something like £18,000.

### 50 " caps "

McIlroy, now 31, joined Burnley in 1949 from Irish League club Glentoran for a fee of about £7,500. He made his First Division debut against Sunderland at Roker Park on October 21st, 1950, and since then has played in 439 league games for the Clarets, scoring 115 goals.

McIlroy has also played in more than 40 F.A. Cup-ties, and four European Cup ties during his time at Burnley. He is one of three Northern Irishmen to have gained more than 50 international "caps," the others being Danny Blanchflower (Spurs) and Billy Bingham (Everton).

*MRS. PEGGY GIBBONS, a Turf Moor cleaner, bids McIlroy good-bye at the ground last night.*

agreed between the two clubs and McIlroy agreed his personal terms and salary with Stoke officials. He received just £300 himself because he had not asked for the transfer, and £600 accrued share of a third benefit. Compare that with today's obscene figures associated with the top players. Waddington had a severe cold and would normally have stayed in bed it was so bad. He had already been to Burnley twice but this third meeting was the crucial one. He was not going to miss the opportunity to add another piece to his jigsaw puzzle.

MAC FOR STOKE AT £25,000-PLUS, was the headline. Potts, Waddington and McIlroy emerged, all smiles, from the room where the signing had taken place and the player whom manager Potts had described as not giving 100% effort, would by the end of the season have a Division Two winner's medal.

"I feel happy and proud to be joining a club with such wonderful traditions as Stoke," said McIlroy. "I cannot wait to get out there with them. They are in the home straight and have sighted the First Division at the end of it. Another great thing is that I shall be playing alongside the man I consider to be the greatest ball-player I have ever seen. Five of the other players I know very well. I have always looked upon Dennis Viollett as a fine player and a wonderful opportunist. I am also looking forward to linking up with one of the friendliest chaps in the game, Jackie Mudie. I shall have players such as Eddie Clamp, Eddie Stuart and Tony Allen behind me. There are good youngsters on the assembly line. Now I am leaving I want to remember only the good times I have had at Turf Moor. I am very happy with all the terms. I am happy it is all over."

In signing the contract he admitted to having the same butterflies in his stomach that he had had years earlier when he had signed for Burnley. The transfer fee was the highest Burnley had received for any player. Ironically, not that much earlier, they had allegedly refused an £80,000 bid from an Italian club.

In between the transfer listing and the move to Stoke, Jimmy wrote in the Press about this traumatic time. It was a candid, dramatic and revealing piece, and certainly made people sit up. It suggested that since the abolition of the common maximum wage, the first ripples of disharmony might have been appearing at the club and that one or two younger players might have been just a little resentful of his star status and higher salary, now that the maximum wage system had been abolished. He likened himself to a general without a baton. It was an eyebrow-raising article.

*"With my future at Burnley possibly limited to days, I have had time to realise that the lift in the pay packet can be a problem that causes tremendous difficulties in many ways for clubs. Are Burnley, in their decision to part with me because they need the cash, setting a trend that other clubs find they will have to follow. Is the pace getting too hot? I will be frank. There has been talk among many clubs of dissension, of discontent, because of the differences in wages. The ink had hardly dried on my contract 18 months ago when it seemed someone made the discovery that I was Burnley's highest paid player.*

*The pessimists and the knockers, and there were a few of them around, at once cried that it would not work. They thought everyone should be paid the same in the Burnley team. My answer was: 'That seems logical when everyone's transfer value is the same'.*

*We have always boasted about the Burnley team spirit being the best. It has been good. But I feel it is no better and no worse than any other team experiencing a similar amount of success. Recently – if it is not due to my imagination – I feel there have been little ripples of dissension in the camp. There have been rumours about the boys, for what rumours are worth, and these bits of chatter have indicated that one or two of the lads are unhappy to find themselves earning less than Jimmy McIlroy.*

*Can I say that there are two ways to look at it? Eighteen months ago they all came out of the manager's office beaming and happy with two-year contracts they signed. Can I now say it is only right for them to honour those contracts? Their angle could be that they feel they are playing as well or better than me, and are entitled to equal reward. And that spells trouble for any club. I can see the pessimists over the lifting of the maximum wage pressing their noses into this and murmuring: "Ah we said team spirit would suffer."*

*This topic was included in my discussion with chairman Lord. His idea, with which I agree, is that it might take a year or two longer for the position to iron itself out. It seems I've been included in the ironing already. One thing is very clear in my mind. The strain on the wages will increase. Demands will grow for better terms.*

*In trying to imagine the attitude of the rest of the team towards Jimmy McIlroy, I am led to the conclusion that a lot of these boys have been living in the shadow of McIlroy and Jimmy Adamson. For a number of years when Burnley have done well, the lion's share of the publicity has gone to us two. The rest of the lads must have felt grossly under-estimated. Will they feel happier now; will their play improve, now that Jimmy McIlroy is 'on his way'? Is it possible there will be new life in the team when I am gone, and good results? I am not kidding myself that there won't be.*

*I am sure a 'Super-League' is on the way. Obviously Burnley want a part of the big-time. The new stand project is designed for that purpose. But they may be with a number of other clubs at this stage finely balanced on the scales as they attempt to live with the giants who have much greater financial assets. I forecast a dramatic pruning of the playing staff before the end of the season.*

*In case you have heard that McIlroy is a cocky type, and have misunderstood, as others seem to have done, let me refer to two of my biggest mistakes during my stay at Burnley. Like a bell ringing an alarm I realise now that I have been wrong to hint and talk jokingly about being a veteran. It seems some folk have the wrong image of McIlroy in their minds. Some may have come to believe it.*

*But my biggest mistake was to allow myself to develop a complex. I have always been a noisy player, shouting, bullying some might call it, pleading. Just to get the best out of others. But there comes a time when some of them tell you to shut up and tell you in no uncertain way. And you do just that. And my mistake was this: I decided that I was going to stop all this. That I was going to stop trying to impress my personality on them. I would move on as usual into the open space and hope their ability or intelligence would help them find me. In that time I became a general without a baton. I feel that the team and I have suffered from it. I think it has been a grave error.*

*As I told Mr Lord, Burnley has been good to me. I like to think I have repaid them. I don't think we owe each other anything.*

(Jimmy McIlroy March 1963)

# Chapter Fourteen

# With Matthews At Stoke

AMONGST JIMMY MCILROY'S many attributes is a delicious sense of humour with an instant, understated dry wit. When I mentioned that Billy Bingham (of whom he talks with great affection) was to be Burnley's new Northern Ireland scout, Jimmy smiled and suggested: "Well, he might find that difficult. He lives in Southport."

Then, the news broke in Burnley that life-long supporter Harry Brooks had written to the town's chief executive to request that Jimmy be made a Freeman of the Borough. "I don't know what it means," said Jimmy, "except that I'm told I can graze cattle anywhere in the town and the last person to receive this honour died in 1882."

Back in 1969, Jimmy Mac's hurt had grown regarding his transfer six years earlier. By 1969 he had played for Stoke City, and had been Oldham Athletic player-manager. From there he had returned to Stoke as coach. But in 1969 the pain of the move still wounded him. He had chosen not to move house, and remained in Burnley, still residing in the place he loved and in which he felt so at home. Burnley won the FA Youth Cup in 1968 but true to form, the best of the players would be sold one by one as the years went by. Lord was still chairman. Potts was still manager, just. He would be moved upstairs, as the saying goes, in 1970, into a meaningless role that reduced him to feeling unwanted and superfluous, replaced by Jimmy Adamson who simply wanted him out of the way. Adamson eventually got his wish, and Potts received a handsome pay-off but a broken heart. Jimmy Mac meanwhile poured out his thoughts on paper.

"Seven thousand fans turned their backs on Burnley Football Club the day I was given away to Stoke City for £25,000," he wrote. He listed all the players that the club had sold, described the furore following his own sale, criticised Bob Lord, and outlined that the greatest hurt he felt was when it was said he'd become complacent and "didn't give enough effort." He stated he didn't believe the reasons given or that it was Potts' decision. He spoke to Lord for an hour and a half in his butcher's factory but all Lord could say was: "What's been done is in the best interests of the club. There was a mention for John Cook (still in 2009, his closest friend); that Lord didn't like this friendship, or the fact that after matches, it was Cook's car not the team coach, that took Jimmy home.

And then Jimmy turned to the topic of Wembley and how he suspected that it was on this day that Lord decided "I was of no further use to Burnley. He wanted desperately to win that Final and he expected Jimmy Mac to turn it on and set Wembley rejoicing in the Cup glories of Burnley." By his own admission McIlroy did not have a good game and nine months later he was gone. He answered the charge of "not trying" by describing how for months he had played with injuries, held together by strapping in the last weeks of the Championship season. At Maine Road in the final game he could hardly walk, "yet I turned out."

## Top-left programme

OFFICIAL PROGRAMME 6d.

№ 2539

Telephone: Stoke-on-Trent 44660    FOUNDED 1863    Telegrams: "Football," Stoke-on-Trent

# STOKE CITY

## FOOTBALL CLUB (1908) CO. LTD.

Directors: G. W. Taylor, (Chairman) C. T. Salmon (Vice-Chairman) G. G. Crowe, F.R.C.S., T. L. Duddell, A. A. Henshall,    Manager: Tony Waddington    Secretary: W. C. Williams

## Top-right programme

# BURNLEY

## FOOTBALL CLUB

### SEASON 1963-64

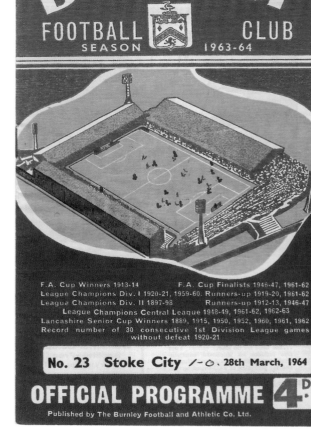

F.A. Cup Winners 1913-14      F.A. Cup Finalists 1946-47, 1961-62
League Champions Div. I 1920-21, 1959-60. Runners-up 1919-20, 1961-62
League Champions Div. II 1897-98      Runners-up 1912-13, 1946-47
League Champions Central League 1948-49, 1961-62, 1962-63
Lancashire Senior Cup Winners 1889, 1915, 1950, 1952, 1960, 1961, 1962
Record number of 30 consecutive 1st Division League games
without defeat 1920-21

No. 23   Stoke City   /- ○ . 28th March, 1964

## OFFICIAL PROGRAMME   4D.

Published by The Burnley Football and Athletic Co. Ltd.

## Bottom-left programme

# STOKE CITY

versus
## BURNLEY

at Victoria Ground
Tuesday, 27th December, 1966
Kick-off 3-15 p.m.

OFFICIAL PROGRAMME 6D

## Bottom-right programme

OFFICIAL PROGRAMME 3d.

№ 4900

Telephone: Stoke-on-Trent 44660    FOUNDED 1863    Telegrams: "Football," Stoke-on-Trent

# STOKE CITY

## FOOTBALL CLUB (1908) CO. LTD.

Directors: G. W. Taylor, (Chairman) C. T. Salmon (Vice-Chairman) G. G. Crowe, F.R.C.S., T. L. Duddell, A. A. Henshall,    Manager: Tony Waddington    Secretary: W. C. Williams

### STOKE CITY

Red and White Stripes    White Shorts

LESLIE

ASPREY (2)      ALLEN (3)

SKEELS (4)    STUART (5)    CLAMP (6)

BRIDGWOOD (7)   DOBING (8)   RITCHIE (9)   McILROY (10)   BEBBINGTON(11)

Referee:
L. J. HAMER
(Bolton)

Linesmen :—
H. Hodson
Yellow Flag
K. A. Winfield
Red Flag

EVANS, B. (11)   McLAUGHLIN (10)   THOMAS (9)   DRAPER (8)   JONES (7)

WILLIAMS (6)    PURCELL (5)    JOHNSON (4)

HUGHES (3)      EVANS, R. (2)

DWYER

White Shirts    White Shorts

### SWANSEA TOWN

_F.A. CUP FIFTH ROUND_

VERSUS

# SWANSEA TOWN

SATURDAY, 15th FEBRUARY, 1964.      Kick-off 3 p.m.

"Hardly any big name is sold without a bust-up," he revealed. Lord's long-running feuds with the Press got a mention, how Gordon Harris was not allowed to write for a local newspaper. After that, the players joked that they weren't even allowed to advertise their houses for sale in some newspapers. "It's so difficult to reconcile that kind of thing with the continual talk of Burnley being a happy family club." In his opinion that atmosphere started to disappear the day he was put on the transfer list "without even a thankyou for services rendered."

He even had difficulty prising his FA Cup bonus from the club after he left. They had beaten Spurs 3 – 0 and were promised £100. It took him six months to get it paid. Lord affected surprise that he should be asked: "After all I've done for you!"

"I don't know what that was supposed to be," said McIlroy," except giving the lads a turkey apiece at Christmas."

"That £100 helped cheer me up on some of those foggy or snowy mornings when I crawled down 66 miles of roads to Stoke. I needed cheering up because from the moment Burnley put me up for sale, a lot of the joy went out of my football."

If there were any consolations, and any reward for the long drive in all weathers to Stoke every day; one was winning a Division Two medal with Stoke, the second was reaching the League Cup Final the following season, and perhaps the best of all was the opportunity to play alongside Stanley Matthews. But Matthews was not the only great player there. There was Jackie Mudie and Dennis Viollett. In defence there were ex Wolves players Eddie Stuart and the formidable Eddie Clamp. At full back was England international Tony Allen. McIlroy rated Viollet, the ex Manchester United man, highly and at United he had played against him and seen him close up several times. He rated him in the Jimmy Greaves class as a striker.

"His nickname was 'Tricky' and I never knew whether it was a result of his football skills or his lifestyle. Dennis survived the crash (Munich) and afterwards became one of the finest strikers in the Football League. He possessed the essential gift all natural goalscorers require – an icy coolness in front of goal. It was something I lacked because I was much cooler in possession back on my own six-yard line. It was only when I joined Stoke City that I really got to know the man. Dennis was one of manager Tony Waddington's shrewdest signings and he quickly became a favourite at the Victoria Ground. In analysing Dennis's skills it is difficult to single out any one that could be described as brilliant or world-class. His strength lay in the fact that he was a superb all-round striker. He was nippy without being lightning fast, good but not brilliant in the air. His awareness of situations was first class and there weren't many in top class football who could find the net as consistently from half chances. On top of all this he was a nice person. There was nothing vicious or nasty in his play; I cannot ever recall Dennis ever being involved in a single vengeful tackle. I admired the man immensely." In the 1962/63 promotion season he scored 23 goals in 37 appearances.

If Viollett was a 'gentleman' on the field, Eddie Clamp more than made up for it. Someone said he would have made Liverpool's Tommy Smith look a namby-pamby. His name was appropriate. A tackle from him with his legs wrapped round an opponent's limbs, was not unlike a car wheel being clamped, except twice as painful. He set himself to be Stanley Matthews 'minder' and his revenge on Chelsea's Ron 'Chopper' Harris in the away game at Chelsea is the stuff of which legends are made.

Don Radcliffe was another of the characters in the Stoke dressing room. "Then there was

Eddie Clamp," said Radcliffe in Simon Lowe's book *Match of My Life*. "Clampy was probably the hardest man I knew. At corners I used to put the ball down to take them and look up to see what he was up to, because I knew that he would be on the lookout for whoever had annoyed him that game. If he found him, he'd wait to see when the ref was looking over at me and the ball, and then head-butt the player. Well, I knew what he was going to do so when I saw him getting near a player I'd quickly take the corner, so the referee was definitely looking my way and wouldn't see what Eddie was up to.

"I remember this one time we played and the other team had this wing-half called Colin Webster who used to play for Manchester United and was one of the original Busby Babes. He had broken full-back George Bourne's leg while playing for United's reserves. It was an injury which finished George. Eddie had heard about this and decided that retribution was in order. Bear in mind that the incident had happened several years earlier, well before Eddie was at the club.

"Anyway at half-time we were walking down the tunnel at Swansea's old ground, the Vetch Field. In the tunnel there was this girder at head height, I'd say about 6 foot 2 inches. It was obvious, as they'd put a sign on it saying, 'Please mind your head'. As we came off the pitch, I was walking behind Webster, with Eddie behind me. Next minute, Clampy grabbed my by the back of the neck, picked me up and put me behind him so he could be next to Webster. He taps Webster on the back and as the lad turns round Eddie's smacked him with his head – right in the middle of his face. His nose was spread all over the place.

"We went into the dressing rooms and the referee comes in and says, 'Mr Clamp, I've heard that you head-butted Webster'.

'No sir, he banged his head on that girder'.

Clamp had played for Wolves and Arsenal before he arrived at Stoke and joked that although he might not be such a good player, he would always manage to pass to a red striped shirt. On the field he was the hardest man in the game. Off the field he was a wonderful man, said Matthews, with nothing but love for his fellow man. "His heart was as big as a bucket." When he arrived in the dressing room he sat by Stan and told him there were some naughty players about; he knew that because he had been one of them, he said. "The days of players kicking you black and blue are over," he told Stan, "because from now on I'm going to look after you."

Clamp stood by the statue of Matthews when it was unveiled at Stoke and, according to Jimmy Greaves; he told Stan that it was the perfect statue. It was too high for dogs to piss on and too low for the pigeons to crap on. It was typical of Clamp to make others laugh with his stories, delivery and antics, says Matthews. Win, lose or draw he lifted other players' spirits.

Matthews had a little story that involved Jimmy McIlroy as well. Playing for England at Wembley, Duncan Edwards set off on a dribble that took him past several Irish players. He passed the ball to Tommy Taylor who then thumped it home. One of the England reserves sitting in the stands, Frank Blunstone of Chelsea, jumped and shouted so loud that his set of false upper teeth shot out of his mouth and landed several rows away. He never found them. "Frank, says Matthews, "never got them back, but Jimmy McIlroy reckons he met a man in County Cork who is still wearing them."

Attendances and belief had soared since the return of Stan to Stoke. They had been in the doldrums for several years until Tony Waddington assembled his team of 'pensioners'.

35, 974 had crammed into the ground to see his homecoming at the age of 46. But Waddington refuted the suggestion that this was a team of 'old crocks' insisting that he only signed 'thoroughbreds'. Having gathered them, Waddington's skill was in letting them get on with the job. How could you possibly coach players like Clamp, Matthews, Mudie, Viollett and McIlroy. They had been doing the job for years. Add to the mix Republic of Ireland international goalkeeper Jimmy O' Neil signed from Everton, home grown Don Radcliffe, Eric Skeels who went on to play 606 games for the club, and Tony Allen, and you had a top class team. The defence was known as 'Waddington's Wall'.

The 1962/63 in Division Two season at Stoke City started badly. The opening game at Leeds was lost and there was no victory for the next six games. At last in September Charlton were beaten 6 – 3 at Stoke. Dennis Viollet scored four of the goals. They then went 18 games unbeaten until Leeds United ended that run. By March they were battling it out for top place with Chelsea and Sunderland. It was at that point that McIlroy arrived. Just behind were Leeds United, Middlesbrough and Huddersfield Town. His debut game was a nightmare and Stoke lost 0 – 6 to Norwich City. Waddington had put Jimmy on the right side of midfield and he was a nonentity. Losing 0 – 6 and played out of position McIlroy wondered what on earth he had let himself in for. For the next game he was moved to his favoured inside-forward position. The change worked immediately and the next game was won 4 – 1. It took them back to the top. At Easter there were three games in four days to play. This was standard practice in those days. Two of them were against rivals Sunderland. 62,138 watched a 0 – 0 draw at Roker Park. 30,000 saw Stoke win 1 - 0 at Cardiff City. Next came the return game against Sunderland. Viollet gave Stoke the lead, a draw seemed likely but a late penalty decision went Stoke's way and Viollet scored.

Promotion was really there for the taking and the excitement in the Potteries mounted. 42,366 people watched the Sunderland game. Not that long ago they had been lucky to get crowds of 8000. Matthews had put Stoke back on the map. Momentum grew.

All this was against the background of the harsh winter of 1963. It had played havoc with fixtures. At Burnley it was the fateful reason why the Liverpool replay was delayed after which McIlroy had been transfer listed. The season was extended and would not end until May 22nd so that in the final four weeks Stoke played seven games. After Easter three games had been lost but Chelsea and Sunderland also dropped points. Everything was set up for a major game at Chelsea. It was too soon to say that the winner would win promotion as a matter of course, but neither side could afford to lose. The date was May 11th.

Stan Matthews describes the day in his autobiography and he begins by saying how tense the dressing room was. It was silent and nervous so Eddie Clamp was asked to stand up and tell one of his long stories to relieve the mood. On completion of the story which ended with them all rocking with laughter, the mood was lifted.

When they went out the crowd was 66,199 and thousands were outside unable to get in. Ron Harris tried unsuccessfully to put Matthews out of the game and Eddie Clamp took his revenge on the young upstart; and it was Jimmy McIlroy who scored the winning goal.

Because of the treatment dished out to him by Harris, Matthews missed the next game. They surprisingly lost it at Bury. Football is like that. A win would have won them promotion. The final game was at home to Luton. 34,000 fans crammed themselves in. A Jackie Mudie goal put them 1 – 0 up and then the scene was set for a Matthews fairytale ending. The man was 47 years old and latching onto a long through ball, rounded the goalkeeper and slid the ball home. 34,000 fans were ecstatic. Promotion was won. The script was perfect and Matthews was voted 'Footballer of the Year'.

But who was it that made the final goal in the Luton game with a perfect through ball for him to run on to? It was Jimmy McIlroy.

In *Match of my Life: Editor Simon Lowe*, sixteen Stoke players relive great games in which they have played. Tony Allen tells the story of Chelsea 0 Stoke City 1, the game that effectively set Stoke up to win promotion. And who scored the solitary goal? It was Jimmy McIlroy.

'We had a fantastic climax to the season with the trip to Chelsea assuming huge importance. It was a vital, vital game. Remember Stoke hadn't won promotion for thirty odd years. Most people couldn't even remember it. And it had been ten years since they had played in the top flight. Before Stan came, the crowds were around the 6-8,000 mark. The club had been in dire straits, but now we were on the verge of some success. Promotion fever was everywhere around the city...

...The great news was that Stan (Matthews) and Dennis (Viollet) were both fit for Chelsea. Our side was at full strength. The week before the game, Stan had been named as Footballer of the Year. That was a red rag to a bull as far as Ron Harris was concerned. He was a young whipper-snapper back then, full of cockney mouth and he publicly declared that he would sort Matthews out. He was beginning to style himself as the 'Chopper' although I don't think the nickname was widely in use at that stage, as he'd only played a few games in their first team over the past couple of years.

He spent the first few minutes of the match trying to kick Stan as hard as he could. Stan hurdled the challenges and avoided most of the kicks, but then Harris connected viciously. That was when Eddie Clamp came into his own. Clampy was a very hard man on the football pitch. I was scared of him and he was on my side! Apparently Eddie and Ron had had their differences during a game when Eddie was at Wolves the season before, so they knew each other well. After Harris had fouled Stan, Clampy goes over to him and says, "You leave him alone now or you'll have me to answer to." And he did leave Stan alone after that, although mainly because he didn't get near him'.

Jimmy Greaves has a different version of events. ' "Listen you little sod," said Clamp menacingly, "if I see you clobber our Stanley again, you'll be taken out of this game on a bloody stretcher." Trouble is Harris continued to clobber Matthews until at last one savage tackle almost took him out of the game. Clamp bristled and fixed his eyes on Harris the next time he had the ball. Clampy took off as hard as a bag of concrete and the tackle was like nothing ever seen before as Harris rose into the air like he was on a springboard. Even after 30 years in the game Matthews reckoned he had never seen a tackle like it as the ball disappeared into the crowd and Harris came back down to earth only semi-conscious. Clamp then stood toweringly over the inert Harris. "I told thee what would happen lad," he snarled. "Next time I won't play the ball first and they'll just slide the stretcher under thee. I always keep a promise." After the game Clamp and Harris shared a beer, Stan had a tomato juice and they all had a good laugh. That's how football was back in those days'.

Harris just wanted to kick Matthews. He'd said so in the papers before-hand, so we knew what he was up to. He was young then and wanted to make a name for himself, but it ended up with his own crowd booing him. They didn't like it at all. They'd actually come to see Matthews play as much as Chelsea win. You wouldn't get that these days, and it

Jimmy's first game back at Turf Moor following his transfer to Stoke City, March 1964. The attendance doubled.

Toss-up with John Angus. "Look at those short shorts", said Jimmy when he saw the picture recently. "They look three sizes too small".

shows you how Matthews captured people's imagination during his career. Even at 48, people wanted to see him play. He had that sort of presence and that aura about him after everything he'd done in his career.....

.....Waddington had set us up to play it tight and look to score on the break. A classic away tactic, I suppose. It worked and we frustrated Chelsea.... Mainly we kept working the ball out to Stan who was tormenting Harris, leaving him on the ground as he tried to make more and more desperate challenges. I remember there is a fantastic picture of Stan in that match. He's running along with Ron Harris lying strewn on the ground having missed the tackle as Stan swerved past him and Eddie McCreadie is looking on in total astonishment in the background. He really did take them totally to the cleaners.

It was from one of these attacks that we finally did score. Matthews passed to Jackie Mudie, who nudged it on to Jimmy McIlroy, arriving on the edge of the area with immaculate timing. He drove the ball right-footed across Bonetti hard and in off the far post. It was a really well worked goal and it hit Chelsea hard, coming about ten minutes before the break.....

.....It was the best performance as a football team that I ever played in. It was a brilliant performance, absolutely brilliant. We deserved to win. And they had a good side out I can tell you.....

..... They were the side that at the start of the season, if you'd put money on anyone going up, it would have been them.... ...The final whistle sounded and we knew we'd pulled off a fantastic result, one which put us right in control of our destiny and that was what we wanted. Better still, it hurt Chelsea, one of our nearest rivals. It was an unbelievable gate of over 66,000. That was the biggest in London outside Wembley all season, and for a Second Division game, but I loved the atmosphere. It was extremely special, and made all the more so because there were thousands of Stoke fans there, who travelled down to cheer us on......

.....We now knew we just needed one more win to guarantee promotion. But to top it all we went to Bury three days later and lost.....

*(Adapted from the Tony Allen chapter, Match of my Life: Know the Score 2007)*

Goalkeeper Jimmy O'Neil tells the story of the tail-end of the season and the final nail-biting game at home to Luton:

'We did need to relax on this occasion, because I think the Bury game had got to us a bit. Mind you, people forget that this was a vital one for Luton too. They needed to win to stand any chance of staying up. They had some good players too, Ron Baynham, Fred Jardine and Ron Davies.

Stan was really buzzing around that day. He used to come back to the penalty area and take the ball from me. But I didn't really like to give it to him, because he'd always have a full-back closely marking him, so I was a bit worried he'd lose the ball.

But that day he turned on another magnificent performance, he had players sliding to unbalance them and he'd be past them. He had incredible balance. Luton didn't know what was going on. Remember it was the middle of May, and they came up with moulded studs on expecting the pitch to be bone dry. In those days you didn't often go out onto the pitch beforehand, so Luton came out just before the game with their moulds on and quickly realised what a quagmire it was and they all had to go back to change their boots.

We had a lucky escape when their left winger Jardine got away and crossed right in

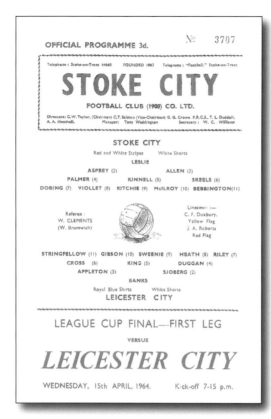

front of us, but their centre-forward couldn't quite reach it, thankfully. I remember how pent up the tension felt in the crowd. The supporters were desperate for us to win, to achieve promotion in front of them that day, and you could cut the atmosphere with a knife. That transmitted itself to the players, I think, as the game was played at a slow pace with a lot of mistakes. The mud didn't help of course.

It was obvious that a flash of inspiration was needed and we had enough quality within our team to provide it. Jackie Mudie had already gone close from one goalmouth scramble, but his shot had been beaten away. When the same thing happened a couple of minutes later, he remained composed and managed to drill the ball past the defenders on the line. I was at the other end, so I couldn't really see what was going on in the melee. All I knew was that the ball hit the net and we were one up.

We got through to the second half unscathed, without too many problems actually. In fact we should have had a nerve-settling second, but Jackie snatched at a better chance than the one he'd scored when Dennis Viollet set him up and he skied the ball over the top. But we couldn't have started the second half any better.

Luton pressed forward straight from the kick-off as they needed to score quickly, but the attack was broken up and the ball fell to Jimmy McIlroy to start a counter-attack. Out of the corner of his eye he spotted one Stanley Matthews haring down the middle of the field, over the mud and puddles as if he was seventeen again. Stan still had a fair turn of speed and he used it on this occasion.

Jimmy found the perfect through ball for Stan to run onto just inside the Luton half and then what happened was pure poetry in motion. Stan raced through the middle with the ball glued to his right foot and about six Luton players all chasing after him, all desperate to stop him. Stan dropped his shoulders so the keeper went down on the edge of the area and then waltzed round him to the left to slide the ball into the net at the Boothen End. It was a truly great goal.

To say the crowd went berserk is an understatement. Delirious, crazy, you name it. The noise was immense. And the release of emotion was incredible too. We knew that was it. And what more fitting player to score the goal that returned Stoke to the top flight than Stan? We didn't really celebrate goals in those days – not like they do today with the choreographed routines and all that malarkey – but Stan was fair mobbed by the lads as he made his way back to the half-way line. Stan was such a cool character that he didn't show emotion on the pitch either, but you could see how exhilarated he was by that goal.

We still had half the match to play of course, but it was to all intents and purposes over. Luton knew they could not score three and we pretty much played out time as they got

The Stoke City promotion team of 1963. Stanley Matthews, middle row, far left, and Eddie Clamp, back row second left. Manager Waddington end right.

used to the idea of being relegated to Division Three. We then heard that Sunderland had been beaten at home 1 – 0 by Chelsea and that meant that we were promoted as Champions. The crowd spilled onto the pitch and mobbed us. I can't remember what happened then. It's all a blur after all these years, but it was wonderful. We eventually managed to get back into the dressing rooms, with the help of some policemen, I think, and then were brought up into the new main stand to wave our thanks to the thousands of people who were now on the pitch. They were chanting "We Want Stan," and quite right too. His goal was the icing on a special cake for everyone at the club, but especially the supporters who had seen the club almost dead on its knees before Stan's return in 1961…  *(adapted from Jimmy O'Neil Match of My Life, 2007).*

I wonder if Jimmy Mac thought about Billy Dougal after that Matthews goal. The goal is on a short clip on *Youtube* if you just do a search on Stanley Matthews. The mud is ankle deep, the conditions horrendous. But there in hazy, faded black and white is Jimmy McIlroy in his own half with the ball. The commentator calls his name and the ball is played through the middle with perfect timing, weight and precision for Matthews to run onto. He runs without another Stoke shirt near him, streaks away from the defenders and rounds the goalkeeper. McIlroy has played Billy Dougal's perfect pass, the perfect ball.

Stoke City were promoted to Division One and incredibly in their first game it was Jimmy Mac who scored both goals.

Promotion, of course, meant that Jimmy McIlroy would return to Turf Moor in season

1963/64 and would play also against Burnley at the Victoria Ground. But before that three coach loads of Burnley supporters made the journey to Stoke City to see their first game in Division One. They went home happily. McIlroy scored both goals as Stoke beat Tottenham 2 – 1.

'At 4-55 this afternoon a roar burst from the Victoria Grounds, Stoke, which was calculated to lift the roof off every house in the vicinity. Stoke City, back in the First Division after ten years' absence, had defeated Tottenham Hotspur, one of the European soccer "greats." And Jimmy McIlroy, pride of Ireland and Stoke, who does not normally hit the headlines as a goal-scorer, was the hero of the day.

Jimmy likes to play deep, laying on his immaculate service of passes for the goal-minded boys. But in front of 44,000 football fanatics, McIlroy scored two wonderful first-half goals to win the match for Stoke and to launch his club into First Division football with a real bang.

"Mac the Knife" scored his first in the 16th minute after the ageless Stanley Matthews had floated over a perfect cross from the left wing. McIlroy had little room to force his shot home, but it was enough, and Spurs' goal scored in the very first minute by Bobby Smith was equalised.

Only half a minute of the first half remained when McIlroy got the all-important winner. This time it was new recruit Peter Dobing who centred the ball after a typical breakaway. McIlroy charged through the middle to score with a first time shot.

Apart from these great goals, McIlroy turned in a tremendous performance as the complete inside-forward. Stoke's other Irishman, ex-Linfield 'keeper Bobby Irvine, also had a good first match of the season.

Although Irvine had little to do against a disappointing Spurs side, he was under tremendous pressure in the closing 15 minutes. Spurs went all out for the equaliser Irvine took some hefty knocks, but he did not put a foot wrong or a hand wrong in 90 minutes.

City, in fact, were masters from start to finish. If Dennis Viollet had played as well as inside colleagues McIlroy and Peter Dobing, Tottenham could have been on the end of a severe beating.

Brown, Baker, Norman and Henry were the only Tottenham players to turn in really useful performances. Blanchflower, Mackay, Greaves and Jones, all these great names, often looked like third-raters. Yes, it was a great First Division come-back for Stoke City; emphatic winners on merit against a team rated possibly the best outfit in the British Isles.' *(Unknown newspaper report)*

Stoke City comfortably held their own in Division One. They reached the final of the Football League Cup, but were beaten over two legs by Leicester City. It was the nearest Jimmy Mac got to further honours and slowly his career was winding down. But that season was still a success; he scored 13 goals which made him third highest scorer and his presence along with the other star names had the added spin-off of attracting good young players to the club so that a youth policy could be developed.

But the following season the end of his first-class career was nearing, and perhaps the saddest headline followed an end of season game in 1965 at Turf Moor when Stoke were beaten 1 – 0 by a lacklustre Burnley. *'Sad return for McIlroy'* was the headline and it referred more to his performance than the final result.

'This was not by any means the brilliant, piercing McIlroy the Burnley fans once cheered. Only so very, very infrequently did we see McIlroy as the maestro. The Irishman looked anything but the master craftsman in the face of tigerish tackling', wrote John Leonard in one Sunday paper.

Keith McNee was even more blunt in the local Press with a particularly poignant headline. *'McIlroy legend dies in a scrappy game'*. His summary did not make happy reading.

'As for McIlroy this was no happy return to the Turf. In fact it was the worst game I have ever seen him play. The Irish star showed one or two flashes of ball skill early on, without ever looking really dangerous. In the second half he was rarely seen. Those who went to see Mac put one over on his former colleagues must have been most disappointed. His languid performance killed the lingering McIlroy legend'.

He would play several more games for Stoke City until January, 1966. But the twilight of his playing career had truly arrived in that April game at Turf Moor.

As 1965 drew to a close he felt sure it was time to end his playing days. He was by then 34 years old, his body ached after every game; he knew the end was approaching. Training was getting more and more difficult, in fact for some time he had trained alone in and around Burnley only travelling to Stoke just once in the week. His last game for Stoke City, with supreme irony, was against Burnley on December 27th, Stoke won 3 – 1.

He hung up his playing boots (or so he thought) and joined the Stoke City coaching staff keen to stay in football and pass on his knowledge gained over 15 years of playing at the top level. Yes he would like to enter management one day and a coaching position at Stoke was the start with Tony Waddington an ideal mentor. His keenest desire was to bring out the best in the young players and to put into practice all his feelings about the game – that you concentrate on what players are good at, that it is a waste of time to concentrate on weaknesses that are never going to get that much better, that too much rigid coaching stifles and restricts natural talent.

So strong were his beliefs that he had once failed an FA coaching course when he challenged the dogma and theories of the 'establishment'.

And then Ken Bates came into his life. In January 1966, just days after accepting the Stoke coaching role, he became manager of Oldham Athletic starting another chapter in his soccer career.

# Chapter Fifteen

# Management, Oldham and Bolton

I WAS WITH Jimmy again. A few days earlier he had returned from a golfing holiday in Spain. The travelling would have taxed anyone. He'd flown out to Spain for a few days, then flown from Spain to Belfast as a guest of the Irish FA to watch a World Cup game. Then the day after that it was fly back to Spain and a few days later had flown back to England.

During a break from going over some of the things that needed checking and changing, he mentioned he had received a letter from Burnley Borough Council. Nobody was supposed to have heard the information the letter contained but somehow the news was out and it genuinely filled him with concern.

The night before I visited him, there had been a Carling Cup-tie at Burnley and Burnley had beaten the Premiership side, Fulham, with one single goal scored with just three minutes to go.

Fellow Irish international Willie Irvine had greeted Jimmy at Turf Moor before the game and congratulated him. "How on earth did he know?" said Jimmy. But the news was indeed out; Jimmy was to be invited to become a Freeman of the Borough and at the end of the week he would be visited by a representative of the Council to discuss it and to indicate if he wished to accept the honour.

He was clearly uncomfortable and apprehensive about all the fuss and limelight to come. "Just what have I done to deserve this, why me?" he asked

The talks with the Borough representative eased Jimmy's worries. He accepted the invitation, even though, yes, he would need to make an acceptance speech. The image of him addressing 300 people at a club dinner some years ago came to mind when he brought the house down with his opening remark: "If only Bob Lord could see me now."

When we got back down to business, I won't say which Burnley manager he was talking about (although he has since left the club) but Jimmy was simply speechless at the language this one used from the touchline. "I just don't understand it; don't see the need for it. Everyone in the stands can hear it." Sadly foul language is endemic in the game.

And who does he think were, and are, the great managers? Of course he has fond memories of Harry Potts, "one of the nicest men in football," and recalls how he had moments of lovely, unintentional, dry humour. 'I want you to go out and play like you've never played before – play well', Harry said to us one day."

It was Jimmy McIlroy's clear and stated ambition to become a manager. "I could go on for hours about the weird and wonderful species of football manager," he wrote in *Right Inside Soccer*, "and for this very reason, it is my ambition to join them one day. Perhaps I shall prove to be more weird than they… but I am determined to try to discover if my ideas are right. The more I look around at team managers, the more I am confident that with so

Jimmy signing as manager at Oldham Athletic with club vice-chairman, Harry Massey.

Surveying the scene and a lot to do. "I can remember the first game as manager. After 20 minutes I turned to assistant Gordon Hurst and said, 'what sort of football is this they're playing?'."

many incompetents doing the job, my chances of success would be, at least, reasonable."

In his book he was critical about certain types of manager. One was Stan Cullis for his 'long-ball', 'powerhouse' style of play. Cullis was "a bald perfectionist prone to sulks, a dressing room tyrant," according to writer John Moyhnihan.

McIlroy criticised the managers who condoned rough play and told their teams to 'get stuck in' at the expense of skill. He was amazed to discover that so many managers when he talked to them still submitted their team selections to the directors. Much of what managers said he described as "stupid… their statements and articles in the Press are a constant source of amusement to me."

He lampooned the managers who yearned for the good old days, when attackers never lost the ball, but defenders always won it. Another type of manager who met his condemnation was the fitness fanatic who drilled his players till they dropped and then after a bad game punished them with more intense physical training.

He was unhappy about the whole notion of "hard fighting football… A good kick with a muddy ball, plenty of bustle in the goalmouth, the ability to withstand the rib-crunching charge, all these are the virtues of British football, because too many managers place false values on their worth."

He was sceptical about new 'scientific' (a sixties buzzword) training methods – the use of weights (they made him ache and lose his balance and he lost his speed off the mark). Then, hurdling became the new thing. It helped him jump higher he admitted but he could still never head a ball. Pressure training, the really strenuous stuff, he deemed unnecessary.

Once you have reached peak fitness then you merely top up that fitness with short training spells.

It was five-a-side games that he loved and saw in them the finest form of training ever devised. And above all, it was what a player did away from the club that determined his fitness levels, the right diet (given minimal thought in his day), the right amount of sleep, and a sensible life-style.

Chapter Thirteen of *Right Inside Soccer* was devoted to coaching ("and its transparent virtues"). Firstly, he considered most of the money the FA spent on coaching to be wasted. He did not believe that all coaching was rubbish but that certainly most of it was. He disliked the way that the FA 'experts' were making a simple game into something that was unnecessarily complicated, with a jargon of its own, and much of the coaching led by people who were never particularly good as players.

Secondly he saw much of the coaching that was taking place as unnecessary interference, stifling the skill that young players had by over emphasising the improvement of weaknesses. His philosophy was simple: take a player's strengths and skills and hone them and polish them and make them even better. Concentrate on the things they were good at, rather than wasting time on trying to improve things that it was too late to improve anyway. It amazed him to think of the thousands of hours wasted on trying to correct a footballer's faults. What would have happened to Stan Matthews if coaches had insisted on making him use his left foot, he argued? What would have happened to Puskas if coaches had insisted on him improving his right foot? In his own case what would have been the use of him spending hours trying to head a ball better?

He was quite proud of the fact that he 'failed' an FA coaching course. He was critical of some of the questions he was asked and the answers that were expected. He asked the examiners if *they* could answer their own questions. He deplored the ever-changing jargon. 'Jockeying' for possession was the word one year but the next year it had become 'curtailing'. He was asked to demonstrate the 'trap pass'. He was nonplussed and asked, "What on earth is that?"

He deplored the new demands being made on 'specialist' players by the FA experts; players like Greaves being asked to work harder in midfield rather than just wait for the ball in scoring areas. He questioned the increasing speed of the game, something he saw as the cause of the increase in poor football in every division. Players, like himself, who slowed the game down to look for the 'perfect pass' were now being told to release the ball early. The faster the game, the less skill he saw. In his own case, at a certain speed he could do things well, at a faster pace he did them less well and was far less accurate.

The managers he did admire included Arthur Rowe in the early fifties at Tottenham who devised the 'push and run' tactics that were so innovative at that time. Today managers say 'pass and move' but Rowe had success with it years ago. "It was superb to watch," says McIlroy all these years later.

Matt Busby was another man he admired. "What did Busby say to you on a Saturday before a game," he asked Dennis Viollett when they were colleagues at Stoke City. 'All he said was to go out and play football and keep on playing football', was the answer. 'Then Busby would ask Jimmy Murphy if he wanted to add anything? No boss you've covered everything, Murphy would say'."

Bill Nicholson at Spurs was always parsimonious with praise: Jimmy Greaves once

Pre-season Oldham Athletic squad with Jimmy and, below, coaching and tactics session in the sun at Oldham.

scored a hat-trick and a Pressman asked him had he said anything to Jimmy? "Why", replied Nicholson. The frustrated Pressman explained he had scored a hat-trick. "Well that's what he's paid to do", replied Nicholson.

It was at Oldham Athletic where he got the opportunity to enter management. It was still an ambition even though he had seen at first hand how players could belittle their managers. Tony Waddington had signed Calvin Palmer from Nottingham Forest, but Tony had never been the greatest of players; in fact he had had a decidedly inferior playing career. In Palmer's first game for Stoke at half-time he was quietly asked by Waddington to stick closer to his man.

Palmer, who knew about Waddington's mediocrity as a player, just turned, and annoyed, looked at him and said quite disparagingly: "And who do you think you are talking to, what street did you play for?"

How Jimmy became a manager is again an example of, if you ask "why me", the answer is very much to do with luck (or bad luck) and being in the right place at the right time.

His great friend John Cook knew Eric Cookson well, and Cookson was a partner with Ken Bates in 'Haworth' a construction and property development company based in Burnley. Jimmy, John Cook and Ken Bates were all at a dinner function one evening, late in 1965, at the Keirby Hotel in Burnley. Cook spent time talking to Ken Bates who had a Burnley season ticket and in passing mentioned that Jimmy was interested in entering football management. Bates, clearly impressed by Jimmy's great playing career, was at this point the Oldham chairman and was pumping money into the club. "Tycoon buys club for Christmas," wrote Don Hardisty in the *Daily Mail*, Bates remembers.

He had seen Jimmy play at Turf Moor many times and was a huge admirer of his genius. It is reasonable to assume that he found the idea of a 'name' manager with a superb playing pedigree appealing, in order to further his ambitions of taking Oldham to the very top.

Jimmy was invited to meet Bates at his home in Cheshire; John Cook took him over; Bates and McIlroy talked, and there and then he was offered the job. The immediate benefit being that the arduous journey to Stoke was replaced by the much shorter journey to Oldham. That apart, it is doubtful that Jimmy knew exactly what he was in for.

One of *the* great players of the First Division, Bobbie Johnstone formerly of Manchester City, had just left the club. But a player that McIlroy did inherit was Albert Quixall of Sheffield Wednesday, Manchester United and England fame. But, he was well past his best (always seemed to be injured when it was an away game recalls Ken Bates) and would feature little once Jimmy arrived. A player Jimmy just missed was the potentially outstanding 18 year old Tommy Hutchison who went on to have a long and distinguished career. He had one trial game at Oldham the day before McIlroy arrived. He heard no more from Oldham and went back to his Scottish club, Dandonald Bluebells. If only Jimmy Mac had seen him that day.

McIlroy was manager at Oldham from January 1966 until August 1968, replacing Gordon Hurst who became assistant manager. Hurst had played for Charlton Athletic in the 1947 Cup Final when Charlton won 1 – 0. When the new man took over Oldham had just 13 points from a possible 44. Relegation looked a definite possibility at the halfway stage of the season, but if Jimmy Mac did just one thing at Oldham, by the end of the season he had steered them away from that threat, although they did also win the Lancashire Senior Cup in 1967.

If the name of Ken Bates today is synonymous with his development and sale of Chelsea, and then more latterly his chairmanship of Leeds United; he was no less ambitious in his younger days at Oldham Athletic where he arrived in December 1965, in his mid-thirties. He loved football and but for problems with one of his feet would loved to have been a professional footballer. He had once stood on the terraces at Queens Park Rangers as a supporter and then later had a Burnley season ticket.

Ken Bates spent three months quietly and privately examining the club, its crowds, recent history and its potential. He discarded Bury, Barrow and Stockport County as possible places in which to invest. Oldham was not a last resort he wrote, he felt it could be fashioned with money and luck into a great club. He saw that they had a tradition of loyal support that for years had not been properly exploited. He had no interest in spending his money on racehorses and speed-boats but more on something he enjoyed doing - football.

His business life began when he was a junior clerk in local government for three years, and then three years in accountancy in the City of London. From there he moved into sand and gravel haulage, quarrying, ready-mix concrete and building. His business interests were wide-ranging, listed in the *Boundary Bulletin* as merchant banking, insurance, investment trusts, property and building, finance, carpets, boat building, toys and overseas development (the Virgin Islands). He was also a Lloyd's underwriter. The *Bulletin* noted that he drove a maroon Rolls Royce and had a huge mansion in Cheshire.

He took over from Chairman Harry Massey who stepped down to become vice-chairman. Massey, as chairman, was in charge of a club that was struggling and was in a financial mess, and he chaired a boardroom that abounded with differences, difficulties and politics. Following an initial telephone conversation, he and Bates met in the Grand Hotel in Manchester during which Bates requested that he could visit the ground.

Massey confessed to being shocked when, even though he had shown him the dire club accounts after the tour of the ground, Bates said he was willing to come along and put money into the club. Once various financial matters had been ironed out he was co-opted onto the board. In a matchday programme in September 1966 Massey announced that it was "salvation day for the 'Latics" when Ken Bates took over.

There is no question that when he took over Bates was all set to put his heart and soul into Oldham Athletic. He was prepared to sink money into the club and ground improvements; there were plans for a new cantilever stand, new players were bought, occasional gates of 14,000+ gave grounds for optimism. The old Third Division had rarely seen a spending programme like it.

His aims and hopes were clear. The club would inaugurate a policy of finding and developing its own stars. The fabric of the club would be converted from the rotting, dilapidated, tumbledown ground into a modern, comfortable stadium with proper facilities. Bright, attractive football would be provided, "not for us ten men in the penalty area… but enjoying matches that we lose as well as those that we win." The magazine type *Boundary Bulletin* (given away free) set new standards and trends in programme production. The target would be the First Division and Europe in the seventies. And finally, the club would be put on a proper financial footing.

The plan was simple; Bates would fund it, McIlroy would mastermind it. The target was Europe, even though they had only just scraped clear of relegation by the end of 1965/66. Paul Doherty became his programme editor at Oldham and later wrote a succinct analysis of exactly what went wrong in Charles Buchan's *Football Monthly*. Inside six months, doubts were emerging. Within a year the fans were openly critical, and after two years Bates told them all he would not spend another penny after the £100,000 he had already ploughed in. Everybody was disillusioned; from Bates, to fans, to manager Jimmy Mac. The question was a simple one... just how had it all gone wrong when there had been a chairman investing his money and such huge, initial ambitions and plans?

A year on from taking over the club, Bates was interviewed by Paul Doherty. He revealed that he had spent more than he thought that he would, but would not continue to do so if people weren't willing to back him. He regarded the signing of Jimmy McIlroy as manager as a masterstroke. But the lack of active support was a major disappointment. "There are plenty of people who are willing to tell you what needs to be done and they don't hesitate to tell you your shortcomings. But there are damned few who will do anything about it... if people want good entertainment at good grounds it has to be paid for... supporters get the club they deserve and pay for."

But the youth policy (nurtured by Jimmy Mac) pleased him enormously and he felt there was a nucleus of very promising young players arriving at the club.

The fact is, however, that it could all have ended unhappily so much earlier had Jimmy Mac not come out of playing retirement, cleaned his boots and taken to the field again. In many of the games in which he played the Press singled him out as the one player worth watching, and the source of the team's inspiration and victory.

Against Darlington in a 4 – 0 win: "Jimmy McIlroy pulled out a five star display that sparkled through a drab, damp winter's afternoon."

Against Scunthorpe in a 1 – 1 draw: "It was a good job McIlroy was playing. Time and time again he tried to open the game up, spraying good passes."

In a 1 – 0 over Queen's Park Rangers: "McIlroy would have none of the big boot. He ventured upfield with the ball at his feet time and time again..... Jimmy McIlroy outstanding... still a fine player."

Against Shrewsbury in a 4 – 1 win: "The irrepressible Jimmy McIlroy planning and feeding was the scourge of the Shrewsbury defence."

Mansfield were beaten 4 – 2: "Ten of the Latics decided to sit on this lead and take a second-half siesta. Jimmy McIlroy was the exception."

Against Sheffield United: "Not until McIlroy slipped into the forward line in the second half, did the attack really discover any real drive, purpose in front of goal and shooting power."

After a game against Rochdale and a win there was a different, novel story. There was one fan, amongst many on the pitch, he just couldn't shake off. The youngster had hold of his shirt and would not let go no matter how Jimmy ran, twisted and turned. After his efforts to free himself failed he turned round to confront the 'attacker' only to find his pursuer holding out a bag of coins. "Take these Jimmy," said the lad. "Sorry it couldn't be more but we had a collection behind the goals and will you buy all the lads a drink." Jimmy, remembering the occasion against Reims in the European Cup when he and the Burnley team were pelted with coins, was quite stunned.

It is probably wrong to say he single-handedly saved the season, but without him it is quite possible that Oldham would indeed have been relegated, so poor were they.

He put his boots on again for one simple reason: "When I suddenly realised the big chasm between the top grade and Third Division stuff, my heart started pounding so hard it could be heard from all over the stands. I suddenly realised my stark responsibility. A manager is only as good as his players and no magician can make a racehorse out of a donkey."

There is a magazine picture of Jimmy Mac and it is memorable for the look on Jimmy's face and his body language. It is the Oldham team picture on the front cover of an old copy of *Soccer Star*. If a picture tells a story, this is the story of a man who is out of place and unhappy.

From the touchline he had no control or influence. On the field he most definitely had. Simultaneously he began to develop his youth policy and Bates happily accompanied him visiting young lads and their parents in their homes in the search for talent. Ken Bates remembers that McIlroy looked at a young lad and had a way of categorising him. He would look at a lad and say "look at him he walks like Alex Elder." Of another one he might say "he runs like Jimmy Adamson." Most of them were from Ireland, but this, in itself, eventually became a source of criticism.

At the beginning of season 1966/67 Jimmy Mac announced that this would be his final playing season. (In fact he would play two more at the very beginning of the next season). The Tuesday, 27th September, 1966 edition of the match programme, the *Boundary Bulletin* made the announcement in a front page article about him.

'It may prove to be a short playing life for the Irishman at Oldham, but there can be no dispute that it has already proved a valuable one. When he acceded to requests to make a comeback (he made his debut on Southend United's ground on Friday night, March 11th) the club was faced with the peril of relegation, but his inspiration and example finally averted the crisis. Since then, the club chairman, Mr Ken Bates, has told Mac to make up his own mind about quitting and settling down entirely behind the scenes. The pressures from taking a dual role, especially in a class of soccer not regularly encountered before, has obviously reshaped his views about the future and the priorities the job should have. "I think I have a different outlook from the one I had when I joined the club last January. The Third Division was a kind of shock to me. I was bewildered by the style of play and the standard of play, more so when I took an active part in it.

"I hope now that I have sampled enough to have formed better opinions. I have had all summer to think about it and I now feel that I am more adjusted to play in it and to manage Third Division players," claimed genial Jimmy Mac.

But Mac had got basic views about soccer management that he had no intention of changing. "The first thing I want to do is to treat the players like grown-ups. If some turn out to be talented schoolboys, they will be treated that way. I want to finish all types of restrictions over fitness and also the code the players have to live to. I want players to be responsible for their own fitness. If they are adult enough and want to make a career in the game they will make sure of this. The responsibility will, I feel, improve their approach and attitude. Those who don't want to bother will not last long enough to be troublesome – they won't be hard to spot," he continued.

What does he think of the past – and the future? "I couldn't have had a more trying baptism than coming to Oldham where a lot of money has been spent and success was expected. It was a hard lesson and I now know what to expect. At times I asked myself had I done the right thing because I had turned down a lucrative offer to stay at Stoke in an

Showing a new player around Boundary Park.

assistant's capacity and was also offered a testimonial.

"But Oldham was a chance to be in charge of players rather than just coaching them. I wanted the responsibility for it all. Being in a desperate relegation position with a Third Division club was not a shattering experience; only a fool would kid himself that such difficult times could not happen to him.

"I don't want to be the manager of an unsuccessful club. I thought that the Stoke crowd were wonderful and deserved success. The Oldham people have been success-starved for so long that I believe, given the slightest encouragement, they could be as fanatical as Liverpool supporters. It may sound flannel, but that is not the intention. I believe it. After all, that's why I'm here.

"I am not under any illusions about the job ahead. But I am attempting to bring a high standard of young player into this club, and I want them brought up my way. It is not conceit that makes me claim my way will be right for them. If it is correct, then the future will be well looked after." '

Jimmy was committed to youth development and making progress. But, in truth, there was little to celebrate, other than the Lancashire Senior Cup, which was not exactly Europe. Players were bought and players were sold. The youths were given their chance but this was a tough division, although on occasions the policy reaped dividends. Colchester were beaten 4 – 0 and the *Daily Mail* reported, "All round this match was a triumph for McIlroy's decision to give youth its fling." The *News of the World* said, "It was a great vindication of manager McIlroy's youth policy."

On tour in Rhodesia, pictured above with Prime Minister Ian Smith, third from right. Second front right is Ken Bates.

During 1966/67 they were in touch with the leaders for most of the season. Early in the season they had actually been top; after 40 games they were within 6 points of second place, but just one win in the last seven games saw the promotion push fade away and attendances began to decline. There were accusations that they had sold their chance of promotion with the sale of players, and a reliance on youth at critical stages had been damaging. The club replied saying that "the foundations for the future were solidly cemented;" the youth policy was well and truly in place, ground improvements were continuing and new social facilities had been opened.

The lack of success, however, continued and supporters looked back in disappointment on a frustrating season. The attendance for the final home game of the season had been a pitiful 2,000. There was no improvement. In his second full season, 1967/68, the season was only saved, after a bad start (just one win in the first twelve games and Oldham in bottom place in the division), by a run of seven consecutive wins and an eventual final place of 16th. Add that disappointing spell to the one at the end of the preceding season, and it made just two wins in nineteen games in total. It was crystal clear then that ambitions and dreams would not become reality and there were drastic economy cuts. It was now a club with a very unhappy boardroom.

Ken Bates eventually announced that he would spend no more money, fed up with what he saw as fans who wanted soccer on the cheap; not prepared to back the club in sufficient numbers; and a Supporters' Club not raising enough money to match his own input. He bluntly told the Supporters' Club they had made a "pretty mess of things in the recent past" and that they had failed miserably to provide an off-field income. "We are tired of failure aggravated by poor book-keeping, secret accounting and a steadfast refusal to co-operate with the directors." £1,800 in six months was just not good enough. A new Supporters' Club was therefore organised responsible directly to the directors: "The new Tangerine Club hopes to rectify these deficiencies and eventually it hopes to raise £20,000 per year for the parent club."

He upset directors with his strong-mindedness and what Paul Doherty described as a "whizz-bang" approach; and fans by telling them bluntly what he thought, and that he couldn't stand ditherers. Conversely, the supporters eventually lost all sympathy for him, finding him unbending and impossible to relate to. From the very start he had offended some of them by replacing Gordon Hurst; he offended more with his loyalty to Jimmy Mac; he upset the pensioners by insisting there could be no price reductions. He annoyed probably all the fans by suggesting that if they wanted to pay Cheshire League prices then they could go and watch Cheshire League football. He fell out with his fellow directors and as a result of a match-day row, one of them, Eric Beard, resigned from the board.

Doherty referred to his "hurricane" style, and if there was one facet to Ken Bates, as applicable now as it was then, it was that he worked at pace, and he had no time for those who could not match that pace. He simply wanted the best for Oldham Athletic.

Yet, he could charm the birds from the trees. Jimmy remembers how, as the debts mounted, all of the directors would be gloomy and despondent before a meeting. "Then Ken would come in to the meeting and tell us all that this player is worth so much, that player is worth so and so, and go through all the team adding up how much they were all worth. By the time he'd finished we all felt on cloud nine and that we had no worries."

Eventually Jimmy Mac too was blamed for the club's ills. He had been able to spend heavily, but then players were sold, especially the goalscorers. Fans could not understand the latter, especially the sale of Kinnell, and saw it as McIlroy's policy. His faith in youngsters began to irritate the senior professionals. Initially, Jimmy Mac did not believe in physically hard training, but after a year he changed his mind. Eventually, too, he came to admit that his demands on his youths were too heavy.

His change of mind on training methods came about after a 0 – 1 home defeat to the top team QPR. In effect his change of mind was a reversal of much that he believed about the way football should be played. It became clear to him that more than skill was needed to win games in the Third Division. "I must say it was this match more than anything else which caused me to revise certain ideas… I think that in our attempt to get a top-class footballing side we have neglected to play the game forcefully enough… something more physical has to go with the ability a side possesses. We are going to go in for a much harder physical training at Oldham."

Accusations of a 'jobs for the boys' policy followed the replacement of chief scout Eric Walker by Bertie Neill. Neill combined the duties of chief coach with scouting in Ireland. He had already prior to the appointment made several young player recommendations. His football pedigree was a good one, though at the time of the appointment he was working in the Civil Service. It was noted however, by those who wanted to be critical that Neill house-hunted in Burnley not Oldham. He was also Jimmy McIlroy's brother-in-law. When there is a winning team such things trouble no-one. When it is an unsuccessful team such things are magnified and criticised.

John Collins from Queens Park Rangers was one of the players signed. In Tim Quelch's book *Never Had it so Good*, he spoke about working with McIlroy.

"I signed for Jimmy McIlroy at Oldham in 1966. He would join in the five-a-sides and so on. He was really strong and so good at shielding the ball. Once he got his arse into you, you had no chance. You couldn't get the ball off him. I don't think he was cut out to be a manager though. It's difficult when you've been that good. You don't really appreciate how hard it is for people less talented than yourself. He didn't really teach us. I'm not sure he knew best how to do this. He expected us to do the things he could do and he could really get the hump if we played badly." Ken Bates nodded his head at these comments by John Collins and added that another example of a great player who found it hard to work with lesser talents was Glen Hoddle.

Despite the lack of success, Ken Bates' loyalty to Jimmy McIlroy was unshakeable; and it was for that reason that Jimmy Mac did not resign far earlier. When he did leave, he said: "I would have left Oldham a long time ago but for the chairman, Ken Bates. He stood by me through thick and thin." Even today, 40 years later, Jimmy clearly has a strong sense of affection for him.

He is quite clear why he left. Ken Bates, convinced that no-one was matching or supporting his input and efforts, appeared less and less at the club, living in the Virgin Islands developing his business interests there. In fairness, however, if Bates was absent because he was disillusioned and losing interest, he could well be forgiven for thinking, is this worth it? He had taken over a club that was in debt, possibly on the edge of closure, mismanaged (he called in the police at one point when he uncovered a season ticket scam); and needed an urgent shake-up, with facilities so rotten that he wouldn't even take his wife to the first games. But after nearly three years he was seeing precious little in return. With

Ken Bates now absent so much, McIlroy was on his own.

Years later in a 2005 *Observer* interview Bates listed Oldham as one of the clubs he had "saved." Given the parlous state it was in when he arrived there is some credence in that. Interviewer Will Buckley also commented that bearing in mind all the flack that comes Bates' way "his achievements tend to be overlooked." When asked by Paul Doherty if he was "dictatorial" he answered that the manager had a free hand on the playing side, the editor of the matchday magazine could print what he chose, that every director had a job and was left to get on with it. "Is that so dictatorial?" he asked. He did add that fools were not suffered gladly.

With the chairman thousands of miles away from Oldham it was left to Jimmy

McIlroy to take the strain and face the supporters alone. It was he who had to meet the directors and the aggravation at board meetings and it was he who had to address one AGM without the support of his chairman. In fact at the AGM he did well, his Irish blarney and sunny optimism winning the day and persuading the vociferous assembly that all would be well. But being left to hold the fort was not what he had signed up for and his resignation was inevitable. He told his own story, a year later, late in 1969. It makes painful reading and reveals all too clearly the problems of management.

*Ken Bates was the money maker. In eight years he'd made a million. I was the expert who would handle his team; Jimmy McIlroy, Wembley finalist, League Champions, 15 years an international. Bates and McIlroy, cash and talent, the combination, they said, could be as renowned as Busby and Edwards; and little Oldham, where we'd teamed together to conquer Europe - into Europe by the seventies.*

*That was the dream. Today they are still picking up the pieces. Today, ex chairman Ken Bates lives in the Virgin Islands, £80,000 worse off.*

*Today I study to be a teacher – and wince when I think of my two and a half years of boardroom squabbles and cash worry; for though Ken Bates put money into the club, the debts still piled up.*

*Before then the boardroom battles had flickered and flared. And once, Bates almost fought in his own directors' box with another board member, Eric Beard, a local schoolteacher. Beard made a remark about an Oldham player and Ken didn't like it. They flared up, threatening to knock each other out of the directors' box. Beard quit immediately after the game.*

*We spent long hours cooped up in a coach, often starting at 8 a.m. and arriving back in the early hours. When it came to paying the meal bills, we sometimes handed over a cheque knowing it would arrive back at the ground almost before we did, for each cheque had to have three signatures and several times it was sent with two. And while it was returned for the third, the*

OFFICIAL MAGAZINE OF    OLDHAM ATHLETIC A.F.C.

# BOUNDARY BULLETIN

Vol. I, No. 4      TUESDAY, 27th SEPTEMBER, 1966.      PRICE 1/-

# 'MAC' DECIDES

## "This is my last season"

JIMMY McILROY, now deep into his eighth month in the twin task as the club's player-manager, has set himself a time for dropping one of his titles and retiring behind the footlights.

"I won't play any more after this season," he has decided.

Jimmy, who will be 35 years old in late-October, is also hoping that the demands on his playing talents may not be too heavy before he officially retires. "I am trusting that the players we have at Oldham will be good enough to keep me out of the team. The opinions I am forming in these early weeks will help me decide, though injuries are complicating the position," he told me.

It may prove to be a short playing life for the Irishman at Oldham, but there can be no dispute that it has already proved a valuable one. When he acceded to requests last March for him to make a comeback—he made his debut on Southend United's ground on Friday night, March 11th—the club was faced with the peril of relegation.

But his inspiration and example finally averted the crisis.

Since then the club chairman, Mr. Ken Bates, has told "Mac" to make up his own mind about quitting and settling down entirely behind the scenes.

The pressures from taking a dual role, especially in a class of Soccer not regularly encountered before, has obviously reshaped his views about the future and the priorities the job should have.

"I think I have a different outlook from the one I had when I joined the club last January. The Third Division was a kind of shock to me. I was bewildered by the style of play and the standard of play, more so when I took active part in it.

"I hope now that I have sampled enough to have formed better opinions. I have had all summer to think about it and I now feel that I am more adjusted to play in it and to manage Third Division players," claimed genial Jimmy.

But "Mac" has got basic views about Soccer management that he has no intention of changing.

"The first thing I want to do is to treat the players like grown-ups. If some turn out to be talented schoolboys, they will be treated this way. I want to finish all types of restrictions over fitness and also the code the players have to live to.

"I want players to be responsible for their own fitness. If they are adult enough and want to make a career in the game they will make sure of this. The responsibility will, I feel, improve their approach and attitude. Those who don't want to bother will not last long enough to be troublesome—they won't be hard to spot," he continued.

What does he think of the past . . . and the future?

"I couldn't have had a more trying baptism than coming to Oldham where a lot of money had been spent and success was expected. It was a hard lesson and I now know what to expect.

"At times I asked myself had I done the right thing because I had turned down a lucrative offer to stay at Stoke in an assistant's capacity and was also offered a testimonial.

"But Oldham was a chance to be in charge of players rather than just coaching them. I wanted the responsibility for it all. Being in a desperate relegation position with a Third Division club was not a shattering experience—only a fool would kid himself that such difficult times could not happen to him.

"I don't want to be manager of an unsuccessful club. I thought that the Stoke crowd were wonderful and deserved success. The Oldham people have been success-starved for so long that I believe, given the slightest encouragement, they could be as fanatical as Liverpool supporters. It may sound flannel, but that is not the intention. I believe it. After all, that's why I'm here.

"I am not under any illusions about the job ahead. But I am attempting to bring a high standard of young player into this club, and I want them brought up my way. It is not conceit that makes me claim my way will be right for them. If it is correct, then the future will be well looked after," Jimmy concluded.

## 1949

## MILESTONES BETWEEN

## 1966

| | | |
|---|---|---|
| 1949 | AUGUST | Signed professional forms for Irish League club Glentoran. |
| 1950 | MARCH | Signed for Burnley after £8,000 deal had been agreed with the Irish club. |
| 1950 | OCTOBER | League debut for Burnley at the age of 19 on October 21st. |
| 1951 | OCTOBER | International debut for Northern Ireland against Scotland, at Windsor Park, Belfast. Lost 3—0. |
| 1955 | AUGUST | Appeared at inside-left for Great Britain team beaten 4—1 by a Rest of Europe side, in Belfast. |
| 1958 | JUNE | Made all five appearances in the Irish team that reached the quarter-finals of the World Cup, only to be beaten 4—0 by France. |
| 1960 | MAY | First Division championship medal with Burnley. |
| 1962 | MAY | In Burnley's F.A. Cup Final team beaten 3—1 at Wembley. |
| 1962 | MAY | In the Burnley side that just missed the famed "double"—they are runners-up in the League. |
| 1963 | FEBRUARY | Burnley put him on the transfer list. |
| 1963 | MARCH | Stoke City pay £30,000 for his services. |
| 1963 | APRIL | His appearance against Wales in Ireland's home international fixture is significant — it's the end of a regular call-up that started in 1952. |
| 1963 | MAY | He collects a Second Division championship medal with Stoke City. |
| 1965 | OCTOBER | Recalled to Irish international team—against Scotland—who beat Scotland 3—2 in Belfast. |
| 1965 | NOVEMBER | Retains his international place on the right wing, against England at Wembley. It's his last appearance. |
| 1966 | JANUARY | Quits his playing career to take over the management of Oldham—and Stoke agree to release him. |
| 1966 | MARCH | Makes a come-back as a player in Oldham colours against Southend United after fee paid to Stoke. |

# MANAGER MAC LOOKS AT THE 'IFS' and 'BUTS'

BOSS Jimmy McIlroy counted off the recent turning points on his fingers as he viewed Latics' temporary leap back onto the promotion fringe before the mid-week set-back at Oxford. IF, he said, one of the two disallowed goals that Ian Towers scored at Walsall in early March had been granted; IF, he quickly warmed to the theme, goalkeeper David Best had been on form at Easter; IF, he continued, Towers had taken more of the chances he has had; IF . . . his voice trailed off.

He weighed up the IFS that have stood between Latics and a prominent promotion placing. The silence was short. " Be fair, every manager in the top six is looking back at the ifs and buts. I never would have guessed the competition would have remained open for so long. How many could have tipped that six clubs would be battling in the last month of the season to take the journey upwards with Q.P.R.?

"Now people are saying that it was silly for us to write off promotion earlier this year. They want me to name a date when I counted our chances had collapsed. I've a simple reply . . . you never write off anything in this game. I never have done. After the experience I had at Burnley, when we were four or six points ahead of the field with three games in hand and nearing the end of the season and we still lost the championship, I know better.

" Any one of six clubs to strike a good run now will win the runners-up place. We have not had that run yet at Oldham. We had a good streak at home, but our away form was a let-down. We are still looking for our first consistent run," Mac told me.

### LOSS OF FORM

Alongside the IFS, what about the regrets ? " If we had been able to keep the team together that started the season for us I claim we could have trotted through to promotion. We can complain about our luck, though. Denis Stevens was injured from the start. He was out for months with his knee injury, and when he returned he never looked like getting his form back.

" Billy Johnston was crocked at Middlesbrough in the sixth game of the season and is only just feeling his way back in the reserves now. Then we have had to contend with key players losing form, something we weren't entitled to expect should

affect us so severely. Players like Jim Bowie, Bill Asprey, David Best and Keith Bebbington for a patch."

And the Oldham chief carried on with his claims: " I stated in the early part of the season, and at a later date, that we were the best footballing side I had seen. I still maintain that on the days the players produce what they are easily capable of we have no equal in the division.

" Every manager knows his players best—I know the extent of ability in my men. What I am disappointed in is the lack of consistency, and there has also been a lack of hardness in the team, too.

" Losing the F.A. Cup replay at Wolves in the circumstances we did was very disconcerting considering the talent we fielded that night.

" I must admit some performances have deflated my optimism a little. The defeats at Colchester (lost 3—2) and at Grimsby (lost 1—0) in the second month of the season are among these disappointing displays to stand out.

" The fact that youngsters were brought in was not a signal that I gave up the promotion chase. Not at all. We were losing too many matches considering the experienced men turning out, so I felt no worse could be done with our younger stars.

" Bear in mind that most of the lads ' blooded ' a few months ago are now in the side which has slipped in behind the leading promotion contenders.

### REGRETS

" The side we set out with this winter was a good one. The injuries were misfortune, loss of form was unfortunate. I wish we could have kept George Kinnell, but I don't think for a moment we could have done so. I know George from our days at Stoke together, and once Sunderland's interest was made clear

I knew that there could be only one outcome.

" Kinnell could possibly have formed a good spearhead to clinch us enough HOME points to be in a better position today. But these are ifs and buts again.

" The fact is that we could still keep in the hunt right up to the death of the season. I don't think it's better to end the season with regrets about missing promotion by one point than have the peace of mind that you are out of the chase in, say, February. If we go close, then it will prove to me that we have a side which would be capable of improving next season and consequently improving on such an effort in the table. Look at today's visitors from London. They finished third last May, and by gosh they've improved on that form in a big way. They must have known then that the signs were there and that the team was bound to mature to be a force in this year's programme," he finished.

And here's how it looks with a handful of games to go:

| | Home | | | | | Away | | | | | |
|---|---|---|---|---|---|---|---|---|---|---|---|
| | P | W | D | L | F | A | W | D | L | F | A | Pts |
| Queen's P. R.. | 39 | 16 | 3 | 1 | 61 | 13 | 7 | 10 | 2 | 33 | 18 | 59 |
| Torquay U..... | 41 | 16 | 3 | 1 | 50 | 14 | 4 | 6 | 11 | 16 | 29 | 49 |
| Bristol R....... | 41 | 12 | 7 | 2 | 43 | 25 | 6 | 5 | 9 | 24 | 33 | 48 |
| Mansfield T.... | 40 | 12 | 3 | 5 | 46 | 32 | 7 | 5 | 8 | 29 | 32 | 46 |
| Watford......... | 39 | 13 | 3 | 3 | 31 | 13 | 5 | 7 | 8 | 21 | 27 | 46 |
| Middlesbro'.... | 39 | 12 | 3 | 3 | 38 | 15 | 6 | 5 | 10 | 33 | 42 | 44 |
| Shrewsbury.... | 40 | 15 | 3 | 3 | 47 | 23 | 3 | 5 | 11 | 22 | 34 | 44 |
| Oldham A...... | 40 | 14 | 2 | 3 | 48 | 13 | 4 | 5 | 12 | 26 | 43 | 43 |

April 15th, 1967. Jimmy reviews season 1966/67 and what "might have been".

*club gained valuable breathing space. It got to the stage eventually when we couldn't even afford a new match ball. We had to buy rejects and rub out the 'reject' stamps so that referees wouldn't notice. One afternoon we couldn't find any ball to play with so secretary Bernard Halford had to dash home for the ball he'd just bought for his son for a Christmas present.*

*The plight was so bad we had to sell George Kinnell, the former Stoke centre-half was sold to Sunderland, and Frank Large to Northampton in a double deal that brought £34,000. (Ken Bates when I showed him this article disagreed that there was a 'need' to sell Kinnell and commented that it was merely a good business deal.)*

*I remember when the board learned of Sunderland's interest in Kinnell, Vice-Chairman Harry Massey said: "If they offer £15,000 I will personally drive Kinnell to Sunderland so that he can sign." I got £20,000 and probably sold our promotion hopes. Later we sold Ken Knighton to Preston for £35,000, a year after I'd bought him for £12,000. But even that kind of cash only barely made an impression on the crippling HP payments we were making for other players.*

*Ken was under constant fire from the rest of the board. When he was away on business trips, I had to take the lot from Vice-Chairman Massey and the other directors. But when he came back to face the attacks, his financial wizardry would convince them that the position wasn't so serious after all. I lost count of the number of times that Massey came in the following morning exclaiming: "No matter how I examine the figures, we still owe £100,000."*

*Ken Bates had such tremendous persuasive powers. While I was in Ireland signing centre-half Alan Hunter, he rang with a message: "Go to South Africa to watch a centre-forward." The boy's experience was confined to the Durban City reserves. What chance had he in the League? I protested, but, luckily for me, received word just before I left for the airport that the boy was playing away from Durban.*

*But we did manage one trip to Africa, which brought a storm of protest and even went as far as the Commons. We defied Whitehall to go on a 10-match tour of Rhodesia. It was a success. What's more important it made a precious £1,000.*

*Ken had geared everything to success, (Ken Bates to this day emphasises that all he wanted was to provide the best facilities) large scale re-building of the dressing rooms and boardroom, a first class medical room and a full-time physiotherapist. That lot cost around £30,000 but during my last summer there was no lavish re-building. Along with trainer Bertie Neil, my brother-in-law, and the apprentices, we painted the dressing-rooms, bathrooms and passages.*

*And then we dug drains on the practice ground from morning to night. We were glorified navvies. I'm convinced that Harry Massey thought I'd done more to earn my wage during those few weeks than all the time I'd been there.*

*But he forgets that I hardly saw my family during the season. Every night I was on the 'circuit' searching for players. At times I ate more food in boardrooms than I did at home and saw more of certain managers than I did of my wife. For what – a manager has to convince his directors that he is enthusiastic and satisfy himself that his previous opinions of a player were correct.*

*But the circuit is like a union, almost every manager, scout and coach follows the herd. And it almost killed me. I was coming back from Middlesbrough after a game when my brakes failed on a moorland road. Luckily it happened on a slight bend and not the countless steep hills and bends I'd just left.*

*The chairman too did his share on the circuit, but it was evident that he was becoming disillusioned. He shielded me from two annual meetings but when it came to the third, and the biggest crisis the board faced, I was thrown to the lions. I was criticised from all angles but I gave them a bit of the blarney, exaggerated a little about the potential of the youth policy, and outlined a great future for the club if the shareholders were willing to be patient.*

*I was shocked by the applause. The shareholders cheered me and one old lady whispered in my ear: "You'd make a great politician Jimmy."*

*But I knew my partnership with Ken Bates would have to be dissolved. The board was making things too hot while he was away in the Virgin Islands. When he decided to live there I wrote explaining the atmosphere and feeling of the directors towards me. I told him he was being constantly attacked by his colleagues in his absence and because of it I couldn't continue.*

*Probably my biggest mistake was not pinning my faith in the established players. Their lack of talent irritated me, for having played with and against some of the world's best I found it almost impossible to work with mediocre players. A pity, they were dedicated and honest. I regret I didn't do more for them.*

*I remember at one time they thought training was too easy so I started running them over to a park two miles away every Monday morning. Then I made them run up a steep hill against the clock. It was murder. One morning I counted nine players being sick on the hill. But their form didn't improve because they now thought they were overtrained.*

*And that's the trouble with the game. The modern player is a top-class athlete. Clubs hire international track stars who introduce murderous schedules. Players run miles against the clock; have pulse counts, lung-capacity testing machines and circuits devised by sadists, all in an attempt to win matches. Players are brain-washed to the extent that if they don't fulfil their quota of miles and circuits, their game will suffer on Saturday.*

*With skill so lacking, a substitute has to be found. A coach cannot teach skill but he can improve fitness and that's what the modern game is all about. Hardness, strength and speed have made the British game superior. Take the World Cup for example. England have still not been fully accepted with the dignity and respect that either Hungary or Brazil commanded. Why – because great footballing teams win fans everywhere and England are not a great footballing side.*

*As with team manager Sir Alf Ramsey, the players are dedicated and give 100% effort, but the side lack flair. Their approach is too methodical, like almost every club in Britain – only to be expected with the number of coaches we have.*

*England's short, sharp, compact style is a bore. Who can honestly say he has been thrilled by watching the 11 players who should be setting an example for all other teams to follow? But as this pattern has been successful, I cannot see Sir Alf changing.*

*Never having seen any other style, young fans will continue to support the game, but other lovers of football must yearn for better days.*

*I tell you; I get more pleasure from watching Tom Finney perform in a charity game than I do watching England. Today's atmosphere is too studied and too professional. But I care how we win. Today's fans feast on the result. My generation had it for dessert. The main course was the performance.*

(Jimmy McIlroy October 1969)

Jimmy wrote this piece 40 years ago and parts of it are as relevant now as they were then. Footballers now must be super-fit athletes. Too many are not born, they are manufactured. Coaching and tactics and systems dominate the game. Flair is a rare commodity; individuality is stifled. Adventurous passing is replaced by a do-not-lose-the-

# OLDHAM ATHLETIC ASSOCIATION FOOTBALL CLUB LIMITED

*versus*

## SOUTHPORT

*on*

**Saturday**

**14th September, 1968**

*at*

**Boundary Park**

*Kick-off—3-15 p.m.*

## Man of the Moment

**KEN BATES**

THERE have not been many moments in Oldham Athletic history quite as important as those which the Club is passing through right now. And at the centre of all the attention is our chairman, Ken Bates, who returned from his home in the British Virgin Islands last Wednesday ready to play his part and say his piece.

The critical meeting, when the future policy will be plotted and the prospects will be weighed, has been booked for Monday when the chairman will travel from his temporary headquarters in London. He spoke to vice-chairman Harry Massey very shortly after his arrival at London Airport, but while the debate was a lengthy one, no indication was given by either director what the likely outcome will be.

So the one big question remains unanswered over the week-end. Is Mr. Bates going to continue playing an active part in Oldham affairs . . . or is he going to carry out a threat which was hinted in some newspapers by following up manager Jimmy McIlroy's letter of resignation with one of his own?

Monday afternoon's meeting seems certain to answer that query since Mr. Bates has provisionally booked his return to the Virgin Islands later the following day. And everyone who knows him appreciate that he's not the man to leave any loose ends unattended.

The chairman has been measuring the situation carefully since he received an urgent cable from McIroy revealing the resignation. Despite attempts by two local evening newspapers to contact him at his home in the B.V.I. no comment has been forthcoming, and since his return to London he has resisted answering all Press questions.

It is clear that there will only be one full statement, and that crucial announcement seems likely to come some time early next week.

The chairman, who has spent heavily since he took his place on the Oldham Board in December, 1965, must still be taken aback at the events which took place during his recent absence. When he returned to his far-off home last month, it appeared that all doubts about the manager's future had been resolved and McIlroy was going to persevere with his plans, weather the criticisms, and see out his five year contract.

But within 48 hours of a 6—0 slamming for the Latics at Brighton, the doubts were being expressed again. Rather unfairly to the Club the manager was quoted as calling the Boundary situation as "seeming hopeless". Soon after that McIlroy (and his brother-in-law Bertie Neill) had quit—as was inevitable after such a depressing statement—to take up employment as coaches with Stoke City.

A major dilemma now remains for Mr. Bates, and it's one which even the best of soccer observers are finding difficult to predict.

It's no secret that McIlroy was hand-picked by the chairman for the job, and he strongly supported his choice in the difficult periods since the new regime took office. On the face of it, the departure of Mr. Bates seems a probability, too.

But Mr. Bates will also be considering the vast investment he made in Latics having a brighter future, and has always maintained that he believes in the Club. He has never been troubled by public opinion in the past, nor has he walked out on battles he has felt could be won. Wiser in the ways of football, and the discretions which are required, his reaction could be to remain—but in a less forceful role.

It's guess-work, I know. Monday seems likely to provide the answer to this key question.

The aftermath of McIlroy's resignation at Oldham.

ball mentality, and playing the safe pass, backwards and sideways. Jimmy frequently asks two questions today – just how many teams are exciting to watch, and just how many individual players would you travel out of your way to pay and see?

It was at Oldham that he played his final game of professional football, two months short of his 36th birthday. It was in a frustrating, home defeat at Boundary Park, 0 – 2 by Peterborough United in September 1967. It was a long way from Europe, Wembley, his First Division winner's medal, and all the glory and adulation he had once enjoyed.

Two days after the opening match of the 1968/69 season, Bates and McIlroy met and the chairman announced that neither of them would be leaving. But, following the first three games, with Bates again away on business in the Virgin Islands, eleven goals conceded and only one scored, Jimmy Mac resigned. For a short period the club was managed by three directors. The defeats continued, Bates returned at the end of September resigning as chairman but remaining as a director. Within six months he had gone.

Jimmy McIlroy said little in any resultant interviews other than, "All I can say is that it has been an experience."

Today, all these years later, he clearly regards it as an unrewarding period and that he was unsuited to management. "I thought I knew enough about the game. I thought I could improve players considerably. I soon learned I couldn't, as much as I wanted to."

*   *   *

After Oldham, Jimmy returned as chief coach to Stoke City and Tony Waddington. But though he was back with talented players he became just as unhappy, as he now battled with uncooperative, senior players and what he saw as lax sloppiness. Plus, he was back to travelling from Burnley to Stoke again in all weathers. By now his son Paul was 15 and the realisation came that he hardly saw him at all other than for just a few minutes at breakfast and a couple of hours on a Sunday. The demands of football weighed heavily on him; wondering how to maintain success, or conversely seeking improvement when things were bad. Sleepless nights came from struggling in the league, pondering over players' weaknesses and faults, making decisions about punishing or fining players, battling with the casual, easy-going atmosphere at the club. On the grapevine Stoke City was known as 'The Haven of Rest' where players in the twilight of their careers went to earn a last good salary in reasonable comfort. He had problems with individual players who questioned and challenged him.

He recalls that in one game George Eastham had made a good pass from which another forward had scored. But it wasn't inch-perfect and the forward needed to pause before shooting. "That was almost a great pass George," Jimmy said to Eastham, in the same way that Billy Dougal used to say the same thing to Jimmy years earlier. Eastham was furious, recalls Jimmy and professed to not having a clue what Jimmy was talking about.

The sum total of his achievements in this period was avoiding relegation. His love of soccer was fast disappearing and he wrote about this period in a piece entitled '*Why soccer sickened me*'. It made for very unhappy reading.

He moved to Bolton Wanderers as assistant manager at a time when they were in the doldrums and it is not unreasonable to say that his involvement there finally ended any of his interest in working within football. Their earlier days of glory, Cup-winners in 1958 and

Assistant manager at Bolton Wanderers. Jimmy pictured with the legendary Nat Lofthouse.

a long history of great players, were over as they fell victim to the abolition of the maximum wage and began to experience all the financial problems that came the way of similar clubs in Lancashire like Blackpool, Preston and Blackburn. It was the city clubs that were beginning to pull away from the pack. Burnley meanwhile would survive a little while longer into the 70s with their scouting system and seemingly endless stream of talent.

Through the sixties manager Bill Ridding strove valiantly to stem the tide at Bolton but it was a hopeless task and one by one the leading players were sold. In 1967/68 the fiery and explosive Francis Lee was sold; centre forward Wyn Davies had gone the season before, and the club were wallowing in the Second Division having been relegated earlier in the decade. Ridding was struggling and change was essential if the club was not to slide further into mediocrity and anonymity, if not the eventual oblivion of Division Three.

Ridding had been at the club for 18 years as manager presiding over their golden decade in the 50s, and 22 years in all including a spell as trainer. It was no fault of his that the club was in decline but simply because of the football facts of life in a changing era.

The directors, therefore, looked to a man who was a club hero and legend in order to solve their problems; instigate a revival, and restore their fortunes. They turned to Nat Lofthouse hoping that this would fire the public, inspire the players and rekindle the town's hopes and imagination. He had been a wonderful player for them and the words 'traditional, old-fashioned centre forward' fitted him like a glove. He wasn't especially big, being not much more than 5' 10" tall, but what there was of him was muscular, powerful, broad and toughened by work underground pushing coal tubs down the mines. His father in fact had a business delivering coal in the 1920s by horse and cart. Hard labour therefore made Lofthouse's stunning physique and strength.

With his legendary goalscoring, his fearless, battering ram style, his hundreds of goals down the years, strength, aggression and superb heading power and two-footed shooting he was a truly iconic player. As a one-club man he was to Bolton what Tom Finney was to Preston and Ronnie Clayton to Blackburn Rovers. Lofthouse was Bolton born and bred and played for no-one else. Legend says that in his very early days he would work eight hours down the pit from the early hours of the morning, then turn out for his club in the afternoon. Many years later in 1958 he scored the Wembley FA Cup Final goal for which he is so well-known, when he clattered into the back of Manchester United goalkeeper Harry Gregg, bundling him and ball over the line after Gregg had knocked a fierce shot up into the air, and turned to catch it as it came down.

Aged 35 he retired as a player and became reserve team trainer and it was in 1968 that he was asked to become manager, accepting the post but later regretting it. Brave and fearless on the field and seemingly indestructible, he was quite the opposite in the manager's chair. "I was the worst manager in the world," he said in later years, being totally unsuited to the job. The player known as 'The Lion of Vienna' because of one particular wonderful game he had against the Austrians and a former 'Footballer of the Year', was a worrier and found it hard to make difficult decisions as manager and face the fans' dissatisfaction.

By the time he replaced Ridding he was chief coach and therefore on the surface the obvious man to invite to take over. But basically he was just too nice a man to do the job. He initially accepted it on a temporary basis and set off to a good start with just one defeat in his first six games. But after that it wasn't long before they were wallowing way down in the bottom half of the table.

This then was the background against which Jimmy McIlroy came into the club as coach. The club had no money, and was heading inexorably towards the Third Division. Jimmy McIlroy, in truth, was going to be able to do little about it. They started 1970/71 well, winning the first two games and scoring six goals but there were only three more wins between then and November. Lofthouse was clearly out of his depth and moved upstairs as general manager. Jimmy McIlroy remembers one instance of Lofthouse's suffering.

"As a player when you collided with him it was like hitting a concrete wall. But there was one day as a manager when he needed some money and was asking the club secretary to change a cheque for him. It was not something he would have ever done but was simply because he didn't want to go to the bank in town and be seen by any of the fans and have to face them."

McIlroy took over. He lasted just two games and 18 days. The home game against Norwich City ended in a 0 – 1 defeat. The next game at Millwall was lost 0 – 2. The history books say that he left on a point of principle because he was expected, and under pressure, to sell the best players to help the club's financial survival. That in fact was true, players were being offered to other clubs at knock-down prices including John Byrom who went to Norwich after the clubs had agreed a fee but then decided to stay at the club. But Jimmy had another reason involving the chairman, Harry Tyldesley.

"The chairman asked me into his office and wanted to pick the team for Saturday with me. I told him that was OK as long as he announced in the programme and the Press that it was his team not mine. He refused, so I left."

One of the players there was a very young centre forward Paul Fletcher, and one of the players that McIlroy was under pressure to sell. Fletcher remembers those days with Jimmy McIlroy and one piece of advice he gave him. "To be a great player you need to be in a great team." Fletcher always felt these words to be prophetic since Fletcher became a key member of the great team at Burnley from 1973 to 1975. It could have gone on to greater glory if chairman Bob Lord hadn't continued selling the best players.

It was Lofthouse who came back into the manager's seat again when McIlroy left; McIlroy having managed to hang on to Paul Fletcher. It was eventual manager Jimmy Meadows who sold him to Burnley for £60,000. Meadows lasted only eleven weeks and Lofthouse took over yet again only to see the club finally succumb and suffer relegation to the Third Division at the end of 1970/71.

It had been a bitter season, and sadly, the 18 day spell as manager was Jimmy McIlroy's last involvement with football as player, coach or manager. If he says today that he just doesn't understand the game any more, it is reasonable to say that the seeds of that lack of comprehension began in the late 60s and the very early 70s. The 'modern' game was passing him by. His era was over.

The cult of the celebrity footballer had certainly been born by then. A growing number of players were no longer 'the bloke next door'. Values and attitudes were changing. He had had enough.

# Chapter 16

# Games To Remember

WHEN JIMMY MCILROY worked some years ago for the *Burnley Express* he came to Turf Moor as a reporter. Now it is just as a spectator. Over the years since he played for the club he saw all the ups and downs, all the triumphs and heartaches, just like the rest of us. In truth it is reasonable to say there have been more downs than ups and more heartaches than triumphs. In recent years he has seen few games at Turf Moor that any of us, let alone Jimmy himself, could honestly say were 'great' games. A 1 – 0 win over Liverpool in the FA Cup just a few seasons ago under Steve Cotterill, and a 2 – 1 win over Tottenham in the League Cup before that under Stan Ternent, and just a handful of league games where the nailbiting tension that comes from the desperate need for a win made them watchable, rather than the football itself. Not until Owen Coyle came to Turf Moor did excitement return on a regular basis.

One memorable game that he attended as a spectator and later wrote about was the 1987 Orient game when Burnley, his club, faced possible extinction in the final game of the season had they lost. In his long and distinguished career, as a player, there are many games that were memorable for him… albeit maybe for different reasons. It would be impossible to list them all but a few of them might be:

1953 Burnley 5 Man Utd 3 FA Cup McIlroy (1)…
1957 England 2 N Ireland 3 Wembley   McIlroy (1)…
1958 Burnley 3 Man Utd 0 League (just after Munich) McIlroy (1)…
1958 Burnley 3 Bolton Wanderers 1… McIlroy (2)…
1960 Burnley 2 Spurs 0 League…
1961 Tottenham 4 Burnley 4 League…
1961 Reims versus Burnley in both legs of the European Cup…
1962 Leicester City 2 Burnley 6 League…
1963 Chelsea 0 Stoke 1 League Two   McIlroy (1)
1963 Stoke City 4 Burnley 4
1964 Stoke City 2 Real Madrid 2, Centenary game (McIlroy 1)
1965 Northern Ireland 3 Scotland 2

There are others such as the European Cup Hamburg game, already covered in a previous chapter, the Maine Road game when Burnley won the title in 1959/60 again mentioned in a previous chapter and several other Burnley books. Only those who were there at Maine Road can imagine the tension of the minutes as the clock ticked down towards the final whistle. In the dressing room afterwards the players were elated but drained, physically and mentally. They celebrated with sherry drunk out of old tea mugs. Margaret Potts remembers the game vividly:

"The stadium was packed, the noise deafening, the atmosphere and sense of occasion like nothing I had ever experienced. Jimmy Mac wasted precious seconds and then minutes holding on to the ball by the corner flag. The referee kept looking at his watch but wouldn't blow the whistle. Mac jigged up and down by the corner flag again. The referee kept looking at his watch. When was the ref going to blow? Burnley fans were whistling and calling and praying. Our nerves were at breaking point. We looked at our watches time and time again… and then we heard that whistle and we heard the wonderful roar of acclamation and relief. We just cheered and clapped and felt so elated."

Then there was the '62 Cup Final; although this is not a game that he remembers with any particular fondness, and it is a game about which enough has been written already in various publications.

There is the Stoke City game that clinched promotion and the title, when he made 'the perfect pass', from which Matthews scored the clinching goal. The list could go on and would certainly include the Ireland-Italy World Cup games and then the games in Sweden.

There were FIVE FA cup games against Chelsea in season 1955/56. None were great games but what was memorable was the number of them, providing one of the longest ever FA Cup marathons. Back then there was no extra time at the end of the first replay. And after that there were yet more replays. The saga began at the end of January 1956 and did not end until three weeks later at White Hart Lane. The first 1 – 1 game at Turf Moor was watched by 45,000 people and Chelsea were the reigning League champions. In atrocious weather the first replay at Chelsea also ended 1 – 1. The second replay was at St Andrews Birmingham on the following Monday. McIlroy made the first goal for Peter McKay with a great pass. McIlroy himself scored the second but the game ended 2 – 2. The Chelsea equaliser came just 14 minutes from the end. The spin of a coin decided that the next venue would be Arsenal. On a part frozen, part waterlogged pitch, the game ended 0 – 0. The clubs tossed again for the replay venue and this time it was White Hart Lane. Chelsea won 2 – 0 and at last the monotony of playing each other was over. With supreme irony just weeks later Burnley beat Chelsea 5 – 0 in a league game at Turf Moor.

The 3 – 0 victory over Manchester United in March 1958 came just weeks after the Munich air crash had decimated the Old Trafford team. It was a match of bad feeling following Chairman Lord's remarks that he felt no obligation to assist United in their hour of need by selling them Burnley's best players. By way of explanation he also commented quite correctly that as a big club they had good reserve players and the finances to recover. Naturally it was his first remark that was widely reported. Although Burnley won 3 – 0, with Jimmy Mac scoring the first goal, the after-effects reverberated for weeks in the Press. This was the game where Pearson for United was sent off, and Lord was accused of labelling Manchester United as Teddy Boys, although he later denied this and revealed it was one of the directors.

There is neither the time nor space to write in detail about every one of these games that Jimmy Mac enjoyed or had some special significance. But one of them is a surprising choice. It was nothing special on the fixture list, was against Bolton Wanderers, had no great importance, but it was the game that Jimmy chose to feature with Chris Barnes in a Burnley matchday programme under the heading, 'Game of my Life'.

It was late in the '57/58 season and Bolton were due to meet Manchester United in the FA Cup Final. He recalled that they were always good, fierce games against Bolton, a derby game.

# CITY OUTCLASSED ALL THE WAY

## By Laurie Simpkin

THERE can be no excuses for Leicester City's 6-2 crash to championship challenging Burnley at Filbert Street last night. For they were outclassed. But I hope there will be no inquests either on this heavy home defeat.

No, the Blues, instead of having nightmares about the scoreline, should try and dream up methods of emulating the scintillating technique of Bob Lord's bargain basement boys.

I enjoyed every one of the 90 minutes of City's troubles. Because Burnley were always entertaining. This was the sort of game that more than anything, can attract the missing millions back to the terraces.

Nobody has written more harsh things about the Filbert Street crowd than this writer. But I must take off my hat to the supporters for the way in which they applauded the side to the dressing rooms at half time and at the end.

## No Magic

But those folk who stayed by the goggle box can be assured that Burnley have found no magic formula for footballing success.

They do the right things quickly and accurately. And they shoot when they get a line at goal.

**A dozen chances — six goals. That is a story in itself.**

Leicester were never allowed to become a compact force. They were always on the stretch. And when any team is under such pressure, cracks will show.

Burnley's rack was built of speed and precision. There was one occasion when they moved the ball so smartly that I timed only a lapse of five seconds from Blacklaw throwing the ball out to Banks saving from Pointer.

## Weaknesses

And there was nothing aimless about Burnley. Nothing at all. Every ball was loaded with intention, measured to perfection. They quickly discovered a weakness in the City armour that other sides have failed to exploit.

And I mean the lack of defensive depth to deal with the ball quickly turned back.

THIS WAS THE WEAPON THAT SANK LEICESTER. THAT GAVE BURNLEY THE FINGER-ON-THE-TRIGGER LOOK.

There will be some diehards, I am sure, who did not enjoy this match—because of the score. I have one piece of advice. See your doctor.

## Never Stopped

While I can't find too high praise for Burnley . . . the side whose only defeat this season was by the same score at Ipswich . . . I pay full tribute to the City.

They never gave up. And they never resorted to clog to counteract Burnley's better brain.

And I say quite sincerely that the Blues have played worse this season and taken home a bonus on pay day.

**My explanation for the score is that in this mood no side in the British Isles would have lived with Harry Potts' well-drilled squad.**

And I include Spurs.

Burnley had scarcely a weakness. Robson was back at his best to eclipse even the gentle genius of McIlroy.

Pointer was a dashing, goal-ravenous leader and there was pace, polish and power on both flanks.

## Overworked

Here it was again Leicester's defensive components having so much individual work to do that there was not the usual amount of propping.

Colin Appleton was the hardest worker on the park for my money. He worked ceaselessly.

BUT NO DEFENCE IN THE WORLD CAN BE REASONABLY EXPECTED TO SURVIVE IF THE BALL COMES BACK FROM ATTACK LIKE A PING-PONG BALL ON THE CREST OF A HURRICANE.

And this was the story. Leicester just could not escape Burnley's defensive grip. The Blues' attackers either found themselves caught in possession or telegraphing passes as the defensive funnel fell into line.

I felt particularly sorry for Graham Cross, playing on the losing side for Leicester for the first time.

## Wrong Position

I shall never agree that inside-forward is the position for which he is best equipped. But he tried so hard. And while City were level early on he and Gordon Wills looked quite a useful pairing.

Gordon Banks has had busier nights without conceding a goal. But apart from one late goal when he fumbled, he can regard this game as quite a good 'un for him.

In the end, Gordon even had the Burnley wing halves and full backs coming through, making the overlap to crack shots at him.

That was the game all over. Burnley were just too good.

**They had what little bit of luck that is always needed to oil a precision machine and it snapped smartly into top gear.**

All I say is Thank You, Burnley for a magnificent evening.

What City must do is learn from the lessons of this display. Especially in the cut back and that thunderbolt shot.

## Opened Well

Leicester started in fine mood and for a few minutes I thought Burnley were really going to have their work cut out.

Appleton and Cross both came not close enough to rounding off work by Wills who began in will-o'-the-wisp mood.

BUT THEN, FOR THE SECOND TIME IN FOUR DAYS THE LANCASTRIANS BEGAN A 6-2 MIDLAND SPREE WITH A 13th MINUTE GOAL.

Harris angled a quick ball out to Robson, tracking parallel to the touch line and he cut in to let go a good pass to his winger who left Banks no chance.

Four minutes later it was 0-2. Harris was the goal-maker. He nursed a fine square pass to the unmarked Connelly . . . a better player last night than when he was capped . . . and the right winger slammed home a fine left-footer.

For this was a two-footed attack. Back went the Blues and an Appleton-Riley-Keyworth move which covered sixty yards in four seconds and three moves ended with the leader heading wide.

## Number Three

It was brief respite for Burnley were three up at the mid-way mark in the half.

Robson got two bites at a ball fifteen yards out after McIlroy had taken Harris's pass to exploit the short pull back and the No. 10 streaked his shot into the net.

Within a minute City had pulled one back. Wills let go a long-angled ball go into the middle and Cross helped it on to his skipper.

**Keeping possession well, despite a double challenge, Walsh's left foot went into overdrive and Backlaw was beaten for the first time.**

But the visitors' three-goal margin was restored after 27 minutes through Connelly. McIlroy began the move which took in Robson before the winger showed his lethal finishing power.

Four minutes after half-time Pointer shot a superb left-footer into the net, just inside Banks right-hand post for goal No. five. But referee R G. New was baffled.

HE SEEMED TO THINK THE CENTRE-FORWARD HAD EXPLODED A HOLE IN THE SIDE NET BEFORE THE SHOT NESTLED AWAY IN A CORNER AND THE LINESMAN FINALLY CONVINCED HIM IT WAS A GOAL.

Burnley were playing with less power but retaining control and it was not until the 66th minute that they ended their scoring spree.

## Banks' Fumble

Adamson, a live wire attacker and a bonny defender, prompted Harris into a break through the middle and Banks fumbled as he went to ground to pick up from Robson.

The big insideman snapped up the chance as the ball ran free and hammered in No. 6 from close range.

And there might have been more goals. Connelly missed a hat trick by the width of a post, Harris and Pointer all had reason to testify to Banks ability.

It is to Leicester's tribute that they staged a minor revival towards the end.

Wills began to operate more in the middle and Blacklaw made two good saves and was beaten by a delicate lob from the wingman which just scraped the topside of the bar.

The fight brought reward in the shape of a second goal for Walsh after 80 minutes.

**The Burnley defenders, funnellers first class, left a channel down which Chalmers steered a good long ball and the Scot turned well and shot well.**

That was it—apart from the ovation which the crowd gave the teams at the end. That was heartening for those of us who campaign for better football.

And it was no more than Burnley deserved.

**Leicester City:-** Banks; Chalmers, Norman; White, King, Appleton (C); Riley (H), Walsh, Keyworth, Cross, Wills.

**Burnley:-** Blacklaw; Angus, Elder; Adamson, Cummings, Miller; Connelly, McIlroy, Pointer, Robson, Harris.

Referee:- R. H. New (Havant). Attendance:- 25,567.

"It was one of those days where running was effortless and I felt I could have run for hours. I genuinely could have played another game at the end of the 90 minutes. I just felt so fit and strong and as performances go it was as near to perfection as I ever felt I played. All through my career, in bed at night, you would analyse your performance and the mistakes you made. That night I slept so soundly there was not one mistake to go over in my mind. The Bolton game was just special for my own personal performance that stood out. But I played in many games when as a team we just clicked and were breathtaking on certain days. Sometimes I even recall wishing I was stood on the terraces watching us when that happened. It must have been beautiful to watch."

He remembers putting the ball accurately on Bobby Seith's head for him to score. Jimmy, in fact, scored twice himself to cap a flawless performance. Burnley won 3 – 1. In the great scheme of things it might not have been the most important of games – but as far as Jimmy is concerned it is one of the best he ever played.

If the Bolton Wanderers game was just another game in the calendar; the Stoke City versus Real Madrid centenary game was not. Played in April, 1963, it was a full-house, gala occasion and pitted McIlroy against players of the calibre of Alfredo di Stefano, Francisco Gento and Ferenc Puskas. He had only moved from Burnley to Stoke a matter of weeks before, and now here he was playing against Real Madrid in a truly prestigious game. Don Ratcliffe who played in the game recalls the occasion:

'The Real Madrid game was a huge game for Stoke City FC to celebrate its centenary. It was big news in the country at the time as we had Real Madrid over here and the last game they'd played in Britain had been the incredible 7 – 3 victory over Eintracht Frankfurt in the 1960 European Cup Final at Hampden park. Having all these big name players over meant that the eyes of the nation were on Stoke. I remember the build-up in the media was all about these great players that would entertain everyone with wonderful football – and I thought, hang on a minute, I can play too you know. Di Stefano was 37 by the way, so he was no spring chicken, although admittedly Stan beat him hands down in those stakes, being 48 and just about to win his second Footballer of the Year award, 15 years after winning the inaugural one.

Memories still lingered of the time Madrid had played a similar friendly at Wolves in 1957 and lost 3 – 2 at Molineux, and they had after all lost the previous season's European Cup Final to Benfica 5 – 3 – so perhaps they were an ailing team. They certainly didn't lack stars; Ruiz, Di Stefano, Gento, Puskas and Santamaria were all among the world's best.

They had been on a tour of European opposition such as Bordeaux and Hamburg in the preceding weeks, after turning down all offers of overseas friendlies until they had clinched their third successive Spanish League title – a feat never before achieved. So this was a special side. They'd beaten all their preceding opponents without conceding a goal.

I remember the night before the game the famous President Don Santiago Bernabau, who created the Real Madrid we all know, and built their stadium which is named after him, said, during the pre-match reception at the North Stafford Hotel where they were staying, "This visit to Stoke is one of the highlights of my life." He obviously hadn't called in at Chell Heath or Fegg Heyes on his way into the city. He meant the club that had discovered Stan Matthews, of course, and it was incredible how Stan's name was known around the world. His arrival really did change the club beyond all recognition.

The timing of the game (April 1963) was good as we were top of the League having gone on a great run since the long break, which an incredibly hard winter had forced us to take, but we'd done really well since the thaw and were confident of going up.

62,000 had seen us draw at fellow promotion challengers Sunderland on Good Friday, while 42,000 had turned up for the return on Easter Monday at the Vic. We'd won that match 2 – 1 thanks to two Dennis Viollet goals and we now looked nailed on for promotion. We could relax and take the Madrid game as a proper celebration game.

As it was, Gento was injured and didn't play, but aside from that, Madrid played their full team. I remember the kick-off as clear as day. Di Stefano just tapped it to Puskas and he flipped it up with his right foot and then hit it on the volley with his left foot. The ball flew the length the field and landed on top of the crossbar. Jimmy O'Neil would never have got it. Straight from the kick off!

After that frightening opening to the match, Madrid controlled things really and it was up to us to get amongst them. That was my job and I relished it along with Eddie Clamp. I got well and truly stuck in. I read the match report from the following day's Sentinel recently, and it describes me as "getting stuck in his own inimitable style."

Madrid were class, though, and kept control for much of the first half, but they only scored once. Di Stefano put a header wide from a few yards out, but then Ruiz broke free and raced clear to hammer home past Jimmy O'Neil. I think we did well to restrict them to one goal in the first half and after we regrouped a bit at half-time, and they made some changes to their team, we came right back into it.

Straight after the restart, Dennis Viollet picked up the ball on the edge of the area from a Jimmy McIlroy pass, beat one player and hit a shot which took a bit of a deflection which helped it into the far corner of the net. Then came my crowning moment. The full-back I was up against, Casado, really wasn't very good. Maybe he was having an off night, but I was skinning him for fun, time after time. I beat him again a few minutes after our first goal for Jimmy McIlroy to score. Now we were suddenly 2 – 1 up against Real Madrid - fantastic.

Ron Andrew came on as centre-half in the first half because of an injury to Eddie Stuart. Ron was still a bit green and he got well and truly done by Puskas, who produced a lovely piece of skill in the area and had Ron flying in to tackle a ball that wasn't there any more. So they got a penalty. Jimmy O'Neil tells this great story about that spot kick. On the afternoon before the match we'd all popped down to watch Madrid training and Puskas was there practising penalties. He cracked every single shot low and hard into the left corner of the goal. Six spot-kicks. When it came to the penalty in the match, Jimmy thought he had it covered. He knew exactly where it was going, so as Puskas hit the ball he flung himself to his right. But Puskas simply rolled the ball into the other corner, leaving Jimmy somewhat red-faced.

Stan had a wonderful game that night. He always raised himself for the big game and he played beautifully that night, causing the Spaniard all sorts of problems. He tired towards the end, though, as he was obviously getting on and Madrid missed a couple of chances to win the match when Amancia went clean through. Bueno hit the post, just as Puskas had earlier. But we survived and I think in the last ten minutes both sides settled for the draw. It was a cracking match and a great result'. *(From Match of my Life, Simon Lowe, Know the Score Books).*

If there was ever one game that Jimmy drools over, it was the night Burnley destroyed Leicester City in September 1961, at Filbert Street, with one of the most devastating displays of football ever seen from a Burnley side. For good measure the previous week they had slammed six past Birmingham City at St Andrews. Twelve goals in two back-to-back away games, if this wasn't an outstanding feat, then nothing was. These two games were part of a run of seven consecutive wins. At Leicester there were long spells when absolutely everything Burnley tried came off and every move was sheer poetry. The Burnley official handbook described the game:

'The match opened at a furious pace with the familiar pattern of the home side going all out for that vital first goal. Burnley's defence stood firm and then in a spell of just nine minutes, Burnley's every pass and every move clicked to bring them a three-goal lead… nothing could stop Burnley… at half-time the Leicester fans, now apparently resigned to the fact that their team was about to be slaughtered, stood to applaud as the teams left the field… they gasped as Ray Pointer netted a fifth with a shot of such power that, as it came out of the net and was kicked away, the baffled referee at first gave a corner… And as the final whistle came with Burnley still weaving those intricate patterns, and having won 6 – 2, these fans stayed on to salute the victors with as much enthusiasm as they could have shown had their own team been at the top.'

The *Leicester Mercury* sang with praise, describing the scintillating technique, the precision and speed, every ball loaded with intention, measured to perfection; no side in the land could have lived with Harry Potts' well-drilled squad. There was scarcely a weakness; pace, polish and power on both flanks, the ball coming back like a ping-pong ball on the crest of a hurricane. And against all this, there was the legendary Gordon Banks in goal. Jimmy McIlroy remembers that no-one, spectators or players, wanted it to end. If there was a football heaven, then this was it.

In a tribute to Jimmy Mac, Frank Keating penned Jimmy's description of the game with what are supposed to be Jimmy's words. Jimmy is sure, however, that although the sentiments may be true, the words are not quite his.

"A sort of purity, an utter untouchable magnificence, possessed us and we blended into one, each truly on song as in a single melody. I think it finished 6 – 3. None of us wanted it to end. Nor did the crowd. Nor the Leicester team. They were as stunned as us at the sort-of, word-perfect drama of it. It was like the opera, when the whole arena stood to applaud us off, as a way of saying they couldn't bear us to go… when it clicked it must have been utterly breathtaking to watch. I can't tell you why exactly, but we found ourselves caught up in the excitement and charm, and elegance and flow. Everything pinpoint exact, and all of us razor sharp and on the very top of our game. I know it's ridiculous but, oh, how I wish I could have been on the terraces actually watching us play."

Of the international games that stand out, England 2 Northern Ireland 3 in 1957 has to be one of them; a match that was written off as a certain win for England.

"At our hotel before the game we were all confident we could beat England," said Danny Blanchflower, "we thought that on the day, we could rise to the occasion and with a better spirit undermine them."

There were great empty spaces on the terraces because the English had stayed away – but the Irish fans were there. Ireland leading 3 – 2 held out against the battering from the English forward line in an unbearably tense finish. Gregg made countless, impossible saves, the ball was kicked off the line a dozen times and when the final whistle went the Irish scrambled over the barriers, dropped their coats and clothes as they ran, and mobbed their players. The exhausted players simply wanted to get back to the bath but the fans surrounded them in joy. Ireland had beaten England, and Jimmy had scored one of the goals. A win was unheard of, unthinkable, but what a wonderful day it was for the Irish, said Henry Rose.

"What a wonderful day for the Irish! Wembley has never seen anything like it since the first Cup Final of 1923. As Mr Griffiths blew the final whistle hundreds of wildly enthusiastic fans burst onto the sacred pitch in celebration of Ireland's first win over England since 1927. Every man jack of their triumphant team was hoisted shoulder high and carried through a mob of cheering fans.

This was a fitting, blood-warming curtain to one of the most exciting and entertaining internationals I have ever seen. Helping to make it a memorable Wembley was a goal for a player on each side; Alan A' Court and Sammy McCrory playing their first internationals.

I find it easy to spare a thought for the beaten warriors of England if only for their magnificent, great-hearted efforts to snatch a draw in those last five thrilling minutes. They forced four corners, had two free kicks just outside the penalty area, Kevan had a header blocked, Edwards was fouled by clubmate Jackie Blanchflower.

The valiant Gregg, surely the best 'keeper in Great Britain, almost broke his back in saving a vicious drive by Clayton. What a storming finish for the millions of TV viewers. But this England team is a long way from being good enough to bring back glory from the World Cup. I think it earned a draw. And I am not speaking because of my 2 – 2 forecast, the only English sportswriter, I think, to concede the Irish a chance of winning.

The posts and bar helped the gallant Gregg. But let us not begrudge their triumph. Don't jump about to any false conclusions about Irish fervour, rough, reckless tackling and the rest. No sir, this was football ability, the pay-off for the Peter Doherty brand of soccer."

One of the Irish tactics had been to negate Johnny Haynes and make him play the passes that the Irish wanted him to make, in other words (shades of Billy Dougal) make him do things he didn't want to do. The victory was crucial, not just because it was against England but because it set up the forthcoming World Cup game with Italy, and gave the Italians something to worry about. "We were a close bunch," said Blanchflower, "and beating England made us feel we could take on anyone."

Of course Jimmy Mac remembers it, especially the goal he scored, thus immortalising himself. But he laughs as he tells the story of it. "It was a penalty. When I took it Eddie Hopkinson went the right way. I actually hit the post, but the ball rebounded and hit Eddie on the head and rolled over the goal-line." One of the England players looked at Danny Blanchflower with an expression of disgust that signified 'you lucky so and so'. But Blanchflower merely grinned and quipped: "Brother, when we do it – we do it clever."

There is a very short clip of film on the *YouTube* website that shows this goal. What is memorable, if not only for the comedy of it, is the undisguised anguish of Hopkinson who flings his cap to the ground and storms around in frustrated fury.

The inimitable Malcolm Brodie also wrote about the game for the *Belfast Telegraph*.

'WEMBLEY, WEDNESDAY WHAT A DAY! This, the showpiece centre of world soccer has never seen anything like it before. The clock hands in front of the Press stand were at 4-12. At that moment referee B. M. Griffiths blew his whistle and Ireland had won 3 – 2 – the first victory over England for 30 years.

And it was the sign for jubilation amongst the few Irish supporters to invade the field.

# Slick Burnley give Wolves a chasing

Despite being challenged by Wolves' right-half Eddie Clamp, Burnley left-winger Brian Pilkington manages to put his centre across.

## WOLVES GET THE SLIP

BURNLEY ................ 4, WOLVES .............. 1.

A LITTLE bird, wearing a black and old gold rosette, whispered that Wolves were storing their power for a special European Cup burst in Belgrade on Wednesday. FORGET IT.

What you shouldn't forget is that Burnley's navigator, Jimmy McIlroy, had his slip showing throughout the 90 minutes—a thigh bandage that helped him to forget a strained muscle.

England left-half Ron Flowers must have been relieved when he saw "Mac" strapped up. Later he could be forgiven for thinking it was a bluff. Jimmy the jewel pulverised them.

Before I'm accused of believing there's only ONE player at Turf Moor, let me praise every other Burnley man. It was telling team work that made Wolves just admiring spectators at times.

### Dangerous

Burnley fans joined chairman Bob Lord and team-manager Harry Potts in asking me afterwards: "What about John Connelly now, then?"

He scored a goal, Jimmy Robson diverted his shot for another and Ray Pointer hit two "smashers" with half chances.

I'm glad to report Connelly played well for my money. Sometimes he came unstuck when he tried to pass left-back Gerry Harris on the outside, but his switching inside was a date with danger for Wolves.

Ray Pointer's fair hair stands out in any football group. At Turf Moor yesterday it seemed to be everywhere, weaving patterns through the Wolverhampton defence. Here Ray nips in to slip the ball past Finlayson for Burnley's third goal.

# McIlroy Superb As Wolves Wilt

JIMMY McILROY: an outstanding display.

They jumped over the greyhound rails on the running track, on the sacred turf, and surrounded the green-clad, victorious Ireland eleven.

Out came the bands to play the National Anthem, but the Ireland players never got a chance to stand in a row. They were lifted shoulder-high by excited green and white scarved Irish fans who jumped and danced and even produced a huge shamrock, on which were the words: "Come on Ireland!"

The players got no opportunity either to walk towards the tunnel. Most of them were carried there by the hoard of followers who simply overwhelmed the police. Yes, a great day for the Irish.

Was the win merited? On the second half showing I would say definitely yes. They got a number of chances and they took them. That was the secret behind this win. Never do I remember such suspense and tingling excitement as there was in the closing half hour.

It was simply exhausting as my eyes travelled continuously from the green sward to my watch. Slowly the minutes ticked away, Ireland 3 England 1; then came the Edwards goal with only ten minutes left.

Ireland had some narrow escapes but they continued to move into attack and perhaps with a little more speed from the inside forward trio, we could have scored a fourth.

It was 4-8, 4-9, 4-10... oh how slowly and inexorably those hands went round, 4-11, 4-12. There goes the whistle – Ireland had done it for the first time in 30 years to become the third country to beat England at Wembley, the others of course being Hungary and Scotland.

Now let's have a quick look at the players. Harry Gregg. One word describes his performance – magnificent. His anticipation was brilliant and in the first half he brought off spectacular saves, some of them from point blank range. Yes, I know no greater 'keeper at the moment than the boy from Coleraine. Perhaps he could be faulted for England's first goal. But how that ball got past, it had only inches to get through.

All praise to the full-backs. They were always competent and confident against the England wingers Douglas and A'Court, in my opinion the two most dangerous opposition forwards. McMicheal beaten frequently by young Douglas, played what I thought was one of his best international performances. And as for Dick Keith he had a brilliant international debut.

And our half-back line must come in for the greatest plaudits of all. They said before the game that England's middle trio was the best in the world. Certainly not in any way superior to Ireland – in fact, it was nowhere as good. Danny Blanchflower has never put in a more superlative display for his country than this one. What a master of the soccer craft he is. He captained the side with a coolness and intelligence which laid the foundations for this Ireland showing.

And his brother Jackie in the middle, completely sewed up his Manchester United clubmate Tommy Taylor, who was lost in the role of a twin centre-forward along with Kevan.

Bertie Peacock, too, was always dominant, always prepared to spring into attack at the slightest opportunity, and the England right flank got little change from the captain of Glasgow Celtic. But, all in all, a glorious middle trio who held the Ireland defence together in the shaky first half and paved the way for the goals in the second.

The Ireland forwards cannot take the same praise even though they did score three goals. In the first half not one of them seemed to click, especially Simpson and McCrory who were slow and ponderous every time they went for the ball. Bingham too, had his moments but generally the line did not function well until the second half. Simpson was really never able to triumph over the commanding Billy Wright. McParland was rarely in the game and the same can be said of Sammy McCrory, until he got the second goal.

Then we began to see some of his skill and opportunism which has earned him fame as a goalscorer with his various cross-Channel clubs. For a while I thought he was going to be a flop but that second goal and his subsequent play ruled him out of that category.

And what of England? As I said after the Cardiff game, this is not the England of old. They are not by any means a class side and on this showing the World Cup is just a mirage'. *(Malcolm Brodie Belfast Telegraph)*

Of all the McIlroy games in Burnley's history, the 4 – 4 draw at Tottenham is one of most talked about. Les Gold, a Spurs fan, can still remember every detail, especially when the fourth goal went in and Burnley were then 0 – 4 down. He remembers that at that point Dave Mackay bowed to the stands in a display of unconcealed arrogance. Burnley Chairman Bob Lord was furious. Les remembers the drenching weather, and that up to this point Spurs had lost just one League game.

Before half-time Burnley managed to pull one goal back. Brown the Spurs goalkeeper could only push out a cunning chip from McIlroy, "a truly great midfield genius displaying majestic poise," and there was Connelly to pounce.  As they left the field Danny Blanchflower came up to McIlroy to jest that it was 4 – 1 and only halftime. Suffice it to say here that the comeback and the final 4 – 4 final score was wonderfully deserved; in fact no one would have been surprised if Burnley had snatched the winner in the final minutes. Alan Hoby in one newspaper wrote:

'The crowd streamed away from this red-blooded masterpiece in the mud warmed and dazzled by one of the finest exhibitions of football I have ever seen in a League match. This was a game – Champions versus Challengers – which excited and electrified every thrilling phase. And what a stirring and sensational comeback we saw from Burnley after being 4 – 0 down. Incredulous then apprehensive, the vast crowd forgot the squalls and the sleet as the score skittered crazily from 4 – 1 at half time to 4 – 2, then 4 – 3 and finally 4 – 4 with 16 palpitating minutes to go. But the fears of these damp, chilly thousands swiftly turned to cheers as they watched Burnley after their mid-week mauling in the European Cup, gloriously live up to their Championship label.'

But another 4 – 4 result that is not talked about quite so often, happened at the Victoria Ground, Stoke City when Burnley were 7th and Stoke were 17th. Only this time McIlroy wasn't playing for Burnley. He was on the Stoke side. It was the first time he had ever played against Burnley and this was an eagerly awaited game with hundreds of Burnley supporters heading for Stoke, part of a 37,000 crowd. Many of them wanted Mac to play well, and indeed show Lord that he had been wrong to sell him. Other fans' loyalties were divided so the result was perfect for the neutrals. McIlroy had been putting in extra training in readiness and it paid off in the first half when he had a superb game, making the first goal for Stoke for good measure. In the second half, however, he would fade. By halftime Burnley were 0 – 3 down and looked to be heading for a drubbing. During halftime the Stoke directors, assuming the game was done and dusted, were jubilant, whilst the Burnley directors were stunned. McIlroy could be forgiven for looking towards the Burnley directors as he walked off with a smile on his face. But in a minute, early in the second half, Burnley scored twice to make it 3 – 2. A defeat still looked inevitable as Peter Dobing made it 4 – 2, but incredibly in the last six minutes Burnley made the score 4 – 4. When Connelly was seen down on the floor holding his face with hardman Eddie Clamp in close attendance, the referee sent Clamp off, and in those days a sending-off was a rare event. John Connelly can still remember the incident. "He was a good player, Eddie Clamp, but he had this temper. I'd cut in, and wellied the ball towards goal and it hit him on the thigh. It really hurt him so I went over and asked was he OK? And he butted me". Harris scored with a bullet shot from the free kick. With only a minute remaining the Stoke goalkeeper mishandled a cross and Harris was there to smack the ball home.

Perhaps it would be fitting to end with a mention of Jimmy's final international appearance when Northern Ireland beat Scotland 3 – 2 in Belfast. It was the game where Willie Irvine of Burnley scored the winner with just a minute to go with an acrobatic overhead kick. 'MAGICAL McILROY AGAIN' was one headline. It was as if being his swansong game it brought out the best in him one last time. He was up to all his old tricks, gave a masterclass; as good as ran the game, even outshining the illustrious George Best.

"McIlroy was the most intelligent and constructive member of the attack. Rarely did he waste a ball and his passing and positioning kept the line on the move. McIlroy was involved in most of the moves. All the build up seemed to centre on McIlroy and his use of the ball was excellent."

How fitting it was that at the end he was hoisted aloft on the shoulders of jubilant supporters. There is an iconic photograph of himself and George Best being carried off in celebration. He no longer has the copy of this picture that was once presented to him. How he would love to find a replacement. It was a reminder of how he finished a distinguished international career with style, and in joyful triumph.

# Chapter Seventeen

# After Football

OCTOBER, 2008, and it was Jimmy's seventy-seventh birthday. Amongst his memorabilia, or at least what is left of it having given so much away, there was a bundle of clippings and old newspaper pages. There was one that I read more than once.

*I want to write this week about a fellow I have known closely for a number of years and to announce his "passing" and also to reflect with anyone who is interested on his fairly long, and I hope, worthwhile career.*

*He is Jimmy McIlroy, the footballer, and he has I think, played his last game. Therefore I have taken it upon myself to write his 'obituary' having been very attached to him all through his career. In fact I am qualified to do so, having shared with him his joys and sorrows, triumphs and disappointments. The end has been impending for some months now. There was a brief flicker of extended hope in his final international game, when he helped Ireland beat Scotland. But that was really a fairy story ending to his home international appearances.*

*Nothing official has been issued yet but somehow I feel that December 27th at Stoke's Victoria Ground was his last serious battle. And again, what a fairy story to finish when he helped his team-mates defeat Burnley, the club which considered him no further use to them three years ago.*

*McIlroy I have heard said, was born under a lucky star, and I won't deny that. But for being blessed with a greater love for football than many other boys he would have been a bricklayer. He would probably never have left his native Irish shores, never met folk in all walks of life, and never have seen some of the wonders of the world.*

*The ex-bricklayer, has I know, suffered many setbacks, but his lucky star saw to it that he was amply repaid with worldly goods. And what but a lucky star would see to it that he favoured as his job the sport he loved so much. This footballer I know admitted to his friends how much he owed to other people for his success. If at times he didn't always show his appreciation, I can tell you that he felt it.*

*He considered soccer a game of skill; and in the last couple of seasons was grieved by the tough and vicious style that has crept in. McIlroy like everyone who is interested in the game, voiced his opinions as to who he thought outstanding performers, and it was obvious that his ratings were based on skill and character.*

*When a long life like this footballing one ends, he expected a great sadness and melancholy – but that wasn't so. Perhaps because he knew better than anyone else that the end was approaching and felt that he had given as much and been as dedicated as most and it was time to make way for the enthusiasm of youth*

*Jimmy McIlroy, the footballer, has inspired me to look for, and if possible, keep his ideals on football. If, in the future an Irish boy wants to come to me and says he wants to play the game the way McIlroy did, then his efforts over the years won't have been in vain.*

Jimmy wrote this beautiful piece about himself in the New Year of 1966. At that point he thought that the game against Burnley had been his last. How was he to know that the Oldham management job would frustrate him so much that he would be reluctantly persuaded to pull his playing boots on again? How was he to know that after just two games as manager at Bolton Wanderers that more frustration and disillusion would provoke him to turn his back on the game he had loved?

Brian Glanville was aghast when I told him that after Bolton Wanderers, Jimmy had spent two years back in the bricklaying trade. "What," he said quite shocked. "Such a wonderful player has to go back to bricklaying. It's an abomination. Can you imagine any of today's highly paid top footballers having to do that when they finish? Of course not, they're millionaires." The indignation was quite apparent in his voice.

"I suppose the truth is I was never really happy as a manager", wrote Jimmy. "As a player I always wanted to stay in the game but then the moment of realisation came after only about five minutes of the first game at Oldham. I could coach all week and try and get ideas across, but then on Saturday afternoon it was all out of my hands. So I came to the conclusion that football is for the players – and anybody else is little more than a hanger-on. So for that reason I registered as a player again and went back out on the field."

More recently he said: "Management was the biggest mistake of my life. I wasn't cut out for management. Right from the very first match I realised that. Once the players crossed the line onto the field I was helpless. There was nothing I could do to improve things. If the players were good they would get you good results and that would make me a good manager but if they couldn't play well, then I couldn't make them into good players.

"Football left me with no great savings or a big bank balance. When I finished at Burnley I had nothing in the bank and it never occurred to me to ask for a backhander when I moved to Stoke. I learned later that manager Tony Waddington had expected me to ask for one because he had put £2,000 aside in case I did. Believe it or not I took a pay cut at Stoke. I was on £80 a week in the season and only £60 in the summer. At Burnley I got the same all year.

"It was an Irish pal of mine called Ernie Gill I worked with first after Bolton. We were both unemployed and we knew there was a lot of demolition work going on in Burnley. It was a case of going down to the Council offices and asking is there any work today. Our job was bricking up windows. We bought an old lorry for £50, went to Accrington to buy the bricks and for two years I really enjoyed it."

There are stories that people were so amazed to see him laying bricks that small crowds gathered to watch. Jimmy McIlroy, the greatest player ever to pull on a Burnley shirt; a Cup Finalist, had played in Europe, possessed a Championship medal, and was now bricking up windows in the grubby, derelict backstreets of Burnley. How was this possible?

"Then, what was then the *Lancashire Evening Telegraph* asked me to join them. They probably thought I could get all the inside information at Turf Moor but, I could never cover a game at Turf Moor as a *Telegraph* reporter. Bob Lord wouldn't allow me in. They took me on to cover Burnley matches, but when he heard of my appointment, Bob Lord banned me from the Press Box.

"Granville Shackleton taught me how to be a journalist. I'd begin by 'phoning the stories in and then gradually began to write them myself. But cost-cutting led to redundancies and I was one of the ones asked to leave. I had no idea what I was going to do but then, unexpectedly, the *Burnley Express* rang up and asked me to join them."

Whilst he was at the *Lancashire Evening Telegraph* Jimmy was a regular feature writer for the Saturday evening *Sports Pink*. In those days he had the fashionable, longer hairstyle with the bushy sideburns. I still have an old *Sports Pink* today, from 1974, and underneath the title 'Jimmy McIlroy writes', his hirsute face beams at the reader. It was a good one to keep and in it he looked back on 'the good old days' and contemplated his own lack of understanding of an ever-changing world. What he wrote is as relevant today as it was then, over thirty years ago.

*"There is nothing wrong with football, and nothing should be changed," I was informed recently by my nephew, a university student, whose opinions are intelligent and warrant consideration. And he added: "Awarding points for goals, changing the offside laws or adopting any of the million and one suggestions won't improve the game as a spectacle."*

*I immediately jumped on him about defensive plans destroying the game and negative football being a bore; insisting, that to open up the game by using the wings and developing an attacking flair, would be more attractive.*

*His look told me I was an idiot. "And what fool manager would attack and leave his defence exposed, or would use the width of the field and disintegrate a solid compact modern formation?"*

*I gave up exasperated – but what he said keeps coming back to me. Having been spawned on a different style I thought was a good one from both a player's and a spectator's point of view, I couldn't agree with his theorising. Then I began to recall the hours I used to spend talking with two former Turf Moor trainers, the late Billy Dougal and Ray Bennion.*

*Hadn't they reminisced about their playing days and hadn't I derided the style and tactics of that era? I thought it ludicrous for full-backs to mark inside-forwards and at the same time be expected to position so as to tackle wingers as well. I can remember their little smiles when they said: "There were some great full-backs in those days, you know. That method of play was the style of the time."*

*Matthews, Finney, Carter, Mannion, Lawton and Haynes were the stars in the method of my era, and just as Bennion and Dougal talk nostalgically of their halcyon days, I and everyone of my vintage would dearly love to turn the clock back, which of course is impossible.*

*Today's stars know nothing of our method and don't want to either. No full-back wants to be exposed to a winger and no winger wants to stand idle on the touchline waiting for the ball to come to him.*

*Today's managers and coaches are the same as people in every walk of life – we copy the latest fashions in clothes, hair styles, holidays, television and cars, and they copy every little change that takes place in the game. And football, like everything else is changing, though ever so slowly, as new ideas are introduced.*

*Today's young fans know no other method of soccer and were it possible to demonstrate ours; they would ridicule it as did my nephew. My generation cannot turn the clock back – so we do the next best thing – we criticise and reminisce, but there is no harm in that.*

*Football is a young man's game. My contemporaries are shocked by what happens on and off the field. Shocked at the brutality of players and at the wanton destruction of property and the pitched battles of young fans, and we feel frightened and helpless because we don't understand it.*

*Every day we grow away from them and every day they develop new ideas, new themes and new tactics. We want everything to stand still, forgetting that every day there are new 14 year olds whose opinions and behaviour differ, if only slightly, from even last year's 14 year olds.*

*Better minds than mine cannot provide answers or alternatives to these happenings. I'm reconciled to accepting the fact that all these events are the result of an ever-changing pattern, and so our generation looks on helplessly.*

*At school I raided orchards for excitement, and although today's behaviour may appear a lot more vicious and callous compared to pinching a few apples, we mustn't forget that it is all done for the same thrills and kicks.*

*We find it impossible to accept that they must go to these lengths for fun, but obviously they do, and what's more they also know we are powerless to do anything about it.*

*Perhaps there is some satisfaction to be gained by my age group from watching today's young both on and off the field by grumbling and reminiscing.* (Courtesy of the Lancashire Telegraph)

It was whilst working at the *Telegraph* that he wrote about the Martin Dobson transfer to Everton. It was a sale in 1974 that took Dobson himself and every Burnley supporter by surprise. But his time had come. No matter that Burnley were at the top end of the top division, Bob Lord needed more income to keep the club afloat and to pay the wages. He always denied it was to pay for the new Stand named after himself; but supporters preferred to call it the Martin Dobson Stand after the sale. McIlroy empathised with Dobson in a piece that was heartfelt and poignant, and in it he saw several parallels to his own sale.

*What a strange effect Martin Dobson's transfer had on me this week… a feeling of re-living the past, of being in someone else's shoes, but, most peculiar of all, knowing that someone else was experiencing exactly the same emotions I had experienced all those years ago. Quotes from Martin of being "dumbstruck… shocked and surprised… surplus to requirements… and going home in a daze to discuss the situation with his wife" all had an alarming ring of familiarity. And, I wondered, did it cross his mind that this was how McIlroy felt on the morning he was told he was to be sold.*

*Like some form of clairvoyance just after the Dobson deal was completed, my wife told me how, she too, felt something unusual about his transfer because she kept wondering what was going through Mrs Dobson's mind, certain that they shared the same feelings and only years apart.*

*Martin and I now know the feeling of numbness, of bewilderment and of hurt pride. I expect that as I did, he will be determined to show his former club that he can still play. Only with time will Dobson convince himself that his transfer was inevitable. When he saw himself in the Everton colours for the first time he may have felt that he was looking at a stranger and that his new image would take some getting used to.*

*Among the thousands of people interested in Burnley Football Club, only I have any idea of what Martin is going through, conditioning himself to accept that instead of being a hero, he is now no longer a Turf Moor player.*

*And before anyone jumps in to remind me that the £15,000 or thereabouts he will collect as part of his percentage of the transfer should anaesthetise the pain, let me speak on his behalf in wagering he would gladly forfeit this sum if he could wake up and find that these few days were only a nightmare. Money cannot take the place of something that was part of your life and it is a poor substitute for a host of wonderful memories and comradeship.*

*In my case, my transfer did not earn me a single penny, but, without making this article sound too much of a sob story, it may interest some to know, that my roots and affections for this little town deprived me of about £10,000 - tax free. The Stoke City directors granted me permission to stage a testimonial game in my third season there on the assumption that I would move to the Potteries instead of travelling every day the 184 miles to the ground and back, and take a coaching post. But I couldn't leave Burnley – it's as simple as that – and when the chance came to take over at Oldham, which meant I could still live in Burnley, I jumped at the opportunity.*

*Naturally, my roots were longer than Martin's because I'd been at Turf Moor longer and I've never been able to tear them up. In my case, without dramatising, my career practically ended the moment I was sold. The Stoke City club was good to me, as I'm sure Martin will find Everton, and the Potteries fans were wonderful, as indeed, he will find the Goodison supporters, but the truth of the matter was that I had become accustomed too much to the Turf Moor atmosphere and I didn't want any other.* (Adapted from 'I know the feeling', Burnley Express September 1974)

It was in the early eighties Jimmy wrote about the Northern Ireland troubles. These were horrendous times in Belfast and several other troublespots. For those of us not directly involved, the atrocities and violence seem a lifetime away now. How quickly we forget from a distance. Making regular visits back to Northern Ireland to see his family he saw at first hand the devastation, fear and tension. In August, 1977, he and his wife Barbara were caught up in a terrifying fire bomb incident in Lisburn late one Thursday night. They drove through the streets as it was actually happening with sparks cascading down on the car roof and the shops burning fiercely.  It was not easy being an Ulsterman then. "Caught in the middle of the madness was like being on a film set," he wrote.

*From the moment you check in and the embarrassing way they go through your luggage and frisk you 'Chicago style' you know your destination cannot be any airport other than Belfast. So thorough is the search that your travelling companions, if interested, can be aware of everything in your case.*

*When I made the trip last week a bag of liquorice black and white mints for my mother were closely scrutinised. After so many years of this procedure I still find it hard to take seriously, maybe because all around you thousands of travellers are leaving without a second glance and certainly without being subjected to a hunt for a dangerous weapon.*

*On my flight there were a number of young, fit-looking lads, with short hair-styles and although in jeans and anoraks, you didn't have to be Sherlock Holmes to deduce they were servicemen returning to complete their tour of duty in Northern Ireland. I found myself looking long and hard at them with a feeling of guilt. Here were young men in the prime of life destined for a terrifying situation where it is impossible to recognise friend from foe, where a moment's relaxation could result in death from a bomb or bullet.*

*Perhaps the guilt stems from the fact that I too, was bound for the same area, yet knowing that I could walk the streets or drive down a country lane with 99% certainty that no-one would have me in the sights of an armalite rifle; while these lads, many of them teenagers, were targets from the moment their plane touched down at Aldegrove.*

*The first-time visitor is quickly reminded of the tragedy that is Ulster, and has been for 13 years, on coming across a heavily guarded road-block with huge ramps to prevent speeding cars just outside the airport.*

*The visitor will also discover that his car can be stopped anywhere, anytime and searched; that before entering hotels, stores or most of the shopping streets in Belfast centre; he is frisked and his belongings gone through. These are just a few of the inconveniences that my countrymen have had to endure since 1969, on top of the fact that they might just get in the way of a stray bullet or be fractionally late to respond to a bomb warning.*

# Like a war film scene

# MY TERROR IN AN IRA FIRE BOMB

**TO BE** caught right in the middle of an all-out IRA fire bomb attack is a terrifying experience and not a pretty sight.

It happened to my wife and I on Thursday n i g h t shortly after 11 pm in my home town of Lisburn.

## Confusion

The town caught the full blast of a Provisional IRA wave of fire bombs that destroyed six shops and hundreds of thousands of pounds of property and stock.

R e t u r n i n g from a friend's house, we first noticed how bright the sky over the town centre was. As we got nearer we ran into a scene like a war film. Flames lit the sky,

## By Jimmy McIlroy

soldiers, police and fire engines were dashing everywhere as first one shop caught fire and became a holocaust and then another.

With fire bombs igniting in such a short space of time all over the town centre causing confusion, and being on the scene while it was actually happening, there had not been time to cordon off roads and we found ourselves in the main street with sparks cascading down on the roof of the car.

I have followed with obvious interest what has been happening in Ulster for years, and sometime ago even arrived on a bombed site only hours after the explosion. But to be caught right in the middle of the madness that has inflicted my homeland was bewildering and sickening.

The worse moment was to be stopped by traffic lights less than 20 yards from the blazing inferno off a large material shop. It seemed hours before the lights changed, and today, looking back, I am still amazed that the occupants in the

other car remained cool and observed the Highway Code — an indication of how acclimatised my countrymen are to the horror of events in their land.

Next morning we strolled through Lisburn to see the extent of the damage and here again the scene was astonishing, but in a different way. Shoppers only paused momentarily to gaze at the destruction.

The people of Lisburn have seen it all before and life had to go on. I heard someone remark: "We were lucky it was only a fire bomb attack and not a gelignite one."

Most shops employ a security officer who searches everyone entering, but a quick search through handbags and baskets cannot detect the tiny appliances that ignite hours after they have been planted.

## Film set

Back home in Burnley today it seems for the past week I have been on a film set instead of a holiday with my family.

Our car was stopped on several occasions for searches, surrounded by armed troops, and at night it was weird to observe the beam of a searchlight from a helicopter, lighting up the ground so powerful that it was possible to read a newspaper.

This is Ulster, and a way of life everyone there has to endure.

● An MP today called on the Prime Minister to recommend to the Queen to cancel next week's Jubilee visit to Northern Ireland.

Mr Marcus Lipton, Labour member for Central Lambeth, said: "I wish I could be as confident as the authorities that all will be well. But even at this late stage, I think the Prime Minister should have second thoughts and recommend the cancellation of the visit."

*One of the first tips I received years ago was make sure when held up at traffic lights that my car wasn't close to an army or police vehicle as they were prime targets for snipers.*

*Having painted a frightening picture, you might well ask, 'Why then risk life and limb by going there'. I can only tell you that my parents live only six miles from Belfast and to date the only 'trouble' they have seen, is what you and I have seen on our television screens.*

*Mind you, when there was a period of intense bombing a few years ago, they did hear the occasional muffled explosion followed by a red glow in the sky. And I wouldn't have to sit long in their front room before they could point out someone going past who had suffered in some way from terrorists through the loss or injury of a relative.*

*On this latest trip I toured the notorious Shankhill Road and the Falls Road areas, the scene of the most horrific bestialities of the conflict, and despite assurances from my guide, there was an undisguised feeling of relief to leave behind those streets of squalor and despair.*

*Graffiti is everywhere, rows of houses are either bricked up or are burnt out shells and pubs are hardly recognisable behind barriers of steel shutters and concrete pillars – yet life goes on.*

*You stare at all this and ask yourself what's it all about and when it is going to end. Who are the people who are responsible for this reign of terror, for the deaths of over two thousand servicemen and civilians, and what cause can possibly justify such wanton destruction of life and property?*

*I used to believe it was simply a Catholic – Protestant religious confrontation stemming from hatreds and fears centuries old. But not any longer.*

*The Provisional IRA is a Marxist group hell-bent on creating a Socialist Ireland, not a Catholic one, and on opposite sides there is a Protestant gang operating on the pretence of defending their sect. But, in actual fact, between them they make sure they keep the situation inflamed to maintain the backing of a people who desperately want to live in peace.*

*I'm convinced too that many of the young men who plant the bombs and aim the rifles are hood-winked into believing their cause is just, while the ambitious men at the top of both organisations are entirely different.*

*In all the areas where violence is rife in Ulster, and I must stress that these are only a small part of the province, it is widespread knowledge that shops and businesses are paying protection money. The irony is that should these payments be allowed to lag, then the 'protectors' move in to beat up the owners or blow up the premises.*

*Both gangs, under false banners, keep the hostilities raging, while caught up in it all is the army who want no part of it but cannot escape from it.*

*It is naïve to talk of pulling the troops out and letting the Northern Ireland people solve the problems themselves, because what Prime Minister is willing to go down in history as the one responsible for the civil war that would surely follow?*

*I see Ulster as an embarrassment to this country, and a financial liability, but England is stuck with it, and with politicians determined not to give an inch, there just isn't an answer.*

*The media in England nowadays only let us have details of the main outrages in Ulster, which is understandable seeing that what at one time was a major story is now almost an everyday happening over there.*

*Only in Irish papers and on television can the whole picture be fully understood.*
*(Jimmy McIlroy 1982)*

A year later in a tribute to Brian Miller, just sacked as Burnley manager, it is interesting that he forecast, quite correctly as it turned out, that Burnley would struggle after they won promotion in 1981/82 unless they added two or three more class players to the side. In reply he was told by one of the directors that all the young players would be a year older and able to hold their own in the new Division. As he penned the piece in January 1983, relegation was looking distinctly possible and a touch of panic was setting in within the club hierarchy, he observed. *(For full article see appendices)*

One of his most memorable newspaper pieces was written in 1987 after the Orient game when defeat would have consigned the club he had served so gracefully to non-league football.

*Never in all the years I've played football have I experienced emotion like I felt at Turf Moor on Saturday – and I blame the fans. It all started when looking from the sponsors' room window and seeing the queues in Brunshaw Road. First, it took me back 25 years to the days when this was a regular scene. Then it hit me. The reason why so many people were paying their first visit to the ground, probably for many seasons, was that they did not want Burnley Football Club to die.*

*And if anything, there was an even greater impact on taking my seat and seeing the terraces and stands looking like a football ground should look – containing hordes of people. Never in all my years in this town have I been made so aware how much the club means to so many. Someone, who should have known better, remarked to me earlier that had 10,000 of these fans been there at the start of the season, Burnley FC would not be in their present plight. With restraint I said: "If Burnley had fielded a team worthy of their support, they would have been here."*

*The atmosphere was electrifying. A man tapped me on the shoulder saying: "This is how much the club means to the people of Burnley and the surrounding areas." The noise as the players lined up for the kick-off was deafening. There was no way the Clarets would lose through lack of support – but there was fear.*

*For the first time ever at a football match, I felt my eyes moist. This was my club, on the brink of humiliation, and here were thousands more who felt the same way. Because of what happened all those years ago when I was transferred, I had always imagined something of my feeling for Burnley FC had died. But on Saturday afternoon my emotions clearly showed. I was as concerned for the future of the club as the most ardent fan out there.*

*At the final whistle, while everyone around was hugging and kissing his or her neighbour, I felt spent and elated, and then sad that the club had to be in its very death throes to awaken interest among its former fans. Now there is some breathing space for the directors to ensure this situation is never repeated. They must work at retaining this new found interest and to be seen in the next few days to be taking concrete steps to build a team worthy of the support of almost 16,000 very relieved fans.* (Burnley Express 1987)

"It was while I was at the *Express* that I went out and about interviewing interesting local people and loved that part of it. The editor must have been happy with what I did. (I always joked that nobody knew more than me about the local ladies' darts leagues). The editor came up to me one day and said I was as good a reporter as I was a footballer.

But then I had a Deep Vein Thrombosis. The consultant asked me what I did and I said 'reporter' and he told me that was no good. I was sitting at a desk for too much of the day, and this would do me no good at all if I continued. So I had to finish and I was barely 60, and living on invalidity benefits."

The shop he opened in 1963 that might have provided him with a healthy income into

Jimmy ventured into the business world with his Ladies' and Gents' outfitters.

his retirement did not last. 'The Separate Shop', ladies and gents' outfitters, at 202 Colne Road, Duke Bar, opened with a full page splash in local newspapers and extensive re-development of the premises. Jimmy Mac brought his sister Muriel and his brother in law Roy Verner to Burnley to run it.

"A lot of footballers when they reach my age, start thinking of something outside the game and many of them go into a newsagent's or tobacconist's business, or into pubs. I don't know of any other player in this line so I may be setting up some kind of record," he wrote about it at the time. Jimmy joked that his speciality would be the ladies swimwear section. Despite its position, well away from the town centre, it did well. But, with all the travel back and forwards to Stoke, Jimmy had less and less time to devote to it. Besides, he recalls now, when he was in the shop he felt like he was in a cage. In hindsight, he says, he was never cut out to be a shopkeeper. "It was a silly thing to do, I had no business experience." He eventually closed it down, and rented out the vacant premises, then finally selling them. Thankfully, unlike so many footballers' retirement ventures, he lost no money on it.

His interest in Burnley Football Club has been rekindled by the excitement of games such as the wonderful Arsenal Carling Cup-tie and the stunning, unexpected victory on a night when the ground was packed, and noise and pulsating excitement took the minds of those who were there back to the long-gone games against Reims and Hamburg. But since he played there have been times when the football at Turf Moor has been so poor he could barely register any interest at all. During those long seven years when the club was in the old Fourth Division, the 'Wilderness Years' we called them, he despaired of ever seeing the club back on its feet again. In 1987 before the victory over Orient he thought it might die forever. But 2008/09 was a good time to be a Burnley supporter. Arsenal was followed by Tottenham when little Burnley were just two minutes away from a Wembley Cup Final. And then in May 2009 there was indeed a Wembley Final and he was there to see Burnley win 1 - 0 and promotion to the Premiership. It was an unforgettable day.

Jimmy's wife Barbara died a few years ago and today he lives alone in the same house he bought for her so many years ago. But the phone never stops ringing and visitors are frequent. He has family very close by, makes regular visits to Northern Ireland, golfs, paints and spends considerable time in the warmth of Spain with his friends the Cooks. The invitations to open or attend various events and functions in the town arrive in his letter box on an almost monthly basis. He cannot walk into any shop or supermarket without being recognised and greeted. Quite simply he has become a symbol of Burnley the town. The names of Burnley and Jimmy McIlroy are inseparable.

## Chapter Eighteen

# The Magic of McIlroy

SOMEWHERE IN THE film *Shakespeare in Love* written by Tom Stoppard, there's a memorable scene.

"How does a play come together?" says the stage manager, played by Geoffrey Rush.

"I don't know, it's magic," is the reply.

You could ask the same about Jimmy McIlroy, and ask how does a 'footballer' come together.

Jimmy himself might well say that it is not magic, but that it is skill, and that the skills he possessed were learned in boyhood with the hours and hours he spent with that tennis ball. But then, I ask myself, why is it that all the rest of us, who played with a tennis ball in our backyards, or in the school playground, didn't go on to become another Jimmy McIlroy.

There is a magic, and it is a magic that cannot be taught. It is something indefinable, something inherent, something natural and instinctive. It is why great painters can paint, and great actors can act. It was in Tom Finney, Stanley Matthews, it was in Jimmy Greaves, it was in George Best. They and Jimmy Mac never really needed coaching. It was why Brian Glanville called his *World Soccer* piece 'The Magic of McIlroy'.

Reporter Don Smith wrote about the same magic of McIlroy shortly after a Burnley win over Tottenham in 1959. He described the same goal that Glanville had seen at White Hart Lane.

'When asked about my outstanding memory, I had no hesitation in recalling an April evening in 1959. Over 32,000 had roared Spurs into a 2 – 1 lead after Albert Cheesebrough had given the Clarets a 1 – 0 early advantage. Time was running out with Burnley facing apparent defeat after a run of eight matches without a loss. Spurs mounted another attack to seal the result but the move broke down on the 18-yard line.

Here Jimmy McIlroy gained possession in the inside left position, slightly left of centre. Mac had been the mainspring of Burnley's raiding power, prompting and inspiring and generally playing too well for the comfort of the home team whose skipper Danny Blanchflower decided to give his personal attention throughout the second half. Consequently when Mac controlled the ball at this particular moment in the fading minutes, Danny snapped into the tackle. McIlroy's flickering footwork outwitted him. Spurs fell back to close ranks.

Instead of releasing the expected forward pass Mac moved forward with deceptive variations in pace, with swerve and sway, the feint to pass and the sudden dart ahead, he weaved a mazy way through a baffled defence in an astonishing solo dribble – a slightly diagonal run into the penalty area where he was at inside right with only goalkeeper Hollowbread to beat.

There was a roar as the keeper came out. Mac realised that Cheesebrough had come up in support and that there was a desperately racing defender rushing back to cover the goal line. Mac coolly slipped a square pass as if to say, "Albert, finish it off." Albert obliged.

The crowd erupted. Probably that last unselfish touch added the final touch of lustre to the incredible run. The whole stand rose, arms waved, they applauded… a Tottenham crowd mark you. They were clapping at the restart as their tribute to a moment of sheer artistry.

It was the finest goal Mac never scored. Yes, one of the three longest dribbles I have ever seen under pressure; a rare and golden cameo of football history'.

Granville Shackleton remembered one piece of sorcery in a piece he wrote called 'The Magic of Mac'. (The word 'magic' seems to be a popular word in any discussion of him).

'He tantalised and baffled experienced opponents to the point of despair and if I had to pick out just one moment of McIlroy magic, this would be it. Burnley were playing Birmingham City at St Andrew's and needing just another goal to really sink the home team's challenge.

He picked up the ball in their half, suddenly swept forward chased by two opponents and ran diagonally to the corner flag on the far side of the field.

I saw him backheel the ball during one of those delicate skips and moments of acceleration and so did about 25,000 other people in the main stand and behind the goal Birmingham were defending.

But his two markers didn't and carried on until Jimmy stopped by the flag, still with his back to them, and started his swaying.

In the meantime Burnley had picked up the ball Jimmy had left behind and with the rest of the defence cursing their two lost colleagues Ray Pointer rammed it into the net.

Then, Mac stopped his doodling and pointed out where the ball now was, to the two defenders'.

Towards the end of March, 1999, Jimmy was surprised and delighted to learn of his inclusion in the Football League's Centenary list. The official invitation, issued by the Football League's then Chief Executive, Richard Scudamore, explained what the occasion was all about.

'At the start of this season, the 100th League Championship, you were recognised as one of the 100 best players ever to have graced professional football in this country. The 100 League Legends were honoured for their individual contribution to the game and to mark this achievement the Centenary Season culminates in a celebration 'Evening of Legends' (London Hilton, evening of 13th May 1999). This will be a unique gathering, never again will so many of football's greatest ever players join together to honour our national game'.

No greater tribute could have been paid to Jimmy McIlroy.

In the writing of this book I have read dozens of written references about Jimmy McIlroy and spoken to no end of people about him, either face to face, or on the end of a telephone many miles away.

Typical was Les Gold who lives near the Spurs White Hart Lane ground in North London, and whose support for them goes back to the fifties. "Jimmy McIlroy," he exclaimed in his broad Londoner voice, "it's a pleasure to talk about him. I saw him play so many times. I know so many players from that era and he was the best. He's the greatest player Burnley have ever had. I'm just so glad you're writing a book about him."

Author Ivan Ponting who has written no end of football books expressed the same

# McIlroy magic beats City super soccer

### By ERIC WELDON: Burnley 4, Manchester City 3

PARDON the superlative—but this game earned a wow rating from first whistle to last. It was tremendous, superb, colossal, in fact, the nattiest Soccer sight at Turf Moor since the same fixture last season. These two clubs have a habit of bringing out the best in each other.

The Irish phantom, Jimmy McIlroy, enjoyed it—after taking about seven minutes to warm up.

Then he began to threaten City's spanking new victory run with a delightful display of Soccer sorcery.

His creation of Burnley's second goal was a good example of his calm genius. His body was poised to go right round Bill Leivers. But suddenly he was flashing down the goal-line to his left.

Ray Pointer glanced home the pass from a yard outside the post.

Joe Hayes had a high old time of it, too. He was the spark that fired the City attack into action. He showed more trickery and speed than a hunted fox. But he had not an ounce of luck with the net in his sights.

Blacklaw's crunching save robbed him of one chance and another was whipped from his whistling boot only three yards out. The end of the game was even more fantastic than the heart-tingling stuff that had gone before.

## Coasting

Burnley seemed to be coasting to a comfy two points with Pointer's goal and another by Pilkington under their belts.

Then in the 79th minute George Hannah scored City's first.

Back stormed Burnley to puncture City's hopes again with two goals from Billy White.

And to cap it all City pulled themselves off the ground to shake Burnley rigid as Hannah again and then Colbridge made it 4—3.

But old-man time was against this fighting City attack. As Burnley punched to save a point the referee whistled time—phew !

Adam Blacklaw, Burnley's 'keeper, was being watched by the Scottish selectors. He made a couple of mistakes.

**BILLY WHITE:** replaced the injured Jimmy Robson and scored twice.

Above: City goalkeeper Bert Trautmann is helpless as Ray Pointer turns a left wing cross from Jimmy McIlroy into the net for Burnley's second goal.

Below: Manchester City's first goal. With Adam Blacklaw unable to hold onto a shot from Billy McAdams, George Hannah is left with a simple chance to reduce the arrears.

sentiments. "Wonderful, it's time someone did a book about him." If Jimmy was worried that no-one would be interested, two publishers expressed immediate interest.

Pete Ellis is typical of the supporters from the sixties who saw Jimmy Mac play, and yet, Pete is from Fareham in the south of England. So many people, years ago, who lived far from Lancashire chose Burnley as their team. Why? They read and heard about Adamson, Connelly, Pointer and the rest, but above all McIlroy. They came to love and admire the skill of their football. In the seventies it was Adamson's team that played with poetry in their feet. Pete wrote to me to say that he had been born in 1947 and later noticed that this coincided with Burnley's Cup Final appearance. At boarding school in Winchester he and a friend played football with a tennis ball (Jimmy Mac would be proud to hear that) allowing themselves only to head it. It was the start of Pete's love affair with football. Like so many young lads he picked a team to follow and fancied a team that played in claret. One of his pals told him: "Well there's Aston Villa and West Ham but there's also this up and coming little side from Burnley who are turning a few heads."

But it was Pete's story of the radio in the English classroom that was most intriguing. "Another thrilling time I had was in the 1961/62 season when the Clarets were in a class of their own. Well I didn't have a radio of my own back then but in our English room we did, but it was totally out of bounds. But Burnley were on a fantastic ride with a possible double looming and most of the media were following them. Anyway nothing was keeping me away from those matches and by hook or by crook I was determined to put up with any punishment if I was caught with the radio in the English room. So I used to sneak in on Cup match days and listen on the school radio. The school was so strict I dread to think what might have happened. Now, today, I can look back and am so pleased I did. I've got all those vivid memories as though it were yesterday."

"I don't know Jimmy personally," wrote Pete, "but the pleasure he gave me in the sixties, and the memories, will live with me to my dying day. I didn't actually get to meet the great man at a book launch at the club last November but would love to have had a chat. But you know what it's like, he never had five minutes to himself, he was continually signing autographs. What a player, God bless."

Somewhere way back in these pages I think I wrote about how we as supporters grow up with our team; how they are part of our boyhood, and we can remember the milestones in our own lives through the events at our football club. Pete wrote to say something similar. "Growing up in my youth, they were my life. I've had some pretty tough experiences and they took away a great deal of pain."

Norman Giller, author of 80 books, one of them being *Fifties Football* and co-author of books with Jimmy Greaves, had this to say: "If Jimmy McIlroy was at his peak today the bidding would probably start at £30million... and Bob Lord would probably want a few pounds of sausages thrown in. When Danny Blanchflower was about to place the ball for his penalty against Burnley in the 1962 Cup Final, Jimmy Mac said to his good friend and countryman: 'Bet you miss it'. Danny, one of the most accurate penalty specialists, duly steered the ball past Adam Blacklaw and as he ran back past Jimmy said: 'Bet I don't'. Give my regards to Jimmy Mac and tell him that I considered Danny and he poetry in motion."

Cliff Jones of Tottenham remembered McIlroy well, having played against Burnley several times and also against Jimmy at International level. Jones was without doubt one of the finest wingers of the time, and always considered Spurs to have been very lucky to have beaten Burnley in the 1961 FA Cup semi-final. Jimmy Greaves said he was so fast that not even wearing an over-coat would have slowed him down.

"Ah Jimmy McIlroy, the 'Prince of Inside Forwards', he was known as," said the former Spurs winger and Welsh international. "He was a lovely player. We had such rivalry between the two clubs. We used to pinch a lot of their free kicks. I played against him so many times and remember the games against him and Burnley well."

"He was a great player," said John Connelly who went on to mention that among his cherished memories of Jimmy are the times he had the ball in the corner not letting anyone take it off him.

"There was one game at Everton one Christmas, it was a record crowd something like 78,000, and we were as good as down to ten men but winning 3 – 0. They had this giant clock at one end and I remember watching that clock in the last minutes with Jimmy in the same corner underneath it with the ball by the flag. And they just couldn't get it off him.

"It was against Wolves where I think he did that for the last time. Ron Flowers told me this story about how they knew Jimmy Mac would hold the ball by the corner flag so they told Eddie Clamp to do something about it. So Jimmy had the ball in the corner, and Eddie Clamp set off towards him from something like 25 yards away. Then with two yards to go he just launched himself at Jimmy and took him, ball, flag and everything six feet over the touchline. They'd figured out how to stop his tricks and in those days you never got sent off for anything like that. I'd guess that was the last time Jimmy ever tried that."

Writer Brian Glanville was delighted to hear the name Jimmy McIlroy after so many years of not knowing how he was or what he was doing. "What a lovely man," was his immediate reaction to my first telephone call. As he went away to fetch pen and paper I could hear him talking. "Chap on the telephone writing a book about Jimmy McIlroy, how wonderful." He came back to the telephone. "Whenever Burnley were in London the two Jimmy's, McIlroy and Adamson, would come to my house for coffee. Then I'd have lunch with the team at Bailey's and go on the coach to the ground with them."

Stanley Matthews felt that Jimmy Mac was the last piece of the Tony Waddington promotion jigsaw and spoke glowingly of him in his autobiography *The Way It Was*.

'Jimmy was a marvellous inside forward. In fact, I am given to say, he was the complete inside-forward. As a person Jimmy was genial. As an inside-forward he was a genius. When play was congested in the middle of the field, up out of the trapdoor would spring Jimmy. A will-o' the-wisp player, he glided rather than ran about the pitch with the ball seemingly hypnotised on the toe of his left boot. A sudden drop of a shoulder and a flick with the outside of his boot, the ball would leave his foot at some acute angle and another rearguard was breached. On releasing the ball, it was if Jimmy disappeared into the ether. He would re-emerge inside the opponent's penalty area, take the return pass and pass again into the net. I say Jimmy passed the ball into the net because more often that not that is what he did. His cool, calculating brain enabled him to size up the situation and choose his spot. Not for him the robust shot into the roof of the net; Jimmy simply guided it between the outstretched hands of the goalkeeper and the post. He succeeded in doing so 150 times during his career. In my time in football, I'd come across players, who, it was said, could make the ball talk. Jimmy could make it sing like an aria and along with Dennis Viollett, he made my life easy at Stoke City.'

Geoff Crambie is a Burnley supporter of nearly 60 years. He went to his first game in

The opening of McIlroy Park in Lagan Valley, Lisburn.

1950 and saw the young 19-year old McIlroy in what might well have been his first game. He is unashamedly a McIlroy admirer and in 2000 wrote this in his local newspaper column after he had taken his grandson Nathan to Turf Moor for his first game. He had heard the news that Jimmy Mac would be opening a new stand which was to be named 'The Jimmy McIlroy Stand'.

'This was an occasion not to be missed and also, more important, this was the ideal match to take grandson Nathan, age seven, to his very first football league game. As we arrived at Turf Moor, both excited, me for the ghosts of the past, Nathan for the things to come, suddenly there was a most tremendous cheer as the dignified figure of Jimmy McIlroy walked across the ground he graced for 13 years.

It was still the same warm Irish smile, although the once coal-black hair had now turned to snow. The crowd of more than 14,000 stood to give a mighty ovation to the great man. Then as I pointed out to Nathan my all-time football hero, who I first saw on this very ground when I was his very age, more heroes of the past strolled onto the pitch. "Look there's Pilky, Robbo, big Brian Miller, the wizard winger John Connelly and stalwart Tommy Cummings".

As the crowd's cheers rang out, Jimmy, surrounded by his team-mates of 40 years ago, cut the tape and the newly named stand was enshrined in glory. As thousands of balloons were released into the December sky, anything that followed had to be an anti-climax. But no, this day had more surprises for us... As the minutes tick by Glen Little and John Mullin team up to play superb football and then, in the very last minute, Andy Payton completes his hat-trick and Burnley have won a marvellous victory by 3 – 2. What a day to remember!'

Harry Brooks in his efforts to have Jimmy made a Freeman of the Borough, wrote this to the Council:

'It is often claimed that Burnley Football Club is the heartbeat of the town and it is indisputable that the club has been a central and significant force in Burnley, through good times and bad, over the past 100 years.

There would be reason enough, then, for the Council to accept my proposal if it were simply to celebrate the contribution of a man widely regarded as the club's finest player. Jimmy McIlroy gave the essence of his footballing life to the town he arrived at in 1950 at the age of 18, fully justifying the intense public outrage in 1963 when he was, in an act of supreme folly, forced out of the club before his playing days were at an end.

How can one encapsulate his unique world-class quality as a player? Grace, style and exceptional skill were allied to pace, strength and unselfish effort in the cause of his team. It is difficult to convey his distinctiveness to anyone who did not see him play. There is no one quite like him in the game today – individual genius of that kind can never be replicated precisely – but those who saw the brilliant young Russian playmaker Arshavin run the European quarter-final against Holland, will have had a flavour of a McIlroy command performance.

But it is not for football alone that the town should honour him. For nearly sixty years in Burnley he has been a fine example of citizenship, lending his name, his presence, his interest and his time, in response to constant requests to support local good causes and worthwhile public events.

Modest almost to a fault, fame never rested more lightly on any man's shoulders.'

Bob Lord paid Jimmy a fine tribute, except this was not *the* Bob Lord but a chap Jimmy used to meet in Scott Park when he took his granddaughter for a stroll in the evenings. This particular Bob Lord was a 94-year old musician who had once played in the dance and music halls in Burnley. They would often chat and this was a fellow who harked back to the days of Halley, Boyle and Watson. He had seen them all, including the wonderful Bob Kelly. Jimmy remembered this particular Bob Lord fondly:

"Darling," Bob once said to Tara. "I hope your granddad doesn't reach 94, there's not much fun." And then one evening he told Jimmy: "Ah McIlroy, you weren't a bad player but Bob Kelly was that much better." And as he said it he held up his thumb and first finger just three inches apart. Jimmy still smiles at the recollection of being told he wasn't quite Burnley's best ever player, and says it was this that always kept his feet on the ground.

In 2002, when a Burnley FC shirt that once belonged to Jimmy Mac came up for auction at Bonhams; (the shirt worn in the European Cup-tie against Reims when Burnley won 2 - 0), it was bought for nearly £4,000. Jimmy had swapped it after the game with French player Raymond Kopa, and it was Kopa who put the shirt and other items up for sale. The successful bidder was Peter Hodson from Cambridgeshire. One of the unlucky bidders, Mervyn Hadfield, another Burnley fan, desperately wanted to buy the shirt for his grandson. Though he did not take the shirt home, he did have his bidding card framed. He penned his thoughts afterwards and called it *Jimmy Mac's Shirt*.

'And there it is, lot '389, in the Bonham auction sale,
Last time I saw it, Jimmy wore it: To me it tells a tale.
Of football played with passion, and verve not oft repeated,
Till Reims, champions of France, trooped off Turf Moor defeated.

Eleven heroes played that night, for Burnley were a team,
As modest Mac has always said, when the Clarets were supreme.
I keep on looking at the shirt as other lots go down,
And I think back to Jimmy Mac and the pride he gave our town.

In the fifties and the sixties with super soccer skill,
Today in his adopted home, there's great affection still.
And now the time has come to bid, I'm full of apprehension,
The auctioneer has made it clear, this lot has claimed attention.

And so it proves, my humble bid, is soon left far behind,
As hundreds turn to thousands, perhaps I shouldn't mind.
At least I tried for Jimmy's shirt, and can't help feeling proud,
It reached the highest price today, and truly stirred the crowd.

As Jimmy Mac so often did, but now before I leave,
I stand before my hero's shirt, and touch the light blue sleeve.
I gaze at it with reverence, the famous number eight.
Over fifty years have passed; it's been a long, long wait.

One lingering look; one final touch, and now I turn to go,
I hear a French voice say to me, "This man, a great one, no?"
I face the Gallic football fan, the question to address,"
"The one who wore this Claret shirt, he is a great man yes."

And suddenly I've no regrets, for here, I'm glad to be.
Though it was priced beyond my scope, the shirt reminded me,
Of what I have that can't be sold, or even put on show.
My priceless memories of that night, Mac wore it long ago.

*(Mervyn Hadfield 2002)*

Even though it had been nearly 40 years since they had last met, Ken Bates referred to Jimmy in his Leeds United programme notes in November, 2008. Bates still remembered what a model player he had been. In his notes he was critical of the modern international world that awards over 100 caps to someone like David Beckham, when the caps have been devalued so much, and have been awarded for appearances in the most meaningless friendly games and for appearing for just minutes as a substitute. He described Jimmy Mac as the Gianfranco Zola of his day and playing in an age when a cap meant something and every one was thoroughly earned.

Burnley FC author David Wiseman devoted several pages to Jimmy in his '*Vintage*

Jimmy's pride and joy – his three granddaughters, from left to right, Tara, Bethany and Catherine McIlroy.

Proud moment in front of one of his European shirts on the night of the Freeman Award.

The Freeman Night with the Lady Mayor and Chairman Barry Kilby.

Family and friends share Jimmy's honour.

*Claret'* book and saw him play throughout the fifties. He makes an observation that makes you wonder. At the end of season 1961/62 Mac was injured with ten games to play. It was those ten games that cost the club dear. Mac missed five of them and was not fully fit in the ones in which he did play. Burnley did not win one of the five games he missed. If only… just two more wins would have won the title again. If Jimmy was placed on the transfer list because he had allegedly "stopped trying" or, "not giving wholehearted effort," then David Wiseman points to a newspaper report that undermines that allegation. It was a game at the end of 1962 against Sheffield Wednesday and Burnley won 4 – 0.

"Despite the ice-rink surface this was a vintage McIlroy who gave a performance his fans won't forget in a hurry… who said McIlroy is finished." Wiseman went to Stoke to see him play after his transfer, but says it just wasn't the same.

On Tuesday, December 9th, 2008, Mac became a Freeman of the Borough of Burnley. The websites and the match programme, the local paper were all filled with fans' tributes. Typical was this from Brian Sellers:

'I was fortunate enough to see you in action during the late 50s and until your departure to Stoke in '63. It is hard to put into words what you and the team meant to the supporters of Burnley Football Club during those vintage years of League Champions, FA Cup finalists and the wonderful European evenings on the Turf. Probably the best example I can give relates to my father who was a lifelong Burnley fan. When he heard the news of your

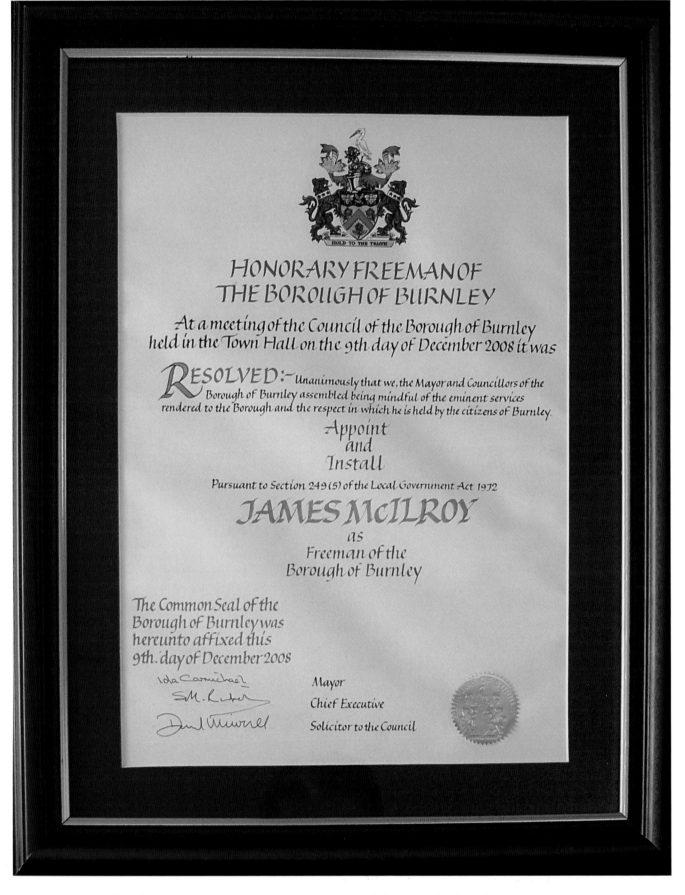

The scroll declaring James McIlroy as Honorary Freeman of the Borough of Burnley.

departure he was so incensed, upset and shocked, he vowed never to pass through a Turf Moor turnstile again and, despite my best efforts during the Adamson era, he kept his word.

Jimmy you leave many lasting memories of how the 'wonderful game' should be played. I can still vividly recall you with the ball at your feet by the opposition corner flag surrounded by 2, 3, or even 4 defenders. Moments later, following a shimmy or two and magic footwork you would be bearing down on goal, leaving the defenders in your wake. Then there was the penalty taking where you almost seemed to mesmerise the opposition goalkeeper, like a rabbit trapped in car headlights. Three or four steps up to the ball, a sway of the hips to leave the keeper rooted to the spot and you would stroke the ball into the bottom corner of the net'.

But Jimmy had worried about the occasion; he had worried about what he would say up on the platform in his response. But his heartfelt speech was a gem, acknowledging both his roots and the place of Burnley in his heart. His words were typical of his modesty.

Jimmy and I had been meeting and talking for much of the year and when Jimmy asked me to be one of his guests at the Town Hall ceremony and at the football club afterwards, I have to say I was quite speechless. It says much about Jimmy that he will never understand why he induces these moments of unashamed admiration in the people who saw him play so many years ago, and even in people who never saw him play when they are in his charismatic company. He has continually questioned the 'need' for a biography about himself as a result of his quite humble modesty. And this, from a man of whom Stan Matthews once said, "Had he been born an Englishman his name would have been one of the biggest in world football."

As I sat and listened to his acceptance speech, and accompanied him to the meal afterwards with his other guests, my mind went back to when he was a player and I was a wide-eyed, young supporter convinced on every Saturday that Jimmy Mac would win us the game, and who every Friday night said a silent little prayer in bed that Jimmy would have a blinder. All these years later I know exactly how I ended my prayer: "And please dear Lord let Jimmy Mac win us the game."

Whilst Jimmy's father, who wanted so much for his son to become a footballer, might never have imagined the fame and glory that would come his way; neither would my father have ever imagined that I, the once hero-worshipping, day-dreaming schoolboy, would one day write the biography of this 'Prince of Inside Forwards'. Life works in mysterious ways.

Today, when Jimmy Mac reads and receives tributes such as these, of course he enjoys them, but at the same time is embarrassed and will be the first to say that he was part of a team; and that he had great players playing alongside him. He remembers the occasion when he and most of the players of that great Championship, and Cup Final team, assembled on Turf Moor for the naming of the Jimmy McIlroy Stand some years ago. He made a short speech in which he said he thought it should be named the Champions Stand. What he omitted to say to the fans that day, and wishes today that he had, is simply this, and perhaps he can say it now:

"What a treat you missed; not having seen these fellows play."

Some of us did and can still see their magic when we close our eyes; Blacklaw, Angus, Elder, Cummings, Miller, Adamson, Connelly, Robson, Pointer, Pilkington, Harris, Bobby Seith, Trevor Meredith, and not forgetting McIlroy himself; golden names from a golden era.

How lucky we were.

# Postscript

PRIL 2009 AND A BIG YEAR is facing him. Burnley Football Club has awarded him a Testimonial in recognition of his services to the club he left in 1963.

There is the 50th Anniversary of the winning of the 1959/60 Division One title to look forward to. The club are planning various functions and events. This makes him smile, not just in anticipation, but also in a sort of benign, humorous acceptance that once again the old players will be brought out of mothballs and dusted down ready for inspection. This thought first occurred to him several years ago at the parade of legends at Turf Moor before a game against Gillingham. "I felt like Captain Mainwaring from Dad's Army. We old players are wheeled out in front of the Burnley fans as often as the BBC does re-runs of Dad's Army."

On top of all this there is not one book but two to publish in October of 2009 to coincide with his 78th birthday. In addition to the biography, he decided he wanted to do something really different, something that as far as we know, no footballer has produced before. The 'scrapbook' that will be produced complements this biography and is made up of items of his memorabilia and those that we have begged and borrowed from collectors. So many items have been gathered that there was never any possibility of including them all unless we had decided to produce a book that was so big it would be unaffordable.

It is a happy accident that the testimonial programme and the two books coincide. The books were started well before the testimonial was announced.

He is no great fan of the football autobiographies that are churned out by the dozen, many of them 'written' by young players in their early twenties, already awash with money, and who have no real story to tell. And always there is the recurring thought in his mind, "Who on earth wants to read about me and just how many people actually remember who I am?"

This last season at Turf Moor has been a good one and I remember him saying after the pre-season game against Glentoran that he had a feeling that there could be a good season ahead. The season's success at Burnley Football Club and the style of play has rekindled his interest. He has felt an excitement that has not been there for some time. There were the wonderful Carling and FA Cup games. Then, with just two games to go at the end of the season Burnley were still in the top six play-off places with a four point lead.

With just the one remaining game to go on the final Sunday, nothing but a win would suffice as Preston North End crept up to within just two points. There was an emphatic 4 – 0 win. He was as nervous as the rest of us prior to that game and just as proud and delighted as the team progressed to the play-offs. Reading were duly disposed of in the play-off semi-finals. The club progressed to Wembley with the prospect of Premiership football just 50 years after Jimmy Mac's title triumph. Jimmy was there at Wembley on May 25th to see Burnley beat Sheffield United 1 – 0, one of a party of nine members of the title team. Images of the night at Maine Road in 1960 flickered through his mind at the end of the game. The town and Burnley FC, Burnley FC and the town, inextricably linked. Little Burnley we say over and again and now in the Premiership. It is a fairy-tale.

"Why me," he continues to ask about himself. It was nearly the title chosen for this biography. Peter Salmon of the BBC provided the foreword for the scrapbook. His words answer the question perfectly and they provide a fitting postscript here for the biography.

'The Burnley I grew up in was tough, industrious and happy. The pubs were teeming, the factory looms were roaring and there was a palpable sense of optimism. It was lively but it wasn't pretty. There were no real heroes to speak of. Just ordinary men and women.

Except one. Jimmy Mac. Everyone in Burnley knew that name. In a workaday mill and pit town, the name was associated with style, flair and even glamour. In a one-club town, one footballer stood several inches taller than the rest. There were other internationals – Pointer, Angus, Miller, Connelly – and later Dobson, James and Thomas. But Jimmy McIlroy was one of a kind. Then like one of those rock superstars, he was taken from us early. This wasn't a drug overdose or plane crash of course. In 1963 Jimmy was transferred, went to play for Stoke, Oldham and then into management briefly with Bolton. But he was lost to us, the people of Burnley, who for more than ten years had idolised and adored him. And somehow it was never the same again – the town or the club. Ten years later we had begun a long slide into the lower divisions. And Jimmy - like those dazzling rock n' rollers never seemed to grow old. Most of us remember him still as the model young athlete with the dazzling smile, square jaw and Tintin-style hair cut.

Like that image, my own reflections are exaggerated. But small towns need heroes too. And Jimmy was ours. He had been a young newcomer from Ireland like so many in the North West, a generation of men and women who moved across after the last war to make good in England. And he made very good. He played nearly 500 times for Burnley, scored 131 goals and whilst at Burnley was capped 51 times for Northern Ireland, the country where his sports-mad family had nurtured his prodigious skills to create the best inside-right in Britain.

I've known Jimmy for more than thirty years. He and his late wife Barbara used to feed me cake and tea and generally humour me when I was dating their daughter Anne, my first proper girlfriend. I played football against their son Paul. Their home in Rosehill was substantial, happy and warm and we've kept in touch ever since, though our lives have changed lots. The funny thing about Jimmy is that you wouldn't know he was a superstar. The only thing he takes to excess is modesty. And maybe golf. Compared to his compatriot George Best or the Beckhams and Rooneys of this generation, he wears his hero status as comfortably as the Marks and Spencer v-neck that's never off his back.

To become a hero you have to win a titanic battle or two. So, there was the First Division Championship in 1959/60 and the following year Jimmy's Burnley were runners up in the Cup and League – the Clarets had begun the sexy sixties as one of the greatest teams in the land. Smoggy Burnley on top of the world. One of my first memories is sitting on my dad's shoulders at the corner of Trafalgar Street as an open top bus brought that legendary team back from Wembley in 1962. I didn't care they had lost – it was just epic – our little Northern team stepping up to the mark against the mighty Tottenham Hotspurs from London. David meets Goliath, with Jimmy McIlroy our midfield general.

Then there was Burnley versus Hamburg in the European Cup on Wednesday 18

January 1961. Glamorous Europe in little, smoky Burnley. I have the match programme still. The mighty German champions were staying at the town's Keirby Hotel, where my mum was a chambermaid. She got legendary centre-forward Uwe Seeler's autograph. Jimmy McIlroy takes on Uwe Seeler – at Turf Moor, our battleground tucked beneath the Lancashire moors. We were on the map, we were on top of the world, we were feeling good about ourselves, we had arrived…

And then, two years later he was gone. It was sudden and traumatic and the stuff of rumour for years. I'm not sure chairman and master-butcher Bob Lord's reputation ever recovered.

So thank goodness for the Jimmy McIlroy books. Memories of a golden era long since gone. When we seemed at the centre of things. The town and the football club. When we had big players who played on a big stage. Still inspiring and still dazzling. And as Burnley FC sets its sights on the top flight once again, it is strangely reassuring. With heroes like Jimmy McIlroy you can conquer the world. Even if those heroes are more at home in carpet slippers and a pullover'.

Perhaps a final few brief statistics will explain why so many people still remember him, and why so many people who never saw him play, still revere his name. They explain why, as the books were being designed at Hudson & Pearson's printing facility in Dunnockshaw, just a couple of miles from his home, the news quickly spread round the factory floor whenever he was in the building. It was no surprise when heads popped round doorways to say hello to him; pictures were politely proffered for signing, or people stepped forward just to say they had seen him play.

When he was sold by Burnley he returned to Turf Moor as Stoke City captain on March 28th 1964. The attendance was 26,868. The previous home game had been just 12,664. For the next home game after the Stoke City visit, it was down to 12,554.

He played 55 times for his country and scored 10 goals.

For Glentoran: 26 games and 9 goals.

For Burnley: 497 games and 131 goals.

For Stoke City: 116 appearances and 19 goals.

For Oldham Athletic: 39 appearances with 1 goal.

Total: 733 games and 170 goals – a truly remarkable achievement.

He was indeed, the prince of inside forwards. His omission from the Preston Museum of Football Hall of Fame is a mystery. Perhaps one day it will be rectified.

As I put the finishing touches to these final words, working in the conservatory that overlooks the garden and a row of houses below, I can see a young lad playing outside his house. He has a tennis ball and is kicking it against the garage door. There is a rich irony in this. These days you don't often see young lads kicking tennis balls around in the street. Jimmy in his day did. I in my own schooldays did. For a few minutes I stop working and watch the lad. I smile – and I'm sure Jimmy would too.

# The Appendices

# Appendix One

**The Matt Busby Foreword to Right Inside Soccer, 1960**

I T IS DIFFICULT to appreciate fully the skill of Jimmy McIlroy. For years he has virtually done the donkey work in a team, which, until their great 1960 Championship triumph, failed to win the top honour in the Cup or the League. Yet for all that, he could be compared favourably with the greatest scheming inside-forwards of all time.

Jimmy McIlroy has the ability to stamp his personality on every match in which he plays. When he is at his best he takes command of the game. When he is off-form, or troubled by injury, he still takes the eye because his magic, so often taken for granted, is missed by the onlookers.

In international soccer affairs, Jimmy has made a tremendous contribution to Northern Ireland's successes. For his club, only those who follow Burnley regularly could calculate his great value.

I have been a personal admirer of the Jimmy McIlroy footballing prowess for many years because Jimmy undoubtedly possesses something, which may be indefinable, but which is shared only by the all-time greats. Subtlety dominates his game and this allied to the ability to read a match and find the open space in a flash makes him a foe to be feared by all opponents.

It should be stressed, too, that Jimmy McIlroy, denied the advantage of physical strength, has reached his present eminence by employing sheer skill, and skill alone. How often the international selectors of England and Scotland must have wished that Jimmy had been born on their side of the Irish Sea.

Among McIlroy's many qualities, his loyalty to Burnley Football Club cannot be over-stressed. Temptations must have been placed in his way, from time to time, by those who feel he could have been a richer man in the colours of one of the 'glamour' teams. But for ten years the loyal supporters at Turf Moor have been able to applaud the dazzling displays of this genius.

Off the field, Jimmy is the ideal type, a young man who lives for his football and likes nothing better than a sensible discussion on all the involved angles of this game.

On the field, he is a model to all aspiring youngsters, scrupulously clean, despite the rather vigorous attentions a player of his calibre invariably receives from opposing defenders. He obviously enjoys every one of the 90 minutes from kick-off to final whistle.

Jimmy has been, and still will be for many years I hope, an asset to Association Football. The game would be better for more McIlroys.

# Appendix Two

## Brian Glanville: The Magic of McIlroy, World Sports, 1960

BURNLEY'S JIMMY MCILROY, at 28, is almost unquestionably the finest inside-forward in Britain: more versatile and fluent than Johnny Haynes, more consistent at international level than Ivor Allchurch, more mature than Bobby Charlton, Denis Law and Jimmy Greaves. McIlroy is above all a stylist and a perfectionist, with an utter mastery of technique. Every pass, every flick, every swerve is studied and controlled.

At a time when British football is pitifully short of outstanding individuals, McIlroy is one of the few players whose place would be secure in any team in the world. After Danny Blanchflower, no one has had more to do with the successes of Northern Ireland in recent years.

McIlroy differs from most Ulster stars in that he does not come from Belfast ("I'm a country yokel," he once told a fan), and in fact he was born in Lambeg. By the time he was 19 he was established in the Glentoran team and Burnley paid £7,000 for his transfer. Today, he must be worth ten times as much in the world market. He made his debut for Northern Ireland at inside-right against Scotland, at Windsor Park, and has stayed ever since.

If McIlroy has a fault, it is perhaps the obverse of perfectionism. Just as the great Austrian forwards of the Vienna school, Sindelar and the rest, found it slightly out of character to score, so McIlroy himself is inclined to play brilliantly in a kind of vacuum. Not that he *cannot* score.

His speed off the mark is amazing. Few who saw it will have forgotten his magnificent burst, half the length of the field, in a League game at Tottenham a year ago. Burnley were a goal down, there was a minute to play, and all seemed over. Suddenly, McIlroy got the ball in the inside-right position and accelerated like a racing car, leaving man after man behind him, boring irresistibly into the Tottenham half. Then, with defence and goalkeeper drawn, he flicked the ball accurately across goal, where Albert Cheesebrough had only to put a foot out and touch it over the line.

White Hart Lane, Tottenham, is indeed a ground for feats by McIlroy. I recall an evening match in 1951. Spurs were again on top but once more McIlroy got possession, accelerated superbly through the defence, and scored.

Today, supported by the sturdy Jimmy Robson, the leggy, bustling Ray Pointer and the deadly John Connelly, he is more suitably assisted in Burnley's attack. When he made up a gifted but fragile inside-forward trio with Peter McKay and Albert Cheesebrough there was too much football and not enough finish. "The impression persists," I remember writing, "that Burnley's tiny forwards could not punch their way out of a paper bag. This was the halcyon period of Alan Brown, an ideal manager for a footballing intellectual such as McIlroy. On the converted farm they used for training, Burnley players practised an infinity of corners, free kicks and throw-ins. Other teams admired and feared them, but results for all that, were good rather than outstanding.

Even now, McIlroy's nonchalance, born out of sheer virtuosity, can sometimes upset the rest of the attack. At Fulham earlier this season, he completely overshadowed Haynes. Burnley dominated the first half, and lost the match 0 – 1. McIlroy who regards haste as a sin, had been superb, but someone must respond to his promptings, someone must shoot, and must hurry through the middle.

In the Irish team, such duties have usually been undertaken by Wilbur Cush and Peter McParland, though team manager Peter Doherty must often ruefully have wondered how many more goals his team would have scored had there been a centre-forward of international stature to respond to McIlroy.

Confidence, of course, has its own nemesis. "Would *you* like to take the penalties next time?" he asked me in the Wembley dressing room, after missing from the spot for the second consecutive international, last November. On both occasions he had strolled up to the ball with almost insulting sangfroid. In Belfast (against Scotland) he had rolled it past the post; at Wembley he shot almost straight at Springett in the England goal. The object, McIlroy explained, was to send the goalkeeper the wrong way; if one failed, then the kick seemed feeble. But it was typical of McIlroy that he should take them like this at all, scorning mere force and speed, turning the whole affair into a sort of private joke and test.

Off the field, he is equally intelligent; a dry, mature, humorous man; married with two children; balanced and at ease in every company. He would like to stay in the game when he finishes playing "to try out some of the things I've learned," and he has his own strong views on coaching.

"There are a lot of coaches being turned out now, with the FA badge," he says, "and I remember them when they were players. Not only were they not good players, but I don't recall them as being intelligent men. You should try to develop a player's strengths rather than work on his weaknesses. If you want two wingers who will hold the ball, and your own wingers aren't doing it, rather than make them change their style you should see if you have any young players in the club who naturally play that sort of game, and work on them. A player does best what he likes to do. Johnny Haynes, for example, doesn't like beating a man."

McIlroy has years of good football ahead of him yet. He's already acknowledged as an outstanding player. By the end of his career he should be recognised as a great one.

# Appendix Three

The *News of the World* Football Annual 62/63
In which Jimmy explains why Burnley failed to do the 'double' in 1962.

JUST AS ROGER BANNISTER crashed the four-minute mile barrier and made it easier for other top-class milers, so did Spurs, in carrying off the 'double', lessen the magnitude of the task for England's top teams. Make no mistake though; it still requires a Herculean effort by the very best sides to emulate this task. Why then did Burnley, whom I consider to be every bit as good as Tottenham, fail so narrowly?

I believe it was due to a variety of reasons, while impossible to pin-point any particular one as the chief culprit. For instance Burnley is a small town, the players are familiar with everyone and to venture out of the house meant discussing our soccer prospects with every person we met, which if course, didn't allow us a moment's mental rest from our ambitions.

Did we over-train or under-train during the last few weeks when the strain was really on? Only by finding ourselves in a similar position again can we find the answer.

If there is such a thing as luck or rub of the green, then it certainly deserted us against Nottingham Forest at Turf Moor about six matches from the finish. Because from that evening, although we seldom turned on peak performances, chances were made, yet the ball would not go into the net.

Fulham may claim that if we lost the breaks in the League we certainly carried them into the Cup, to knock them out of the semi-final. I won't accept this because I feel the scales were finely balanced in most Cup rounds.

In both games with Fulham, I was practically a passenger over the entire 180 minutes with a bad ankle injury, not having recovered for the replay, and even with this advantage, Fulham never caused me as much worry as Leyton Orient did in the 4th Round replay at Brisbane Road.

As for the Final, my conclusion was that there was little between the teams. When we equalised I sensed that Spurs' shoulders drooped in despair, only to be lifted almost immediately by what is termed in soccer as a 'silly' goal (one that should never have been scored) and that goes for their first goal as well.

Still, despite our big disappointments, I have the pleasant feeling that reaching Wembley won't be as difficult again, besides conditioning the mind for another assault on the 'double'.

Being so near to the summit of a wonderful achievement has really whetted our appetites for another attempt at it. Maybe next year I'll be in a position to tell you how we accomplished it.

# Appendix Four

From the Gillette Book of Cricket and Football 1963
'I owe a lot to kicking a tennis ball'

IT IS A FALLACY that I refuse to acknowledge the benefits of coaching, because any success I've merited is due in no small measure to the hours of coaching I've received since I first kicked a ball in a little Irish village. I believe that I, and any coach, can improve a boy's knowledge of football.

The greatest inside-forwards I've known weren't necessarily the best ball players, although it's a tremendous advantage to have complete control of the ball, to kill it dead in an instant, and to be able to use both feet easily and accurately.

I'm certain I owe a lot to the countless hours spent kicking a tennis ball against the wall of my home, when my pals were tired of soccer, and using my imagination as an opponent, conjuring up all sorts of incidents I was likely to encounter in a match, such as a defender rushing in to tackle and being forced to play the ball first-time from all heights and angles. I'm convinced this 'self-coaching' developed my skills, timing and balance, because in my imaginative wonderland I captured the pace and excitement of a real game; and it's only in matches skills are nurtured into peak performances.

It's possible, too, Irish as it may sound, that I was fortunate my schooldays happened during the war years, when footballs were practically non-existent, and touch and ball-sense was fostered with the only balls occasionally available – tennis balls. Today's young footballers have much better facilities, better playing surfaces, and proper footballs. With the professional footballer's lot vastly improved, there is a meaningful incentive to make the grade in the game. Well-meaning people with limited knowledge of soccer, used to pass on advice and coaching in my very early teens; tips such as, shoot, often on greasy surfaces, or get rid quickly against rugged opponents, all of which was well meant, but useless at the time, because I played football according to instinct and was solely concerned in playing football the only way I knew how.

Even at seventeen, and a professional with the Irish League club Glentoran, I can't remember absorbing much of the tactics or the team talks prior to every match. By Irish standards I was playing so well that in March 1950, at the age of 18, Burnley bought me, and it wasn't until arriving in England that I realised how much of the game I still had to learn. Football is similar to any professional career, in that, years of study and experience, or to be more explicit, years of playing, thinking, and talking amongst footballers are needed, before a boy feels he knows a little of what his job is all about.

Naturally every team position is important, but that of inside-forward is vital. Here is usually found the brains of the side, the schemer, who if partnered by a goal-snatching inside-forward, goes a long way towards forming the nucleus of a good team.

Generally, inside forwards are classed in one of two categories – the striker and the schemer, his type of style being determined by the boy's make-up or character.

I enjoy playing behind the other four forwards, just in front of my wing-halves, where I try to position myself so as to receive the ball from them and then, either with a first-time pass, or by holding it for a few seconds to enable a colleague to run into an attacking position, and a way to goal may be created if passed accurately.

Deep-lying inside forwards need stamina to cover the entire field for 90 minutes, confidence to hold the ball long enough until someone takes up an advantageous position and courage to keep on looking when things aren't going well.

If a boy thirsts for goals, as Jimmy Greaves does, he becomes a striker, and I don't expect him to burn up his energy seeking the ball. He must save himself for lightning sprints and darts around the penalty area in his quest for goals. What a lot of people fail to realise is just how strength-sapping those sprints are, which leads to this type of forward often being called lazy. Nevertheless if my poaching partner scores week after week, I don't grumble about running a few extra yards for him.

Trying to blot inside-forwards out of the game are the wing-halves. Some are highly skilled, often poor tacklers, but brilliant ball-players and clever at starting attacks. Others are noted more for their defensive assets, their tackling and positional play. A good team has one of each type, and I prefer to oppose the footballing wing-half, because he allows me that yard extra in which to receive the ball and control it, and it turns out to be a test of skill, not one of strength and stamina.

His counterpart tackles hard, sometimes too hard for my liking, marks closely and on the whole is a spoiler. When opposite this type I'm happy if I have my regular wing-half behind me, with Burnley it's Jimmy Adamson, with Ireland it's Danny Blanchflower, both great players, both of whom I've played with so long as to be able to almost read each other's thoughts.

If they see I'm tightly marked, they hold the ball whilst I sprint away from them, taking my opponent with me, until I reverse sharply, gaining enough space to collect their pass. Or, I draw him to the wing or into the centre, leaving a space for Jimmy Adamson or Danny to surge forward. Adamson and I have spent years talking, planning, and plotting to reach the understanding we have.

In our early days at Turf Moor we were encouraged to work out moves together by our two trainers Billy Dougal and Ray Bennion, but half the time we coached each other. Ray and Bill introduced us both to new skills, such as, hitting a 'dipper' shot, a shot that drops suddenly due to top-spin; dribbling by stepping over the ball from side to side; and shielding it from an opponent with the body.

I respect these veteran coaches simply because they were experienced enough to know that for each individual certain skills come naturally and easily, and they never insisted we relentlessly attempted the ones we disliked.

I believe in showing a boy in his teens everything I can do with a ball, encouraging him to discover in as many ways as possible that the ball can be played by all parts of the body, and allowing him to pursue the skills which appeal to him.

Whether you are a striker or a schemer; one thing is essential – fitness. To the ambitious youngster this is the easiest part of football to attain, or perhaps I should say, it should be. Any boy who loves the game won't have to be bullied into reaching peak fitness. He should derive immense pleasure and pride from the feeling of fitness; his game will benefit and the satisfaction gained in out-running an opponent will be worth that extra bit of training he had to grit his teeth to withstand. For me, the pre-season training is the worst. When all those surplus pounds collected during the summer break have to be lost, and the emphasis is on pressure and circuit training. Still, it's the modern trend and anyway it only lasts a few weeks until we are back at the type of training I like best – five-a-side. It is the finest practice I can think of. It produces every move in the game; it can be conditioned to make players part quickly, improve their stamina, and make them think and move quickly into a narrow space.

There are many ways to fitness, but boys must realise that training doesn't finish at the ground. All the good work can be nullified by lack of thought. Too much food, not enough sleep or fresh air are examples of the harm a young footballer can do to himself. But if he really loves soccer, his determination to reach the top will provide the will-power to resist all temptation. *(Jimmy McIlroy 1963)*

# Appendix Five

**I can't believe it. How did I go wrong?**
**Jimmy McIlroy**

I FEEL SHOCKED, bewildered, amazed. I have never known the real meaning of those words until now. The definitions were brought home with hammer blows by a statement made to me this morning by manager Harry Potts.

It was 10.30 a.m.; the sun was shining and everything looked good to me when I walked into the ground. Then came the words: "The board have decided to place you on the transfer list."

Harry Potts is just about the nicest fellow I know in football. We have been pals since the moment he arrived to take charge at Turf Moor. So the shock of being told that Burnley no longer wanted me is dwarfed only by the shock of hearing Harry say; "You will admit in the past I have been good to you. I feel that you have not reciprocated."

The Irish are noted for their repartee. We are never at a loss for words – but this time I can honestly say I was struck speechless. All sorts of things flashed through my mind but not one of them was related to the playing side in my connection with Burnley. What was the reason for this? Had I done something against the grain? Had I said something out of turn? Had I used a word or said something detrimental about the club, the manager or the board? I could not think of a thing.

It baffles me although there have been times when I have mildly criticised the team, including myself. In fact, I think I have often been my own biggest critic. But at that moment, and even now, just a few hours later, I still cannot think of the reason for this amazing turn in my career. It leaves me completely baffled.

When I look back there were a lot of things during that interview I should have asked to satisfy myself. There are no doubt a lot of things many of the fans want to know. I suppose my pride won't allow myself to ask those questions of my manager and the Burnley club either now or later.

If I have not been playing well enough, is it a good enough reason for my transfer. That is a matter of opinion. Another thing I forgot to ask was how long had my playing satisfied or displeased the manager?

Surely it is only reasonable to expect if he was disappointed before Christmas he would have taken me on one side and given me a severe talking to or perhaps achieved a better result by dropping me. Since Christmas we have played four games, won two, drawn one and lost one. Against Sheffield Wednesday we won 4 – 0. The manager seemed pleased after that; next a tough game against Tottenham. He seemed highly pleased after that. Next came the Cup-tie at Liverpool.

Here was a case in point of one of the finest compliments Burnley could pay me. On many occasions they have done this – asking me to play knowing I was not 100% fit. Maybe I was foolish to damage my reputation, and I am not going to say it out of pure, unselfish loyalty to the club. But if there was a reason for playing me in this condition it was apparently that even strapped up they felt that I could be of some help to the rest of the lads.

I have been asking myself all day if losing the Liverpool match has anything to do with all this. I feel it might have been the straw that broke the camel's back. I am certain there has been a lot leading up to it but I don't know what it was a lot of, to use an Irishism. Talk of my saying the wrong thing after the Anfield match is just talk. I certainly did not make any remarks that any Burnley officials could have taken exception to.

Now I feel as if I have been kicked in the stomach.

I ask myself: Am I finished? Does every manager in the game think I am finished or will there be someone with faith still left in me?

Beggars can't be choosers. Now at the ripe old age of 31, I will have to take what is offered me and be happy with it.

If there is the slightest consolation for me in this sad moment it is that Danny Blanchflower was not much younger when he made a wonderful move to Tottenham.

Now I come to a personal matter. Unknown to most folk in Burnley I have been negotiating to open a business in the town. The venture involves my sister and brother and brother in law in Ireland. We had reached a point where they had given up their jobs in Ireland and been across to weigh up the whole project.

There has, no doubt, been much conjecture about all the happenings of today. Now the fans have my side of it and I think that is only fair in the circumstances.

The reason I say that is that people are saying that something must be covered up. If there is any other reason than those mentioned by Potts this morning, I only wish I knew.

At home now everyone is walking round on tip toe, talking in hushed voices almost as if there was a bereavement in the house. I feel as if there is a body lying around the corner shrouded and still… and the body is Jimmy McIlory.

The more I think on past events the more baffling it is. I think of Mr Bob Lord our chairman. I can only say quite honestly that he has been for me and for Burnley a chairman I would not have swapped for any other chairman in the land.

*(Jimmy McIlroy Daily Express Tuesday February 1963)*

# Appendix Six

**I talk with my chairman. I feel almost happy about it.**
**Jimmy McIlroy**

TOLD BURNLEY CHAIRMAN Bob Lord yesterday that I may quit soccer. That I may finish while I am at the top. I don't think Mr Lord took me very seriously. So I repeat it here. And I am quite serious about it.

The business venture in the town that I have been negotiating involves the whole family. It excites me so much that I cannot suppress a rapidly growing enthusiasm towards the whole scheme.

No one but me in Burnley has any idea how deeply I have been contemplating this move and I admit the seed has grown.

I now feel quite clear-headed and almost happy about the events of Monday when manager Harry Potts told me I was on the transfer list.

The magic has come because of that long interview yesterday with Mr Lord. My mission yesterday was to see Bob Lord. I could not rest. My sleep was broken by a torrent of suggestions pouring on me from all quarters; and some of my own.

I had to see Bob Lord.

But another shock hit me between the eyes before I came into his presence. On the door next to Mr Lord's meat factory in large, white, painted letters were splashed the words: WE WANT McKILROY SACK POTTS.

I wish I hadn't seen it. I wish it hadn't been written, even if it could be considered nice from my angle to know that someone cared about my future.

The unpleasantness of being responsible or rather indirectly responsible for the Turf Moor sensation is not regarded by me to be something to be proud of. It is something I never wanted to happen.

Now I have come to definite conclusions. I feel the whole affair is the result of not one cause but a chain of incidents that have brought about the present circumstances. I don't want to sound heroic but my talk with Mr Lord has convinced me that what has taken place was intended to be in the best interests of the people involved. Whether it was the right thing to do or the right way to go about it, only time will tell.

For even the intention behind the act of the person defacing Mr Lord's door was to the person who wrote it good. But the method used was not good. And this is how I feel about the method Harry Potts employed to inform me he had placed me on offer for transfer.

I talked for an hour and a half with Mr Lord. We have had similar sessions before. Sometimes on opposite sides of the fence, more often as virtual team-mates in planning Burnley's future. This time it was a simple case of a player asking for a simple explanation. And so it should have been on the face of it to all who are interested; but not to me.

I knew or imagined that there was something deeper; something that the board or

268

manager could not, or would not reveal at this moment because they considered it not in the best interests of the club to do so.

I wasn't naïve enough to expect any information from the chairman.

Mr Lord started off by telling me the decision was entirely the manager's. But after 90 minutes talk, talk, talk, he finished up by saying; "What has been done is in the best interests of the club."

I accept that. I don't expect anyone, or a football club, to do anything that will harm themselves.

I kept on stressing that the only explanation I found feasible was that MONEY was the root of all the trouble. If there was any other reason I could not think of it.

I kept thinking of the huge stand project which has been promised and the colossal expenditure involved. I kept thinking of our limited gates.

I kept thinking of the tales other players have spread about regarding the fantastic salaries they are earning and how it must only cause our young star players to review their position.

If I were manager Potts I would brace myself for a few of these youngsters coming into my office at the termination of their contracts and asking for considerably more than they have received in the past two years.

I thought that meeting these terms will present a problem. All this and more at my meeting with Mr Lord made me think hard; and I think I am on the mark.

I left Mr Lord on good terms. In fact, we shook hands. Now I await the return of Mr Potts from Peterborough to ask him two questions.

One – is my affair a club matter entirely? Two – is it a team matter?

If it is a club matter then I assure everyone there is no personal conflict involved and it can only be a matter of finance.

Should it be the latter this is entirely unacceptable. If it was a team matter I would have been dropped or replaced by someone considered better.

I must begin to sum up. I believe now more than ever that money is the root of all evil, especially when applied to the business of professional football.

Looking back on my short interview with Harry Potts I cannot help but recall the feeling that it was as painful for him to say the words as it was for me to hear them.

Being as close to him as I have been, I sensed that he was desperately searching for the words. I think he used words he did not really mean, I don't bear the slightest grudge.

Those who know of my affinity with Danny Blanchflower must be wondering what he thinks about all this. He came on the telephone late last night in a devil of a sweat with the words pouring so quickly from him that I could just make out… "this is stupid… this is nonsense."

For the first time since I met him there was no wisecrack passed.

But there was enough said for me to realise how concerned he was about me. And, I might add, if it is of any interest to Mr Lord, Danny was also concerned about the chairman AND Burnley. He is an admirer of both.

*(Newspaper article Jimmy McIlroy February 1963)*

# Appendix Seven

**My pay packet brings ripples of discontent.**
**Jimmy McIlroy**

I HAVE FOUGHT for and believed in the lifting of the maximum wage. I still believe in it and I think it will never now be removed. It is part of our system.

Now, with my future at Burnley possibly limited to days, I have had time to realise that the lift in the pay packet can be a problem that causes tremendous difficulties in many ways for the clubs.

Are Burnley, in their decision to part with me because they need the cash, setting a trend that other clubs will find they have to follow? Is the pace getting too hot?

I will be frank. There has been talk among many clubs of dissension, of discontent because of the differences in wages.

The ink had hardly dried on my contract 18 months ago when it seemed someone had made the discovery that I was Burnley's highest paid player.

The pessimists and the knockers, and there were a few of them around, at once cried that it would not work. They thought everybody should be paid the same in the Burnley team. My answer was: "That seems logical when everyone's transfer value is the same."

We have always boasted about the Burnley team spirit being the best. It has been good. But I feel it has been no better and no worse than any other team experiencing a similar amount of success.

Recently – if it is not due to my imagination – I feel there have been little ripples of dissension in the camp. There have been rumours about the boys, for what rumours are worth, and those bits of chatter have indicated that one or two of the lads are unhappy to find themselves earning less than Jimmy McIlroy.

Can I say that there are two ways to look at it? Eighteen months ago they all came out of the manager's office beaming and happy with two-year contracts they had signed. Can I say now it is only right for them to honour those contracts?

Their angle could be that they are playing as well or better than me, and are entitled to equal reward. And that spells trouble for any club.

I can see the pessimists over the lifting of the maximum wage pressing their noses into this and murmuring: "Ah we said team spirit would suffer."

The topic was included in my discussion with Chairman Lord. His idea, with which I agree, is that it might take a year or two longer for the position to iron itself out. It seems I've been included in the ironing already.

One thing is very clear in my mind. The strain of the wages will increase. Demands will grow for better terms.

In trying to imagine the attitude of the rest of the team towards Jimmy McIlroy, I am led to the conclusion that a lot of these boys may have been living in the shadow of McIlroy and Jimmy Adamson.

For a number of years when Burnley have done well, the lion's share of the publicity has gone to us two. The rest of the lads must have felt grossly underestimated.

Will they feel happier now? Will their play improve, now that Jimmy McIlroy is on his way?

Is it possible there will be new life in the team when I have gone, and good results? I am not kidding myself that there won't be.

I am sure a 'super league' is on the way.

Obviously Burnley wants a part of the big time. The new stand project is designed for that purpose. But, they may be with a number of other clubs at this stage finely balanced on the scales as they attempt to live with the giants who have much greater financial assets. I forecast a dramatic pruning of the playing staff before the end of the season.

In case you have heard talk that McIlroy is a cocky type and have misunderstood, as others seem to have done, let me refer to two of my biggest mistakes during my stay at Burnley.

Like a bell ringing an alarm I now realise that I have been wrong to hint and talk even jokingly about being a veteran. It seems some folk have the wrong image of McIlroy in their minds. Some have come to believe it.

But my biggest mistake was to allow myself to develop a complex. I have always been a noisy player on the field, shouting, bullying, some might call it, pleading. Just to get the best out of the others.

But there comes the time when some of them tell you to shut up and they tell you in no uncertain way. And you do just that.

And my mistake was this: I decided that I was going to stop all this. That I was going to stop trying to impress my personality on them. I would move as usual into the open space and hope their ability and their intelligence would help them find me.

In that time I became a general without a baton. I feel that the team and I have suffered from it. I think it has been a grave error.

As I told Mr Lord, Burnley has been good to me. I like to think I have repaid them. I don't think we owe each other anything.

*(Newspaper article Jimmy McIlroy February 1963)*

# Appendix Eight

### The Mystery of McIlroy in Distress
### Danny Blanchflower March 1963

WHEN I PICKED up an evening newspaper last Monday and read that Jimmy McIlroy had been put on the transfer list by his club, I was as shocked as everyone else seemed to be. "Oh no," were my first thoughts as I read it. "Now I'm going to get a lot of letters from Burnley fans again telling me to keep my big head out of their and McIlroy's business".

This first happened some years back when Jimmy enjoyed some publicity at the expense of asking his club for a move. I had been at Turf Moor with Tottenham on the Saturday afternoon and he had asked me round to his home for some tea.

We were both to travel to Belfast for an international match the following week. Jimmy said nothing to me and the first I knew about it was when I picked up the newspapers in Belfast and the sporting headlines screamed it out.

He didn't say a word to me about it and I didn't ask him. I wasn't convinced that he wanted to move. I wrestled with the thought that perhaps he had connived in some way with the Belfast Legion of Pressmen, or that they had conned him into it, so that they could splash a story worthy of their names across the morning papers.

But I dismissed this as very unlikely, although I wasn't altogether surprised when the whole thing blew quickly by and Jimmy was still at Turf Moor.

Of course the Burnley fans blamed me. They read in the papers that I had been round to his house for tea, and that was all they needed to know. I got the rude letters until they had forgotten it and every time after that when Jimmy and the club had a difference, I was the logical root of the trouble.

But as I read the evening paper, I was to realise that this time it was different. Burnley manager Harry Potts had admitted that the move had not been made at the player's request, but when pressed for further information he replied: "I have no comment. It is a club matter."

Jimmy had turned up at Turf Moor for training and had been beckoned to the manager's office. Mr Potts had told him that following a meeting of the directors it had been decided to place him on the transfer list. He was shocked and bewildered. It had come out of the blue and he had not had time to think about it.

I gave him a few hours to think about it and then I tried to reach him on the phone. I didn't know his number so I rang some friends to see if they could help. Eventually David Coleman of the BBC advised me to get through to the Burnley exchange and ask them to tie me up with him.

"Pleased to meet ya," the supervisor at the Burnley exchange said when I told who I was and what I wanted. "What's happening up there?" I asked him.

"Aye it's a pity," he responded. There was a tone of great understanding in his voice as if some deep instinct had prepared him to accept the idea that you could not always expect the best of men to tread the wisest and most sensible paths.

"Does your reserve team want a good, deep-lying inside forward?" McIlroy chided me when I finally got through to him.

"No chance," I ribbed, "Haven't you heard, that's my job now."

"Anyway," I said, "what the hell's going on up there?"

"I honestly don't know," answered Jimmy. "I've been trying to think what the reason can be. Harry Potts said he wasn't satisfied with my play. But I've… "

"Don't accept that," I interrupted. "You don't play a man all season and then suddenly transfer him because you think he's not playing well. You gee him up a bit, or you drop him for a couple of matches."

As we talked the matter over I could see that Jimmy really was bewildered. His pride had been hurt and that was easy to understand. It is not funny when you are King by vote of the taxpayers, acclaimed by the popular Press, praised for years by your Prime Minister and then suddenly the Chief Whip calls you into his office and tells you that you are to be deported just as soon as they can find somewhere to send you.

McIlroy was an idol in distress. He would find that just as suddenly as the manager had uttered those words so the whole nature of his relationship with the club would change. There would be a sort of vacuum around him in the dressing room as he changed for training and hung his clothes on the familiar peg. He would feel isolated in a sort of outer-space eeriness. They would all pretend to be normal but most of them would feel a little uneasy. The others would watch him, wondering what he was thinking and how he was taking it. They might regret what had happened to him, but only because it could happen – maybe all the more – to them.

Some of them who deep down hated his guts would be glad about it, although they would try not to show it. Most of them would look away not wishing to face anybody about it, not even too willing to question themselves about it in case they would find something deep down within themselves that they didn't really like.

In a way they would all be pleased and relieved. They had been living in the shadow of McIlroy. It was always McIlroy. He got most of the slaps on the back. He was getting more money than them. It was some true stroke of justice as far as they were concerned. If he got the biggest deal, he was entitled to the biggest kick.

Bob Lord wasn't willing to talk about it. You could tell he was treading on thin ice. He said it was Harry Potts' idea but he didn't actually say that the board were against it. Harry Potts was quietly admitting it, but he didn't seem to be doing it with much conviction.

"Following a board meeting…"he had told McIlroy, "it had been decided to put you on the list. And then he said something about doing a lot of favours for Jimmy but that the player had not reciprocated.

That sounded a bit funny and phoney to me. Perhaps Harry Potts sincerely thought he had done Jimmy a lot of favours, but you do not transfer a player because you have been favourable towards him. That sounded like a guilt excuse, an effort to justify some action you're not quite sure about, or one that you cannot logically explain.

A day or two went by and nobody was any the wiser. I phoned Jimmy again. He'd had a man to man talk with Bob Lord but had got no satisfaction. Bob had continued to say it was in the best interests of the club and that it was Harry Potts' idea. Jimmy had challenged his chairman with the question of financial difficulties at the club. They are putting up an expensive new grandstand soon. But Jimmy felt that Bob had evaded the question although he thinks that Bob probably feels that he didn't.

I have always had a respect for the Burnley club. They have managed to keep pace with and ahead of most other clubs with better resources. They have been prudent. They have not spent large sums of money on players and they have managed to sell some at sizeable prices. They have taken a pride in the welfare of their players and I have sometimes thought they were living above their means.

Bob Lord is known as a rough diamond. He is ambitious for himself and the club. He usually means well and he usually does well. But rough diamonds have not got the polish and perhaps that is what frustrates Bob and the Burnley club a bit. I'm not saying I think any the less of them for not appearing to have the finishing polish, but perhaps they feel a bit anxious about it themselves and it is this frustration that causes them to do things that shock people.

Remember how they stamped out of that hotel in New York? Perhaps they are used to better conditions that what they got there, but they could have done it with more tact.

Remember how they accused Manchester United of being Teddy Boys just after Munich? Perhaps there was something in what they said, but they seemed to add to the hysteria instead of subduing it.

Then there was the night that Harry Potts ran onto the field in a European Cup tie. Anybody can understand a manager's feelings. He wants his players to get a fair deal and he wants his team to win. But does that suggest that Harry Potts is a bit more impulsive than what he seems to be? He seems such a nice bloke. Or does it mean he has no real control at Turf Moor? And that it reflects in his action of no control over himself at critical moments?

I phoned Turf Moor on Wednesday to ask him about McIlroy. When I got through a man's voice informed me that they hadn't got back from Peterborough where the team had been playing a fixture. They were due back at any moment. I told the voice who I was and asked him to tell Harry that I would phone again in about a quarter of an hour and that I would like to have a chat with him. When I phoned back, a different voice answered. They were back from Peterborough but he didn't know if Harry was around. He had a look in the manager's office and out on the ground. Harry wasn't around. He didn't know anything about my message.

"Can I speak to Mr Potts?" I phoned again the next afternoon.

"Who wants to speak to him?"

I told the voice.

"I'll see if he's here," he said without much conviction. Harry wasn't around.

So what gives with McIlroy? It must be finance. That's a club matter. When they beat Tottenham, Bob Lord and his merry men probably thought they would win the Cup. But Liverpool had other ideas. Another Cup run to Wembley would have brought thousands of pounds to the kitty. Maybe they were counting on that. And on the added support a good Cup run would bring to their League matches.

It's been a hard winter. Funds are low all round. McIlroy is getting more money than all the others. Perhaps the others are starting to ask questions. Perhaps the others are starting to ask for the same? Simple solution: Sell McIlroy, get some cash in; cut the feet from under the others with regards to asking for more. That's better for the club in the long run or it would seem to be?

But why don't they come out and say that? Well it's all about the polish and their anxiety. It's pride. When you are trying very well to keep up with the Joneses, you can't admit that you are a bit short at times.

But to the danger they haven't realised. A big new Stand is a wonderful thing, as Sheffield Wednesday will tell you. Takes foresight; but you can never be sure. It's no good if you haven't got a good team and nobody will come to sit in it.

Burnley and McIlroy have been good for one another. If partnerships like this are made in heaven, then God or man here, somewhere has gone astray.

*(Newspaper article Danny Blanchflower March 1963)*

# Appendix Nine

**Selling Mac will balance the budget**
**Bob Lord**

ALL AT TURF MOOR are not insensible to our supporters' feelings from time to time, and the latest move in the case of Jimmy McIlroy being placed on the transfer list was not done in the heat of the moment, or hastily, in any shape or form.

The action was committed after very careful thought, and I, on behalf of all connected with the Company and the club, once again ask all our supporters to believe that we have done the job because we are of the opinion that it was the course which had to be taken after considering all angles of the situation.

I think it is true to say that I fought as much as anyone in football for the abolition of the maximum wage for footballers and believe me, I did not arrive at the conclusion that it would be for the best, without exploring the possible consequences which would accrue. One had to consider what changes it would bring about in football generally, and also I had to think how it would concern Burnley Football Club.

Burnley, to my way of thinking, is a great town, which has suffered depression perhaps as much as any other town in the country. It contains folk who can take the good with the bad, the smooth with the rough, the bad weather with the good, and always come up smiling. I was born into it, and it is a part of me, but since my early boyhood days I have always realised that it is not a big town, and that the population is small in comparison to some other Lancashire towns.

In that respect, there is obviously less chance of the institutions, organisations or clubs of the town being quite so successful as those places where the population is greater. Therefore, in my humble estimation, I believe quite candidly, that Burnley Football Club has got to be very shrewd, very thoughtful and careful, in how it conducts its business in order to keep and maintain a successful First Division Club.

My directors and myself are of the opinion that, no matter how successful in playing results we are, we shall have to be content with average gates of between 25,000 and 30,000 per match, and I have no hesitation in stating quite emphatically that the revenue from that figure at the proceeds we charge will not allow us to run the club successfully.

Everyone in football knows that Burnley Football Club have, during the last ten years at least, employed a hundred per cent youth policy. In fact, I don't know of any other League club who has done that in the past, or does now.

We contrive and manage to find our players in the raw. We have a wonderful scouting system, the members of which are organised, efficient, loyal, conscientious, and in no small degree, successful.

However, not all of the captures manage to make the grade after lots of hard work by the manager Mr Potts and his capable team of coaches and trainers. We have from time to time managed to help some of them obtain positions with other lower league clubs but never forget, all these youths have got to be paid wages. Much money is spent on their training and coaching, but we believe at Turf Moor, that it is generally money well spent.

Further, all the players have to have conditions equal to the best at the very least. All this costs money.

Therefore, occasionally, in order to balance the budget, we have to sell players, who for some reason or another do not fit into our plans.

HENCE, THE TRANSFER OF JIMMY MCILROY.

One must not forget that we have more than played the game with Jimmy, and he more than anyone knows that to be true.

Far from the manager instructing him to do this and that, he has generally pleased himself; make no mistake about that fact.

He was paid a wage and was expected to give of his best, both for the club and for the benefit of all the other players on Burnley's books, and on his own admission, he quite truthfully admits that perhaps he has been complacent.

Many people have said that he could have been placed in the reserves team, and my answer to that is, that the end product would have been just the same, and no-one more than he knows better.

In conclusion, we at Turf Moor believe that we have acted in the best interests of the club.

Perhaps to many people that reads silly at the moment, but I am confident time will tell that we were right in our actions. In football we have to think of everyone, and I am sure that the eleven players who represent Burnley on the field of play will give us all they have got.

Successful First Division football is Burnley's aim. We intend to keep it that way, but as I have said before, perhaps our ways and actions will not always be understood by everyone. Nevertheless, I believe we know where we are going.

*(Bob Lord 1963)*

# Appendix Ten

### Dusty – a real gentleman
### In which Jimmy pays tribute to Brian Miller

DUSTY MILLER is a gentle giant. As a player he was a great fellow to have in your side, as honest as they come, a man who loved life, who spoke no evil of anyone, and above all, he was a close mate of mine. Ask me to name anyone else I've known in football warranting the same praise and I'd be flummoxed – that is the measure of the esteem in which I hold this man.

One of nature's gentlemen, Brian Miller travelled much further along the road to success than did a heck of a lot more talented players, mainly on sheer honest endeavour. He was a big man, with strength to match, yet never once in all the years we played together in Claret and Blue jerseys, can I recall one single incident when he used this power illegitimately, though often his size and enthusiasm seemed to strike terror into the hearts of opposing forwards.

I gathered this from chatting to players from other clubs and it was a job to choke back a chuckle on hearing some of them considered that Miller was a big, dirty so and so. The truth was that Brian couldn't kick or hurt anyone had he tried, because he simply didn't know how. Occasionally in mock defence of him I'd tell these moaners that my wife was more capable of inflicting pain than he was.

We travelled the world together and even though I shared a room with Jimmy Adamson, the bond with Dusty was stronger because we seemed to have more in common.

One typical deed he performed, which probably he has long forgotten, meant more to me than ever he could have imagined. It was when I was no longer wanted by Burnley and sold to Stoke City. On arriving at Norwich City's ground for my first game with for the Potteries side, I found a good wishes telegram from Brian. For my sins, I cannot remember ever thanking him for the gesture, but the memory of that telegram remains something special.

I left Turf Moor against my wishes and my family was distraught, yet from among all the lads I'd played with for seasons, sharing great triumphs and bitter disappointments, he was the only one to let me know he cared.

My world was upside down when Burnley let me go, and now I have an opportunity to let Brian and his family know that I feel for them. His axing as Burnley manager hasn't come as a big surprise because it is the norm in football that when a team does badly, a scapegoat, usually the manager has to be found.

Towards the end of last season, just before Burnley clinched promotion, I was in the company of Miller and some Burnley officials at an Alan Stevenson testimonial dinner, and with the Clarets looking certs to go up, my old mate was being feted like a hero.

In conversation with a prominent official, I suggested that unless two or three class

Brian Miller, a one-club man who served Burnley Football Club in every capacity with honesty, dedication and distinction.

players were bought the side would struggle in the Second Division, only to be told that their young players would be a season older, more experienced and therefore able to hold their own in the higher class.

Well, Dusty wasn't given the money to strengthen his squad to any degree and it matters little if that official now knows it is unwise to rely on young players, regardless of their promise. Relegation now looks a distinct possibility and a touch of panic seems to have set in. The man who was a Messiah six months ago is now deemed a failure and has been discarded.

Brian Miller may have left the soccer limelight this week, perhaps for good, but as far as I'm concerned the memory of him bursting through with strength and no small measure of skill, week in and week out, in that Claret and Blue number 6 jersey, with the enthusiasm of a schoolboy, fills me with a warm glow.

He was a humble footballer who recognised his limitations – assets when it was a case of backs to the wall, in other words, a man who sweated blood for Burnley FC.

Brian, old pal, you no doubt feel you still have something to offer the game, but whether or not you have the chance to prove it again, I just want you to know that in my book, you were every bit as successful in the 'hot-seat' as you were on the field.

*(Jimmy McIlroy Burnley Express January 1983)*

# Appendix Eleven

### An old has-been at 60
### In which Jimmy Mac interviews himself to celebrate his birthday

NORMALLY I DECIDE who to interview, but this time I've been requested (ordered) to dig up an old has-been for no other reason than the fact that today he celebrates his 60th birthday. Normally I look forward to a good chat with my subject, eager to learn as much as possible about him or her. But in this instance, it so happens that I, and most of you as well, know only too well just about everything there is to know about him – having been bored for decades with exaggerated details of his own career rammed down our throats time after time. I met him vowing not to ask him the usual humdrum soccer questions, at the same time worried that we might then run out of chat very soon.

**"You're known as a modest man. Is this true?"**

"There's no such thing as a modest footballer," he said, attempting what passed for a modest smile. "Especially in a town this size, where everyone recognises you. It's only because I'm better than most at disguising conceit."

**"What's special about reaching 60?"** was the only question I could think of next.

"Nothing really," was his answer. "Though way back last November when I lay against a park wall fighting for breathe as a result of blood clots following a varicose vein operation, I have to admit that reaching 60 seemed wishful thinking."

**"If you were half as good as reports that some older fans would have us believe, why then did you remain in a little town like Burnley?"**

That silly little grin appeared again and he replied: "First of all I'm a much, much better player now, than I was then, because in none of the stories told today, do I make a mistake, give a bad pass, or have a stinker - and I can assure you I had my share of all three.

"But I stayed here for two reasons; one being that with a maximum wage in existence there was no financial advantage playing for Arsenal, Spurs or Manchester United, because everyone earned the same."

He added: "The real reason was that I fell in love with this little town from the moment I moved from my tiny Irish village in 1950.

"One Saturday after looking around the stand at Highbury and seeing celebrities from all walks of life, I thought this is the kind of audience I'd like to show off in front of every week – if only the ground and spectators lock stock and barrel could be lifted and transported here." And do you know, for the first time, he almost sounded sincere.

Unable to think of anything else, I had to ask a question he'd been asked a thousand times.

**"Undoubtedly there have been many great moments in your career – which one stands out the most?"**

"I've had one inspired moment in my life that I don't mind mentioning," he said. "With my wife I was in the company of an outstanding young Clarets star years after I'd hung up my boots, when a little clever Dick asked, 'Don't you wish you were playing today and earning as much as this fellow?'

"In a flash I had my arm round my wife, saying, 'But sure I wouldn't have met this little treasure' – and I swear I could feel her growing inches taller."

It wasn't quite the answer I was seeking, so I tried again.

**"What was your worst moment?"**

"Next to the morning when Burnley put me on the transfer list," he said, "it happened this year, walking along the promenade with my father in Newcastle County Down, and a lady stopped us saying, 'My son and I have been discussing you two and I've decided you are brothers'."

His little grin this time definitely wasn't genuine as he declared: "My father really did grow ten feet tall, but it wasn't the first time he's received similar boosters.

"Once outside Anfield approaching kick-off time, a Liverpool fan heard the name McIlroy mentioned and he turned to my father asking, 'Are you not playing today?'

The old has-been smiled weakly and told me his father has repeated this story 100 times, while he, modestly, has only told one or two people about the time he was taken for his father's son. I didn't attempt to work it out – I let him ramble on.

"During a 5-a-side training session in Barcelona's Nou Camp Stadium I was coaching Stoke City on tour," he said. "A number of Barcelona directors were watching and when my name cropped up one of them turned to the Stoke Chairman saying, 'Ah McIlroy, his son was in the Burnley side that officially opened our stadium'.

"I was 38 at the time," he said with unbridled conceit. Now certain I should have refused this interview, I could think of nothing else to ask him other than:

**"What does it feel like to be 60?"**

"Disappointing," he said. "I thought by this time I would be confident, wise and sure of myself. Instead I feel just as naïve and simple as the day I landed here off the Heysham boat. By now I'd had more than enough. I concluded with what are you doing these days? And I wish I'd kept my mouth shut when he replied: "I used to talk a load of rubbish *and now I write it."*

(*Jimmy McIlroy Burnley Express 1991*)

# Appendix Twelve

**In which Jimmy wrote his thoughts about football in 1962.**

**(See next five pages)**

# KEEP IT SIMPLE

### BY JIMMY McILROY

UNNY, but losing the Cup Final wasn't so upsetting as I thought it would be. It was a good sporting game, which could easily have gone the other way.

As for the League Championship—well, we lost the run of the ball at the vital period of the season over Easter and Ipswich Town were good enough to take advantage of our lapse. I think

Jimmy McIlroy, inside forward star of Burnley and Ireland

**Jimmy McIlroy in a Burnley training session in rural surroundings at Burnley's training camp at nearby Padiham**

that Ipswich may be more successful in the European Cup than many people expect. Burnley put in a spirited effort in 1961, and last season Spurs went one better by reaching the semi-final. They tend to under-estimate British clubs in Europe, and I'd like to see Alf Ramsey's team surprise them.

In my view, British football is still the best because our top teams are able to perform well on mud, slush, frosty or hard grounds whereas clubs like Benfica and Real Madrid are never at their best when asked to play on anything but the hard surfaces they are used to at home.

And in Britain there isn't a great deal to choose between the top sides like Ipswich, Spurs, Everton, Sheffield Wednesday, Rangers, Celtic and Burnley. That's a good thing, because one really outstanding club, like Real Madrid has

been, can put a nation's football standard out of perspective. The close-matching of the British clubs I have mentioned leads to tense and exciting competition, such as we enjoyed last season, with each set of supporters knowing their side has a chance of topping the table and tilting for European honours in the season to follow.

There is a difference in character between these teams. Spurs have bought the players they need and blended stars of the four home nations into a successful combination, Everton are following their example. Ipswich and Burnley, on the other hand, are not rich clubs and have had to rely mostly on homegrown talent. Either method can be successful as we have seen, particularly if the team's policy is to play good football—good, *thoughtful* football—no matter what.

Wolves have known success in the recent past, and perhaps they will soon be back as strong as ever. Frankly, I don't much care for their style of power-play with liberal use of the long ball, fight and effort, but it has got good results so who can blame Wolverhampton for thinking their ideas are the right ones ? Their failings last season were not so much due to a faulty system as lack of the right players to fit into that system.

Every manager has his own idea about how to win—all he needs is the players. At Burnley, Mr Potts is lucky because he has a group of players who like to try and play skilful football and who blend their individual qualities together to fit into a system. For instance, in John Connelly, I have a wing partner who is tremendously fast and deadly accurate in his shooting. By giving me the ball, and then haring off towards goal at top speed, John knows that there is a fair chance that I will be able to push the ball forward to a position from which he will have a goalscoring opportunity. We have managed to notch quite a few goals with this simple tactic.

Spurs have their own equally simple and effective moves which have been devised to use the talents of their players to best advantage. And it is just the same with Benfica, the present European Cup holders. Tactics, you see, are not magic, but a common-sense way of bringing the best out of the players you have in your team.

It's a fallacy to say that you can't buy success

"Since I have been getting into the box and looking for goals it has been surprising how many chances have come my way."

—Real Madrid and Spurs have proved otherwise. But buying a player at a star price doesn't mean he will be a star. Teams have failed so often in the past by buying foolishly, or allowing themselves to be panicked into buying. And I'm glad to say that Burnley have also proved that you don't have to buy in order to be successful—with patience and imagination you can fashion stars from the raw material to be found on your own doorstep.

To return to that memorable Cup Final—oddly enough I had the feeling right from the 3rd Round when we beat Queen's Park Rangers by 6-1 that Burnley would go right through to Wembley. It was the first season I could remember being able to listen to the draw on the radio without getting a sinking feeling in the tummy.

Leyton Orient gave us a big fright by drawing 1-1 at Turf Moor, and I can still picture Dave Dunmore heading against the crossbar in the last few minutes of the replay when we led 1-0. Orient had the misses, but we got the goal that mattered, so it seemed my confidence was justified.

We were glad to be drawn at home against

Everton, because the skilful Toffeemen were for some strange reason less dangerous away from home last season. We had less trouble than we expected to win 3-1.

Penultimately came the tough sem-final battle with Fulham, which we were frankly lucky to win 2-1 after a 1-1 draw. It had been Burnley v. London in our two stiffest matches on the road to Wembley, and now we were due to meet a third London team in a match that was billed in advance as " The Cup Final of the Century."

Here at length our luck deserted us. As I have said, it could have gone either way, but it was at least a splendid game played throughout in a good spirit and Spurs were good value for their " double."

My first Cup Final will certainly rank amongst the most memorable of the matches in which I have played since leaving my native village of Lambeg in Northern Ireland twelve years ago. There have been dozens of other games which stand out for one reason or another, and to be truthful I think the thing that has given me as much satisfaction

"I admit I'm not the world's best header of the ball, but I try to keep my eyes open and use my forehead in the approved manner," says Jimmy

as any of them has been my regular daily training. It is the feeling that if you wake up a little sluggish you can go down to the ground for a spot of training and by the end of it you feel on top of the world. Fitness has given me a lot of pleasure, and because I generally feel livelier and fitter than the average man in the street I am able to make a fuller day for myself.

Such success as I have been lucky enough to win in football is largely due to my love of the game, and the fact that I have enjoyed playing it and practising it at every conceivable opportunity for as long as I can remember. Sometimes I get a little worried because boys today do not get the opportunity to play as much football as I did when I was young—there are so many other attractions—and this is likely to affect the standard of play in years to come.

If a boy enjoys football, and plays it at every opportunity he is well on the way to becoming a good player. There is very little extra advice I can give him. Personally I have always played by instinct, and I am sure that is the best and only satisfactory way.

Nevertheless, I would like to help others to get as much pleasure as I have done, so from time to time I search for ways to get boys to think about the game and their approach to it. Wingers, for example, should never be content simply to get the ball across into the centre— they should have a purpose behind their kick. If a winger is clear of the full back he will have time to select the forward best placed to receive a pass. He can at least try to form a mental picture of how the players are grouped in the goalmouth.

Wing halves must realise that they must give as much thought to defence as to attack, according to the run of the play, while full backs and goalkeepers can often turn defence into instant attack with one shrewdly placed clearance.

We call inside forwards "the donkeys" because they are always fetching and carrying for the other players, but the role you play depends upon your style. If you have the goal-poaching ability of a Jimmy Greaves it would be wrong to expect you to lessen your potential by running about all over the place.

As a centre-forward you must develop goal-

**Jimmy McIlroy, like all star players, has learnt to bring the ball under control quickly with any part of the body**

sense above all other things, and the only way to do this is to get as often as possible into your opponents' penalty area. It is only recently that I have remedied my own weakness in this respect, and since I have been getting into the box and looking for goals it has been surprising how many chances have come my way.

Some of you football fans may find what I have written very elementary, but then soccer is a simple game seen at its very best when it is played that way. The skill comes in by perfecting the simple actions so that you can perform them quickly and accurately in the right place at the right time, and that is something you can only learn to do by practice. Good luck to you all !

**Jimmy McIlroy makes a spectacular overhead "scissors" kick during a practice match**

**Quickness off the mark is an essential quality for players**

# Source Material

World Cup 1958: John Camkin, Sportsman's Book Club 1959
Right Inside Soccer: Jimmy McIlroy 1960
Soccer with the Stars: Billy Bingham, Stanley Paul, 1962
My Fight for Football: Bob Lord 1962
The Soccer Syndrome: John Moynihan, Simon and Schuster 1965
This One's On Me: Jimmy Greaves, Barker Ltd 1979
Oldham Athletic Complete Record: Garth Dykes, Breedon 1988
Keeping the Dream Alive Oldham Athletic: Stewart Beckett, 1991
The Post War History of Bolton Wanderers: Ponting and Hugman 1992
The Clarets Collection: Ray Simpson, Burnley Football Club 1996
Danny Blanchflower a biography: Dave Bowler, Gollancz 1997
Masters of Soccer: Maurice Edelston & Terence Delaney, Heinemann
Who's Who of Stoke City: Tony Matthews
101 Stoke Golden Greats: Simon Lowe
The Way It Was: Stanley Matthews, Headline 2000
The Glory Years Remembered: Mike Prestage, Breedon 2000
Viollet: Cavanagh and Hughes, Empire Publications 2001
Glentoran A Complete Record: Roy France, 2001
Broken Dreams: Tom Bower, Simon and Schuster 2003
My Autobiography: Tom Finney, Hodder Headline 2003
No Nay Never Volume One a Burnley FC Anthology: Dave Thomas 2004
The Heart of Football: Jimmy Greaves, Time Warner 2005
Harry Potts Margaret's Story: Dave Thomas, Sportsbooks 2006
Match of My Life Stoke City: Simon Lowe, Know the Score 2007
The Clarets Chronicles: Ray Simpson, Burnley Football Club 2008

Charles Buchan's Football Monthly December 1955
Soccer Star Monthly August 1959
World Sports: Brian Glanville 1960
Empire News and Sunday Chronicle Football Annual 1960/61
News of the World Football Annual 1962/63
The Gillette Book of Cricket and Football: Gordon Ross 1963
The Boys' Book of Soccer for 1963
All Stars Football Book 1963
Soccer the British Way 1963
Charles Buchan's Football Monthly November 1968

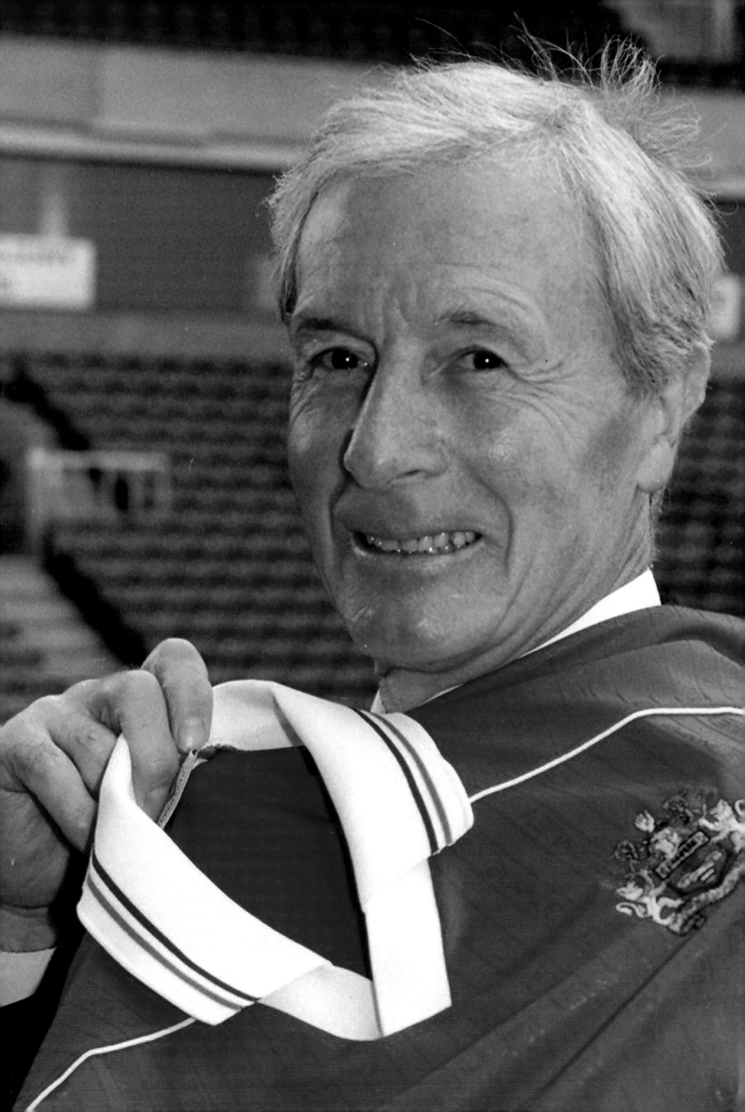